WITHDRAWN
CEDAR MILL LIBRARY

D0438117

Copyright © 2016 by Michael I. Days

Cover design by JuLee Brand
Cover image by Todd Plitt/Getty Images
Cover copyright © 2016 by Hachette Book Group, Inc.

Hachette Book Group supports the right to free expression and the value of copyright. The purpose of copyright is to encourage writers and artists to produce the creative works that enrich our culture.

The scanning, uploading, and distribution of this book without permission is a theft of the author's intellectual property. If you would like permission to use material from the book (other than for review purposes), please contact permissions@hbgusa.com. Thank you for your support of the author's rights.

Center Street
Hachette Book Group
1290 Avenue of the Americas
New York, NY 10104
centerstreet.com
twitter.com/centerstreet

First Edition: September 2016

Center Street is a division of Hachette Book Group, Inc.
The Center Street name and logo are trademarks of Hachette Book Group, Inc.

The publisher is not responsible for websites (or their content) that are not owned by the publisher.

The Hachette Speakers Bureau provides a wide range of authors for speaking events. To find out more, go to www.HachetteSpeakersBureau.com or call (866) 376-6591.

The excerpt from "Praise Song for the Day" © 2009 by Elizabeth Alexander, is used with the permission of Elizabeth Alexander and Graywolf Press.

Library of Congress Cataloging-in-Publication Data has been applied for.

ISBNs: 978-1-4555-9662-1 (hardcover), 978-1-4555-9661-4 (ebook)

Printed in the United States of America

RRD-C

10 9 8 7 6 5 4 3 2 1

OBAMA'S LEGACY

WHAT HE ACCOMPLISHED AS PRESIDENT

Michael I. Days

CENTER STREET

New York   Boston   Nashville

At his second inauguration, President Obama paused to look back at the crowd that packed the mall before leaving the platform at the U.S. Capitol in Washington, D.C. Standing behind him were First Lady Michelle Obama, their daughters, Malia and Sasha, and his mother-in-law, Marian Robinson, January 21, 2013. (Official White House Photo by Lawrence Jackson)

OBAMA'S LEGACY

To my mother,
Helen B. Days

President Obama had a friendly exchange with Pope Francis after a private audience at the Vatican on March 27, 2014. The president invited the pope to visit him at the White House, and he did in September 2015. (Official White House Photo by Pete Souza)

Contents

INTRODUCTION   1

PART I: A MAN OF THE PEOPLE

CHAPTER 1: The Young   11

CHAPTER 2: Women   20

CHAPTER 3: African Americans   36

CHAPTER 4: LGBT   58

CHAPTER 5: Immigrants   69

CHAPTER 6: The Disabled and the Elderly   75

CHAPTER 7: Veterans   81

CHAPTER 8: Prisoners   89

CHAPTER 9: Workers   94

PART II: A MAN OF ACTION

CHAPTER 10: The Economy   101

CHAPTER 11: Defense   116

CHAPTER 12: Diplomacy   125

CHAPTER 13: Justice   136

CHAPTER 14: Labor   148

CHAPTER 15: Education   153

CHAPTER 16: Housing and Urban Development   162

CHAPTER 17: Transportation   166

CHAPTER 18: Homeland Security   172

CHAPTER 19: Agriculture   176

PART III: A MAN OF CONVICTION

CHAPTER 20: Health   181

CHAPTER 21: Energy and the Environment   189

CHAPTER 22: Technology   197

Conclusion: Seeds of Change   205

Epilogue   207

Chronology   211

Acknowledgments   215

Notes   217

Bibliography   249

Index   279

OBAMA'S LEGACY

President Obama announced a New START Treaty at the White House on March 26, 2010, joined by (from left) Admiral Mike Mullen, Secretary of State Hillary Clinton, and Secretary of Defense Robert Gates. (Official White House Photo by Pete Souza)

Introduction

So much anticipation filled the air the night of November 4, 2008: Election Night. The daily, even hourly, chant had been "Hope and Change!" This came from a youngish black man who was waging a credible run for president, a run that was hard to fathom in an America that still seemed so focused on race. The country was paying attention, as was the rest of the world, and, indeed. much of the country was being inspired. One might have thought that the gods had anointed Barack Hussein Obama to ascend to the presidency of the world's most powerful nation. How could this even have been possible?

As editor of the *Philadelphia Daily News*, I had worked with my chief lieutenants to convey the historic nature of the race to our readers. In fact, we may have been the first mainstream paper in the country to declare that Obama would be our next president. Veteran political columnist John Baer wrote the day after the Super Tuesday primaries, nine months before the general election, that Obama would win both the Democratic nomination and the general election because of his ability to attract new voters, his momentum, and his demonstrated ability to galvanize.

Still, he had to get it done. The polls said he would, but they had been wrong before, especially with elections involving African Americans. Polls often overestimated the strength of black candidates' support. It had happened to Harold Washington in his bid to become mayor of Chicago in 1983. He won, but by a much narrower margin than the double-digit lead that polls predicted. Then something similar happened to Jesse Jackson in 1988 when polls overestimated the size of the white vote he would get in the Wisconsin Democratic presidential primary, when he came in second, after Michael Dukakis. Polls were also wrong when David Dinkins ran for mayor of New York City in 1989. Like Washington, Dinkins won, but by a narrow two-point margin after polls had shown him with a double-digit lead a few days before the election. The phenomenon even had a name then—the Bradley Effect, named after former Los Angeles mayor Tom Bradley. Back in the early '80s, Bradley ran for governor of California, and polls indicated throughout that he was leading in the race, but when all the votes were counted, he fell short.

It turns out, many whites would tell pollsters that they supported a black candidate but would not actually vote as they had indicated. As the theory goes, the white voters gave pollsters a socially desirable answer but voted their true instincts.

So there was that factor weighing heavily. You could sense history in the air, but it wasn't clear whether the history would be that Obama got really close, closer than any other person of color to the presidency, or that he would win.

Then, the news broke about a couple of hours before midnight. Barack Obama would be the forty-fourth president of the United States, winning with 53.8 percent of the popular vote. We had planned our coverage, our front page, knowing that even with digital outlets' becoming more common as news sources for readers of all stripes, they still sought newspapers as keepsakes on major occasions—and this would certainly be one. As one of the country's premier tabloids, we wanted to produce a signature paper, a signature front page.

My offices then were on Broad Street, one of Philly's main thoroughfares. The week before, the Phillies had beaten the Tampa Bay Rays to take the World Series, and all kinds of folks had arrived from all directions and paraded up and down Broad Street, celebrating the unexpected win. Days later, on this Tuesday night, the joy seemed even more palpable. That same street quickly filled with even more jubilant crowds, mostly college kids embracing and shouting, "O-BA-MA!"—knowing that they were part of history and that they had played a key role in his election.

Sandra Shea, our editorial page editor, emerged from the building heading onto Broad Street with our front page, holding it high so that the throng could see. It was a simple close-up of a smiling Obama with his last name in bold letters. I popped out to check it all out, then dashed back into the newsroom to watch the cable coverage and to make sure that we were, as we say in our business, making deadline, and doing so with spot-on coverage of this amazing night.

Once stories were turned in and edited, reporters and editors pulled up chairs around the television at the city desk to witness history. Among them was Kitty Caparella, a since-retired reporter who had covered the mob for years. She knew that I always kept my cool demeanor and largely kept my personal feelings to myself. I am an old-school journalist who believes the public need not know your personal leanings and they most certainly should not be reflected in the stories that grace the newspaper. Still, Kitty and I had been friends for a very long time, and she knew that, like many, I had not believed that my fellow Americans, given the nation's racial history and our ongoing racial strife, would actually elect an individual of color to the country's highest office.

When I joined my colleagues around the television, Kitty turned to me and asked, "Well, what are you thinking now?"

I really was not thinking. It was one of those few moments in life, like one's graduation or marriage or the arrival of your children or the birth of your grandchildren, that was definitely breathtaking. These are the moments, captured vividly in your memory, that you carry to the grave.

Then the moment of exultation passed.

I don't think that the average citizen who believed in hope and change realized then how difficult Obama's pledge would be to fulfill. Obama acknowledged during his final State of the Union address, on January 12, 2016, that it was "one of the few regrets of my presidency that the rancor and suspicion between the parties has gotten worse instead of better. I have no doubt that a president with the gifts of Lincoln or Roosevelt might have better bridged the divide."

Dick Polman, a noted national political analyst based in Philadelphia, posted on his personal Facebook page on January 13, 2016, that the president was being hard on himself, as neither Lincoln nor Roosevelt had fared well against their rival parties. Polman wrote, "Lincoln died because of his era's bloody divide; prior to his dying he endured four years of 'baboon' insults, and worse. As for FDR, he was thoroughly hated; his wife was smeared as a 'n—r lover.' And worse...In a 1936 speech he simply said of his right-wing opponents: 'They are unanimous in their hate for me—and I welcome their hatred.'"

So maybe it's just proof that there is not anything new under the sun.

I argue that, especially given the Republican establishment's aggressive push to see him fail, Obama's legacy and his historic accomplishments have been all the more remarkable. Obama's accomplishments have come against a backdrop of criticism or open defiance from conservatives, lack of cooperation in Congress, and racially tinged commentary—really, have we ever had another president who has repeatedly had his citizenship questioned? I believe the answer is no.

Paul Krugman, an economist of significant note, wrote for *Rolling Stone* that he believed Obama was one of the most successful presidents in the country's history. "Obama has done more to limit inequality than he gets credit for...The financial aid in Obamacare—expanded Medicaid, subsidies to help lower-income households pay insurance premiums—goes disproportionately to less-well-off Americans," Krugman wrote.

The economic indicators, that the stock market is stronger, that the unemployment rate is down significantly, that Obama led us safely out of the Great Recession, can't be refuted. History will view him as a transformational president largely because of his signature achievements: the passage of the Affordable Care Act and the Supreme Court's upholding of it, the legalization of same-sex marriage, and, dare I say, ridding the planet of one Osama bin Laden. He should get credit for those accomplishments, especially considering the financial crisis that was ongoing when he assumed the presidency in 2008.

He also should get credit for keeping his swagger, his cool. At the 2015 White House Correspondents' Dinner, Obama smartly employed Keegan-Michael Key, the comedian who has come to be known for his character Luther, Obama's "anger translator." Obama spoke deftly and calmly about climate control, Ebola, and immigration, as well as about how happy he was to be at yet another correspondents' dinner. Luther ranted, in turn, about what a chore the dinner is, what he deemed to be FOX's out-of-control biased coverage of everything, and CNN making the Ebola challenge seem like it would be the end of the world. Ultimately, they seemed to become one at the dais as the president's own tone became angrier, prompting Luther to recoil and spurt, "You don't need an anger translator; you need counseling." It was all definitely laugh-out-loud hilarious, but the moment seriously crystallized the many challenges that the forty-fourth president has had in the now 24/7 news cycle.

This book will examine Obama's accomplishments in spite of all those challenges in a straightforward, factual manner. It is not about what his ideas, plans, or promises were; it is about what he actually got done. As he entered his final months in office, the evidence indicated he had been tremendously successful and effective by objective measures in his two terms in office. On economic indicators alone, his achievements are impressive. He is credited with the longest streak of job growth in U.S. history, a two-thirds reduction in the federal budget deficit (from 9.8 percent of gross domestic product in fiscal year 2009 to 2.5 percent in October 2015, according to the Treasury Department and the Office of Management and Budget). The stock market continued to be a tad temperamental, but it continued to outperform the record lows that Obama found when he assumed office, and it rebounded to record highs.

Still, for a great many Americans the data is just that: data. It doesn't capture how they feel about Obama.

I attended a 2016 Martin Luther King Jr. Day gathering that included about five hundred folks, mostly black, nearly all college-educated, who, no doubt, had benefited from Dr. Martin Luther King Jr.'s dream. Even the location of the event, the Westin in Princeton, New Jersey, a fashionable hotel in one of the nation's most elite suburbs, perfectly captured the hope and change that Obama represents in spite of the withering challenges.

The Reverend Doctor Cory L. Jones, senior pastor of the Tabernacle Baptist Church in Burlington, New Jersey, reminded those gathered of how much they loved the president, how much they had rejoiced in his election in 2008 and his reelection in 2012. It was, Jones said, "the something that seemed impossible" for a black man in America. Jones, relatively new in his pastorate at Tabernacle Baptist, recalled that he had received an email from a parishioner at a neighboring church shortly after his arrival in New Jersey. The gentleman was particularly perturbed that this African American church prominently displayed a portrait of the country's first African American president, and he urged the pastor to remove it. Jones said the man believed that no Christian church should support Obama given his enthusiastic support and legislative success in the legalization of same-sex marriage and his ongoing support of legalized abortion.

No doubt, these are two significant issues that have been taboo, theologically, in many Christian churches. Yet you will not find a poll that has support for Obama within the black community anywhere below 90 percent, regardless of ideology. Reverend Jones got nothing but applause and nodded agreement from those gathered that day to celebrate King's birthday.

The fact that Obama is the first and only person of color thus far elected to be the most powerful person on our planet makes his accomplishments all the more noteworthy. Elizabeth Alexander captured it well when she read her poem, "Praise Song for the Day," at Barack Obama's first inauguration on January 20, 2009. In part, she proclaimed:

Say it plain: that many have died for this day.
Sing the names of the dead who brought us here,
who laid the train tracks, raised the bridges,
picked the cotton and the lettuce, built
brick by brick the glittering edifices
they would then keep clean and work inside of.

Obama had already set the theme earlier in his inaugural address, calling for resolve amid an "uncertain destiny." That resolve despite the many obstructions has been a hallmark of his presidency. That resolve will serve his legacy well. I have no doubt that history will view him as one of America's most effective presidents.

In one role in particular, he has no peer—as our counselor-in-chief, our pastor-in-chief. Who will ever forget how Obama, surprisingly, belted out "Amazing Grace" at the funeral for Clementa C. Pinckney, a senior pastor and South Carolina state senator? Pinckney and eight of his parishioners had been slaughtered during a prayer service by a "guest" who said he had hoped to ignite a race war. (See chapter 3.) President Obama has been remarkable, passionate, and even visibly angry after each of the mass shootings during his tenure, which are too numerous to mention. He has helped to heal us with words and with song, and with resolve.

It is that same resolve that has helped him push through an agenda of change and to power through a wall of opposition, ignoring slights and staying the course to make "hope and change" more than a slogan.

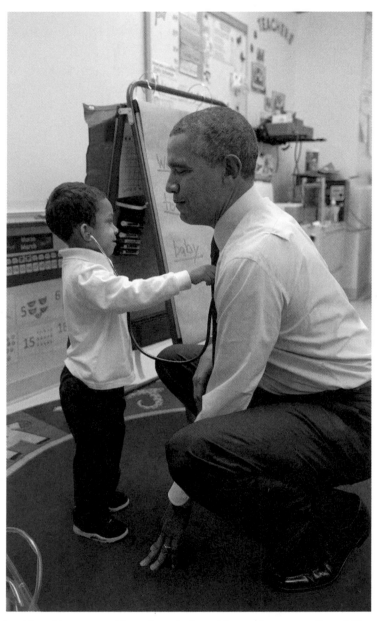

When President Obama saw this student playing with a stethoscope at Powell Elementary School in Washington, D.C., during a visit on March 4, 2014, he asked the child to check his heartbeat. (Official White House Photo by Pete Souza)

PART I

A MAN OF THE PEOPLE

★ ★ ★

You have to love the picture taken in the Oval Office, with the lanky President Obama bent over so that five-year-old Jacob Philadelphia can touch his hair. Jacob is the son of a former White House staffer, and Jacob had asked the president, in a hushed tone, if the president's hair was like his. Obama reportedly invited Jacob without hesitation to touch his hair to see for himself.

Obama instinctually understood that what the boy was asking went well beyond the lad's touching his hair. In a very personal way, Jacob wanted to see if this very powerful man had been just like him when he was a little boy. If Obama's hair felt like his, maybe he, too, could be the president of his country someday.

That interaction happened back in 2009. Now, that young man talks about someday becoming a U.S. president, or a test pilot.

In many ways, one might argue that Obama's response to the boy is a window into what makes Obama tick. He is criticized as being aloof and unable to connect with the common man or woman, yet the issues that he has been passionate about more than suggest that his actions and policies have often come from his own life experience as a kid of African ancestry who didn't always fit in, a son of an often-single, struggling mother, and a grandson of a professional woman who often found herself up against the glass ceiling. It is those and other life experiences that likely have benefited people who have often been marginalized in the land of plenty. Obama has forever changed the trajectory of their lives.

This section examines the actions and policies that seem inspired by

Obama's life history. They include a focus on education; on women's and children's health; and certainly on equal rights for women, gays and lesbians, and people of color, especially black and Latino young men. This section also looks at Obama's impact on developing policies that have lessened the prison population. The number of Americans incarcerated has dropped for the first time in thirty-two years.

President Obama's initiatives and policies have touched the lives of many individuals, including the most vulnerable among us.

CHAPTER 1

The Young

"There are few things as fundamental to the American Dream or as essential for America's success as a good education. This has never been more true than it is today. At a time when our children are competing with kids in China and India, the best job qualification you can have is a college degree or advanced training."

President Obama, April 24, 2009

President Obama got down on his hands and knees playfully to look tiny Ella Rhodes directly in the eye as she was crawling around during a visit to his office. She is the daughter of Ben Rhodes, his deputy national security adviser, June 4, 2015. (Official White House photo by Pete Souza)

President Obama's education and health initiatives are giving millions of children a chance for a better life and a brighter future. Many have benefited from his education initiatives and his health care programs.

President Obama's concern for the young and their admiration of him shine through in countless White House photographs—scenes of him getting down on the floor to play with a baby, running with children or letting a young boy touch his hair. Beyond the "photo ops," however, is a solid record of initiatives intended to benefit this generation of youth and future generations.

Education stands at the top of this list. In his first address to a joint session of Congress on February 24, 2009, President Obama announced a goal for the nation to have the highest proportion of college graduates in the world by 2020 to allow U.S. workers to compete in the global economy. "I ask every American to commit to at least one year or more of higher education or career training," he said. "This can be community college or a four-year school; vocational training or an apprenticeship. But whatever the training may be, every American will need to get more than a high school diploma. And dropping out of high school is no longer an option. It's not just quitting on yourself, it's quitting on your country—and this country needs and values the talents of every American. That is why we will provide the support necessary for you to complete college and meet a new goal: by 2020, America will once again have the highest proportion of college graduates in the world."

In 1990, the U.S. was first in the world for the proportion of the population of twenty-five to thirty-four years old with four-year degrees, according to the White House. By 2009, the U.S. ranked number twelve.

"We also suffer from a college attainment gap, as high school graduates from the wealthiest families in our nation are almost certain to continue on to higher education, while just over half of our high school graduates in the poorest quarter of families attend college," a White House statement read. "And while more than half of college students graduate within six years, the completion rate for low-income students is around 25 percent." This came at a time when higher education was more vital than ever to fill the jobs available and to ensure the financial security of families. "The 2020 goal is the North Star guiding all our efforts to improve education," U.S. Department of Education Secretary Arne Duncan wrote in *Forbes* magazine in August 2010. "Roughly 60% of Americans will have to earn college degrees and certificates by 2020 to regain our international lead, compared with about 40% today. And the truth is that America can only have the best-educated, most competitive workforce if parents, students, educators and entire communities begin to rethink and remake the educational status quo."

According to the U.S. Department of Education,

- Bachelor's degree holders typically earn 66 percent more than high school graduates and are less likely to be unemployed.
- College graduates will earn about $1 million more over a lifetime than will workers without postsecondary education.
- By 2020, two-thirds of job openings will require postsecondary education or training

Yet college education had become more and more a luxury item, out of reach for many high school graduates. The Department of Education said tuition at four-year colleges had more than doubled over the previous three decades, and the average debt for a bachelor's degree graduate more than doubled from 1992 to 2012 to $27,000. Pell Grants covered only about 30 percent of the cost of an education at a four-year public college, even after major increases in Pell Grants under the Obama administration.

To regain the lead in college-degree attainment for the U.S., Obama promoted an agenda to make college more affordable and to assure that students are college-ready. His actions included investing heavily in early education, as well as in elementary and secondary education, and creating the Race to the Top program, which rewarded states for effective school reforms in K–12 education.

At the same time, he increased funding for financial aid to college students and reformed student-loan programs by ending the role of private banks in the lending system through the Health Care and Education

Reconciliation Act of 2010. According to the U.S. Department of Education, the Obama administration increased total annual aid to students by more than $50 billion from 2008 to 2016 and tax benefits by more than $12 billion. The administration said it raised the maximum award for Pell Grants to low-income and middle-class students by more than $1,000 since 2008 to $5,730 for the 2014–15 award year and expanded the number of recipients by one-third. The Department of Education under the Obama administration proposed expansion of Pell Grants to cover summer classes to help students earn degrees faster.

It also launched a pilot program to use Pell Grants for education for federal and state prisoners, ending a twenty-year ban on such aid for inmates, the vast majority of whom are young black and Hispanic men. While only Congress can lift the ban, the administration used its authority to run short-term experimental programs for a limited number of prisoners. Secretary Duncan said that restoring Pell eligibility to prisoners was another way to increase college affordability and completion rates. Lawmakers, like Representative Donna Edwards, D-Md., who sponsored a bill that would lift the ban, and House Education Committee ranking member Bobby Scott, D-Va., a cosponsor of the bill, cite a 2013 Rand Corporation study paid for by the Justice Department that found that every dollar invested in prison education programs saved four to five dollars in incarceration costs later. That study found that prisoners in education programs were 43 percent less likely than others to return to prison within three years, and 13 percent more likely to have jobs after they have served their time.

"We want to do even more, developing experimental sites that will make Pell Grants available to programs that award credentials based on demonstrated competency, to incarcerated adults seeking an independent, productive life after release, and to adult learners who enroll in short-term certificate programs that provide job-ready training," Duncan said.

As part of the American Recovery and Reinvestment Act of 2009, which Obama signed, the administration created the American Opportunity Tax Credit to help families pay for college. In 2016, the credit would benefit ten million students and families, according to the Department of Education.

The American Recovery and Reinvestment Act of 2009, known as the Stimulus or the Recovery Act, was signed on February 17, 2009, by President Barack Obama tc stimulate the economy to avoid a depression.

The Obama administration also tightened standards for for-profit colleges that many say prey on students. The Education Department issued regulations to protect students from becoming overburdened by loans. The rules hold "career colleges" accountable for student outcomes. "Career colleges must be a stepping stone to the middle class. But too many hard-working students find themselves buried in debt with little to show for it. That is simply unacceptable," Secretary Duncan said in an Education Department announcement of the regulations in October 2014. "These regulations are a necessary step to ensure that colleges accepting federal funds protect students, cut costs and improve outcomes. We will continue to take action as needed." Under the rules, for a school to participate in taxpayer-funded federal student aid programs, the estimated annual loan payment of a typical graduate could not exceed 20 percent of his or her discretionary income or 8 percent of total earnings.

In 2015, Obama also announced proposals to make two years of community college free and to expand training programs for technical jobs, and members of Congress introduced legislation in July of that year to carry out the plan. The free-tuition plan, known as America's College Promise, would cover tuition for up to two years at qualifying community college programs, as long as a student maintained a 2.5 GPA.

Children's Health

Children have also benefited from the president's health care initiatives. Standing right beside the president, watching him closely when he signed legislation to overhaul the national health care insurance system was Marcelas Owens, an eleven-year-old Seattle boy who began lobbying for reforms after his twenty-seven-year-old uninsured mother died. His family epitomized the many families with children who gained health coverage under the Affordable Care Act.

The Gallup organization found that the uninsured rate dropped nearly six percentage points after the fourth quarter of 2013, which was the last quarter before the Affordable Care Act's requirement for Americans to carry health insurance took effect. Gallup said the latest quarterly rate then, 11.4 percent in the second quarter of 2015, down from 11.9 percent in the first quarter, was the lowest quarterly uninsured rate recorded since Gallup and Healthways began daily tracking of the data in 2008. The 2015 second quarter results were based on approximately 44,000 interviews with U.S. adults, April 1 to June 30, 2015. Gallup said the monthly trend indicated that "the decline in the uninsured rate took place late in the first quarter—after the February 15 deadline to purchase health insurance—and that the lower rate held steady throughout the second quarter. The uninsured rate fell to 11.3 percent by March, and the April, May and June averages were similar."

This law also provided relief to young adults without medical insurance by allowing them to stay on their parents' plan until age twenty-six if they were not covered at work. Many young people work in jobs that do not provide such insurance, but they aged out of their parents' plans earlier before the Affordable Care Act took effect.

On February 4, 2009, President Barack Obama also signed the Children's Health Insurance Program Reauthorization Act, expanding coverage to four million previously uninsured children and covering eleven million children in all. President George W. Bush had twice vetoed similar legislation.

"In a decent society, there are certain obligations that are not subject to tradeoffs or negotiation—health care for our children is one of those obligations," Obama said in signing the law.

The Children's Health Insurance Program Reauthorization Act of 2009, a law signed February 4, 2009, authorizing the Children's Health Insurance Program (CHIP), provides matching funds to states for health insurance to cover children in families of modest income who are not eligible for Medicaid.

Aid to Families

The American Recovery and Reinvestment Act, which Obama signed, expanded the Child Tax Credit to cover an additional ten million children in working families and created a new Make Work Pay tax credit, which, according to the Internal Revenue Service, provided up to $400 for working individuals and $800 for couples filing jointly in 2009 and 2010.

The act also included an additional $2 billion for the Child Care and Development Block Grant, $1 billion for Head Start, $1.1 billion for Early Head Start, and a $20 billion increase for the Supplemental Nutrition Assistance Program (SNAP), formerly known as Food Stamps. It also had funds for the Special Supplemental Nutrition Program for Women, Infants, and Children (WIC) and for food banks. The Recovery Act added 64,000 slots to Head Start and Early Head Start.

In his 2013 State of the Union address, President Obama called on Congress to expand access to high-quality preschool for every child in America. In 2014, the Department of Health and Human Services launched a $500 million competitive grant opportunity to support the expansion of Early Head Start and the creation of Early Head Start–Child Care Partnerships. The Department of Education announced a $250 million Preschool Development Grants competition to enhance state programs and expand access to preschool for four-year-olds.

> The Healthy, Hunger-Free Kids Act of 2010, signed on December 13, 2010, funded child-nutrition programs and free-lunch programs in schools for five years.

President Obama also signed the Healthy, Hunger-Free Kids Act of 2010, which set new nutrition standards for school meal programs and allocated $4.5 billion to fund them. The standards came about as part of First Lady Michelle Obama's initiative to fight childhood obesity through her Let's Move! campaign. The law authorized funding for five years and set federal policy for school lunch and breakfast programs, the Special Supplemental Nutrition Program for Women, Infants, and Children (WIC), and other programs.

Marcelas Owens: Child Activist

Marcelas Owens, far right, was among the guests when President Obama delivered remarks on the health insurance reform bill at the Department of Interior. Others are, from left, Vice President Joe Biden and Vicki Kennedy, widow of Senator Edward M. Kennedy, March 23, 2010. (Official White House photo by Pete Souza)

The fifth-grader at Seattle's Orca K–8 school began lobbying for changes in the health care system after his mother, Tiffany Owens, became ill and died.

She was an assistant manager at a Jack in the Box when bouts of diarrhea and vomiting forced her to miss so much work that she lost her job and with it, her insurance, in October 2006, according to the *Seattle Times*. Uninsured and ineligible for Medicaid, she did not seek care until she ended up in an emergency room. She was eventually diagnosed with pulmonary hypertension, a serious condition involving the arteries in the lungs, and died at age twenty-seven in June 2007. That left Marcelas, then aged seven, and his two younger sisters in the care of their grandmother, Gina Owens, who had been active for years with Washington Community Action Network, the state's largest consumer-advocacy group. Her daughter's death mobilized her and her grandson to focus on the health care issue.

Marcelas told his story to Senator Patricia Lynn "Patty" Murray, Democrat of Washington, at a rally for health insurance. She mentioned it on the

Senate floor and spoke about it to President Obama and Vice President Joseph Biden.

Marcelas took part in a rally in Washington, D.C., organized by Health Care for America Now, a nationwide lobbying campaign. "I want health care to be for everybody," he said.

After the passage of the health care act, Marcelas was at the president's side to see it signed.

In remarks before the signing, President Obama said, "Marcelas lost his mom to an illness, and she didn't have insurance and couldn't afford the care that she needed. So in her memory he has told her story across America so that no other children have to go through what his family has experienced."

Marcelas went on to work for other reforms and to encourage others to get involved in political action.

"When it got passed, it showed me that things could actually get done, and it made me want to make change on other things," he said.

CHAPTER 2

Women

"I didn't run for President so that the dreams of our daughters could be deferred or denied. I didn't run for President to see inequality and injustice persist in our time. I ran for President to put the same rights, the same opportunities, and the same dreams within the reach for our daughters and our sons alike. I ran for President to put the American Dream within the reach of all of our people, no matter what their gender, or race, or faith, or station."

President Obama, March 8, 2010

The president talked with Justice Elena Kagan and Chief Justice John Roberts before Justice Kagan's investiture ceremony at the Supreme Court, October 1, 2010. (Official White House photo by Pete Souza)

President Obama demonstrated a commitment to protecting the rights of women, placing women in high-profile positions, and providing avenues for women to thrive. He signed legislation to make it easier for women to prove pay discrimination, appointed women to high office, and protected women's health and reproductive choices. The president expanded funding to prevent violence against women. He supported the opening of military combat roles to women.

The first legislation President Obama signed into law was the Lilly Ledbetter Fair Pay Act, which effectively extends the statute of limitations to file a claim for discrimination in pay. "It is fitting that with the very first bill I sign—the Lilly Ledbetter Fair Pay Act—we are upholding one of this nation's first principles: that we are all created equal and each deserve a chance to pursue our own version of happiness," President Obama remarked.

Lilly Ledbetter was a production supervisor at a Goodyear tire plant in Alabama who filed a discrimination action shortly before taking early retirement in 1998. When she started work at the company, her earnings were on par with men's, but as she approached retirement, she was making hundreds of dollars less per month than did a group of her male peers. According to court documents, Ledbetter earned $3,727 per month, while the lowest-paid male area manager received $4,286 per month and the highest-paid male manager was at $5,236 a month. She sued the company for discrimination.

As of the U.S. Supreme Court decision in *Ledbetter v. Goodyear Tire & Rubber Co.* on May 29, 2007, the clock on the statute of limitations for such a lawsuit began when the employer made the decision that created the discriminatory pay. The Lilly Ledbetter Fair Pay Act, which was signed on January 29, 2009, two days after it passed the House, amended the Civil Rights Act of 1964 to specify that the clock for the 180-day statute of limitations for filing a lawsuit asserting pay discrimination restarts with each paycheck that continues the inequitable pay. A bill seeking to reverse the *Ledbetter* decision had failed in the previous Congress.

Women's groups had argued that the Supreme Court ruling meant that a company needed only to keep its discriminatory pay practice secret long enough to get away with it. Writing the dissenting opinion to the Supreme Court decision, Justice Ruth Bader Ginsburg argued: "The Court's insistence on immediate contest overlooks common characteristics of pay discrimination. Pay disparities often occur, as they did in Ledbetter's case, in small increments; cause to suspect that discrimination is at work develops only over time. Comparative pay information, moreover, is often hidden from the employee's view. Employers may keep under wraps the pay differentials maintained among supervisors, no less the reasons for those differentials." She said that a worker might overlook small discrepancies initially, "particularly when the employee, trying to succeed in a nontraditional environment, is averse to making waves. Pay disparities are thus significantly different from adverse actions 'such as termination, failure to promote…or refusal to hire,' all involving fully communicated discrete acts, 'easy to identify' as discriminatory," Ginsburg wrote.

In other actions in support of pay equity, President Obama signed an executive order in 2014 prohibiting federal contractors from retaliating against employees who discuss compensation with each other. He also instructed the secretary of Labor to issue regulations requiring federal contractors to inform the Department of Labor of compensation paid to their employees, including data broken down by sex and race.

Under the Obama administration, the Equal Employment Opportunity Commission (EEOC) has obtained more than $91.5 million in monetary relief for victims of sex-based wage discrimination, according to the White House.

The Lilly Ledbetter Fair Pay Act, signed January 29, 2009, amends civil rights laws to specify that, to calculate the 180-day statute of limitations, each time discriminatory compensation is paid can be considered a new violation.

Lilly Ledbetter: Equal-Pay Plaintiff

Lilly Ledbetter was born Lilly McDaniel, April 18, 1938, in Jacksonville, Calhoun County, Alabama, the daughter of J. C. McDaniel, a mechanic at Anniston Army Depot, and Edna Smith McDaniel, a homemaker, according to the *Encyclopedia of Alabama*. She grew up working on her grandfather's cotton farm and graduated from Jacksonville High School in 1956. She married Charles Ledbetter the same year, and they had two children.

Before Ledbetter worked at the Goodyear Tire & Rubber plant in Gadsden, Alabama, in 1979, she worked as a manager at H&R Block and as an assistant financial aid officer at Jacksonville State University.

At Goodyear, she was the only female area manager when she learned, reportedly through an anonymous note, that she made far less than some male peers. In 1998, she filed a claim with the Equal Employment Opportunity Commission (EEOC).

Subsequently, she was transferred to a less-desirable job. Ledbetter soon took an early retirement. She filed a lawsuit in the U.S. District Court for the Northern District of Alabama claiming wage discrimination under Title VII, as well as several other complaints. Her claims on disparate pay and involuntary transfer came to trial, and a jury concluded that she had suffered pay discrimination and awarded her more than $3.5 million in back pay and punitive damages. A judge reduced the amount to $360,000 in keeping with a legal cap on damages payable under Title VII of the Civil Rights Act of 1964. Goodyear appealed and the U.S. Court of Appeals, Eleventh Circuit found that the claim was outside the statute of limitations. Ledbetter appealed to the U.S. Supreme Court, which ruled 5-4 in favor of the company in May 2007. Goodyear argued and the Supreme Court ultimately agreed that Ledbetter was "time barred" from pursuing a claim involving pay decisions made more than 180 days before she filed her charge with the EEOC.

Women on the Court

Obama's greatest achievement may be assuring that the court itself was more representative of the nation as a whole. Obama appointed two women to the Supreme Court, including the first Latina ever to serve as a justice. The addition of his appointees, Sonia Sotomayor and Elena Kagan, joining Ruth Bader Ginsburg, brought the total number of women on the court at one time to three, a record. Ginsburg became the second woman on the court, when President Bill Clinton appointed her in 1993, and Sandra Day O'Connor, whom Ronald Reagan appointed in 1981 and who retired in 2006, was the first. Obama appointed Sotomayor to fill the vacancy upon the retirement of Associate Justice David H. Souter, and he later appointed Kagan to replace John Paul Stevens when he retired.

Announcing Sotomayor's nomination on May 26, 2009, Obama said, "When Sonia Sotomayor ascends those marble steps to assume her seat on the highest court of the land, America will have taken another important step towards realizing the ideal that is etched above its entrance: Equal justice under the law."

In choosing her, the *Washington Post* said he selected "the most controversial of his potential nominees" at the time. His options included three other women with whom he was familiar and whom he had interviewed for the nomination: Judge Diane P. Wood of the U.S. Court of Appeals for the Seventh Circuit, Solicitor General Elena Kagan, and Homeland Security secretary Janet Napolitano. Sotomayor, not one to hold her tongue on issues of gender and ethnicity or the role of the judiciary, was the least popular among conservatives, but Obama was impressed with her experiences in life and in the law.

The *Washington Post* said Obama presented Sotomayor "as the embodiment of the qualities he seeks in a judge: a rigorous intellect, an appreciation of the limited role of the judiciary" to interpret the law impartially. Introducing her in the East Room, he said, "We need something more. For as Supreme Court Justice Oliver Wendell Holmes once said, 'The life of the law has not been logic; it has been experience.' Experience being tested by obstacles and barriers, by hardship and misfortune; experience insisting, persisting, and ultimately overcoming those barriers. It is experience that can give a person a common touch and a sense of compassion; an understanding of how the world works and how ordinary people live. And that is why it is a necessary ingredient in the kind of justice we need on the Supreme Court."

That viewpoint, that anything other than strict interpretation of the law should influence a judge's decisions, did not sit well with many conservatives, and it was not long before the nominee was stirring up controversy. She was asked in Senate confirmation hearings about remarks that she had made referring to "a wise Latina." For years, she had spoken about how her experiences, traditions, and even foods as a Latina woman had influenced her and how she hoped her experiences would help her arrive at better judicial decisions than someone with a narrower range of experiences might. "I would hope that a wise Latina woman with the richness of her experiences would, more often than not, reach a better conclusion," she had said in a number of speeches that were made available to the Senate for review as part of the confirmation process.

In at least one speech, she had added, "than a white male who hasn't lived that life." Some Republicans interpreted that as racism. Senators asked about it at her confirmation hearings, and the conservative media pilloried her for it. Sotomayor apologized and said that it might have been a poor choice of words. She won confirmation and took her seat on the court on August 8, 2009.

Presented with his next opportunity to nominate a Supreme Court justice, Obama again chose a woman, Elena Kagan, a former dean of Harvard Law School, out of a pool of male and female candidates. He had named Kagan as solicitor general of the United States in 2009 and considered her for the seat that went to Sotomayor instead. This time he nominated Kagan to the Supreme Court on May 10, 2010. She won confirmation, and she joined the court on August 7, 2010.

Of Kagan's appointment, Obama said, "She has won accolades from observers across the ideological spectrum, not just for her intellect and record of achievement, but also for her temperament." She had a reputation as a deeply intellectual, open-minded consensus builder, according to various press accounts.

With the appointments of two smart liberals, President Obama has assured himself the opportunity to have an impact on the court for years to come. In an article about Obama's judicial legacy, Jeffrey Toobin, writing in the *New Yorker*, noted that Obama has used his power to shift the balance of the federal courts in ideology and demographics. "Obama has had two hundred and eighty judges confirmed, which represents about a third of the federal judiciary," Toobin wrote. In addition to the two Supreme Court appointments, he noted that Obama had put 53 people on the circuit courts of appeals, 223 to the district courts, and 2 to the court of international trade. "When Obama took office, Republican appointees controlled ten of the thirteen circuit courts of appeals; Democratic appointees now constitute a majority in nine circuits. Because federal judges have life tenure, nearly all of Obama's judges will continue serving well after he leaves office," Toobin wrote.

The article also noted that 42 percent of Obama's judgeship appointments were to women, compared to 22 percent under George W. Bush and 29 percent under Bill Clinton, and 36 percent of Obama's judges were members of minority groups, double the 18 percent for Bush and more than Clinton at 24 percent.

Obama took pride in this legacy, telling the *New Yorker* in an interview: "I think there are some particular groups that historically have been underrepresented—like Latinos and Asian-Americans—that represent a larger and larger portion of the population. And so for them to be able to see folks in robes that look like them is going to be important."

After the death of U.S. Justice Antonin Scalia in February 2016, the president nominated Judge Merrick B. Garland of the U.S. Court of Appeals in D.C., a popular centrist. Republican leaders in the Senate declared that they would not act on the nomination.

Sonia Sotomayor: Wise Latina from the Bronx

Sonia Sotomayor was a judge of the United States Court of Appeals for the Second Circuit when President Obama chose her for the nation's highest court. President Bill Clinton had appointed her to the appeals court and President George H. W. Bush had appointed her as a judge on the United States District Court for the Southern District of New York.

Born in the Bronx, New York, in 1954 to Puerto Rican parents, she was raised along with her brother in public housing mostly by their mother, a nurse, after their father died when she was nine. She became an avid reader and excelled in her academic work in Catholic schools, urged on by her mother, who emphasized the importance of education. Sonia Sotomayor graduated summa cum laude from Princeton University and later earned a juris doctorate from Yale Law School, where she was an editor of the *Yale Law Journal.* From 1979 to 1984, she was an assistant district attorney in New York and was a partner in a law firm before her appointment to the U.S. district court.

Elena Kagan: A Trailblazer for Women

Elena Kagan was born in New York City in 1960. She grew up in Manhattan as the daughter of a teacher and a lawyer. She also graduated summa cum laude from Princeton and went on to earn a master of philosophy from Oxford in 1983 and a juris doctorate from Harvard Law School in 1986. She served as a clerk to Judge Abner Mikva of the U.S. Court of Appeals for the D.C. Circuit and for Justice Thurgood Marshall of the U.S. Supreme Court. She worked for a Washington law firm and became a law professor at the University of Chicago Law School and later at Harvard.

Kagan worked in the Clinton White House as associate counsel to the president and later deputy assistant for domestic policy. She was the first woman to become dean of the Harvard Law School and the first woman to serve as solicitor general.

At age fifty, she became the youngest justice and the only one on the court at the time without previous experience as a judge. However, as solicitor general, she had been the Obama administration's chief lawyer arguing high-profile cases before the Supreme Court and assisting the Justice Department in preparing cases for argument before the Supreme Court.

The Secretary

Obama's choice for secretary of State was also a bold move. Making Hillary Clinton a leading figure on the world stage was not only a magnanimous move but also a strategic one. As the *New York Times* noted, after considerable wooing and negotiating, she was to become "the public face to the world for the man who dashed her own hopes for the presidency."

"President-elect Barack Obama and Mrs. Clinton fought perhaps the most polarizing nomination battle in decades, but in recruiting her for his cabinet, Mr. Obama chose to turn a rival into a partner, and she concluded she could have a greater impact by saying yes than by remaining in the Senate," the *Times* reported before she was appointed.

In selecting Clinton, he chose someone who was a symbol of achievement for women. He also gave her a highly visible platform to enhance her credentials and standing for her next drive to win the presidential nomination. The *Times* reported that its sources said Obama "concluded after the election that the problems confronting the nation were so serious that he needed Mrs. Clinton's stature and capabilities as part of his team, notwithstanding their past differences."

Already the only U.S. first lady to be elected to public office in her own right, Hillary Rodham Clinton became the nation's only first lady to join the cabinet. On January 21, 2009, she won confirmation by the Senate, resigned from the Senate, and took the oath of office as secretary of State. She left the position after Obama's first term.

President Obama also named Janet Yellen as chairman of the Federal Reserve, on October 9, 2013, making her the first woman to head it. Yellen, sixty-seven, succeeded Ben S. Bernanke, whose term had expired. She had served as vice chair since 2010.

He also appointed Loretta Lynch as the attorney general, the first African American woman to serve in that position.

Women Appointed by Obama

Here are some of the major appointments of women President Obama has made:

CABINET LEVEL

Hillary Clinton: Secretary of State
Janet Napolitano: Secretary of Homeland Security
Hilda Solis: Secretary of Labor
Kathleen Sebelius: Secretary of Health and Human Services

Loretta Lynch: Attorney General
Sally Jewell: Secretary of the Interior
Penny Pritzker: Secretary of Commerce
Sylvia Mathews Burwell: Secretary of Health and Human Services
Gina McCarthy: Administrator, Environmental Protection Agency
Lisa Jackson: Administrator, Environmental Protection Agency

OTHER PROMINENT POSITIONS

Janet Yellen: Chairman of the Federal Reserve
Cecilia Muñoz: Director, White House Domestic Policy Council
Valerie Jarrett: Senior White House Adviser
Anita Breckenridge: Deputy Chief of Staff for Operation, White House
Shailagh Murray: Assistant to the President and Senior Adviser
Susan Rice: National Security Adviser
Samantha Power: Ambassador to the United Nations
Karen Mills: Small Business Administrator
Maria Contreras-Sweet: Small Business Administrator
Julia Pierson: Director, U.S. Secret Service
Caroline Kennedy: Ambassador to Japan

SUPREME COURT

Sonia Sotomayor   Elena Kagan

COURT OF APPEALS

Beverly B. Martin   Nina Pillard
Barbara Milano Keenan   Carolyn B. McHugh
O. Rogeriee Thompson   Nancy Moritz
Jane Branstetter Stranch   Robin S. Rosenbaum
Mary H. Murguia   Cheryl Ann Krause
Kathleen M. O'Malley   Julie E. Carnes
Susan L. Carney   Pamela Harris
Morgan Christen   Jill A. Pryor
Jacqueline Nguyen   Kara Farnandez Stoll
Patty Shwartz   *Myra C. Selby
Jane Louise Kelly   *Jennifer Klemetsrud Puhl
Patricia Ann Millett
*Appointed January 2016, pending confirmation

Women's Health

Women were major beneficiaries of Obama's health reforms. The Affordable Care Act incorporated major provisions that protect women by preventing insurance companies from denying them coverage or raising premiums based on gender or preexisting conditions, including pregnancy. More than 4.3 million women and girls enrolled in coverage through the Health Insurance Marketplace in the first open enrollment period, according to a White House fact sheet, and many more gained coverage through Medicaid.

Opposition to the act was formidable, and it continued to face challenges in Obama's final months in office. On January 8, 2016, President Obama vetoed legislation that would have repealed the health care plan and blocked federal funding of Planned Parenthood. The bill had passed the House 240-181, and the Senate, 52-47. Neither margin was enough to override a veto, however.

In a message to Congress, the president said, "Rather than refighting old political battles by once again voting to repeal basic protections that provide security for the middle class, members of Congress should be working together to grow the economy, strengthen middle-class families, and create new jobs. Because of the harm this bill would cause to the health and financial security of millions of Americans, it has earned my veto."

Under the act, most insurance plans must also cover preventative services, including contraception, mammograms, HIV testing and counseling, domestic-violence counseling, and testing for gestational diabetes with no deductibles, copayments, or coinsurance. The White House estimates that nearly thirty million women were eligible for those services because of the Affordable Care Act.

The administration also issued new rules in August 2014 to cover women whose companies objected to paying for contraception on religious grounds after the Supreme Court sided with Hobby Lobby in a case challenging the law's provisions. As a result of the contraceptive benefits, a report published in *Health Affairs* in July 2015 noted that the costs of pregnancy prevention declined quickly and starkly after the act went into effect.

The average percentages of out-of-pocket spending for oral contraceptive pill prescriptions and intrauterine device insertions both dropped by 20 percent (June 2012 to June 2013) after implementation of the Affordable Care Act mandate, the report said. Out-of-pocket expenses for the pill dropped 38 percent, and those for the IUD declined 68 percent. Costs for other forms of birth control declined dramatically as well.

Cancer researchers also found that the number of young women diagnosed in the early stages of cervical cancer had increased because of the law, improving their chances for better outcomes. Early diagnosis became possible because younger women who previously would have been uninsured were eligible to remain on their parents' policies until age twenty-six under the Affordable Care Act and thus were getting the recommended early screenings, the American Cancer Society research indicated.

The Patient Protection and Affordable Care Act, signed March 23, 2010, is a law intended to increase the quality and affordability of health insurance, provide coverage for the uninsured, and reduce health care costs.

Obama's Vetoes

President Obama has used his veto power sparingly but pointedly. According to the American Presidency Project, he had vetoed 9 bills as of January 19, 2016, in comparison with 12 for George W. Bush, 37 for Bill Clinton, 44 for George H. W. Bush, and 78 for Ronald Reagan. None of President Obama's vetoes has been overridden by Congress. He is the first president since Lyndon B. Johnson not to have any vetoes overridden.

Here is a list of his vetoes as listed on whitehouse.gov:

- **December 30, 2009** H.J.Res. 64. Department of Defense Appropriations Act, 2010. Continuing Appropriations, fiscal year 2010. In a memorandum of disapproval, the president said, "The enactment of H.R. 3326 (Department of Defense Appropriations Act, 2010, Public Law 111-118), which was signed into law on December 19, 2009, has rendered the enactment of H.J.Res. 64 (Continuing Appropriations, FY 2010) unnecessary. Accordingly, I am withholding my approval from the bill. (The Pocket Veto Case, 279 U.S. 655 [1929])."

- **October 12, 2010** H.R. 3808. Interstate Recognition of Notarizations Act of 2010. Legislation to require any federal or state court to recognize any notarization made by a notary public licensed by a state other than the state where the court is located when such notarization occurs in or affects interstate commerce. In a statement explaining the veto, the White House said it was returning the bill for closer review of the impact on consumers, particularly in regard to mortgages. Consumer advocates had raised concerns about the possibility of fraud related to electronic records of notarization.
- **February 24, 2015** S. 1. Keystone XL Pipeline Approval Act. Legislation to authorize TransCanada Keystone Pipeline, L.P., to construct, connect, operate, and maintain a pipeline, running from Alberta, Canada, to Nebraska, and cross-border facilities specified in an application filed by TransCanada Corporation to the Department of State on May 4, 2012. (See chapter 21.)
- **March 31, 2015** S.J.Res. 8. Providing for congressional disapproval under chapter 8 of title 5, United States Code, of the rule submitted by the National Labor Relations Board relating to representation case procedures. A joint congressional resolution disapproving an NLRB rule to make it easier for workers to hold a vote on whether to unionize. (See chapter 9.)
- **October 22, 2015** H.R. 1735. National Defense Authorization Act for Fiscal Year 2016. An act to authorize appropriations for fiscal year 2016 for military activities of the Department of Defense, for military construction, and for defense activities of the Department of Energy, to prescribe military personnel strengths for such fiscal year, and for other purposes. (See chapter 11.)
- **December 18, 2015** S.J.Res. 23. A joint resolution providing for congressional disapproval under chapter 8 of title 5, United States Code, of a rule submitted by the Environmental Protection Agency relating to "Standards of Performance for Greenhouse Gas Emissions from New, Modified, and Reconstructed Stationary Sources: Electric Utility Generating Units."

- **December 18, 2015** S.J.Res. 24. A joint resolution providing for congressional disapproval under chapter 8 of title 5, United States Code, of a rule submitted by the Environmental Protection Agency. A joint resolution to disapprove an EPA rule "Carbon Pollution Emission Guidelines for Existing Stationary Sources: Electric Utility Generating Units." A White House statement explaining the veto said the resolution "would nullify the Clean Power Plan, the first national standards to address climate-destabilizing greenhouse gas pollution from existing power plants." (The Pocket Veto Case, 279 U.S. 655 [1929]).
- **January 8, 2016** H.R. 3762, Restoring Americans' Healthcare Freedom Reconciliation Act. An act to provide for reconciliation pursuant to section 2002 of the concurrent resolution on the budget for fiscal year 2016. Legislation that would have repealed the health care plan and blocked federal funding of Planned Parenthood. (See chapters 1, 2, and 20.)
- **January 20, 2016** S.J.Res. 22. A joint resolution providing for congressional disapproval under chapter 8 of title 5, United States Code, of a rule submitted by the U.S. Army Corps of Engineers and the Environmental Protection Agency relating to "Clean Water Rule: Definition of 'Waters of the United States.'" Congressional opponents had argued that it went too far in extending the definition of waters on private lands entitled to environmental protections.

Reproductive Rights

The president has also maintained a solid stand in favor of women's right to choose abortion. In a speech to Planned Parenthood supporters in 2013, he vowed to defend women's rights with regard to reproductive health. "As long as we've got to fight to make sure women have access to quality, affordable health care, and as long as we've got to fight to protect a woman's right to make her own choices about her own health, I want you to know that you've also got a president who's going to be right there with you, fighting every step of the way," he said.

In January 2015, he threatened to veto legislation that would ban abortion after twenty weeks' gestation on grounds that it was scientifically specious and represented a violation of women's privacy. The legislation's supporters argued that a fetus is capable of feeling pain at twenty weeks, but opponents disputed that. The bill was known as H.R. 36—the Pain-Capable Unborn Child Protection Act. It passed the House on May 13, 2005, but Democrats blocked it from consideration in the Senate on September 22, 2015. Such legislation inevitably would have faced a challenge because it violated the Supreme Court's prevailing ruling that abortion is legal until the fetus is viable outside the womb.

Violence against Women

Obama also expanded funding to prevent violence against women. On March 7, 2013, he signed reauthorization of the Violence against Women Act, which provided $660 million over five years for legal assistance, transitional housing, counseling, and support hotlines to victims of rape and domestic abuse. First authorized in 1994, the act had lapsed in 2011, and women's advocates cited Republican opposition to renewal as part of the oft-referenced "war on women" during the 2012 elections.

Women's advocacy groups credited the act with a 58 percent drop in sexual assaults against women and girls over the past fifteen years. According to a Justice Department survey, in 2010, 270,000 rapes or sexual assaults were reported, down from 556,000 in 1995.

"One of the great legacies of this law is that it didn't just change the rules; it changed our culture. It empowered people to start speaking out. It made it okay for us, as a society, to talk about domestic abuse," Obama said at the signing. "It made it possible for us, as a country, to address the problem in a real and meaningful way. And it made clear to victims that they were not alone—that they always had a place to go and they always had people on their side."

Women in Combat

The Obama administration became the first to permit women to serve in any capacity for which they are qualified in the military. On December 4, 2015, President Obama endorsed Defense Secretary Ash Carter's order that the military open all combat roles to women, calling it a "historic step forward."

Carter said, "To succeed in our mission of national defense, we cannot afford to cut ourselves off from half the country's talents and skills." At a Pentagon press conference, he announced that beginning in 2016, women would be eligible to serve in all combat jobs, including 213,600 formerly male-only positions in fifty-two different specialties, which would include elite special operations units. "As long as they qualify and meet the standards, women will now be able to contribute to our mission in ways they could not before," Carter said. "They'll be allowed to drive tanks, fire mortars, and lead infantry soldiers into combat. They'll be able to serve as Army Rangers and Green Berets, Navy SEALs, Marine Corps infantry, Air Force parajumpers and everything else that was previously open only to men."

Two women, Army Captain Kristen Griest and First Lieutenant Shaye Haver, became the first to complete Army Ranger school, in August 2015.

Echoing Carter's enthusiasm for the long-debated and controversial move, the president said in a prepared statement. "When we desegregated our military, it became stronger. In recent years, we ended 'Don't Ask, Don't Tell' and allowed gay and lesbian Americans to serve openly—and it's made our military stronger. Over recent decades, we've opened about 90 percent of military positions to women who time and again have proven that they, too, are qualified, ready and up to the task. In the wars in Afghanistan and Iraq, our courageous women in uniform have served with honor, on the front lines—and some have given their very lives." He said the Defense Department's action would open "the remaining 10 percent of military positions, including combat roles, to women."

CHAPTER 3

African Americans

"If I had a son, he'd look like Trayvon. When I think about this boy, I think about my own kids."

President Obama, March 23, 2012

Many people in the audience joined in as President Obama started singing the hymn "Amazing Grace" while delivering the eulogy of the Reverend Clementa C. Pinckney, one of the church shooting victims in Charleston, South Carolina, June 26, 2015. (Associated Press photo/David Goldman)

President Obama, often portrayed as reluctant to address racial issues, found his voice as a leader on matters of race at crucial times and used it effectively when the times called for it. He spoke out forcefully against the killing of unarmed men and took concrete actions to investigate police departments and to curtail the transfer of military equipment to municipal police departments. He launched an initiative to help young black and Latino males and increased funding for historically black colleges and universities. He inspired record voter turnout among African Americans and increased interest in political participation.

It was a signature moment in the presidency of Barack Hussein Obama when he broke into song on June 26, 2015, to comfort the grieving after the fatal shootings of nine black people in Charleston, South Carolina. The president of the United States "raised" a hymn, looking and sounding as comfortable doing so as any pastor in a black church would on any given Sunday. He chose a beloved standard, "Amazing Grace."

A repentant British slave trader, turned abolitionist and Anglican minister, wrote the words in 1772. Yet, it is a song that resonates with Christians today, both black and white, and many in the audience took the cue to join in: "I once was lost, but now am found/Was blind, but now I see."

In his remarks, Obama, channeling both our sorrows and our hopes for a better America, said, "For too long, we've been blind to the way past injustices continue to shape the present. Perhaps we see that now. Perhaps this tragedy causes us to ask some tough questions." He addressed the need for action to improve the state of race relations. "None of us can or should expect a transformation in race relations overnight. Every time something like this happens, somebody says, 'We have to have a conversation about race.' We talk a lot about race. There's no shortcut. We don't need more talk."

He had come to speak at the funeral of the Reverend Clementa C. Pinckney, the pastor and state senator who was among the nine fatally shot by a white supremacist gunman they had welcomed into their midst for a Bible study at Emanuel African Methodist Episcopal Church, one of the nation's oldest black churches.

Dylann Storm Roof, a twenty-one-year-old white man, had sat among them for an hour before he began venting against blacks and shooting, killing the victims, who ranged in age from twenty-six to eighty-seven. Authorities charged him with multiple counts of murder and attempted murder, as well as with federal hate crimes.

"Maybe we now realize the way a racial bias can infect us even when we don't realize it, so that we're guarding against not just racial slurs, but we're also guarding against the subtle impulse to call Johnny back for a job interview but not Jamal," the president said.

The very fact that a black man sits in the White House makes a statement. What that statement is remains open to interpretation. After Obama's election, black folks could finally look their children square in the eye and honestly tell them that they, too, could be president. Many black parents had raised their children to believe it, even as the elders suspected it would never be true. To the amazement of many, including me, finally it had been accomplished.

Just seeing a black man on television every day acting in his role as the leader of the free world with his swagger and coolness was uplifting for African Americans. Seeing him as a loving husband and caring father, living in the White House with four beautiful black women spanning three generations, his wife, Michelle; daughters, Malia and Sasha; and mother-in-law, Marian Shields Robinson, was an antidote to the negative images of black men the media too often present. Various news reports even touted the beneficial "Obama Effect" on politics, race relations, and possibly even academic achievement for young people.

Still, while many postulated that his election meant we had reached "postracial" nirvana, it seems clear that has not happened given the upheaval we have seen in our streets and on our campuses over police shootings, excessive use of force, and racially motivated acts of other kinds.

Many African Americans have also complained that Obama "talks down" to black audiences and that he has not "done enough" for them— whatever "enough" might be. A study by Daniel Q. Gillion, a University of Pennsylvania researcher, found that Obama had talked less about race in his first two years of office than any Democratic president since John F. Kennedy was in office.

Others have pointed out that the fact that he is black put Obama in the awkward position of not being able to do too much for African Americans specifically, lest he appear to be playing favorites. It was a "damned if he did, damned if he didn't" dilemma. As *New York* magazine put it in an article in October 2015, "The Paradox of the First Black President": "In a country whose basic genetic blueprint includes the same crooked mutations that made slavery and Jim Crow possible, it is not possible to have a black president surrounded by black aides on Marine One without paying a price. And the price that Obama has had to pay—and, more important, that African-Americans have had to pay—is one of caution, moderation, and at times compromised policies: The first black president could do only so much, and say only so much, on behalf of other African-Americans. That is the bittersweet irony of the first black presidency."

Indeed, it is difficult to separate out specific items on Obama's long list of accomplishments that solely or clearly target black people as beneficiaries. However, his record includes many initiatives that address issues that disproportionately affect African Americans, as well as major reforms that touch the lives of all Americans.

In a meeting with six black American journalists in February 2013, Valerie Jarrett, a senior adviser to the president, defended the president's record on behalf of African Americans. As George E. Curry, a prominent writer and editor, reported it on Afro.com, Jarrett said:

If you look at the president's record in the first four years, if you look at his major domestic policy accomplishments, they disproportionately do benefit the African-American community...If you look at the Affordable Care Act—roughly 9 million African-Americans uninsured will have health insurance today—if you look at the president's Recovery Act and subsequent budgets...If you went through the menu of tax incentives and unemployment that disproportionately benefit the African-American community, time and time again—I think unemployment insurance has been extended like nine times—every single time we had to fight the Republicans to get that done.

Race and the Law

As the president of all the people, Obama did seem reticent to talk about race for a long time, but when he did, his voice resonated in a way that none of his predecessors' voices could have. He has often used his platform to speak to racial issues in a profound way, as when he expressed his empathy by declaring in March 2012 that Trayvon Martin could have been his son.

The fatal shooting of the unarmed teenager occurred when a neighborhood watch captain confronted and followed him for no apparent reason other than that he looked "suspicious" while walking through the gated community where his father's fiancée lived.

Obama had kept silent, to the dismay of many black leaders, as thousands of people took to the streets and blew up social media to protest that police had not even arrested the shooter. Aides had said the president was unlikely to address the case that was then still under investigation by local as well as federal officials under his command.

"We here in the White House are aware of the incident, and we understand that the local FBI office has been in contact with the local authorities and is monitoring the situation," Jay Carney, the White House press secretary, said. "Our thoughts and prayers go out to Trayvon Martin's family, but obviously, we're not going to wade into a local law-enforcement matter."

A few days later, Obama broke his silence at a press conference about the World Bank, in the Rose Garden, saying, "My main message is to the parents of Trayvon Martin. You know, if I had a son, he'd look like Trayvon," Obama said. "All of us as Americans are going to take this with the seriousness it deserves."

The fact that he spoke to this issue was "evidence of Obama's evolution and rising comfort level in dealing with the matter of race," the *Washington Post* declared.

After a jury acquitted George Zimmerman of killing Martin in July 2013, igniting a tsunami of protests and commentary throughout the country, Obama stepped into the fray again. He popped into the White House Press Room at the time slotted for a routine briefing and delivered remarks about the case. "The reason I actually wanted to come out today is not to take questions, but to speak to an issue that obviously has gotten a lot of attention over the course of the last week—the issue of the Trayvon Martin ruling. I gave a preliminary statement right after the ruling on Sunday. But watching the debate over the course of the last week, I thought it might be useful for me to expand on my thoughts a little bit."

He recalled his comments from a year earlier. "Another way of saying that is Trayvon Martin could have been me thirty-five years ago," he said. "And when you think about why, in the African American community at least, there's a lot of pain around what happened here, I think it's important to recognize that the African American community is looking at this issue through a set of experiences and a history that doesn't go away."

Continuing his remarks, the president spoke directly to the issue of racial profiling. "There are very few African American men in this country who haven't had the experience of being followed when they were shopping in a department store," he said. "That includes me. There are very few African American men who haven't had the experience of walking across the street and hearing the locks click on the doors of cars. That happened to me—at least before I was a senator. There are very few African Americans who haven't had the experience of getting on an elevator and a woman clutching her purse nervously and holding her breath until she had a chance to get off. That happens often."

These are things black men complain happen to them almost daily, but to have the president say them was a watershed moment for many of us. When we as ordinary black men describe such incidents to our white associates or colleagues, we are almost never believed, or the incidents are dismissed as insignificant or overblown. Would it make a difference that white people were hearing it from President Obama?

Action accompanied Obama's rhetoric. The Justice Department conducted an independent investigation but ultimately concluded that the evidence regarding events surrounding Martin's death was insufficient "to prove beyond a reasonable doubt that Zimmerman's actions violated the federal criminal civil rights statutes."

Obama also had the Department of Justice (DOJ) investigate several police departments as shootings of unarmed black men by officers and deaths in custody began to seem epidemic and as protests snowballed.

In the midst of the uproar over a video of the shooting of Laquan McDonald by a Chicago police officer, Attorney General Loretta Lynch announced on December 7, 2015, that the U.S. Justice Department would investigate whether Chicago police habitually violated laws or the U.S. Constitution in their policing. The "pattern or practice" investigation was to focus on the "use of force, including racial, ethnic and other disparities in use of force, and its systems of accountability," according to the department announcement. The Federal Bureau of Investigation had already entered an investigation specifically into the McDonald case in April and its inquiry was still in progress.

A police dash-cam video that was excruciating to watch and even harder to comprehend showed police officer Jason Van Dyke shooting McDonald on October 20, 2014, as he was running away from officers, contradicting their official statements that he was lunging toward them with a knife, posing a threat. Anyone watching the video could clearly see that an officer fired sixteen shots at the retreating seventeen-year-old, even pumping bullets into the youth as he lay on the ground, sixteen shots in about fifteen seconds. It appears that none of the officers present rendered McDonald assistance after the shooting, and he died later at a hospital.

No charges were filed either in the case of Ronald Johnson, who was killed by Chicago police eight days before McDonald.

Mass protests over the McDonald shooting and the brazen cover-up sprang up in Chicago after the video's release, including a rally on Black Friday that virtually shut down commerce along a stretch of the city's famed "Miracle Mile."

Months earlier, the City of Chicago had paid McDonald's family $5 million although the family had not filed a lawsuit, but officials resisted pressure and Freedom of Information requests to release the video for thirteen months until a judge finally ordered the release. The officer who killed McDonald remained employed by the department at a desk job after the deadly shooting. Authorities charged him with first-degree murder on November 24, the day the video was released, and released him about a week later on a $1.5 million bond.

An account of the Justice Department's announcement of an investigation on CNN.com noted that such investigations were "nothing new to President Barack Obama's administration. Many cities have fallen under the federal microscope during his administration." The *Washington Post* also noted the Obama administration's record on the investigation of policing issues. "Under Obama, Attorneys General Loretta

Lynch and her predecessor, Eric Holder, have used patterns-or-practices investigations to aggressively probe police departments for potential constitutional violations, investigating dozens of departments since 2009," the *Post* reported. "These probes have found patterns of excessive force by police in Cleveland; Albuquerque; the Los Angeles County Sheriff's Department; Portland; New Orleans; Seattle; Puerto Rico; and Warren, Ohio."

The investigations are authorized under a law Congress passed after the widely viewed videotaped beating of Rodney King by Los Angeles police officers and the subsequent acquittal of four officers in the case, which generated riots in April 1992.

In its investigations, the Justice Department gathers information from people inside and outside the police department, observes police through ride-alongs, and reviews documents. Investigators do not look at individual cases for potential criminal violations, but they do look at incidents for patterns, according to the Justice Department.

In August 2014, Attorney General Holder announced a "pattern or practice" investigation into the Ferguson, Missouri, police department after he visited the community in the wake of the shooting of Michael Brown, another unarmed black teenager, by a police officer. The Justice Department also undertook an investigation into whether the officer, Darren Wilson, should face federal civil rights charges.

On March 4, 2015, the Justice Department announced that while evidence examined in its investigation into the fatal shooting did not support charges under the civil rights laws, it had found that the Ferguson Police Department engaged in a pattern or practice of conduct that violated the Constitution under the First, Fourth, and Fourteenth Amendments. "As detailed in our report, this investigation found a community that was deeply polarized, and where deep distrust and hostility often characterized interactions between police and area residents," said then attorney general Eric Holder. "Our investigation showed that Ferguson police officers routinely violate the Fourth Amendment in stopping people without reasonable suspicion, arresting them without probable cause, and using unreasonable force against them. Now that our investigation has reached its conclusion, it is time for Ferguson's leaders to take immediate, wholesale, and structural corrective action. The report we have issued and the steps we have taken are only the beginning of a necessarily resource-intensive and inclusive process to promote reconciliation, to reduce and eliminate bias, and to bridge gaps and build understanding."

About a year later, on February 10, 2016, the Justice Department filed a civil rights lawsuit against Ferguson, the day after the city rejected an agreement to overhaul its criminal justice system and address the abuses found. "Their decision leaves us no further choice," Attorney General Loretta Lynch said at a news conference announcing the suit.

Better Policing

President Obama also established a task force on policing and rolled back the use of certain military equipment by municipal police.

On December 18, 2014, President Obama signed an executive order establishing the Task Force on 21st Century Policing, charged with offering recommendations on how the police can fight crime and build public trust.

Charles H. Ramsey, the Philadelphia police commissioner, and Laurie Robinson, a George Mason University professor, chaired the task force. It included law-enforcement representatives, community leaders, youth, and academic experts. The White House said the task force took testimony from more than one hundred witnesses in public hearings across the country and reviewed hundreds of written submissions.

In May 2015, Obama unveiled its final report, which included nearly sixty recommendations. Among them were that the federal government should

- Create and fund a national crime and justice task force to review and evaluate all components of the criminal justice system to make recommendations for comprehensive criminal justice reform.
- Promote programs that take a comprehensive approach to addressing the core issues of poverty, education, health, and safety.
- Establish a law-enforcement diversity initiative to help assure that police departments reflect the demographics of the community.
- Require law-enforcement agencies to collect data on all officer-involved shootings, whether fatal or nonfatal, and deaths in police custody. Agencies should be required to maintain and report the data to the federal government.

- Create a mechanism for investigating complaints and issuing sanctions for inappropriate use of equipment and tactics during mass demonstrations.
- Support training to help law-enforcement agencies take advantage of technology and tactics for best practices in twenty-first-century policing.
- Encourage development of "less than lethal" technology to help control combative suspects.
- Reevaluate zero-tolerance strategies directed at adolescents.
- Promote higher standards for police training, ongoing education, and incorporation of research on policing and encourage higher education for police.
- Support continuing research on mental health checks for officers, as well as fitness, resilience, and nutrition.

The Justice Department's Office of Community Oriented Policing Services said it had already begun putting some of those recommendations into action.

On May 18, 2015, President Obama issued an executive order that banned the transfer of certain kinds of military equipment to local law-enforcement agencies, following the recommendations of a multi-agency working group in his administration. The decision came in reaction to the paramilitary response to protests in Ferguson and elsewhere as demonstrations over police killings sprang up across the country. Television viewers and rights advocates were alarmed and outraged to see police who seemed all too happy to don full riot gear to confront peaceful marchers and roll along in armored trucks, armed with tear gas and assault rifles. Many citizens were unaware that local departments had such extensive arsenals at the ready and that they often obtained the equipment from the federal government through the Defense, Justice, and Homeland Security offices.

The president's order immediately banned transfer of armored vehicles that use tracks, bayonets, grenade launchers, camouflage uniforms, and large-caliber weapons and ammunition.

"We've seen how militarized gear can sometimes give people a feeling like they're an occupying force, as opposed to a force that's part of the community that's protecting them and serving them," Obama said in a speech in Camden, New Jersey.

He said other equipment that might be necessary in emergencies, such as aircraft, wheeled tactical vehicles, mobile command-and-control units, battering rams, and protective riot gear, would go on a "controlled equipment list." To acquire it, police departments would have to meet national policing standards, track the use of the equipment, and receive federal approval to sell or transfer any of it.

"We're going to prohibit some equipment made for the battlefield that is not appropriate for local police departments," Obama said.

Beer Diplomacy

One reason for the president's caution in speaking out on the Trayvon Martin killing was the harsh criticism he had faced when he commented on the arrest of Dr. Henry Louis Gates Jr. Police charged the professor, an African American who was one of the most prominent academics in the nation, with disorderly conduct on July 16, 2009, after an encounter at his home in Cambridge, Massachusetts. He was the Alphonse Fletcher Jr. University Professor and director of the Hutchins Center for African and African American Research at Harvard University and was world renowned for his books, documentaries, PBS series on genealogy, and countless honors.

A caller had reported a possible break-in after seeing the professor trying to open the jammed lock to his own home, assisted by his driver, after returning from a trip to China. Reports that the caller specifically said the would-be burglars were black were refuted.

According to a police report, Gates refused to step outside to speak with an officer and initially resisted handing over his identification, though he ultimately did. The officer reported that when he told Gates that he was investigating a possible break-in, Gates opened the front door and exclaimed, "Why, because I'm a black man in America?"

Gates produced identification after the officer followed him into the home. According to the professor's account, the officer repeatedly refused to give his name and badge number as requested.

Police said they arrested the professor for "loud and tumultuous behavior in a public space." "While I was led to believe that Gates was lawfully in the residence, I was quite surprised and confused with the behavior he exhibited toward me," the officer, Sergeant James Crowley, said in the report.

Police released Gates after four hours and dropped the charges a few days later.

Asked about it at a press conference on national television, Obama said the police "acted stupidly" in making the arrest.

"I don't know, not having been there and not seeing all the facts, what role race played," Obama said.

What he didn't say was that Gates, then fifty-nine years old, of relatively small stature, a man who had walked with a limp for most of his life, could hardly have posed a threat to the officer. Moreover, because of his documentaries and series on PBS, Gates was highly recognizable to millions of people all over the world, and the local police should have known him.

The president prefaced his remarks by admitting that he was "a little biased" toward Gates, who had been teaching at Obama's alma mater since 1991, because they were friends, and he noted that the arrest had come after Gates had shown identification proving he lived there. That said, the president added, "I think it's fair to say, No. 1, any of us would be pretty angry; No. 2, that the Cambridge police acted stupidly in arresting somebody when there was already proof that they were in their own home; and, No. 3 . . . that there's a long history in this country of African-Americans and Latinos being stopped by law enforcement disproportionately."

That did not go over well in some quarters, notably among law-enforcement groups, and Obama had to backpedal a bit, saying he regretted the remarks.

On July 24, showing up unannounced at a White House press briefing, Obama said he had just had a conversation with the arresting officer and felt "he was an outstanding police officer and a good man." Obama added,

> And because this has been ratcheting up—and I obviously helped to contribute ratcheting it up—I want to make clear that in my choice of words I think I unfortunately gave an impression that I was maligning the Cambridge Police Department or Sergeant Crowley specifically—and I could have calibrated those words differently. And I told this to Sergeant Crowley. I continue to believe, based on what I have heard, that there was an overreaction in pulling Professor Gates out of his home to the station. I also continue to

believe, based on what I heard, that Professor Gates probably over-reacted as well. My sense is you've got two good people in a circumstance in which neither of them were able to resolve the incident in the way that it should have been resolved and the way they would have liked it to be resolved.

Nevertheless, Obama seized upon the episode as a "teachable moment" on race relations by inviting Gates and Crowley to the White House for what quickly became known as the "beer summit."

Obama took issue with some critics who said that as president he should not have spoken at all on such a local matter. "I have to tell you that that part of it I disagree with," he told the press in the briefing room. "The fact that this has become such a big issue I think is indicative of the fact that race is still a troubling aspect of our society. Whether I were black or white, I think that me commenting on this and hopefully contributing to constructive—as opposed to negative—understandings about the issue, is part of my portfolio."

On July 30, joined by Vice President Joe Biden, the president of the United States sat down in the Rose Garden for a brief chat with the two men at the center of the controversy as they enjoyed beverages and snacks. After the encounter, the president said, "I have always believed that what brings us together is stronger than what pulls us apart...I am confident that has happened here tonight, and I am hopeful that all of us are able to draw this positive lesson from this episode."

The Pew Research Center, a nonpartisan fact tank that studies public policy issues and trends, said the Gates episode was "the largest single event explicitly tied to race in the way it was covered during the year... Nearly one-fifth of all coverage studied during the year relating to African Americans (19.4%) had to do with Gates' arrest and the ensuing controversy, including Obama's remarks," Pew reported.

HBCU Funding

President Obama increased funding and focused government resources on historically black colleges and universities. He signed an executive order on February 26, 2010, renewing the White House Initiative on Historically Black Colleges and Universities (HBCUs) as part of the Department of Education. (President Jimmy Carter first signed an executive order in 1980 establishing a program to expand the educational capacity of HBCUs, and presidents since then have continued some sort of initiative for such institutions.)

The initiative's mission was to coordinate government and private efforts to strengthen the capacity of HBCUs to participate in federal programs, foster private and public partnerships, improve communications with HBCUs, share best practices, and explore new ways to improve the relationship between the federal government and HBCUs. The order also established a president's board of advisers on HBCUs.

The White House also announced at that time that its 2011 budget included

- $98 million in new money for HBCUs at the Department of Education—$13 million, a 5 percent increase for the Strengthening HBCUs Program, and $85 million in mandatory funding for HBCUs in the Student Aid and Fiscal Responsibility Act, then pending.
- $20.5 million to provide HBCUs with access to financing for capital projects, including $279 million in new loans in 2011, more than $100 million more than in 2010.
- $64.5 million for the Strengthening Historically Black Graduate Institutions Program, a $3.1 million or 5 percent increase.
- $103 million for a comprehensive science and technology workforce program at the National Science Foundation to engage undergraduates at historically black, tribal, and Hispanic-serving colleges and universities, a 14 percent increase for these activities.

The White House also noted that the increase in the Pell Grant maximum award to $5,710 in 2011—$160 over the 2010 level—and future increases above inflation would benefit all students. In 2011, students attending HBCUs were to receive about $900 million in Pell Grants, an increase of nearly $400 million during the Obama administration.

In spite of these actions, African Americans have criticized the president for remarks he has made about the need for HBCUs to make sure their graduation rates are competitive. Answering a question from a student of Southern University at a town hall in Baton Rouge, Louisiana, about the value of an HBCU education, he said in part:

Well, first of all, the role of the historically black colleges and universities in producing our leadership and expanding opportunity—training doctors and teachers and lawyers and ministers who change the landscape of America—I hope most people know that story, and if not, you better learn it. Because it has been powerful and continues to be a powerful tradition.

And I will tell you that if you have done well at an HBCU and graduated, and you go to an employer and are making the kind of presentation you make or a Morehouse man makes or a Spelman young lady makes, you will do just fine. I don't think it's true that actually people don't take—or discount that tradition. And you will be credentialed. You'll succeed.

I do think that there's a range of challenges that HBCUs face. Some are doing great; some are having more difficulty...We have been very supportive of HBCUs over the last several years. And to their credit, the previous administration had supported them, as well. There are some HBCUs that are having trouble with graduation rates. And that is a source of concern. And what we've said to those HBCUs is we want to work with you, but we don't want a situation in which young people are taking out loans, getting in debt, thinking that they're going to get a great education and then halfway through they're dropping out.

Now, some of it is those HBCUs may be taking chances on some kids that other schools might not. And that's a positive thing, and that has to be taken into account. But we also have to make sure that colleges—any college, HBCU or non-HBCU—take seriously the need to graduate that student and not load them up with debt.

The *Journal of Blacks in Higher Education* reported that "the graduation rate of African-American students at the nation's historically black colleges and universities (HBCUs) tends to be much lower than the graduation rate for black students at the nation's highest-ranked institutions. Yet the graduation rate at a significant number of HBCUs is well above the nationwide average for black student graduations...at an extremely low rate of 42 percent." Rates are based on students completing a bachelor's degree within six years of enrolling.

The highest rate was at Spelman College, at 77 percent, which was higher than the black student graduation rate at thirteen of fifty-six high-ranking predominantly white colleges and universities. Morehouse and Fisk colleges had rates of 64 percent. Only four other HBCUs had rates of 50 percent or more, and at twenty-four HBCUs—nearly one-half of all HBCUs in the journal's survey—two-thirds or more of all entering black students did not go on to earn a diploma. The lowest graduation rate was at the University of the District of Columbia with 7 percent earning a bachelor's degree.

Studies have attributed the low numbers to cuts in state funding, philanthropy, and student aid, as well as the fact that HBCUs serve many students who are low-income, first-generation college enrollees. Obama seems to have accounted for that in his remarks, which were in keeping with his overall focus on increasing U.S. college graduation rates. (See chapter 1.)

My Brother's Keeper

On February 27, 2014. Obama addressed the needs of young men of color directly when he signed a presidential memorandum establishing the My Brother's Keeper Task Force, an interagency effort to coordinate and evaluate approaches to helping them. The White House announcement said:

> For decades, opportunity has lagged behind for boys and young men of color. But across the country, communities are adopting approaches to help put these boys and young men on the path to success. The President wants to build on that work. We can learn from communities that are partnering with local businesses and foundations to connect these boys and young men to mentoring, support networks, and skills they need to find a good job or go to college and work their way up into the middle class. And the Administration will do its part by helping to identify and promote programs that work.

Obama also initiated the My Brother's Keeper Alliance to create partnerships with the private sector and encourage nonprofits to raise $200 million in five years for programs focused on young men of color. (The name of these programs comes from Genesis 4:9, from the question

Cain poses to God after he has killed his brother, Abel, and God asks him where his brother is: "Am I my brother's keeper?")

The My Brother's Keeper Alliance challenges communities to enact policies, programs, and partnerships to improve the lives of young people. According to the White House, nearly two hundred mayors, tribal leaders, and county executives across forty-three states and the District of Columbia had accepted the My Brother's Keeper Community Challenge by the fall of 2015.

The six goals of the My Brother's Keeper Challenge are to ensure that all children

- Enter school cognitively, physically, socially, and emotionally ready.
- Read at grade level by the third grade.
- Graduate from high school.
- Complete postsecondary education or training.
- Find employment when they are out of school.
- Remain safe from violent crime.

At an event promoting the alliance, on May 4, 2015, at Lehman College, in the Bronx in New York, President Obama said,

You all know the numbers. By almost every measure, the life chances of the average young man of color are worse than his peers'. Those opportunity gaps begin early—often at birth—and they compound over time, becoming harder and harder to bridge, making too many young men and women feel like no matter how hard they try, they may never achieve their dreams.

And that sense of unfairness and of powerlessness, of people not hearing their voices, that's helped fuel some of the protests that we've seen in places like Baltimore, and Ferguson, and right here in New York.

The president said the alliance was an idea that his administration had pursued in the wake of Trayvon Martin's death. "We wanted the message sent from the White House in a sustained way that his life mattered, that the lives of the young men who are here today matter, that we care about your future—not just sometimes, but all the time," Obama said.

The White House brought together a broad coalition of leaders in the public and private sectors, the president said, "all united around the simple idea of giving all our young people the tools they need to achieve their full potential. We were determined not to just do a feel-good exercise, to write a report that nobody would read, to do some announcement, and then once the TV cameras had gone away and there weren't protests or riots, then somehow we went back to business as usual," Obama added. "We wanted something sustained. And for more than a year, we've been working with experts to identify some of the key milestones that matter most in every young person's life—from whether they enter school ready to learn, to whether they graduate ready for a career. Are they getting suspended in school? Can we intervene there? Are they in danger of falling into the criminal justice system? Can we catch them before they do? Key indicators that we know will make a difference."

Obama told the audience that he personally planned to make this cause part of his life's work. "This will remain a mission for me and for [my wife] Michelle not just for the rest of my presidency but for the rest of my life," he said.

The media quickly jumped on this statement as the harbinger of where Obama planned to focus his energies and his influence in his postpresidential years. It was a declaration of what he wanted at least part of his legacy to be.

Some lesser known, but far-reaching, actions he has taken in the interest of black people and other protected groups include increasing funding for civil rights enforcement and initiating more vigorous enforcement activity. (See chapter 13.)

Trayvon Martin: Somebody's Son

Trayvon Benjamin Martin was born on February 5, 1995, to Sybrina Fulton and Tracy Martin. They divorced when he was four, but both remained involved in his life. Fulton was an employee for Miami-Dade County's housing agency, and Tracy Martin was a truck driver.

Trayvon was a junior at Dr. Michael M. Krop High School, where he was a good student. He had taken advanced English and math. The young man was interested in aeronautics, his family said, and was preparing for his SAT.

He had no juvenile record and no criminal record, despite some media efforts to portray him as a thug. He reportedly had minor disciplinary issues at school, including some suspensions over tardiness, evidence of marijuana residue in his book bag, and "tagging" or drawing graffiti.

He lived with his mother and older brother, a college student, in Miami Gardens, Florida.

At the time of his death, he was visiting at the home of his father's fiancée, Brandy Green, in a gated community, The Retreat at Twin Lakes, in Sanford, Florida.

Trayvon Martin's family described him as kind-hearted, giving, and not prone to violence, according to a column by Charles M. Blow in the *New York Times*. Martin would spoon-feed his quadriplegic uncle, babysit his young cousins, and bake cookies for them, the family said. They described how he earned money by painting houses, washing cars, and working the concession stand at Pee Wee football games.

The facts of the case were widely reported (sometimes with varying details):

He was unarmed when he was confronted by George Zimmerman on February 26, 2012, after going to buy some Skittles candy for Green's fourteen-year-old son and a can of AriZona iced tea for himself at a 7-Eleven convenience store.

The tall, slight seventeen-year-old known as Slimm was walking along wearing a hooded sweatshirt as he headed back to Green's town home when Zimmerman, a volunteer neighborhood watch coordinator, drove by, noticed him, and called the police. According to the recording, Zimmerman said, "We've had some break-ins in my neighborhood, and there's a real suspicious guy." He said the person was "just walking around looking about" but that he looked as if "he is up to no good or he is on drugs or something."

Zimmerman reported that the person had his hand in his waistband, and muttered, "These assholes. They always get away." He told the dispatcher that the young man was running, and defied the dispatcher's instructions not to pursue him. Four minutes later, when police arrived, Martin lay facedown in the grass with Zimmerman standing over him, near the rear of Green's town home. The youth was declared dead but was not identified and remained listed as a John Doe in the morgue overnight. His father, who had been out to dinner with his fiancée, reported him missing that night, but did not learn of his fate until police showed him a picture of the corpse the next day.

Police took Zimmerman into custody the night of the shooting, but they questioned him and released him without charges. He claimed Martin threatened and attacked him. A friend who was on the phone with Martin during the encounter disputed that, as did witnesses who heard or saw parts of the encounter. Police said they had no evidence to refute Zimmerman's claim that he had acted in self-defense, and that Florida's Stand Your Ground law gave him the right to defend himself with lethal force.

Protests erupted across the country as demands for an arrest and full investigation went viral on social media, forcing traditional media to cover it 24/7 and officials to look at the case more closely. Hoodies like the sweatshirt Martin was wearing became symbolic of the case.

As Blow wrote in the *Times*:

> To believe Zimmerman's scenario, you have to believe that Trayvon, an unarmed boy, a boy so thin that people called him Slimm, a boy whose mother said that he had not had a fight since he was a preschooler, chose that night and that man to attack. You have to believe that Trayvon chose to attack a man who outweighed him by 100 pounds and who, according to the Sanford police, was wearing his gun in a holster You have to believe that Trayvon chose to attack even though he was less than a hundred yards from the safety of the home where he was staying. This is possible, but hardly sounds plausible. The key is to determine who was standing his ground and defending himself: the boy with the candy or the man with the gun.

Black Appointees

African Americans who have served in top positions in the Obama administration include the following:

Eric Holder: Attorney General
Loretta Lynch: Attorney General
Anthony Foxx: Secretary of Transportation
Jeh Johnson: Secretary of Homeland Security
Valerie Jarrett: Senior White House Adviser
Susan Rice: National Security Adviser
Reggie Love: Special Assistant to the President
Patrick Gaspard: Director of the White House Office of Political Affairs,
    later Ambassador to South Africa
Bill Burton: Deputy Press Secretary, White House
Van Jones: White House Environmental Adviser
Broderick Johnson: Chairman of the My Brother's Keeper Task Force
Marlon Marshall: Deputy Director, White House Office of Public
    Engagement
Melody Barnes: Director, Domestic Policy Council

Unwavering Support

Even with the talk among some that Obama did not do enough for African Americans, black support for Obama has never wavered. His approval ratings among blacks have been the highest for any ethnic group, and the percentage of African American voters who voted for him in both presidential elections is unprecedented—95 percent in 2008 and 93 percent in 2012. Both his poll and voter turnout numbers throughout his tenure attest to that reality.

According to U.S. Census Bureau data analyzed by the *Cook Political Report*, African Americans made up 10 percent of those who voted in 2000 and 11 percent in 2004. That percentage increased to 13 percent in 2008 and remained the same in the 2012 election. In fact, the black turnout of 66 percent exceeded the white turnout by 2 points.

In addition, a recent *Cook* report noted that without the black vote,

Obama would not have carried Florida, Maryland, Michigan, Nevada, Ohio, Pennsylvania, and Virginia—all huge battleground states rich with electoral votes.

Jonathan Capehart, the noted *Washington Post* columnist, wrote on January 22, 2016, that Obama was "wildly popular" in the African American community with a 91 percent approval rating, six points higher than the previous week.

Obama's successes have encouraged other blacks to seek political office, and his very public support of former Newark mayor Cory Booker helped propel him into the U.S. Senate. Obama's influence will no doubt affect politics for many years to come.

For black Americans, Obama, faults and all, has been "the one" they have been waiting for.

CHAPTER 4

LGBT

"We've made real progress in advancing equality for LGBT Americans in ways that were unimaginable not too long ago."

President Obama, June 26, 2015

President Obama spoke during a reception for LGBT Pride Month in the East Room of the White House as First Lady Michelle Obama listened, June 30, 2014. (Associated Press photo/Manuel Balce Ceneta)

President Obama has used his powers and influence broadly to end discrimination against lesbian, gay, bisexual, and transgender people at home and abroad. Notably, he ended the military's Don't Ask, Don't Tell policy and appointed gay and transgender people to prominent positions. He signed legislation to punish hate crimes based on sexual orientation or gender identity. The president changed his position to support same-sex marriage and declared that his administration would not defend the Defense of Marriage Act.

In November 2015, *Out* magazine named President Obama its "Ally of the Year," and he became the first sitting president of the United States to pose for the cover of a gay magazine.

The magazine covers news and culture for gay and lesbian readers. In its cover article, *Out* noted that Obama had reversed his position on same-sex marriage in 2012, evolving from his earlier view that "marriage" applied only to male-female couples to support marriage equality by the end of his first term. "For someone who at first seemed coy, even awkward, on the subject, President Obama's evolution on marriage equality has been something to behold. He came to office reiterating that marriage was an institution reserved for a man and a woman, and continued to hold that line throughout most of his first term, even while advancing other important legislation, including the repeal of 'don't ask, don't tell,'" the magazine said.

Out also cited his order prohibiting federal contractors from discriminating on the basis of sexual orientation or gender identity, passage of the Matthew Shepard and James Byrd, Jr., Hate Crimes Prevention Act, his efforts to end a ban on transgender military service, and his efforts to diversify the judiciary. It also lauded him for the nomination in November 2015 of the first openly gay person to head a military branch, Eric K. Fanning as secretary of the army. "Whichever way you look at it, this president and his administration have ushered extraordinary change into the lives of LGBT Americans," *Out* said.

In short, on Obama's watch, the legal status of lesbian, gay, bisexual, and transgender people has emerged from the Dark Ages. Most notably, on September 20, 2011, he officially ended the Pentagon's policy of Don't Ask, Don't Tell (DADT). The policy, in effect since February 1994, allowed gay people to serve in the military only if they kept the fact of their sexual orientation to themselves and did not engage in "homosexual conduct." With Obama's long-standing support of the idea, Congress passed legislation to end the policy after a waiting period. President Obama signed the repeal into law on December 22, 2010.

The law delayed the repeal until sixty days after the president, secretary of Defense, and chairman of the Joint Chiefs of Staff certified that the military was prepared to lift the ban without harming military readiness. However, a federal appeals court ruling on July 6, 2011, barred further enforcement of the ban on openly gay service members serving in the U.S. military. President Obama, Secretary of Defense Leon Panetta, and Admiral Mike Mullen, chairman of the Joint Chiefs of Staff, sent the certification to Congress on July 22, setting the official end of the policy on September 20.

When the appeal went into effect, Obama said, "Today, the discriminatory law known as 'Don't Ask, Don't Tell' is finally and formally repealed. As of today, patriotic Americans in uniform will no longer have to lie about who they are in order to serve the country they love. As of today, our armed forces will no longer lose the extraordinary skills and combat experience of so many gay and lesbian service members. And today, as Commander in Chief, I want those who were discharged under this law to know that your country deeply values your service." The new law allowed those who were discharged solely because of their sexual orientation to reapply for military service.

A year after the repeal, the Palm Center, an academic research institute at the University of California, Santa Barbara, released a study concluding that the repeal had no negative effect on military readiness, contrary to predictions by opponents of the move. In fact, the report said the repeal had had positive effects. "Our conclusion...is that DADT repeal has had no overall negative impact on military readiness or its component dimensions, including cohesion, recruitment, retention, assaults, harassment or morale," the report said. "Although we identified a few downsides that followed from the policy change, we identified upsides as well, and in no case did negative consequences outweigh benefits. If anything, DADT repeal appears to have enhanced the military's ability to pursue its mission."

When President Bill Clinton announced the DADT policy on July 19, 1993, he called it "a major step forward." Before then, gays were banned from military service, period. While the new policy would allow them to serve, so long as they remained deeply closeted, Clinton admitted it wasn't ideal. He had campaigned on a promise to lift restrictions on gays in the military but compromised in the face of opposition.

"It is not a perfect solution," Clinton said then. "It is not identical with some of my own goals. And it certainly will not please everyone, perhaps not anyone, and clearly not those who hold the most adamant opinions on either side of this issue."

A movement to repeal the policy grew as attitudes toward homosexuality shifted and the hypocrisy of the policy became more apparent. The Palm Center report noted that public opinion had changed in the years since the policy went into effect, with polls showing most Americans were in favor of ending the ban when it ended.

> The Don't Ask, Don't Tell Repeal Act of 2010, signed December 22, 2010, is a law that established a process for ending the policy in effect since 1994 that barred gays, lesbians, and bisexuals from serving in the United States Armed Forces unless their sexual orientation remained secret.

The repeal did nothing to lift a ban on transgender people's serving in the military, but on July 13, 2015, Defense Secretary Ash Carter announced that he was establishing a working group to study how they might serve openly in the military. In the meantime, any decisions to separate people from service for reasons related to their transgender status had to be made by an undersecretary of Defense.

"At my direction, the working group will start with the presumption that transgender persons can serve openly without adverse impact on military effectiveness and readiness, unless and except where objective, practical impediments are identified," Secretary Carter said.

In February 2013, the Pentagon also extended some new benefits to the spouses of gay personnel, including housing privileges, use of recreational facilities, and joint duty assignments.

In response to the Supreme Court ruling that struck down the Defense of Marriage Act, the Department of Defense (DOD) announced on August 14, 2013, that it would extend other benefits to same-sex spouses of uniformed service members and DOD civilian employees with valid marriage certificates. The benefits included health care coverage, housing allowances, and survivor benefits.

Same-Sex Marriage

The president came out in favor of same-sex marriage near the end of his first term, and when the Supreme Court issued its decision that gay couples nationwide had the right to marry, Obama welcomed it. "Our nation was founded on a bedrock principle that we are all created equal," he said. "The project of each generation is to bridge the meaning of those founding words with the realities of changing times... Progress on this journey often comes in small increments, sometimes two steps forward, one step back, propelled by the persistent effort of dedicated citizens. And then sometimes, there are days like this when that slow, steady effort is rewarded with justice that arrives like a thunderbolt."

After North Carolina banned gay marriage in May 2012, Robin Roberts of ABC News asked President Obama in an interview if he was still opposed to it. He told her he had been "going through an evolution on this issue." He noted that before the Defense of Marriage Act (DOMA), marriage had been a state matter, not a federal one. According to a transcript from the network, the president continued:

> I've stood on the side of broader equality for the L.G.B.T. community. And I had hesitated on gay marriage in part, because I thought civil unions would be sufficient...
>
> But I have to tell you that over the course of several years, as I talk to friends and family and neighbors. When I think about members of my own staff who are incredibly committed, in monogamous relationships, same-sex relationships, who are raising kids together. When I think about those soldiers or airmen or marines or sailors who are out there fighting on my behalf and yet, feel constrained, even now that Don't Ask, Don't Tell is gone, because they're not able

to commit themselves in a marriage. At a certain point, I've just concluded that for me personally, it is important for me to go ahead and affirm that I think same-sex couples should be able to get married.

In February 2011, President Obama informed Congress through a letter from Attorney General Eric Holder that the administration had determined that the Defense of Marriage Act was unconstitutional and that the Justice Department would no longer defend the law in court. Obama had pledged the repeal of DOMA as early as 2008, but his administration continued to defend the law during Obama's first two years in the White House.

"The President and I have concluded that classifications based on sexual orientation warrant heightened scrutiny and that, as applied to same-sex couples legally married under state law, Section 3 of DOMA is unconstitutional," Holder said.

DOMA had defined a marriage to be constituted of a man and a woman for the purposes of federal law, and the letter said the administration would continue to comply with it throughout the federal government as long as it was on the books.

On June 26, 2013, the Supreme Court, in *United States v. Windsor*, struck down a significant part of the 1996 law declaring that gay couples married in states where same-sex marriage was legal must receive the same federal benefits—health, tax, Social Security, and other—that heterosexual couples received. That ruling did not go so far as to say that the right to marry extended to gay couples no matter where they lived.

Obama praised the decision and announced that the federal government would move quickly to comply. "We welcome today's decision, and I've directed the Attorney General to work with other members of my Cabinet to review all relevant federal statutes to ensure this decision, including its implications for Federal benefits and obligations, is implemented swiftly and smoothly," he said.

Two years later, on June 26, 2015, the Supreme Court ruled in *Obergefell et al. v. Hodges, Director, Ohio Department of Health*, on behalf of fourteen same-sex couples and two men whose same-sex partners were deceased. The court said the right of due process and equal protection under the Fourteenth Amendment require a state to license a marriage between two people of the same sex and to recognize such a marriage when it was lawfully licensed and performed out of state.

James Obergefell: The Name on the Case

After being together for decades, James Obergefell and John Arthur of Cincinnati, Ohio, decided to get married after the Supreme Court struck down the Defense of Marriage Act's ban on federal recognition of same-sex couples' marriages in *United States v. Windsor* on June 26, 2013.

Arthur had been diagnosed with amyotrophic lateral sclerosis (ALS) in 2011, a fatal neurological disease that paralyzed him and confined him to bed, and Ohio did not recognize same-sex marriage. So they flew to Baltimore-Washington International Airport to marry in Maryland, where it was legal, on July 11. Arthur's aunt performed the ceremony on a specially equipped medical plane.

"We landed at Baltimore, sat on the tarmac for a little bit, said 'I do,' and 10 minutes later were in the air on the way home," Obergefell, a Realtor and IT consultant, said for an article on *BuzzFeed*.

Eight days after they wed, the couple sued for recognition of their marriage. Realizing Arthur had little time left, they wanted Obergefell to be listed on the death certificate as his spouse, but knew that Ohio would not grant that distinction. Arthur died three months later, and the quest to secure and protect the right to have his spouse's name on his death certificate is what eventually landed the case, through twists and turns and reversals, in the Supreme Court with Obergefell's name as the lead petitioner.

A federal judge had ruled in favor of Obergefell and Arthur, but the state of Ohio challenged the ruling and won. Obergefell appealed and took it all the way to the Supreme Court. His case was eventually combined with others from four states. On January 12, 2016, he was a guest in First Lady Michelle Obama's box for the State of the Union address.

Hate Crimes

On October 28, 2009, President Obama signed a law for which he had advocated, making it a federal crime to assault someone because of his or her gender, sexual orientation, gender identity, or disability. It was part of an expansion of the federal hate-crimes law and was attached to a $680 billion defense-authorization bill.

The hate-crimes law was named for two people who were tortured and killed in 1998: Matthew Shepard, a gay University of Wyoming student who was kidnapped, beaten, tied to a fence, and left for dead in October, and James Byrd Jr., an African American man who was chained behind a pickup truck and dragged to death by white supremacists in Jasper, Texas, on June 7.

Joe Solmonese, president of the Human Rights Campaign, the largest gay rights group in the nation, called the hate-crimes measure "our nation's first major piece of civil rights legislation for lesbian, gay, bisexual and transgender people."

Addressing that group a few weeks before signing the law, Obama said, "Despite the progress we've made, there are still laws to change and hearts to open. This fight continues now, and I'm here with the simple message: I'm here with you in that fight."

The legislation extended provisions of a law enacted in 1968 that made it a federal crime to attack individuals because of their race, religion, or national origin. It allows judges to impose stiffer penalties on crimes motivated by hate and allows the Justice Department to assist police departments in investigations of such crimes.

Legislation to extend the law to cover crimes motivated by anti-gay sentiments had been tied up in Congress for years, by opposition and delaying tactics by conservatives. Democrats eventually attached it to the defense bill to prevent Republicans from blocking it.

President Obama signed the bill in the presence of Dennis and Judy Shepard, the parents of Matthew; relatives of Byrd; and the family of the late senator Edward M. Kennedy, who had long worked on behalf of the legislation before his death on August 25, 2009. The president said, "You understood that we must stand against crimes that are meant not only to break bones, but to break spirits—not only to inflict harm, but to instill fear...that the rights afforded every citizen under our Constitution mean nothing if we do not protect those rights—both from unjust laws and violent acts."

Presidential Appointments

President Obama has also appointed more openly gay officials than any president in history.

The *Huffington Post* reported that he had set a new record in 2010, less than halfway through his first term. Activists estimated he had made more than 150 such appointments at various levels of government, surpassing the previous record of 140 that President Bill Clinton made during two full terms.

Obama's gay appointees included John Berry as director of the Office of Personnel Management; Nancy Sutley, chairwoman of the White House Council on Environmental Quality; Fred Hochberg, chairman of the Export-Import Bank; and David Huebner, ambassador to New Zealand and Samoa.

In an interview with the *New Yorker* in October 2014, the president seemed particularly proud of his gay appointees to the judiciary. "When I came into office, I think there was one openly gay judge who had been appointed. We've appointed ten," the president boasted.

He also named the first openly transgender presidential appointee, Amanda Simpson, to be the deputy assistant secretary of Defense for operational energy, and he appointed the first openly transgender White House staff member, Raffi Freedman-Gurspan, a former policy adviser at the National Center for Transgender Equality, to be a recruitment director in the Office of Presidential Personnel.

The president also took other actions on behalf of LGBT people, including the following:

* His administration announced a clarification of rules on July 1, 2010, to prohibit gender- and sexual-orientation-based discrimination in housing.
* The president reaffirmed gay partners' rights to make medical decisions for each other and visit each other in hospitals, by presidential memorandum on April 15, 2010.

Global Impact

Not only has President Obama advanced the rights of LGBT people domestically, but he has also stood up for LGBT people all over the globe. Addressing the United Nations General Assembly on September 21, 2011, he said, "No country should deny people their rights because of who they love, which is why we must stand up for the rights of gays and lesbians everywhere."

Eight weeks into his first term, in March 2009, Obama reversed the previous administration's position opposing a U.N. declaration supporting the decriminalization of homosexual activity worldwide.

In October 2014, the U.N. Human Rights Council adopted a landmark resolution in support of LGBT rights, promoted by the U.S., and in September 2015, a dozen U.N. agencies issued a joint call for countries to end violence against gay, lesbian, bisexual, and transgender people. The agencies said they were "seriously concerned" that millions of people around the world face widespread human-rights violations. The statement urged nations with laws that criminalize same-sex acts between consenting adults to repeal them.

In December 2011, Obama also issued a groundbreaking presidential memorandum on global LGBT issues, directing U.S. agencies working abroad "to ensure that US diplomacy and foreign assistance promote and protect the human rights of LGBT persons." The president said in the memorandum, "I am deeply concerned by the violence and discrimination targeting LGBT persons around the world whether it is passing laws that criminalize LGBT status, beating citizens simply for joining peaceful LGBT pride celebrations, or killing men, women, and children for their perceived sexual orientation."

Todd Larson, senior LGBT coordinator, U.S. Agency for International Development, said Obama's orders "demonstrated that he was an ally not just to LGBT Americans but to LGBT people everywhere, and that if the United States is to truly defend human rights and dignity, it must reach out beyond its own borders to people who are persecuted, detained and sometimes killed for whom they love."

As the first U.S. president to visit Kenya, his father's home country, Obama also spoke out against the oppression of gays there when someone asked him about it at a joint press conference with President Uhuru Kenyatta of Kenya. "As somebody who has family in Kenya (half-siblings and other paternal relatives) and knows the history of how the country so often is held back because women and girls are not treated fairly, I think those same values apply when it comes to different sexual orientations," he said. "I believe in the principle of treating people equally under the law, and that they are deserving of equal protection under the law and that the state should not discriminate against people based on their sexual orientation," Obama said. "I'm unequivocal on this."

The Kenyan leader was equally unequivocal. He said that while the United States and his country shared some values, "there are some things that we must admit we don't share—our culture, our societies don't accept."

Homosexuality is widely viewed as antithetical to religious and cultural beliefs in Kenya and elsewhere on the continent. Homosexual conduct is punishable in Kenya with up to fourteen years in prison.

In the press conference, the Kenyan leader quickly pivoted to other topics, saying, "For Kenyans today, the issue of gay rights is really a non-issue. We want to focus on other issues that really are day-to-day issues for our people."

Obama did not back off from his remarks, but he denied that relations between the two countries were strained and vowed to return to Kenya, perhaps after he left office. "And my hope is that some of the philanthropic work that I do after my presidency is over builds on some of the things that we've been doing now," he said.

CHAPTER 5

Immigrants

"My fellow Americans, we are and always will be a nation of immigrants. We were strangers once, too. And whether our forebears were strangers who crossed the Atlantic, or the Pacific, or the Rio Grande, we are here only because this country welcomed them in, and taught them that to be an American is about something more than what we look like, or what our last names are, or how we worship. What makes us Americans is our shared commitment to an ideal—that all of us are created equal, and all of us have the chance to make of our lives what we will."

President Obama, November 20, 2014

President Obama, Vice President Biden, and some aides met with a group of people representing undocumented immigrants in the Oval Office. Seated clockwise from the president were Melissa McGuire-Maniau; Mehdi Mahraoui; Angie Kim; Cecilia Muñoz, director of the Domestic Policy Council; Valerie Jarrett, senior adviser; Julie Chavez Rodriguez, associate director of the Office of Public Engagement; Kate Kahan, legislative director of the Center for Community Change; Diana Colin; Kevin Lee; Miguel Leal; and Justino Mora, May 21, 2013. (Official White House photo by Pete Souza)

President Obama used his executive powers to grant young, undocumented immigrants brought to the country as children a reprieve from deportation, allowing them to work and pursue their education. He later issued an order to extend coverage to other undocumented immigrants.

On June 15, 2012, President Obama announced the Deferred Action for Childhood Arrivals (DACA) policy. He took executive action after Congress failed to pass legislation known as the DREAM Act to grant conditional permanent residency to young, undocumented immigrants. DREAM stands for Development, Relief, and Education for Alien Minors. The legislation was first introduced in Congress in 2001 with bipartisan support, but opponents who argue that it rewards and encourages illegal immigration have blocked it.

The policy exempts qualified undocumented immigrants who entered the country before the age of sixteen and before June 2007 from deportation and allows them to receive work permits. The policy helps young people who came into the country as children with their families and who remained undocumented through no fault of their own.

Speaking about the policy from the Rose Garden, Obama said,

These are young people who study in our schools, they play in our neighborhoods, they're friends with our kids, they pledge allegiance to our flag. They are Americans in their heart, in their minds, in every single way but one: on paper. They were brought to this country by their parents—sometimes even as infants—and often have no idea that they're undocumented until they apply for a job or a driver's license, or a college scholarship.

Put yourself in their shoes. Imagine you've done everything right your entire life—studied hard, worked hard, maybe even graduated at the top of your class—only to suddenly face the threat of deportation to a country that you know nothing about, with a language that you may not even speak.

On August 15, 2012, the United States Citizenship and Immigration Services began accepting requests for consideration of deferred action for childhood arrivals on a case-by-case basis. An estimated 900,000 people were eligible for consideration when the program began, according to the Pew Research Center. The Brookings Institution found that more than half a million people had applied for DACA through June 2013. Of those, the institution said 72 percent had been approved and 1 percent denied, and the remainder were still under review. According to a Pew Research Center analysis of government data, through March 31, 2014, 86 percent of 643,000 applications accepted had been approved.

While the deferred-action order did not provide the equivalent of lawful status, permanent residence, or citizenship, those granted deferral would not be deported for a renewable two-year period and could receive Social Security numbers and authorization to work.

Applicants had to show that they

- Entered the United States without inspection before June 15, 2012, or their lawful immigration status had expired as of June 15, 2012.
- Came to the United States before the age of sixteen.
- Had continuously resided in the United States since June 15, 2007.
- Were present in the United States on June 15, 2012, and at the time of application.
- Were under the age of thirty-one as of June 15, 2012.
- Were enrolled in school, had graduated, or had obtained a certificate of completion from high school, had a general educational development certification, or had been honorably discharged from the Coast Guard or U.S. armed forces.
- Had not been convicted of a felony, significant misdemeanor, or three or more misdemeanors, and did not otherwise pose a threat.

Obama had called for comprehensive reform of immigration laws along with tighter controls on our borders. With legislation blocked by the Republican leadership in the House of Representatives after it passed the Senate, Obama announced on November 20, 2014, that he would take executive action to address immigration issues. "I continue to believe that the best way to solve this problem is by working together to pass that kind of common sense law," he said. "But until that happens, there are actions I have the legal authority to take as President—the same kinds of actions taken by Democratic and Republican presidents before me—that will help make our immigration system more fair and more just."

The orders called for a crackdown on illegal immigration at the border, prioritization on deporting criminals, and a requirement that some undocumented immigrants pass criminal background checks and pay taxes to remain in the U.S.

Astrid Silva: DREAM Act Activist

In his statement announcing the immigration policies on November 20, 2014, President Obama mentioned the name of Astrid Silva as an example of hard-working immigrants who come to the United States seeking opportunity.

"These people—our neighbors, our classmates, our friends—they did not come here in search of a free ride or an easy life. They came to work, and study, and serve in our military, and above all, contribute to America's success," the president said.

"Astrid was brought to America when she was four years old," Obama said. "Her only possessions were a cross, her doll, and the frilly dress she had on. When she started school, she didn't speak any English. She caught up to other kids by reading newspapers and watching PBS, and she became a good student."

Obama detailed how Silva, the daughter of a landscaper and a house cleaner, grew up in Las Vegas as the family lived in fear of filling out paperwork, forced "to live mostly in the shadows," lest their undocumented status be discovered.

Two days after the president's announcement, Silva, a twenty-six-year-old college student and immigrant organizer for the Progressive Leadership Alliance of Nevada, wrote about her own story in *USA Today*. At first, she had missed hearing him call her name, she said, but soon recognized that he was talking about her and how her family migrated to the U.S. from Mexico across the Rio Grande on a tire raft.

Silva recalled what living in the shadows was like. "I loved school and I even won the top student 'gladiator' award in seventh grade. With the award came a trip to Washington, D.C. I was thrilled at the prospect of seeing the nation's capital, but my parents said no," she wrote. "They said no when I wanted to be a cheerleader. They said no when I wanted to attend a magnet school. They kept saying no. In my teen angsty way, I was annoyed. I thought they were being unfair. As I grew up, I started to understand that they weren't being unfair, they were afraid. They were afraid they'd have to show papers and people would discover we were undocumented."

As the president noted, she ignored her parents' order not to apply to the magnet school. She attended and excelled, graduating at the top of her class, eventually earning two associate's degrees at a community college, she said.

All the while, the family continued to live in fear. They were afraid they would be separated when her father got a deportation order. It was eventually stayed but could be invoked again. The family was unable to attend her grandmother's funeral in Mexico because without papers they would not be able to leave the United States and return.

"That's when I realized I couldn't sit idly by and watch families being torn apart because of our broken immigration system," Silva wrote. "I knew I had to act. With my friends, we created a DREAMers group, DREAM Big Vegas, to fight for comprehensive immigration reform."

She also started writing to Senator Harry Reid, Democrat of Nevada, about her situation as an undocumented American, and he used her name in a speech in the Senate.

In her article, Silva thanked the president for his executive order. "President Obama's bold action means that millions of families like mine will no longer live with the perpetual anxiety that they may not be together to celebrate birthdays, anniversaries, graduations and holidays," she wrote.

Silva added that comprehensive legislation was still necessary to provide permanent security so millions of immigrants need never live in fear again.

The executive actions Obama announced would give an estimated five million undocumented workers the chance to apply for work authorization and relief from deportation. The primary beneficiaries would be parents of U.S. citizens, legal permanent residents with at least five years' continuous presence, and a larger pool of deferred-action, DREAMer applicants. His orders would also increase funding for border patrols and raise pay for immigration-enforcement agents.

However, in response to a lawsuit by twenty-six states, a federal district judge issued a preliminary injunction to block the action, and an appeals court upheld the injunction. On November 20, 2015, Obama appealed to the Supreme Court, and on January 19, 2016, the court announced that it would hear the case.

The White House issued a statement saying the administration was pleased that the Supreme Court took the case: "The deferred action policies announced by the President in November 2014 will provide greater opportunities for immigrants to contribute to our society...The policies will make our communities safer. They will make our economy stronger. And they are consistent with the actions taken by presidents of both parties, the laws passed by Congress, and the decisions of the Supreme Court. We are confident that the policies will be upheld as lawful."

If so, it would be a tremendous victory for Obama and for the DREAMers.

CHAPTER 6

The Disabled and the Elderly

*"We all know too many people with disabilities are still unemployed—
even though they can work, even though they want to work, even
though they have so much to contribute."*

President Obama, July 20, 2015

Before an event commemorating the twentieth anniversary of the Americans with Disabilities Act, President Obama talked with, from left, Representative Steny Hoyer, D-Md.; Representative James Sensenbrenner, R-Wisc.; Cheryl Sensenbrenner; Representative James Langevin, D-R.I.; and Senator Tom Harkin, D-Iowa, July 26, 2010. (Official White House photo by Pete Souza)

President Obama used his executive powers to expand job opportunities in the federal government to disabled people and used the Affordable Care Act to provide them with health services. He also signed a law allowing disabled people to open tax-free savings accounts.

At a celebration to mark the twenty-fifth anniversary of the Americans with Disabilities Act, President Obama pledged to "tear down barriers" that still hamper people with disabilities. The Americans with Disabilities Act (ADA) was signed into law on July 26, 1990, by President George H. W. Bush.

Speaking before a packed house in the East Room of the White House on July 20, 2015, Obama said, "Days like today are a celebration of our history. But they're also a chance to rededicate ourselves to the future—to address the injustices that still linger, to remove the barriers that remain." He detailed some of his administration's accomplishments on providing greater support and opportunities for disabled people. However, he said, much more work remains to be done, particularly in the area of employment—especially access to fair pay, training, and technology—and vowed to continue to work on those issues.

Among other accomplishments, Obama recalled that he had issued an executive order on July 26, 2010, to establish the federal government as a model employer of individuals with disabilities. This order resulted in jobs in the federal workforce for nearly 60,000 workers with disabilities in the first four years, according to the White House. "As the Nation's largest employer, the Federal Government must become a model for the employment of individuals with disabilities," the order said. "Executive departments and agencies must improve their efforts to employ workers with disabilities through increased recruitment, hiring, and retention of these individuals. My Administration is committed to increasing the number of individuals with disabilities in the Federal workforce."

In his remarks at the ADA celebration, he also noted that his administration had "strengthened the rules for federal contractors to make sure they have plans in place for hiring people with disabilities." He added, "I'm hoping more employers follow suit, because Americans with disabilities can do the job, and they're hungry for the chance and they will make you proud if you give them the chance."

The president said that his administration had "created the first office within FEMA [the Federal Emergency Management Agency] dedicated to disability, so that when disaster strikes, we're prepared to help everybody, including those with physical or mental conditions requiring extra help." He also noted the appointment of the first special adviser for international disability rights at the State Department.

Access to Health Care

Although Obama did not mention it that day, Americans with disabilities also stand to benefit greatly from the Affordable Care Act because of its key provisions that bar discrimination based on preexisting conditions, ban caps on lifetime benefits, and prevent insurance companies from discriminating based on medical history or genetic information.

The act also establishes a form of long-term-care insurance that can help those with disabilities remain in their homes by providing funds to pay for community support services. The law also provided community-based care for Medicaid recipients.

For older Americans, the Affordable Care Act provides Medicare participants free annual wellness visits so they can consult with their doctors and formulate a plan to help them remain healthy. Under the health law, Medicare also provides free preventative care like cancer screening and cholesterol testing, which has saved the elderly money and given them a chance to live longer, healthier lives.

The law also gradually closes a gap in prescription-drug coverage, known as the "doughnut hole," and provides a 50 percent discount on brand-name prescription drugs and 20 percent on generic ones, saving the elderly even more money. Before the Affordable Care Act became law, many older people experienced an insurance-coverage gap in which they were responsible for the cost of prescription drugs up to $4,550 for the year. The discounts on prescription drugs are to grow each year until the doughnut hole ends in 2020, when senior citizens will pay a $310 deductible and 25 percent of prescription costs.

Advocates for elderly Americans applauded when the Supreme Court upheld the major components of the Affordable Care Act in June 2012, a *New York Times* blog reported. "This is great news for seniors on Medicare," Paul Nathanson, executive director of the National Senior Citizens Law Center, a nonprofit advocacy group, was quoted as saying in a conference call.

The Medicare reforms that went into effect after the law was enacted in 2010 could have vanished if the law had been overturned. The court ruled on challenges to the act brought by a group of states and a federation of businesses over the mandate requiring individuals to have health insurance or face tax penalties, and over penalties for states that did not participate in the Medicaid expansion called for in the act.

The *Times* blog cited data from the American Association of Retired Persons that about 2.2 million people had taken advantage of the free wellness-exam benefit the previous year.

With the gradual closing of the doughnut hole and prescription discounts, Medicare users could save an average of $650 a year, said Max Richtman, head of the National Committee to Preserve Social Security and Medicare, on the same call. "That's real money, especially for seniors," he said.

The article noted that the court's action to protect the Affordable Care Act preserved several initiatives for services to support elderly and disabled people at home, rather than in nursing facilities, as well as provisions to help spouses protect their assets when one must spend down to qualify for Medicaid.

Kevin Prindiville, deputy director of the National Senior Citizens Law Center, said, "The act is going to improve health for seniors in a variety of ways."

Special Education

During his first presidential campaign, Obama promised to "fund the Individuals with Disabilities Education Act." The 1975 law committed the federal government to funding 40 percent of the cost of special education, but it was covering only about 16 percent, according to DisabilityScoop.com, which tracks news on developmental disabilities.

On February 17, 2009, Obama provided for $12.2 billion in additional funds as part of the American Recovery and Reinvestment Act of 2009. The act provides funds to state and local agencies to ensure that children with disabilities have access to a free, appropriate public education and that infants and toddlers with disabilities can get early-intervention services. The president's budget proposal for 2016 also included additional funding for disability programs.

Savings for Disabled

In December 2014, the president also signed a law that passed with bipartisan support in Congress and allows disabled people to open tax-free accounts in which they can build savings without losing their Social Security, Medicaid, and other government benefits. The Stephen Beck Jr. Achieving a Better Life Experience Act (ABLE), allows individuals with disabilities and their families to save up to $100,000 for education, medical and dental care, job training, housing, transportation, and other expenses. Contributions to the account grow tax-free and withdrawals for disability-related expenses are also tax-free. Previously, disabled individuals with more than $2,000 in savings could lose public benefits.

The bill passed the Senate as part of a tax package on December 16, 2014, and President Obama signed it into law three days later.

Stephen Beck Jr.: Advocate for the Disabled

Stephen Beck Jr. died at the age of forty-four in his home in Burke, Virginia, on December 8, 2014, before the Achieving a Better Life Experience (ABLE) Act that he had long championed got through Congress.

The ABLE Act had passed the House on that December 3 by a wide bipartisan margin of 404-17. After Beck's death, the bill's author, U.S. Representative Ander Crenshaw, Republican of Florida, filed to have its name changed to the Stephen Beck Jr. Achieving a Better Life Experience Act of 2014.

"The disability advocacy community has lost a true champion, and my thoughts and prayers go out to Steve's family, friends, and colleagues," said Crenshaw.

Beck was assistant vice president of operations for Dominion Electric Supply Co. Inc. in Chantilly, Virginia. He had also served as chairman of the National Down Syndrome Society and the Down Syndrome Association of Northern Virginia Board of Directors.

Along with other parents, he helped conceive of and advocated for ABLE as a way to help his teenage daughter who had Down syndrome to save for her future.

CHAPTER 7

Veterans

"We have a sacred duty...When they [soldiers] come home, we're supposed to be there for them. We've been able to systematically add resources to the VA."

President Obama, July 21, 2015

President Obama greeted World War II veterans at the Seventieth French-American Commemoration D-Day Ceremony in Colleville-sur-Mer, France, at the Normandy American Cemetery and Memorial, June 6, 2014. (Official White House photo by Pete Souza)

President Obama issued an order to protect veterans using the Post-9/11 GI Bill from exploitation by colleges, especially for-profit institutions, and signed legislation to provide veterans with better health care, while increasing accountability for officials responsible for their care.

———————

President Barack Obama and Michelle Obama traveled to Fort Stewart, Georgia, home to the army's famed 3rd Infantry Division, on April 27, 2012, to meet with ten thousand soldiers and their family members. As the service people and families stood witness, he signed an executive order to protect veterans from unscrupulous practices by colleges, particularly for-profit schools, to reap their Post-9/11 GI Bill benefits.

Some institutions had recruited disabled veterans and those with post-traumatic stress disorder without providing adequate academic support and counseling; encouraged veterans to go into debt for their education; and failed to provide accurate information about the education they could provide, the president said. "The executive order . . . will make life a whole lot more secure for you and your families and our veterans— and a whole lot tougher for those who try to prey on you," Obama told the service people.

The White House said the president was acting on this issue even though some members of Congress had introduced legislation to address it because the administration felt it should do as much as it could to help veterans immediately.

The president's order

- **Required colleges to be more transparent about their outcomes and financial aid options for students.** It requires use of the Know Before You Owe financial aid form, for every college student in the Department of Defense's tuition-assistance program and the GI Bill program. This form informs students about tuition and fees, available federal financial aid, estimated debt upon graduation, and graduation rates.

- **Required the Department of Defense (DOD) to establish rules governing educational institutions' access to military installations** to bar those known for deceptive or predatory recruiting and marketing practices.
- **Directed the U.S. Department of Veterans Affairs (VA) to register the term "GI Bill" to prevent fraudulent marketing** by external websites and programs that resemble official government sites or suggest that veterans' benefits are only available at certain schools.
- **Established a centralized complaint system for students** receiving military and veterans' educational benefits.
- **Required colleges participating in the military and veterans' education-benefit programs to provide clear educational plans for students**, academic and financial aid counseling services, and to make it easier for service members to reenroll and/or receive a refund if they must leave school for service-related reasons.
- **Required the DOD, the VA, and the Department of Education to develop improved measures of student outcomes**, such as completion rates for veterans, and a plan for collecting this data.
- **Ordered the VA and DOD to strengthen the enforcement and compliance** functions and to act on complaints of improper activity.

An analysis by *U.S. News and World Report* found that efforts initiated under the executive order on the GI Bill were having an impact as of February 2014 as a result of new websites established to help military students file complaints and compare information on schools. It said the VA had "a thoroughly modern, online college comparison tool to enable veterans to figure out where they might use their GI Bill...Veterans using the GI Bill suddenly have a 21st century VA. Prior to this, veterans had to visit 17 different sites at different federal agencies to try to get a sense of their GI Bill benefits and their college options."

The *U.S. News and World Report* article also noted that President Obama had warned in his State of the Union address that in the face of an intractable Congress he would wield the "power of the pen," or executive orders, more.

"Would the VA have done this on its own, without an executive order? Unlikely...But that's why our system of government includes a commander in chief. And it's why the president has the power to order federal agencies to act," the article said. "The dramatic changes at VA this week are perfect evidence of the 'power of the pen,'" the article continued. "This is especially true because Congress did produce a related law, passed shortly after the president's action—but it was watered down by profit-making private education companies with a financial interest in accessing the GI Bill."

The Veterans of Foreign Wars (VFW) saluted the president for issuing the order. "The VFW is big on education, but we are even bigger on the proper administration and oversight of a new GI Bill we fought for 10 years to get enacted," said Richard L. DeNoyer, national commander. "The VFW has worked very hard to get these protections created, and the president's Executive Order will go far to crack down on the predatory recruiting practices and poor performance of all schools who participate in the Post-9/11 GI Bill."

Access to Care

In the wake of a scandal over the timeliness of care afforded veterans, on August 7, 2014, the president signed the Veterans' Access to Care through Choice, Accountability, and Transparency Act of 2014. The law included provisions to make the VA more accountable, expanded survivor benefits and educational opportunities, and provided for improvements in care for victims of sexual assault and veterans with traumatic brain injuries.

The president traveled to Fort Belvoir, Virginia, to sign the reform bill and to address the issue of mismanagement at some VA facilities and the reports of cover-ups in cases in which veterans did not receive proper care or were left waiting for long periods for appointments. The legislation passed Congress with overwhelming bipartisan support.

"Over the last few months, we've discovered some inexcusable misconduct at some VA health care facilities—stories of our veterans denied the care they needed, long wait times being covered up, cooking the books," Obama said. "This is wrong. It was outrageous...Working together, we set out to fix it and do right by our veterans across the board." He said the administration had "already taken the first steps to change the way the VA does business. We've held people accountable for misconduct. Some have already been relieved of their duties, and investigations are ongoing."

President Obama said the law would

- Help the VA to hire more doctors and more nurses and to staff more clinics.
- Allow veterans who don't live near a VA facility or can't get an appointment within a reasonable time to receive treatment elsewhere.
- Give the secretary of the VA authority to remove senior executives quickly if they fail to meet standards for competence and conduct.

"If you engage in an unethical practice, if you cover up a serious problem, you should be fired. Period. It shouldn't be that difficult," Obama said. "And if you blow the whistle on an unethical practice, or bring a problem to the attention of higher-ups, you should be thanked. You should be protected for doing the right thing. You shouldn't be ignored, and you certainly shouldn't be punished."

Mental Health

In 2012, President Obama directed federal agencies to coordinate efforts to ensure that veterans, service members, and their families received the mental health services they needed, including suicide-prevention efforts. Under that effort, the VA increased mental health staffing, expanded the capacity of the Veterans Crisis Line, and created partnerships to improve services and coordinate research efforts.

On August 26, 2014, the president announced nineteen additional executive actions to improve mental health services to active military personnel and veterans and families and to expand research on mental health issues.

Mental Health Services for Military and Veterans

According to a fact sheet issued by the U.S. Departments of Defense and Veterans Affairs, the White House executive actions on August 26, 2014, included

IMPROVING SERVICE MEMBERS' TRANSITION FROM DOD TO VA AND CIVILIAN HEALTH CARE PROVIDERS

- DOD will ensure that all service members leaving military service who are receiving care for mental health conditions are automatically enrolled in the inTransition program.
- VA revised its drug formulary policy to ensure that service members leaving military service and enrolling in the VA health care system maintain access to mental health medication prescribed by an authorized DOD provider.
- DOD and VA will work together to develop a single joint, comprehensive plan for service members transitioning from DOD to VA with multiple, complex, severe conditions such as traumatic brain injury (TBI), psychological trauma, or other cognitive, psychological, or emotional disorders.

IMPROVING ACCESS AND QUALITY OF MENTAL HEALTH CARE AT DOD AND VA

- VA will pilot the expansion of peer support beyond traditional mental health sites of care to veterans in primary care settings. Peer specialists are veterans trained to help other veterans and will work with primary care teams to help improve the health and well-being of veterans being treated in primary care settings.
- DOD initiated action to eliminate quantitative limits for mental health care. DOD said it was working with Congress to bring its mental health and substance use disorder care coverage up to full parity with medical or surgical conditions.
- DOD moved mental health care to operational units, (1) expanding to all services a behavioral health data portal to allow providers, patients, and clinical leaders to access data for mental health conditions and substance use disorders, even in austere settings such as deployed operational units, (2) aggregating and analyzing data on the effectiveness of

mental health care delivery models and outcomes, and (3) designing a study on the effectiveness of such care.

- DOD has also expanded eligibility for nonmedical counseling through a 24/7 resource for service members and their families, and family life counselors at installations, child development centers, and youth centers.

IMPROVING TREATMENTS FOR MENTAL HEALTH CONDITIONS INCLUDING POST-TRAUMATIC STRESS DISORDER (PTSD)

- Convening the White House BRAIN conference featuring numerous panels on PTSD and TBI
- Advancing cutting-edge PTSD research through a new $78.9 million, five-year research program to develop new, minimally invasive neurotechnologies to manage diseases and support healing
- Launching a longitudinal project focused on the early detection of suicidality, PTSD, and long-term effects of TBI, and other related issues in service members and veterans
- Conducting a $34.4 million national clinical trial involving 1,800 veterans on strategies to prevent suicides among those who have survived a recent attempt

RAISING AWARENESS ABOUT MENTAL HEALTH AND ENCOURAGING INDIVIDUALS TO SEEK HELP

- First Lady Michelle Obama and Dr. Jill Biden's Joining Forces initiative will help the VA to raise awareness about its three hundred vet centers, and encourage veterans and their families to seek help at these facilities.
- The VA expanded suicide-prevention training. It required Veterans Health Administration clinicians to renew online training for suicide-risk management every three years. All other staff members who interact with veterans will participate in the "Operation SAVE" suicide-prevention training every two years. DOD will also expand existing mental health training for all service members and improve chaplain training to recognize and refer service members in need to mental health care.
- DOD and VA expanded mental health awareness campaigns to reduce stigma surrounding mental health care, encourage people experiencing

mental health problems to get help, and emphasize to commanders the importance of mental fitness.

- In partnership with Veterans Affairs, the Treasury Department will begin a new initiative to include mental health awareness training for volunteer tax preparers at more than two hundred facilities in the next three years as part of an existing initiative.

IMPROVING PATIENT SAFETY AND SUICIDE PREVENTION

- DOD will ensure that opiate-overdose-reversal kits and training are available to every first responder on military bases or other areas under DOD's control.
- DOD and VA launched new programs to make it easier for service members, veterans, and their families to safely dispose of unwanted prescriptions, reducing the opportunities for abuse.
- DOD will implement a policy to facilitate requests for at-risk service members or at-risk military family members to voluntarily secure their firearms and to encourage friends or community groups to help improve firearm safety for veterans in distress.

STRENGTHENING COMMUNITY RESOURCES FOR SERVICE MEMBERS, VETERANS, AND THEIR FAMILIES

- DOD and VA will disseminate their new military cultural competency course to three thousand community mental health providers.
- The Treasury Department and the Department of Veterans Affairs are working together to identify communities in need of veteran mental health facilities and develop targeted outreach to community development entities in those markets.

CHAPTER 8

Prisoners

"When they describe their youth, these are young people who made mistakes that aren't that different from the mistakes I made, and the mistakes that a lot of you guys made. The difference is that they did not have the kind of support structures, the second chances, the resources that would allow them to survive those mistakes."

President Obama, July 16, 2015

Charles Samuels, director of the Bureau of Prisons, right, and Ronald Warlick, a correctional officer, led President Obama on a tour of the El Reno Federal Correctional Institution in Oklahoma, July 16, 2015. (Associated Press photo/Evan Vucci)

Under President Obama's administration, the federal prison population dropped for the first time in thirty-two years. He initiated reforms in the federal prison system and commuted the sentences of nonviolent drug offenders as part of his efforts to push for national legislation to reverse the trend of mass incarceration and encourage states to do likewise. He ended the use of solitary confinement for juveniles in federal prison and curtailed its use for other inmates.

President Obama became the first sitting president ever to visit a federal prison when he stepped inside the El Reno Correctional Institution in El Reno, Oklahoma, in July 2015. Inside the walls of the prison, he spoke at length with six prisoners.

The forty-five-minute conversation with nonviolent drug offenders while seated around a table was recorded, at the president's invitation, for an HBO, VICE documentary on criminal justice. The special report, "Fixing the System," made its debut in September 2015.

The visit was part of Obama's campaign to reduce the prison population by reforming sentencing laws, improving the juvenile-justice system, and eliminating the school-to-prison pipeline, while providing meaningful rehabilitation of prisoners and effective programs to help those who have served their time reenter society.

In the same week, he commuted the sentences of forty-six nonviolent drug offenders and outlined his plans for remaking the criminal justice system to the National Association for the Advancement of Colored People at its annual conference in Philadelphia.

"In too many places, black boys and black men, and Latino boys and Latino men, experience being treated different under the law," Obama said there. "Mass incarceration makes our country worse off, and we need to do something about it."

In October 2015, a bipartisan group of senators introduced legislation proposing the kind of comprehensive reforms the president sought, and House members introduced similar legislation. In the private sector, a broad coalition of advocacy groups and foundations supported the proposed reforms.

The United States accounted for less than 5 percent of the world's population in 2014, according to the U.S. Census, yet it has about 22 percent of the global prison population, according to the International Centre for Prison Studies. The United States also has had the highest prison population rate in the world. At 716 per 100,000 people, the U.S. rate is more than five times higher than most nations.

During the prison visit, Obama said, "We have a tendency sometimes to almost take for granted or think it's normal for a black youth or a Latino youth to be going through the system in this way. It's not normal," he said. "It's not what happens in other countries. What is normal is teenagers doing stupid things. What is normal is young people making mistakes."

The president acknowledged that some criminals do need to be in prison. "I don't have tolerance for violent criminals," he said. "We need to keep our communities safe."

The phenomenal U.S. rates are largely a result of a crackdown on drugs during the crack epidemic in the 1990s and of disparate sentences imposed for possession of crack and powder cocaine.

Former president Bill Clinton acknowledged in a CNN interview in May 2015 that strict federal sentencing rules adopted on his watch helped to pack the prisons. Clinton signed a crime bill in 1994 that included the federal "three strikes" provision, which mandated life sentences for criminals convicted of a violent felony after two or more prior convictions, including drug crimes.

"The problem is the way it was written and implemented is we cast too wide a net, and we had too many people in prison," Clinton said. "And we wound up...putting so many people in prison that there wasn't enough money left to educate them, train them for new jobs and increase the chances when they came out so they could live productive lives."

From 1980 to 2013, the federal prison population rose from twenty-four thousand to more than two hundred thousand, according to the Bureau of Justice Statistics. The federal prison population recently dropped for the first time in thirty-two years, Attorney General Eric Holder announced in a speech to the National Press Club on February 17, 2015. The decline was small but encouraging after decades of increases.

Solitary Confinement

In July 2015, President Obama directed the Justice Department to review the use of solitary confinement in U.S. prisons.

In an op-ed piece in the *Washington Post* on January 25, 2016, "Barack Obama: Why We Must Rethink Solitary Confinement," the president announced that he was sharply curtailing the use of solitary confinement in federal prisons following recommendations from the Justice Department. The president cited the effects of solitary confinement on prisoners' mental health, recalling the case of Kalief Browder. The sixteen-year-old from the Bronx remained in solitary confinement for two years on Rikers Island awaiting trial on a charge of stealing a backpack. He was released without ever standing trial and attended college briefly but took his own life at twenty-two, never having fully recovered mentally from the trauma of his prison experience, the president said.

"Research suggests that solitary confinement has the potential to lead to devastating, lasting psychological consequences," he wrote. "It has been linked to depression, alienation, withdrawal, a reduced ability to interact with others and the potential for violent behavior...Those who do make it out often have trouble holding down jobs, reuniting with family and becoming productive members of society."

He banned solitary confinement for juveniles and for those imprisoned for low-level infractions. Obama also announced that he was expanding treatment for the mentally ill and increasing the amount of time inmates spend outside their cells while in solitary confinement.

"In our criminal justice system, the punishment should fit the crime—and those who have served their time should leave prison ready to become productive members of society," Obama said. "How can we subject prisoners to unnecessary solitary confinement, knowing its effects, and then expect them to return to our communities as whole people? It doesn't make us safer. It's an affront to our common humanity."

He estimated that as many as one hundred thousand people were in solitary confinement in U.S. prisons. Obama said his action applying to federal prisons would affect about ten thousand inmates in solitary confinement "and hopefully serve as a model for state and local corrections systems." He said federal prisons had already reduced the use of solitary confinement by 25 percent since 2012.

President Obama noted that the Justice Department had found solitary confinement necessary in certain circumstances to protect prisoners or staff. "In those cases, the practice should be limited, applied with constraints and used only as a measure of last resort," Obama said.

CHAPTER 9

Workers

"When you make sure everybody gets a fair shot and a fair shake, and you're fighting for decent wages for workers, and making sure they've got decent benefits, when you reward people who are playing by the rules—that's how everybody does better. That's how America gets ahead."

President Obama, September 8, 2015

Terrence Wise, a fast-food worker, introduced President Obama at the White House Summit on Worker Voice, October 7, 2015. (Associated Press photo/Andrew Harnik)

By executive order, President Obama extended sick leave benefits to thousands of people who work for federal contractors. This followed similar orders to increase wages, improve working conditions, expand overtime compensation, and ban discrimination based on sexual orientation.

As Congress repeatedly declined to adopt labor reforms in the private sector that he advocated, President Obama changed the lives of hundreds of thousands of working people by using his executive power to order federal contractors to change some labor practices. On Labor Day, September 7, 2015, President Obama signed an executive order requiring companies that contract with the federal government to provide paid sick leave to workers. They would have to offer an hour of paid leave for every thirty hours an employee worked, up to seven paid days per year, including time for family care. As a result, three hundred thousand American workers who work for companies that have contracts with the federal government became eligible for paid sick leave. The rules were set to go into effect in 2017, allowing contractors time to factor any added costs into their bids for government work.

Obama announced the order in Boston during a Labor Day breakfast and rally sponsored by the Greater Boston Labor Council. In his speech, he urged Congress to extend paid leave to millions more Americans through the Healthy Families Act, which would apply to employers with more than fifteen workers.

"Right now, about 40 percent of private-sector workers—44 million people in America—don't have access to paid sick leave," the president said in his Boston speech. "You've got parents who have to choose between losing income or staying home with their sick child...Let's face it—nobody wants a waiter who feels like they have to come to work when they're coughing or contagious. But if they don't have sick leave, what are they going to do?"

Extending the benefit to others would require an act of Congress, but the Republicans controlling Congress opposed legislation, arguing that it would raise costs for businesses and consumers.

The president also required companies that bid on federal contracts of more than $500,000 to disclose publicly all previous violations of labor law, including unpaid claims for back wages, and he made it illegal for federal contractors with more than $1 million in contracts to force employees into arbitration to settle workplace discrimination accusations.

USA Today reported that Obama had signed "at least 15 executive orders and presidential memoranda aimed at contractors, dictating their hiring and firing practices, compensation policies and working conditions...With his executive orders, Obama is using the government's buying power not just to get a better deal for the taxpayer, but also to set economic and social policy on minimum wage, paid leave and paycheck fairness—issues the Republican-controlled Congress has not acted on," USA Today said. "The White House is hoping that the orders send a message to the economy at large, and have an effect far beyond the public sector."

"When the president issues an executive order, it reinforces that we care," Anne Rung, administrator of the White House's Office of Federal Procurement Policy, was quoted as saying. "That kind of statement can not only drive greater economies and efficiency in the federal government, it can have a trickle-down or multiplier effect on the economy at large."

If Congress enacted similar reforms for the private sector, millions more workers would benefit.

President Obama used the power of the veto, his first after Republicans took control of the Senate in January 2015, to thwart their efforts to halt a National Labor Relations Board (NLRB) rule making it easier and faster for workers to hold a vote on whether to join a union. On March 31, 2015, the president rejected a joint resolution for congressional disapproval of the NLRB rule. "Because this resolution seeks to undermine a streamlined democratic process that allows American workers to freely choose to make their voices heard, I cannot support it," President Obama said.

The NLRB rule fast-tracked the union-organizing process by allowing some documents to be filed electronically, instead of mailed, and allowed workers to vote before employers could proceed with legal challenges. Opponents had said it would create "ambush" organizing elections without giving employers time to present a case against unionization.

Politico reported on September 1, 2015, that with an Obama-appointed Democratic majority, the NLRB had issued

> a string of rulings that favor unions—including six pro-labor decisions in just the past few days. On Thursday, the NLRB issued a momentous 3-2 ruling along party lines that may make it easier for McDonald's to unionize, reversing a 34-year precedent. The board subsequently issued five additional decisions ruling for unions on less-momentous matters ranging from whether a worker may demand that a union rep be present during a drug test (yes) to whether an employer may exclude union reps from voluntary peer review committees (no). Two of these new rulings were made public Monday, concluding a flurry of NLRB votes from a board that observers say is more pro-union than any since the early 1980s.

The NLRB was the source of much contention between President Obama and the Senate after he made supposed "recess" appointments unilaterally, and the Senate successfully contested all the way to the Supreme Court that it was not technically in recess when the appointments were made. The two sides eventually reached a compromise to fill the seats on the NLRB.

"As a management-side lawyer for 40 years," Michael Lotito of Littler Mendelson, a San Francisco–based law firm handling labor and employment issues for management, told *Politico*, "I certainly have not seen such an activist board as this one on behalf of labor. Nothing close."

Larry Cohen, former president of the Communications Workers of America, was quoted as saying: "The quality of this board is the best ever. The NLRB appointments is one place where President Obama would get a perfect score."

Through the NLRB, *Politico* predicted, Obama "may end up doing more for the struggling labor movement than any president in three decades."

President Obama discussed the economy during a town hall meeting in Racine, Wisconsin, on June 30, 2010. (Official White House Photo by Pete Souza)

PART II

A MAN OF ACTION

★ ★ ★

Presidents visibly age and for good reason. Maybe it is that security briefing report a president reads every morning. Maybe it is having the safety of the United States, the weight of the world on your shoulders, day in and day out, that does it. Whatever it is, it is more than an axiom.

When Barack Obama was elected, the United States was on the precipice of an economic meltdown. The auto industry seemed certain to be sold off or dismantled, and the unemployment rate was 7.8 percent. It rose to just over 10 percent before beginning to decline.

In addition, Osama bin Laden, that outsized symbol of terrorism, was still on the loose more than seven years after being responsible for the attacks that forever altered the American psyche. In addition, we were still actively at war in Iraq and Afghanistan.

After the swearing-in and dancing at the many inaugural balls for the momentary celebration of being America's first black president, the party was over.

More than a few economists have said that without significant intervention on many fronts, the country could have lurched from a terrifying recession into a great depression. Economists say Obama's multi-layered strategy saved us and has set us on the path to economic stability.

Still, the country's constant battle against terrorism, and, increasingly, homebred terrorists, continues to be a developing story for the man who won the Nobel Peace Prize in his first year as president

This section will explore Obama's efforts to stabilize the economy, keep its citizens safe, and improve our relationships abroad.

It will also explore the positive impact of the American Recovery and Reinvestment Act, Obama's posture on defense and homeland security, the numerous questions surrounding justice for all, and the myriad other issues that, no doubt, define him as a man of action.

CHAPTER 10

The Economy

"I came in during the worst recession any of us have ever seen. And we've worked to rebuild our economy on a new foundation—to make it stronger for everybody."

President Obama, September 8, 2015

President Obama visited the Alcoa Davenport Works factory in Bettendorf, Iowa, to discuss the critical role manufacturing plays in the U.S. economy. He toured the plant, which is the manufacturing hub for Alcoa's $3 billion aerospace business, with, from left, Klaus Kleinfeld, Alcoa chairman and CEO; Malcolm Murphy, vice president and general manager, Davenport Works and Satellites; and Charles "Skip" McGill, president of the United Steel Workers Local 105, June 28, 2011. (Associated Press photo/Carolyn Kaster)

President Obama inherited an economy teetering precariously on the edge of a major depression. He signed an economic recovery package that reversed the course, presided over its execution, and put the nation on a pathway toward prosperity.

On Christmas Eve 2015, Treasury Secretary Jacob J. "Jack" Lew declared that after seven years in office, President Obama had officially turned around the dismal economy he had inherited. "Where we are now, we're seeing steady growth," he said. "We've seen enormous job creation over this period of time, we're seeing the unemployment rate around 5 percent, and we're seeing that growth in spite of the fact that there's a lot of headwinds from a slower global economy," he said in a December 24 interview with Maria Bartiromo on FOX Business Network.

As DailyNewsBin.com, a political news website, put it, Lew "confirmed what economists and those familiar with economic policy have already known: the U.S. economy has been growing at a steady rate for several quarters, private sector job growth is consistently high, the unemployment rate has been reduced all the way down to the five percent level which economists view as ideal, and the stock market has grown tremendously. This all occurred even as President Obama reduced the annual federal deficit by seventy-two percent."

When Barack Obama took office on January 20, 2009, the economy was buckling under the weight of the Great Recession, which began in December 2007, and was on the brink of a depression.

As Lew said in the FOX interview, "You look at where we were seven years ago, the economy was in a free fall. We were losing millions of jobs. We had an unemployment rate of 10 percent. We had a deficit that was skyrocketing out of control," Lew told Bartiromo, according to the video. "I think the United States is in a far better place than it was seven years ago."

In October 2014, Paul Krugman, the Nobel Prize–winning economist and an unlikely champion of Obama, wrote in *Rolling Stone* that Obama had "emerged as one of the most consequential and, yes, successful presidents in American history." Krugman said he was making this declaration in spite of misgivings he had, and that Obama's success came despite the bitter opposition from the right and after some near missteps in the interest of compromise. "Back in 2008, when many liberals were wildly enthusiastic about his candidacy and his press was strongly favorable, I was skeptical," Krugman wrote.

Krugman defended his pessimism and tempered his praise with caveats but cited among Obama's accomplishments the Affordable Care Act, the Dodd-Frank Wall Street Reform and Consumer Protection Act of 2010 (discussed later in this chapter), and the economic-stimulus plan. "You'd never know it listening to the talking heads," Krugman wrote, "but there's overwhelming consensus among economists that the Obama stimulus plan helped mitigate the worst of the slump... The bottom line on Obama's economic policy should be that what he did helped the economy, and that... the United States coped with the financial crisis better than most countries facing comparable crises have managed. He should have done more and better, but the narrative that portrays his policies as a simple failure is all wrong."

Economic Recovery

On February 17, 2009, President Obama signed the American Recovery and Reinvestment Act, the economic-stimulus package that, along with other adjustments. reversed the tide. The law aimed to preserve jobs, create new ones, and provide some relief for those most affected by the recession, while investing in infrastructure, education, health, and renewable energy.

In his first joint speech to Congress, on February 24, 2009, President Obama said:

I know that for many Americans watching right now, the state of our economy is a concern that rises above all others. And rightly so. If you haven't been personally affected by this recession, you probably know someone who has—a friend; a neighbor; a member of your family. You don't need to hear another list of statistics to know that our economy is in crisis, because you live it every day. It's the worry you wake up with and the source of sleepless nights. It's the job you thought you'd retire from but now have lost; the business you built your dreams upon that's now hanging by a thread; the college acceptance letter your child had to put back in the envelope. The impact of this recession is real, and it is everywhere.

But while our economy may be weakened and our confidence shaken; though we are living through difficult and uncertain times, tonight I want every American to know this:

We will rebuild, we will recover, and the United States of America will emerge stronger than before...

The fact is, our economy did not fall into decline overnight. Nor did all of our problems begin when the housing market collapsed or the stock market sank. We have known for decades that our survival depends on finding new sources of energy. Yet we import more oil today than ever before. The cost of health care eats up more and more of our savings each year, yet we keep delaying reform. Our children will compete for jobs in a global economy that too many of our schools do not prepare them for. And though all these challenges went unsolved, we still managed to spend more money and pile up more debt, both as individuals and through our government, than ever before...

Well, that day of reckoning has arrived, and the time to take charge of our future is here.

Now is the time to act boldly and wisely—to not only revive this economy, but to build a new foundation for lasting prosperity. Now is the time to jumpstart job creation, re-start lending, and invest in areas like energy, health care, and education that will grow our economy, even as we make hard choices to bring our deficit down. That is what my economic agenda is designed to do, and that's what I'd like to talk to you about tonight.

It's an agenda that begins with jobs.

As soon as I took office, I asked this Congress to send me a recovery plan by President's Day that would put people back to work and put money in their pockets. Not because I believe in bigger government—I don't. Not because I'm not mindful of the massive debt we've inherited—I am. I called for action because the failure to do so would have cost more jobs and caused more hardships. In fact, a failure to act would have worsened our long-term deficit by assuring weak economic growth for years. That's why I pushed for quick action. And tonight, I am grateful that this Congress delivered, and pleased to say that the American Recovery and Reinvestment Act is now law.

Over the next two years, this plan will save or create 3.5 million jobs. More than 90 percent of these jobs will be in the private sector—jobs rebuilding our roads and bridges; constructing wind turbines and solar panels; laying broadband and expanding mass transit.

Because of this plan, there are teachers who can now keep their jobs and educate our kids. Health care professionals can continue caring for our sick. There are 57 police officers who are still on the streets of Minneapolis tonight because this plan prevented the layoffs their department was about to make.

Because of this plan, 95 percent of the working households in America will receive a tax cut—a tax cut that you will see in your paychecks beginning on April 1st.

Because of this plan, families who are struggling to pay tuition costs will receive a $2,500 tax credit for all four years of college. And Americans who have lost their jobs in this recession will be able to receive extended unemployment benefits and continued health care coverage to help them weather this storm.

> The American Recovery and Reinvestment Act of 2009, known as the Stimulus or the Recovery Act, is a law signed on February 17, 2009, by President Barack Obama to avoid a depression and stimulate the economy.

Experts say the Great Recession began in December 2007. In September 2010, the *New York Times* blog Economix, citing the Business Cycle Dating Committee of the National Bureau of Economic Research, reported that it was apparent that the recession had ended in June 2009. "As many economists had expected, this official end date makes the most recent downturn the longest since World War II," the blog said. "This recent recession, having begun in December 2007, lasted 18 months. Until now the longest postwar recessions were those of 1973-5 and 1981-2, which each lasted 16 months. The newly-declared end date to the recession also confirms what many had suspected: The 2007-9 recession was the deepest on record since the Great Depression, at least in terms of job losses."

As the committee noted, its declaration after months of careful consideration to pinpoint the date did not mean the economy was fully recovered; it meant only that June 2009 was when the economy hit bottom and began to spring back. The finding was based on a number of indicators.

The Congressional Budget Office estimated in 2012 that the economic-stimulus package was pumping $831 billion into the economy, which continued to rebound. In October 2015, under President Obama, the U.S. economy set a new historical record for private-sector job growth with 268,000 new jobs in that month. Businesses had added 13.5 million jobs during sixty-eight consecutive months of private-sector job growth, according to the Bureau of Labor Statistics (BLS). The unemployment rate fell to 5 percent.

PoliticusUSA, a website with the slogan "Real Liberal Politics," reported on November 6, 2015: "Unemployment rate ticked down, wages grew, and overall the economy added 271,000 jobs in October—which makes the last three years the strongest years for job creation since...oh, 2000. Ho-hum. This is what Republicans refer to as a horrible economy that they claim to want to 'fix.' (To see what that looks like, recall 2007, 2008, 2009 ish.) This is what the 'job-killing ObamaCare' has done to us. This is what 'job-killing taxing the wealthy' looks like. LOL."

In his Labor Day speech in Boston in September 2015, Obama took some credit: "It's working folks who helped power our economy to 66 straight months of private-sector job growth [as of that August]—the longest streak on record. Five and a half straight years—13.1 million new jobs overall," he said. "The lowest unemployment rate in seven years."

Deficit Declines

The Obama administration also reported on October 15, 2015, that the federal budget deficit had fallen to its lowest level since he took office because of increased tax receipts and a stronger economy.

The deficit declined $44 billion, or 9 percent, over the previous fiscal year, to $439 billion for the fiscal year that ended September 30, 2015, the Treasury Department and the Office of Management and Budget reported. "Under the president's leadership, the deficit has been cut by roughly three-quarters as a share of the economy since 2009—the fastest sustained deficit reduction since just after War II," Treasury Secretary Lew said in a statement released with the figures.

The statement said the $439 billion was also "$144 billion less than forecast in President Obama's FY 2016 Budget. As a percentage of Gross Domestic Product (GDP), the deficit fell to 2.5 percent, the lowest since 2007 and less than the average of the last 40 years. In dollar terms, the FY 2015 deficit was the lowest since 2007 as well."

Auto Industry and Manufacturing

Obama is widely credited with rescuing the auto industry from collapse, and often cites this accomplishment in his remarks "We had an auto industry that was flat on its back when I came into office," he said in his 2015 Labor Day speech. "Now, we're on track to sell more cars and trucks this year than we have in more than a decade."

The top three American automakers, General Motors, Chrysler, and Ford, turned to the government in late 2008 for help when they were on the verge of collapse. Their crisis resulted from a global financial crisis, a credit crunch at home, and rising fuel prices that decimated sales of the sport-utility vehicles and pickup trucks that had been their bread and butter. If the major automakers failed, the argument went, they would drag a huge network of suppliers with them and sink the already abysmal economy into a depression.

While the bailout began at the end of President George W. Bush's tenure with short-term loans to GM and Chrysler, Obama's administration had to decide whether to extend additional aid, and what form it might take, or let the two automakers fail. (Ford was able to forego federal money, yet nevertheless supported the bailouts.)

Obama set up a task force to study the options and eventually ordered GM and Chrysler to go through bankruptcy to reorganize, streamline, and shed expenses as a condition of getting federal money. The bailout, highly controversial and widely unpopular at the time, included a government takeover of 60 percent ownership in General Motors.

The U.S. Treasury department announced in December 2014 that the government had recovered $70.42 billion of the $79.68 billion it gave to General Motors, Chrysler, Ally Financial, Chrysler Financial, and automotive suppliers. "This program was a crucial part of the Obama administration's effort to stop the financial crisis and protect the economy from slipping into a second Great Depression," Treasury Secretary Lew said at the time. The $9.26 billion loss was far less than had been anticipated in 2009, and the auto industry was rebounding.

In 2013, the Center for Automotive Research (CAR) estimated that the nation would have had about 2.6 million fewer jobs in 2009 and about 1.5 million fewer jobs in 2010 if the two automakers had gone out of business. CAR also estimated the government had saved $105 billion in lost taxes and savings for such social-service expenses as food stamps, unemployment benefits, and medical care.

"Now, it's clear that the bailout was a solid success," Robert J. Samuelson, *Washington Post* economics columnist, wrote on April 1, 2015. Samuelson continued:

> The revitalized auto industry has been a pocket of strength in a lackluster economic recovery. Motor vehicles and parts have provided 25 percent of the recovery's gain in manufacturing, despite representing only 6 percent of manufacturing's value added. Since mid-2009, the number of manufacturing jobs increased by 256,000, up 41 percent from the low of 623,300. Dealerships and parts stores added another 225,000. (All gains are as of mid-2014.)
>
> GM and Chrysler are also more competitive. As conditions for government aid, the companies closed several dozen plants, pared billions of debt, adopted lower wages for new workers and slashed the number of dealerships. The companies returned to profitability in 2010 and recouped some of their lost market share. In mid-2014, the Big Three (Ford avoided federal aid) had a market share of 45.1 percent, up from its 2009 low of 43.7 percent but below the pre-crisis 50.5 percent.

Financial Reform

On July 21, 2010, President Obama signed the Dodd-Frank Wall Street Reform and Consumer Protection Act, legislation intended to prevent the kind of financial crisis that had set off the Great Recession. The Obama administration originally proposed legislation in June 2009.

Versions were introduced in both houses—in the House of Representatives by Representative Barney Frank (D-Mass.), chairman of the Financial Services Committee, and in the Senate by Senator Chris Dodd (D-Conn.), chairman of the Senate Banking Committee, so the law was eventually named after the two men. It received final passage in Congress on July 15, 2010.

Among its provisions, the law

- Expanded federal banking and securities regulation to a wide range of financial companies.
- Created a council of federal regulators to monitor risks to the financial system.
- Provided regulators with new powers to oversee or dismantle failing companies.
- Created a powerful regulator to protect consumers of financial products.

The *New York Times* reported that at a signing ceremony "Democrats and White House officials were euphoric about passage of the legislation," even as Wall Street groups signaled that they would be circling the regulators to try to influence how they might carry out the new law.

In 2015, the Republican-controlled Congress persisted in efforts to undo portions of the law at the behest of Wall Street lobbyists, and calls for repealing it were a staple of the GOP presidential primary campaign in 2016.

The Dodd-Frank Wall Street Reform and Consumer Protection Act is a law signed July 21, 2010, by President Obama, to improve accountability and transparency in the financial system, to end the "too big to fail" bank policies, to end bailouts, and to protect consumers from abusive practices in financial services.

Stock Market

Dow Jones Industrial Average

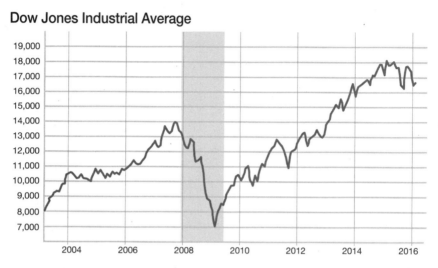

During President Obama's tenure, the stock market has reached record highs, springing back from historic lows under the previous administration.

While it is debatable whether a president can claim the credit or take the blame for the stock market's performance, during President Obama's tenure, the stock market has reached record highs, springing back from historic lows. At the close of the day of his first inauguration, January 20, 2009, the Dow Jones Industrial Average stood at 7,949.09. As of March 31, 2016, it was 17,685. On Inauguration Day 2009, the NASDAQ closed at 1,440.86 and the S&P 500 was at 805.23. On March 31, 2016, the Nasdaq closed at 4,870, and the S&P 500 at 2,060.

Investopedia, an investment education site based in Alberta, Canada, noted that the January 20, 2009, figure represented "the lowest inaugural performance for the Dow since its creation" and that the S&P 500 and NASDAQ had similar declines, as did other indicators. It was not an auspicious day for the markets.

"While the economic backslide may have seemed to indicate that the American public was less than confident in their newly elected leader, the dip was instead widely credited to continued lack of confidence in the failing economy left behind by the previous administration," *Investo-*

pedia said. "Under former President Bush, the stock market took a 2.3 percent fall on an annualized basis, reflecting the 1 percent increase achieved during his first four years and the 5.5 percent decline suffered during his second term. If nothing else, the historic lows of the Bush administration and the shaky beginnings of the Obama years definitely indicate an economy in flux. Good news, however, was not too long in coming."

By September 12, 2014, *Investopedia* said the Obama administration had "overseen an impressive upswing in the stock market." The Dow was then at 16,987.51. "More importantly, it has maintained a healthy average between 14,719 and 17,162 for the past 52 weeks," *Investopedia* said. "Though there have been intermittent downturns, the Dow's general upward trend speaks well for the Obama administration's efforts at economic recovery."

Jobs

Kevin Drum, writing for *Mother Jones*, in an article from December 28, 2015, titled, "Obama's Economic Performance Is Even Better Than It Looks," referenced an updated chart Paul Krugman had posted on NYTimes.com. The graphic compares private employment gains during the Obama administration to those in the Bush administration. His headline was "Obama: The Job-Killer" (a mocking reference to the predictions by Obama critics) but the lines clearly show jobs rising precipitously under Obama after an early dip, and jobs hitting bottom under Bush after sinking early on and then rising moderately for a time.

Drum also updated a chart comparing total government expenses under the two presidents' administrations, showing steady increases in the Bush years and declines under Obama that even out on the low side. The columnist explained:

Bush inherited a mild recession and got a huge fiscal boost. Obama inherited a deep recession and got a huge fiscal headwind. Even so, Obama's employment performance has been far better than Bush's.

As it happens, I don't think presidents have a dramatic effect on the economy. But they have some. John McCain wouldn't have fought for stimulus spending or extensions of unemployment insurance. He would probably have appointed more conservative

Change in private employment

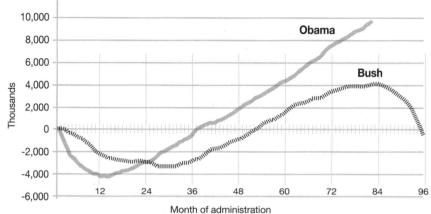

Month of administration

Source: Paul Krugman blog, "Obama The Job Killer," *New York Times*, December 27, 2015

This chart is based on one that Paul Krugman, the *New York Times* op-ed columnist, presented in his blog, showing private employment gains trending upward during the Obama administration, compared with the levels during the George W. Bush administration.

members of the Fed, who might have tightened monetary policy sooner. He would have insisted on keeping the portion of the Bush tax cut that goes to the rich.

So Obama deserves some of the credit for this. George Bush squandered his political capital on tax cuts for the wealthy and soft regulation of Wall Street. We saw the results of that. Obama spent his political capital on stimulus and health care and the social safety net. The result has been a sustained recovery despite a net decrease in government spending over the past six years. Not bad.

In January 2009, the month Obama took office, nonfarm payroll employment dropped by 598,000, and the unemployment rate rose from 7.2 to 7.6 percent, the BLS reported. Its report, issued about two weeks into his term, said payroll employment had declined by 3.6 million since the start of the recession in December 2007. "About one-half of this decline occurred in the past 3 months. In January, job losses were large and widespread across nearly all major industry sectors," the report said. "Both the number of unemployed persons (11.6 million) and the unemployment rate (7.6 percent) rose in January," it said. "Over the past 12

Total government expenditures

State + local + federal, inflation adjusted

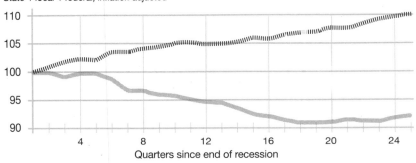

Quarters since end of recession

Source: Kevin Drum blog, "Obama's Economic Performance Is Even Better Than It Looks," *Mother Jones*, December 28, 2015

This chart comparing total government expenditures under the George W. Bush and Obama administrations is based on one presented by Kevin Drum for *Mother Jones*. With the start of recovery indexed to 100, in Bush's administration, the total government spending was about 10 percent higher twenty-five quarters after the beginning of the recovery. In Obama's case, total spending was about 8 percent less.

months, the number of unemployed persons has increased by 4.1 million and the unemployment rate has risen by 2.7 percentage points."

Throughout Obama's first year in office, unemployment rates continued to rise, peaking at 10.2 percent in October 2009, the highest rate seen since April 1983, according to BLS data. The *New York Times* said in November 2009 that as the rate reached "double digits for the first time in 26 years, it suddenly seemed possible that the nation might yet confront the worst joblessness since the Great Depression. In the six decades since the government began compiling such data, the highest level of unemployment came at the end of 1982, when it hit 10.8 percent. Despite the widespread assumption that the recession has already ended, and even as the economy has resumed growing, the government's latest snapshot of the labor market...testified to the uncomfortable truth that expansion had yet to translate into jobs."

The worst was over, however. The jobless rate hovered at 9.8–9.9 for a few months, the start of a bumpy but definitive decline.

In January 2016, as the final year of Obama's term began, the BLS reported that total nonfarm payroll employment increased by 151,000 the month before, and the unemployment rate was 4.9 percent, a low not seen since the recession took hold in 2008.

Black unemployment was at 8.8 percent in January 2016, after falling to 8.3 percent in December 2015, the lowest rate since 2007 (before the Great Recession began), and down from 9.4 percent in November, the BLS reported on February 5, 2016. Black unemployment had peaked at 16.8 percent in 2010.

Homes

On May 20, 2009, President Obama signed the Helping Families Save Their Homes Act and the Fraud Enforcement and Recovery Act into law, legislation addressing the mortgage-fraud and foreclosure problems that had set off the recession.

"These landmark pieces of legislation will protect hardworking Americans, crack down on those who seek to take advantage of them, and ensure that the problems that led us into this crisis never happen again," said President Obama.

The Fraud Enforcement and Recovery Act gave the federal government more leverage to crack down on the practices that cost thousands of families their homes or put them at risk. It expanded the Department of Justice's powers to prosecute and set up a bipartisan commission to investigate the practices that created the mortgage crisis and try to prevent such a crisis from reoccurring.

"Four months ago today, we took office amidst unprecedented economic turmoil," the president said before signing the bills. "And ever since that day we've worked aggressively across all fronts to end this crisis and to build a new foundation for our lasting prosperity. Step by step, I believe we're moving in the right direction." He noted that both bills had passed Congress with bipartisan majorities and praised lawmakers in what he called "one of the most productive congressional work periods in some time."

He said the Helping Families Save Their Homes Act would help responsible homeowners, prevent avoidable foreclosures, and keep families in their homes. It also required banks to honor renters' leases to prevent unfair evictions when owners had not paid their mortgages. The law also provided resources to prevent homelessness for families with children.

The other bill was aimed at "the twin scourges of mortgage fraud and predatory lending," the president said, adding,

Last year, the Treasury Department received 62,000 reports of mortgage fraud—more than 5,000 each month. The number of criminal mortgage fraud investigations opened by the FBI has more than doubled over the past three years. And yet, the federal government's ability to investigate and prosecute these frauds is severely hindered by outdated laws and a lack of resources.

And that's why this bill nearly doubles the FBI's mortgage and financial fraud program, allowing it to better target fraud in hard-hit areas. That's why it provides the resources necessary for other law-enforcement and federal agencies...to pursue these criminals, bring them to justice, and protect hardworking Americans affected most by these crimes.

The president also said at the signing,

I know my administration will be judged by various markers. But there's only one measure of progress that matters to me, and that's the progress that the American people see in their own lives, day to day, because right now, despite progress, too many Americans are hurting. They're Americans desperate to find a job, or unable to make ends meet despite working multiple jobs; Americans who pay their bills on time but can't keep their heads above water; Americans living in fear that they're one illness or one accident away from losing their home—hardworking Americans who did all the right things, met all of their responsibilities, yet still find the American Dream slipping out of reach.

CHAPTER 11

Defense

"It's harder to end a war than begin one. Indeed, everything that American troops have done in Iraq—all the fighting and all the dying, the bleeding and the building, and the training and the partnering—all of it has led to this moment of success."

President Obama, December 14, 2011

President Obama was headed for a press briefing on defense strategy accompanied by Defense Secretary Leon Panetta, right, and Army General Martin E. Dempsey, chairman of the Joint Chiefs of Staff, at the Pentagon, January 5, 2012. (Department of Defense photo by Erin A. Kirk-Cuomo)

President Obama directed a bold operation to raid Osama bin Laden's hideout and kill him. He ended U.S. involvement in the war in Iraq in 2011, bringing the troops home, but rejoined the fight against radical terrorists there in 2014.

On matters of defense, President Obama has acted decisively and boldly to protect the nation.

During an October 2008 debate with John McCain, the Republican presidential candidate, then candidate Obama vowed, "If we have Osama bin Laden in our sights and the Pakistani government is unable or unwilling to take them out, then I think that we have to act, and we will take them out. We will kill bin Laden...We will crush Al-Qaeda. That has to be our biggest national security priority."

In his first term, Obama actively engaged in planning for, and ultimately approved, the raid on Osama bin Laden's secret compound, which resulted in his death on May 2, 2011. The leader of the militant group Al Qaeda was killed in Pakistan in an operation led by the U.S. Central Intelligence Agency—and carried out by Navy SEALs of the U.S. Naval Special Warfare Development Group.

Al Qaeda had claimed responsibility for the September 11, 2001, attacks on the World Trade Center, the Pentagon, and a hijacked airliner headed for Washington, D.C., which crashed in a field in Somerset County, Pennsylvania. Al Qaeda had also been the culprit in the 1998 bombings of the U.S. embassies in Kenya and Tanzania. Yet its leader had eluded capture for more than a decade after the 9/11 attacks, and the fact that he remained at large meant the attacks had still been an open wound for many Americans.

A *New York Times* obituary, titled "The Most Wanted Face of Terrorism," detailed how bin Laden had built "a borderless brotherhood of radical Islam...into a multinational enterprise for the export of terrorism."

Before the raid, U.S. intelligence believed that Osama bin Laden had crossed the Afghan border to hide out in Pakistan, and advisers informed the president that they thought they had pinpointed his location at a compound under surveillance there. This began months of intense strategizing and debate with direct supervision by the president in consultation with various advisers, according to news reports at the time. The result was a daring helicopter mission that dropped Navy SEALs inside the complex.

In an address to the nation after the successful operation against Osama bin Laden, the president said:

> Shortly after taking office, I directed Leon Panetta, the director of the CIA, to make the killing or capture of bin Laden the top priority of our war against al Qaeda, even as we continued our broader efforts to disrupt, dismantle, and defeat his network.
>
> Then, last August, after years of painstaking work by our intelligence community, I was briefed on a possible lead to bin Laden. It was far from certain, and it took many months to run this thread to ground. I met repeatedly with my national security team as we developed more information about the possibility that we had located bin Laden hiding within a compound deep inside of Pakistan. And finally, last week, I determined that we had enough intelligence to take action, and authorized an operation to get Osama bin Laden and bring him to justice.
>
> Today, at my direction, the United States launched a targeted operation against that compound in Abbottabad, Pakistan. A small team of Americans carried out the operation with extraordinary courage and capability. No Americans were harmed. They took care to avoid civilian casualties. After a firefight, they killed Osama bin Laden and took custody of his body.
>
> For over two decades, bin Laden has been al Qaeda's leader and symbol, and has continued to plot attacks against our country and our friends and allies. The death of bin Laden marks the most significant achievement to date in our nation's effort to defeat al Qaeda.

Al Qaeda quickly confirmed the death of its leader and vowed revenge, while world leaders hailed the move.

U.N. Secretary-General Ban Ki-moon declared Osama bin Laden's death "a watershed moment in our common global fight against terrorism," the Reuters news service reported. "The crimes of al Qaeda touched most continents, bringing tragedy and loss of life to thousands of men, women and children," Ban told reporters. "This is a day to remember the victims and families of victims here in the United States and everywhere in the world."

Americans at home expressed relief. According to an overnight opinion poll by the Pew Research Center for the People and the Press and the *Washington Post*, Obama's approval rating shot up to 56 percent, from 47 percent the previous month, with 38 percent disapproving in the May 3, 2011, poll. In the overnight survey of 654 adults, 72 percent said they felt "relieved" by Osama bin Laden's death, while 60 percent felt "proud," and 58 percent said they were "happy."

The End of Qaddafi

Similarly, the U.S. helped to topple the regime of Muammar Qaddafi in March 2011, when the U.S. joined military action by a coalition of countries to defend Libyan civilians and support rebel troops. The dictator was overthrown and killed on October 20 of the same year by rebels, ending his forty-two-year reign.

President Obama reacted to the news of Qaddafi's death in a statement in the White House Rose Garden: "[This] is a momentous day in the history of Libya. The dark shadow of tyranny has been lifted. And with this enormous promise, the Libyan people now have a great responsibility—to build an inclusive and tolerant and democratic Libya that stands as the ultimate rebuke to Qaddafi's dictatorship."

He said the U.S. would "look forward to the announcement of the country's liberation, the quick formation of an interim government, and a stable transition to Libya's first free and fair elections."

President Obama acknowledged that the road ahead would be difficult for Libya. "We're under no illusions—Libya will travel a long and winding road to full democracy," he said. "There will be difficult days ahead."

Indeed, Libya has remained torn by rival factions, even as international efforts continue to restore stability, but the president could not have predicted then the attacks on the U.S. consulate and another compound on September 11, 2012, in Libya by radical protesters that killed the ambassador, another diplomat, and two CIA operatives.

War in Iraq

Recalling another promise from his first presidential campaign, Obama announced that he was ending U.S. involvement in the Iraq War. He said on October 21, 2011, that the United States would withdraw virtually all of its troops from Iraq by the end of that year. "After nearly 9 years, America's war in Iraq will be over," Obama said. He said the last Americans on the ground would leave "with their heads held high, proud of their success, and knowing that the American people stand united in our support for our troops."

Addressing returning troops at Fort Bragg, North Carolina, on December 14, 2011, he said, "As your commander in chief and on behalf of a grateful nation, I'm proud to finally say these two words—welcome home, welcome home, welcome home."

The president said the war had cost 4,500 American lives, 60,000 Iraqi lives, and more than $1 trillion. At the height of the conflict, 170,000 U.S. troops were serving in Iraq.

U.S. involvement had begun, along with a coalition of other nations, in 2003 with an invasion to topple the repressive regime of Saddam Hussein and purportedly to counter the threat that he was holding weapons of mass destruction (WMDs) and harboring Al Qaeda. Hussein was captured in December 2003 and executed three years later after trial by a special Iraqi tribunal and conviction of crimes against humanity. Meanwhile, fighting in Iraq dragged on as insurgents emerged to oppose the new government and the occupying military.

The conflicts in Iraq continued after the U.S. military drawdown, and the situation deteriorated. In 2014, Obama announced that he was approving new missions in Iraq. He revealed on August 7, 2014, that he had authorized limited airstrikes against Islamic militants in Iraq to avert the fall of the Kurdish capital, Erbil.

In a statement from the White House, the president said:

First, I said in June—as the terrorist group ISIL [Islamic State in the Levant] began an advance across Iraq—that the United States would be prepared to take targeted military action in Iraq if and when we determined that the situation required it. In recent days, these terrorists have continued to move across Iraq, and have neared the city of Erbil, where American diplomats and civilians serve at our consulate and American military personnel advise Iraqi forces.

To stop the advance on Erbil, I've directed our military to take targeted strikes against ISIL terrorist convoys should they move toward the city. We intend to stay vigilant, and take action if these terrorist forces threaten our personnel or facilities anywhere in Iraq, including our consulate in Erbil and our embassy in Baghdad. We're also providing urgent assistance to Iraqi government and Kurdish forces so they can more effectively wage the fight against ISIL.

The president said that at the request of the Iraqi government, he had also approved an operation to have U.S. military aircraft drop food and water to tens of thousands of Iraqis, members of a religious minority, who had fled militants and became isolated on a barren mountain range.

As ISIL has marched across Iraq, it has waged a ruthless campaign against innocent Iraqis. And these terrorists have been especially barbaric towards religious minorities, including Christian and Yezidis, a small and ancient religious sect. Countless Iraqis have been displaced. And chilling reports describe ISIL militants rounding up families, conducting mass executions, and enslaving Yezidi women.

In recent days, Yezidi women, men and children from the area of Sinjar have fled for their lives. And thousands—perhaps tens of thousands—are now hiding high up on the mountain, with little but the clothes on their backs. They're without food, they're without water. People are starving. And children are dying of thirst. Meanwhile, ISIL forces below have called for the systematic destruction of the entire Yezidi people, which would constitute genocide. So these innocent families are faced with a horrible choice: descend the mountain and be slaughtered, or stay and slowly die of thirst and hunger.

I've said before, the United States cannot and should not intervene every time there's a crisis in the world. So let me be clear about why we must act, and act now. When we face a situation like we do on that mountain—with innocent people facing the prospect of violence on a horrific scale, when we have a mandate to help—in this case, a request from the Iraqi government—and when we have the unique capabilities to help avert a massacre, then I believe the United States of America cannot turn a blind eye.

The president concluded his remarks, saying, "Earlier this week, one Iraqi cried that there is no one coming to help. Well, today America is coming to help."

The president vowed that these military operations would not drag the U.S. back into the conflict in Iraq against militants from ISIL (also known as ISIS, for the Islamic State of Iraq and Syria, or simply as the Islamic State), but on February 11, 2015, President Obama submitted a resolution to Congress to seek formal authorization to use military force against ISIL, limiting engagement to three years and prohibiting the use of "enduring offensive ground forces."

However, ten months later the Associated Press reported that the U.S. had a little more than three thousand troops in Iraq, including advisers and trainers.

Over New Year's Day weekend 2016, the U.S. and its allies announced that they had carried out twenty-six strikes against ISIL in Iraq.

War in Afghanistan

On May 25, 2014, over the Memorial Day holiday weekend, President Obama made a surprise visit to U.S. troops at Bagram Air Base in Afghanistan to thank them for their service and to begin talks on how much military force would remain in Afghanistan after the end of the year, when the U.S. would end its combat role there.

Speaking to three thousand troops inside a huge hangar near the capital city of Kabul, he promised that the war would end and many of them would never see another tour of duty in Afghanistan.

Less than a year and a half later, on October 15, 2015, President Obama announced that he was ending the withdrawal of American military forces from Afghanistan and would maintain troop presence there through the end of his term. The president said it was vital to U.S. security interests that some force remain there at a time when the Taliban, the Islamic fundamentalists, as well as Al Qaeda and militants from the Islamic State, were a major threat in Afghanistan.

Obama said he would keep about 9,800 troops in Afghanistan through much of 2016 and reduce the force to about 5,500 before his term ended in early 2017.

In his statement announcing the decision to keep troops there, the president recalled, "Last December—more than 13 years after our nation was attacked by al Qaeda on 9/11—America's combat mission in Afghanistan came to a responsible end. Today, American forces no longer patrol Afghan villages or valleys. Our troops are not engaged in major ground combat against the Taliban. Those missions now belong to Afghans, who are fully responsible for securing their country.

However, he said he was authorizing the continued military presence to provide training and support for counterterrorism efforts. "As Commander-in-Chief, I will not allow Afghanistan to be used as safe haven for terrorists to attack our nation again," he said. "Our forces therefore remain engaged in two narrow but critical missions—training Afghan forces, and supporting counterterrorism operations against the remnants of al Qaeda. Of course, compared to the 100,000 troops we once had in Afghanistan, today fewer than 10,000 remain, in support of these very focused missions."

He said the situation in Afghanistan remained precarious and dangerous as the Taliban had exploited the situation when U.S. troops withdrew from various areas. "The Taliban has made gains, particularly in rural areas, and can still launch deadly attacks in cities, including Kabul," he said. "Pressure from Pakistan has resulted in more al Qaeda coming into Afghanistan, and we've seen the emergence of an ISIL presence. The bottom line is, in key areas of the country, the security situation is still very fragile, and in some places there is risk of deterioration."

Even in a limited role, the U.S. forces have continued to suffer some casualties, on the order of twenty-five a year, as opposed to nearly five hundred in 2010, according to the president. The deaths of six U.S. soldiers whose convoy was attacked by a suicide bomber near Bagram Air Base just before Christmas in 2015 underscored the dilemma the president faced in risking American lives to support the Afghans in fighting terrorists who posed a global threat. In addition, a U.S. service member died and two others were wounded on January 5, 2016, during operations in southern Afghanistan, the Pentagon said.

Veto on Defense Funds

A few days after his Afghanistan announcement, on October 22, 2015, President Obama exercised his veto power for only the fifth time in his presidency. He used it to block a defense-authorization bill, the National Defense Authorization Act (NDAA) for 2016, saying that the legislation constituted an end run around budget limitations for the military and would restrict the transfer of detainees at Guantánamo Bay. The White House said Obama had vetoed the bill because it would allow an account for contingencies to become a slush fund to pay war costs and avoid budget restrictions.

The *New York Times* said the decision "signaled his determination to use the defense bill as a bargaining chip to push Republicans to abandon strict spending limits on military and domestic programs enacted in the 2011 Budget Control Act."

Signing his veto message publicly with reporters assembled around his desk, he said, "My message to them is very simple: Let's do this right. We're in the midst of budget discussions. Let's have a budget that properly funds our national security as well as economic security. Let's make sure that we're able in a constructive way to reform our military spending to make it sustainable over the long term."

On November 25, 2015, the president signed a revised version of the bill, which he said had altered the provisions to which he had objected. "I am therefore signing this annual defense authorization legislation because it includes vital benefits for military personnel and their families, authorities to facilitate ongoing operations around the globe, and important reforms to the military retirement system, as well as partial reforms to other military compensation programs," he said.

CHAPTER 12

Diplomacy

"I face the world as it is, and cannot stand idle in the face of threats to the American people. For make no mistake: Evil does exist in the world. A non-violent movement could not have halted Hitler's armies. Negotiations cannot convince al Qaeda's leaders to lay down their arms. To say that force may sometimes be necessary is not a call to cynicism—it is recognition of history; the imperfections of man and the limits of reason."

President Obama, December 10, 2009

Cuban president Raúl Castro and President Obama greeted each other before a bilateral meeting at the United Nations headquarters, September 29, 2015. (Associated Press photo/Andrew Harnik)

President Obama improved America's image and standing in the world from the beginning of his term. When he unexpectedly received the Nobel Peace Prize in his first year in office, he took it as a "call to action" and used his acceptance speech to weigh the costs of war against the benefits for keeping peace. He restored relations with Cuba, reached significant agreements on nuclear arms with Russia and Iran, and negotiated a major trade deal with twelve Pacific nations.

President Obama's diplomatic accomplishments reversed a sharp decline in world opinion of the U.S. during the previous administration. According to a BBC World Service poll of twenty-eight countries, global views of the United States improved markedly from 2009 to 2010. For the first time since the BBC started tracking, in 2005, views of the United States' influence in the world were more positive than negative on average, the survey found.

The United States was viewed positively on balance in twenty of twenty-eight countries, with an average of 46 percent now saying it had a mostly positive influence in the world, while 34 percent said it had a negative influence.

"Compared to a year earlier, negative ratings of the United States have dropped a striking nine points on average across the countries surveyed both years, while positive ratings are up a more modest four points," the survey report said.

The Norwegian Nobel Committee announced on October 9, 2009, that it had chosen Obama, not quite ten months after his inauguration, for his "extraordinary efforts to strengthen international diplomacy and cooperation between people." It cited his work toward nuclear nonproliferation and creating a "new climate" in international relations.

The decision was met with skepticism at best and outrage at worst. When the announcement was made in Oslo, gasps could be heard from the audience, Reuters reported. The committee's choice was a "stunning decision that honored the first-year U.S. president more for promise than achievement," Reuters said. Some critics thought that it was merely premature, others that it was undeserved. A *New York Times* op-ed piece by Timothy Egan recalled five years later that "as near as anybody could tell, it was the only Nobel ever given for future good ntentions."

Even Obama seemed stunned, saying he would accept it as a "call to action" to stand up to the challenges the world presented. "I do not view it as recognition of my own accomplishments but rather an affirmation of American leadership on behalf of aspirations held by people in all nations," he said.

Only two other sitting presidents had won the Nobel Peace Prize, Theodore Roosevelt in 1906 for negotiating peace in the Russo-Japanese war and resolving a dispute with Mexico, and Woodrow Wilson in 1919 for founding the League of Nations. To Wilson's disappointment, the U.S. Congress refused to ratify the treaty that created the league and to join it. Jimmy Carter won the Nobel Peace Prize more than two decades after leaving office for his untiring diplomacy and humanitarian efforts.

The head of the prize committee defended the decision to award the prize to Obama. "Only very rarely has a person to the same extent as Obama captured the world's attention and given its people hope for a better future," said Thorbjørn Jagland, chairman of the Nobel committee. "In the past year Obama has been a key person for important initiatives in the U.N. for nuclear disarmament and to set a completely new agenda for the Muslim world and East-West relations."

He also explained that the purpose of the award was not merely to reward the winner, but to "enhance" that individual's efforts to promote peace. "We do hope that this can contribute a little bit to enhance what he is trying to do," he said. "It is a clear statement to the world that we want to advocate and promote (the efforts toward peace)."

In accepting the award on December 10, 2009, President Obama acknowledged the "considerable controversy" his selection had fueled. "In part, this is because I am at the beginning, and not the end, of my labors on the world stage. Compared to some of the giants of history who've received this prize—Schweitzer and King; Marshall and Mandela—my accomplishments are slight...But perhaps the most profound issue surrounding my receipt of this prize is the fact that I am the Commander-in-Chief of the military of a nation in the midst of two wars."

He went on to discuss at length when and under what conditions war might be necessary and just:

> More and more, we all confront difficult questions about how to prevent the slaughter of civilians by their own government, or to stop a civil war whose violence and suffering can engulf an entire region.
>
> I believe that force can be justified on humanitarian grounds, as it was in the Balkans, or in other places that have been scarred by war. Inaction tears at our conscience and can lead to more costly intervention later. That's why all responsible nations must embrace the role that militaries with a clear mandate can play to keep the peace.
>
> America's commitment to global security will never waver. But in a world in which threats are more diffuse, and missions more complex, America cannot act alone. America alone cannot secure the peace...I understand why war is not popular, but I also know this: The belief that peace is desirable is rarely enough to achieve it. Peace requires responsibility. Peace entails sacrifice. That's why NATO continues to be indispensable. That's why we must strengthen UN and regional peacekeeping, and not leave the task to a few countries.

Engaging Cuba

As he neared the end of his service as chief commander and chief diplomat, President Obama was leaving a clear record of achievement, not the least of which was renewing diplomatic ties to Cuba and setting in motion a plan to normalize relations.

On December 17, 2014, President Obama ordered the restoration of full diplomatic relations with Cuba and announced plans to open an embassy in Havana. It was a surprise announcement that came at the end of eighteen months of secret talks to end a stalemate that had begun a lifetime earlier.

"We will end an outdated approach that for decades has failed to advance our interests, and instead we will begin to normalize relations between our two countries," said Obama, addressing the nation on television from the White House. He said the deal would end a "rigid policy that is rooted in events that took place before most of us were born," including him.

After Fidel Castro seized power in 1959 and established a cozy relationship with the Soviet Union, President Dwight D. Eisenhower imposed a trade embargo against Cuba in 1960 and broke off ties in January 1961. His successor, President John F. Kennedy, tried ousting the dictatorship with an invasion at the Bay of Pigs, which went awry in 1961 and faced off with Castro over the presence of Soviet missiles in Cuba in 1962.

Obama had a long-standing desire to fix the relationship with Cuba, according to an account in the *New York Times* of how the thaw in relations had come about. He relaxed some travel restrictions in 2011, but would not press forward while Cuba held a U.S. government contractor in prison for delivering satellite telephone and computer equipment to Cuban civilians. After Obama's reelection in 2012, he made Cuban relations a priority and authorized secret negotiations. Pope Francis encouraged Obama and Cuban leader Raúl Castro to talk, and the Vatican hosted a meeting to finalize terms. Finally, Obama and Raúl Castro, the brother and successor of Fidel, spoke by telephone to confirm a deal.

The deal included the release of the contractor, swapped for some Cuban prisoners held in the U.S., but did not include a lifting of the trade embargo. Only Congress can do that, and it seemed unlikely that would happen before Obama left office.

U.S. Secretary of State John Kerry (who succeeded Hillary Clinton in February 2013) formally reopened our nation's embassy in Cuba with a flag raising on August 14, 2015. "For more than half a century, U.S.-Cuba relations have been suspended in the amber of Cold War politics," the secretary said. "It's time to unfurl our flags and let the world know we wish each other well."

The three marines who had lowered the flag at the U.S. embassy in 1961—Larry Morris, Francis "Mike" East, and Jim Tracy—were there to see the flag hoisted and participate in the ceremony.

Curbing Iran

After twenty months of negotiations, Iran and six world powers, led by the United States, reached a historic agreement on July 14, 2015. The agreement limits Iran's nuclear capability and represents the biggest diplomatic triumph of Obama's presidency, according to the *New York Times*. The agreement restricts the amount of nuclear fuel that Iran can keep on hand and makes it more difficult for Iran to produce a bomb quickly. Iran accepted limits in return for the lifting of international oil and financial sanctions.

The deal faced some opposition in Congress, but Obama vowed that he would "veto any legislation that prevents the successful implementation of this deal."

Obama said the agreement was "not built on trust—it is built on verification." The president emphasized that whatever the objections might be, this deal was better than having no deal at all, with the prospect of an unmonitored and highly dangerous nuclear arms race in the volatile Middle East. "Put simply, no deal means a greater chance of more war in the Middle East," he said.

Opponents in Congress tried but failed to kill the deal within a sixty-day review period, which ended in September. Democrats in the Senate blocked a procedural motion that would have allowed a disapproval resolution to be considered before the time ran out.

The provisions of the Iran deal began to go into effect on October 18, 2015.

President Obama hailed the Senate vote as "a victory for diplomacy, for American national security, and for the safety and security of the world." He said, "I am heartened that so many senators judged this deal on the merits, and am gratified by the strong support of lawmakers and citizens alike."

Pope Francis, speaking before the U.N. General Assembly, on September 25, 2015, praised the agreement as "proof of the potential of political good will and of law, exercised with sincerity, patience and constancy." He added, "There is urgent need to work for a world free of nuclear weapons...with the goal of a complete prohibition of these weapons."

In early January 2016, Iran detained ten American sailors after their boats drifted into Iranian waters, but quickly released all ten sailors. A few days later, the U.S. and Iran agreed to a prisoner swap. The outcomes of both of these incidents were widely viewed as diplomatic breakthroughs resulting from the negotiated nuclear deal. Before that accord, relations between the U.S. and Iran had been severed ever since the 1979–81 hostage crisis, when Iranian revolutionaries held Americans hostage for 444 days.

In the January 2016 prisoner exchange, Iran freed four Americans, and the U.S. released seven Iranians who had been convicted in the U.S. for violating nuclear sanctions against Iran. The freed Americans, all of whom were of Iranian descent, were Jason Rezaian, a *Washington Post* reporter; Amir Hekmati, a former marine; the Reverend Saeed Abedini, a pastor from Boise, Idaho; and Nosratollah Khosravi-Roodsari, whom U.S. officials declined to identify further at the time of the release. He elected to remain in Iran after gaining his freedom.

The prisoner swap also came just as economic sanctions that had isolated Iran for years were lifted. That took place after the International Atomic Energy Agency confirmed that Iran had complied with the agreement.

"This prisoner release personifies the persistence and wisdom of the Obama administration's diplomatic efforts," Reza Marashi, research director for the National Iranian American Council and a friend of the reporter, wrote in the *Huffington Post*. "It simply could not have happened without dialogue between the U.S. and Iran. The nuclear deal helped begin that dialogue and create the political space necessary for prisoners to be freed. Like the release of 10 U.S. sailors, this exchange is a direct result of the nuclear deal."

Agreement with Russia

On April 8, 2010, President Obama and Russian president Dmitry Medvedev signed an agreement at a ceremony in Prague in the Czech Republic to reduce nuclear stockpiles for each of their nations by about a third. The new Strategic Arms Reduction Treaty (START) replaced a 1991 agreement, which had expired the previous December.

"This day demonstrates the determination of the United States and Russia—the two nations that hold over 90 percent of the world's nuclear weapons—to pursue responsible global leadership," Obama said. "Together, we are keeping our commitments under the Nuclear Non-Proliferation Treaty, which must be the foundation for global nonproliferation."

The Russian president said reaching the accord was a "win-win situation." He said, "This agreement enhances strategic ability and, at the same time, allows us to rise to a higher level of cooperation between Russia and the United States."

The signing represented the culmination of long and difficult negotiations over issues such as verification.

The U.S. Senate ratified the new START by a vote of 71-26 on December 22, 2010, and the treaty went into effect on January 26, 2011, following the Russian ratification process. Supporters in the Senate defeated some Republicans' efforts to alter the treaty that would have effectively killed it, but to appease opponents, supporters accepted amendments to a resolution accompanying the treaty.

John Kerry (D-Mass.), then a senator and the chairman of the Foreign Relations Committee, championed the treaty in the Senate and appealed to his colleagues to support it. "This is one of those rare times in the United States Senate . . . when we have it in our power to safeguard or endanger human life on this planet," he said. "More than any other, this issue should transcend politics."

After the vote, Kerry said, "The winners are not defined by party or ideology. The winners are the American people, who are safer with fewer Russian missiles aimed at them." He said the treaty would send a message to the world that the U.S. was ready to work with Russia and other nations to reduce the spread of nuclear weapons to other countries. "With this treaty, we send a message to Iran and North Korea that the international community remains united to restrain the nuclear ambitions of countries that operate outside the law," Kerry said.

Trade Deal

President Obama negotiated the Trans-Pacific Partnership (TPP) to secure more favorable trade terms for U.S.-made products. Twelve nations, including Australia, Canada, Japan, Mexico, Chile, and Peru, reached agreement on October 5, 2015, after nearly a decade of negotiations. For the U.S, the treaty will require congressional approval.

As "the largest regional trade accord in history," it represented the culmination of five days of intense negotiations in Atlanta among trade ministers who had failed to come to agreement a few months earlier, according to the *New York Times*. The *Times* called it "a hallmark victory" for Obama, who still had to persuade Congress to ratify it in the face of opposition from some Democrats and Republicans.

In a statement issued by the White House, the president said:

> I've spent every day of my presidency fighting to grow our economy and strengthen our middle class. That means making sure our workers have a fair shot to get ahead here at home, and a fair chance to compete around the world. My approach to trade has been guided by a unifying principle: leveling the playing field for American workers and businesses, so we can export more products stamped Made in America all over the world that support higher-paying American jobs here at home...When more than 95 percent of our potential customers live outside our borders, we can't let countries like China write the rules of the global economy. We should write those rules, opening new markets to American products while setting high standards for protecting workers and preserving our environment...
>
> This partnership levels the playing field for our farmers, ranchers, and manufacturers by eliminating more than 18,000 taxes that various countries put on our products. It includes the strongest commitments on labor and the environment of any trade agreement in history, and those commitments are enforceable, unlike in past agreements. It promotes a free and open Internet. It strengthens our strategic relationships with our partners and allies in a region that will be vital to the 21st century. It's an agreement that puts American workers first and will help middle-class families get ahead.
>
> Once negotiators have finalized the text of this partnership, Congress and the American people will have months to read every word before I sign it. I look forward to working with lawmakers from both parties as they consider this agreement.

Three major organizations representing business—the U.S. Chamber of Commerce, the National Association of Manufacturing, and the

Business Roundtable—endorsed the agreement and were poised to help Obama lobby Congress to ratify it in 2016.

"No trade agreement is perfect, and the TPP is no exception," Chamber president Thomas J. Donohue said in issuing his organization's endorsement on January 6, 2016. "However, the benefits of a trade agreement lie in how it is interpreted, implemented, and enforced. With that in mind, we're rolling up our sleeves to work with the administration, Congress and our TPP partners to ensure the agreement is implemented in a way that maximizes its commercial benefits, including market access, rules, and intellectual property protections. We intend to see this job through to the end—to the agreement's entry-into-force and beyond."

Trade Initiatives

The Obama administration trade initiatives also include

- On March 11, 2010, President Obama announced a National Export Initiative to improve conditions that directly affect the private sector's ability to export with the goal of doubling exports over five years.
- On November 12, 2010, President Obama announced the Energy-Smart Communities Initiative (ESCI) to support the energy-efficient buildings, transport, and electric power grids for sustainable development and long-term job creation for the Asia-Pacific region, led by the United States and Japan. He also announced the U.S.-Japan Economic Harmonization Initiative; the U.S.-Japan Dialogue to Promote Innovation, Entrepreneurship, and Job Creation; and the U.S.-Japan Policy Cooperation Dialogue on the Internet Economy to further strengthen economic ties between the United States and Japan.
- On November 19, 2012, at the U.S.-ASEAN Leaders Meeting in Phnom Penh, Cambodia, President Obama and leaders of the ten Association of Southeast Asian Nations (ASEAN) states announced the launch of the U.S.-ASEAN Expanded Economic Engagement (E3) initiative to expand trade and investment ties between the United States and

ASEAN, creating new business opportunities and jobs in all eleven countries.

- On July 1, 2013, President Obama announced the launch of Trade Africa, a new partnership between the United States and sub-Saharan Africa to increase internal and regional trade within Africa, and expand trade and economic ties among Africa, the United States, and other global markets.

- On June 19, 2013, the president directed the White House Rural Council to bring together federal resources to help rural businesses and leaders take advantage of new investment opportunities and access new customers and markets abroad.

- On January 27, 2015, President Obama announced the Indian Diaspora Investment Initiative, $4 billion of new initiatives aimed at boosting trade and investment ties and financing social development ventures in the country.

CHAPTER 13

Justice

"The arc of the universe may bend toward justice, but it doesn't bend on its own."

President Obama, August 28, 2013

While discussing his actions to tighten rules on gun sales, President Obama had to pause as tears welled up when he mentioned the schoolchildren who had been killed in December 2012 in a mass shooting in Newtown, Connecticut, January 5, 2016. (Associated Press photo/Carolyn Kaster)

President Obama has used his power to pardon and reduce sentences far more often than his recent predecessors and created an initiative to grant more clemency in the final months of his presidency, especially for nonviolent drug offenders. The president, delivering on a campaign promise, made the elimination of disparities in sentencing for crack and powder cocaine possession a major pillar of his efforts to foster justice and reduce the prison population. He signed a bipartisan bill on August 3, 2010, significantly reducing the disparities. With the help of his attorneys general, he has pursued an aggressive civil rights agenda. The president also took executive action to tighten restrictions on gun purchases.

In December 2015, President Obama commuted the sentences of 95 people, bringing his total commutations granted to 184, more than the previous five presidents combined, according to the White House. George W. Bush granted 11; Bill Clinton, 61; George H. W. Bush, 3; Reagan, 13; and Carter, 29, according to a White House chart extracted from Justice Department data.

Article II of the Constitution gives the president "Power to grant Reprieves and Pardons for Offences against the United States, except in Cases of Impeachment," essentially unlimited power to reduce sentences or grant pardons for a federal crime. A reprieve or commutation is a lessening of a sentence. Presidential pardons eradicate the legal effects of a conviction, restoring full rights.

A *New York Times* editorial on December 31, 2015, titled "Mr. Obama's Trickle of Mercy," criticized Obama for not using his power to pardon and commute sentences more often to address the sentencing disparities for drug crimes. While conceding that he had used it far more than his modern predecessors had, the paper urged him to do more to process applications of thousands of others waiting for justice as he entered the final months of his presidency: "The presidential power of mercy is explicit in the Constitution, it is virtually unlimited, and presidents once used it far more freely to correct injustices," the *Times* said. "It is a 'tool

Reducing sentences

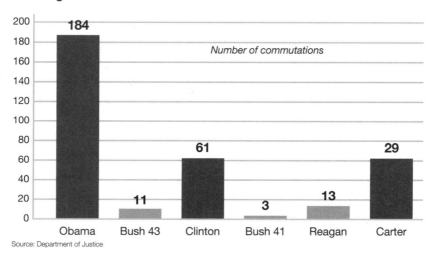

On December 18, 2015, President Obama commuted the federal prison sentences of 95 men and women, primarily nonviolent offenders. That brought his total to 184 commutations, more than the total for the last five presidents combined.

of public morality,' as one former federal prosecutor put it. If Mr. Obama truly wants to reinvigorate this moribund process, he has a year left to do it. The job requires only two things: a pen and the political will. There is no question that Mr. Obama has the pen."

Clemency Initiative

The president, however, had already shown that he had the political will to do it. As part of the drive to reduce the prison population and administer justice, as the *Times* noted, President Obama did set in motion a plan to release hundreds, perhaps thousands, more federal prisoners before his term ends, if applications can be filed and processed in time. He announced a clemency initiative in April 2014 to shorten the sentences of federal inmates, particularly nonviolent drug offenders, who would have gotten less time under current law.

Apparently, the application process was bogged down, and few cases were advancing. In mid-2015, the Obama administration warned lawyers for federal inmates who might be eligible for presidential clemency to expedite their filings because "the clock is running" on his presidency.

In early January 2016, the Justice Department also signaled that it was preparing to step up the pace of reviewing applications by doubling the force of lawyers on staff to handle the filings. The Office of the Pardon Attorney, which handles the cases, posted a job listing for attorney advisers on the Justice Department's website. In mid-January 2016, U.S. Pardon Attorney Deborah Leff announced that she was leaving the post by the end of the month, clearing the way for the president to name a replacement.

When the clemency initiative was announced, Deputy Attorney General James Cole said the purpose was "to quickly and effectively identify appropriate candidates, candidates who have a clean prison record, do not present a threat to public safety, and were sentenced under out-of-date laws that have since been changed, and are no longer seen as appropriate."

The primary focus was to shorten sentences of inmates serving long prison terms because of a disparity between the treatment of powder cocaine and crack cocaine in federal law. Obama had signed legislation in 2010 to reduce that disparity, but the clemency order was not limited to such cases.

The Justice Department said the clemency initiative was open to prisoners who

- Were serving a federal sentence in prison and, by operation of law, likely would have received a substantially lower sentence if convicted of the same offense today.
- Were nonviolent, low-level offenders without significant ties to large-scale criminal organizations, gangs, or cartels.
- Had served at least ten years of their sentence.
- Did not have a significant criminal history.
- Had demonstrated good conduct in prison.
- Had no history of violence prior to or during their current term of imprisonment.

In an interview with the *Huffington Post* in March 2015, the president said he planned to use his power to grant early release "more aggressively" as his term wound down. As of December 2014, he had granted only eighteen commutations, the *Huffington Post* said.

He said in the interview that he had used that power infrequently because of problems in the Office of the Pardon Attorney inherited from the previous administration. "I noticed that what I was getting was mostly small-time crimes from very long ago," Obama said. "It would be a 65-year-old who wanted a pardon to get his gun rights back. Most of them were legitimate, but they didn't address the broader issues that we face, particularly around nonviolent drug offenses. So we've revamped now the DOJ office. We're now getting much more representative applicants."

He announced his new initiative after the head of the office resigned, but the process still appeared to be seriously bottlenecked. Thousands were applying, and none were being approved at that time.

"I think what you'll see is not only me exercising that pardon power and clemency power more aggressively for people who meet the criteria— nonviolent crimes, have served already a long period of time, have shown that they're rehabilitated—but also we're working with Democrats and Republicans around criminal justice reform issues," Obama said.

He said he was also encouraged to see that criminal justice reform and elimination of some mandatory minimum sentences that had con-tributed to the massive incarceration and criminalization of nonviolent crime was a "rare area where we're actually seeing significant bipartisan interest." Consensus had been building that the draconian sentencing policies adopted in the 1980s to deal with the crack epidemic had over-shot the mark, leading to the burgeoning prison populations and disrup-tion of lives on a grand scale.

"If we can get some action done at the federal level, that will make a difference in terms of how, I think, more and more states recognize it doesn't make sense for us to treat nonviolent drug offenses the way we do," Obama told the *Huffington Post*.

Although the president has authority over federal prisons, he can do little to stop the states from overzealous sentencing and to reduce the state prison populations other than to set the model and hope they would follow the federal government's lead.

Sentencing

On August 3, 2010, President Obama signed into law the Fair Sentenc-ing Act (FSA), which reduced the disparity in the amounts of powder cocaine and crack cocaine a suspect trafficked in order to trigger mandatory minimum sentences. The law eliminated the mandatory minimum sentence for simple possession of crack cocaine, as evidenced by the small amount possessed.

Under the 2010 law, 28 grams (about one ounce) of crack cocaine triggers the five-year mandatory minimum penalty, and 280 grams of crack cocaine triggers the ten-year mandatory minimum penalty. Under the old law, 5 grams of crack triggered the same five-year minimum sentence as 500 grams of powder cocaine would, according to the Justice Department. Under the newer law, powder cocaine quantities triggering five- and ten-year mandatory minimum penalties remain at previous levels, 500 and 5,000 grams.

Fair Sentencing Act of 2010
Change in quantities for mandatory minimum sentences

Statutory penalty	Crack cocaine		Powder cocaine	Ratio	
	old law	new law		old ratio	new ratio
5-year mandatory minimun	5 grams	28 grams	500 grams	100:1	18:1
10-year mandatory minimun	50 grams	280 grams	5,000 grams	100:1	18:1

Source: U.S. Department of Justice

This law reduced the disparity in the amounts of powder cocaine and crack cocaine sold that would trigger mandatory minimum sentences. Under the new law, 28 grams (about one ounce) of crack cocaine would trigger the five-year mandatory minimum penalty, while 280 grams of crack cocaine would trigger the ten-year mandatory minimum penalty. Under the old law, five grams of crack triggered a five-year minimum sentence, the same sentence 500 grams of powder cocaine would.

The American Civil Liberties Union (ACLU) pointed out that the 2010 law reduced the sentencing disparity from a ratio of 100:1 to 18:1. "The scientifically unjustifiable 100:1 ratio meant that people faced longer sentences for offenses involving crack cocaine than for offenses involving the same amount of powder cocaine—two forms of the same drug," the ACLU said. The organization noted that the 18:1 ratio had resulted from a political compromise and that ultimately no disparity in sentencing should exist for equal amounts of crack or powder cocaine; the ratio should be 1:1.

"On average, under the 100:1 regime, African Americans served virtually as much time in prison for non-violent drug offenses as whites did for violent offenses," the ACLU said. "The FSA represents a decade-long, and truly bipartisan, effort to reduce the racial disparities caused by the draconian crack cocaine sentencing laws and to restore confidence in the criminal justice system—particularly in communities of color."

> The Fair Sentencing Act, signed into law by President Barack Obama on August 3, 2010, reduced the disparity between the amount of crack cocaine and powder cocaine needed to trigger certain federal criminal penalties. It also eliminated the five-year mandatory minimum sentence for simple possession of crack cocaine.

In 2011, the U.S. Sentencing Commission, an independent agency of the judiciary that establishes sentencing policies and practices for the federal courts, voted to apply the new guidelines retroactively to individuals sentenced before the law was enacted.

The National Association for the Advancement of Colored People (NAACP) welcomed the commission's action, saying, "This means that more than 12,000 men and women currently incarcerated for crack cocaine possession, more than 10,000 of whom are African-American, will be eligible for an adjustment of their sentences."

The NAACP said its members "know all too well the devastating impact the 100 to 1 sentencing disparity has had on our communities. Most authorities estimate that more than 60% of those who use crack cocaine are white. Yet in 2006, 82% of those convicted and sentenced under federal crack cocaine laws were African American. When you add in Hispanics, the percentage climbs to above 96%. Thus the communities served by the NAACP have a clear and crucial stake in the Fair Sentencing Act." The organization added that it was pleased with the U.S. Sentencing Commission's decision.

An ACLU report in 2006 said that racial disparities in use or possession stem from the affordability of crack, compared to powder cocaine. "Because of its relatively low cost, crack cocaine is more accessible for poor Americans, many of whom are African Americans. Conversely, powder cocaine is much more expensive and tends to be used by more affluent white Americans," the report said.

The report also said that whites were less likely to be prosecuted for drug offenses, when prosecuted were more likely to be acquitted, and if convicted, they were much less likely to be sent to prison.

The report recalled that the rationale for the harsh sentences for crack stemmed largely from the hysteria and myth surrounding the drug in the early 1980s when it was thought to be far more lethal and addicting than powder cocaine.

The ACLU report said,

> Many of the assumptions used in determining the 100:1 ratio have been proven wrong by recent data. For example, despite many of the misconceptions at the time . . . numerous scientific and medical experts have determined that in terms of pharmacological effects, crack cocaine is no more harmful than powder cocaine—the effects on users is the same regardless of form . . . In addition, research indicates that the negative effects of prenatal crack cocaine exposure are identical to the negative effects of prenatal powder cocaine exposure. Other assumptions, such as the epidemic of crack use by youth, never materialized to the extent feared.

When Attorney General Eric Holder addressed the National Press Club on February 17, 2015, announcing the first reduction in the federal prison population in more than thirty-two years (see chapter 8), he also cited the Smart on Crime Initiative undertaken by the administration. In addition to a broad package of reforms, it aimed to discourage federal prosecutors from pursuing harsh minimum sentences for low-level, nonviolent drug criminals and to shift resources to fighting more serious crime.

In 1980, the federal prison population was about 24,000. By December 2013, the figure was about 216,000, down from 218,000 a year earlier, according to the Bureau of Justice Statistics. "This newly unveiled data shows we can confront over-incarceration at the same time that we continue to promote public safety," Holder said.

A report on the Smart on Crime Initiative in August 2013, the result of a review he had ordered of the criminal justice system, cited the high cost of maintaining prisons as an incentive to pare the prison populations:

> Our prisons are over-capacity and the rising cost of maintaining them imposes a heavy burden on taxpayers and communities. At the state level, costs for running corrections facilities have roughly tripled in the last three decades, making it the second-fastest rising expense after Medicaid. At the federal level, the Bureau of Prisons comprises one-third of the Justice Department's budget.
>
> This requires a top-to-bottom look at our system of incarceration. For many non-violent, low-level offenses, prison may not be the most sensible method of punishment. But even for those defendants who do require incarceration, it is important to ensure a sentence length commensurate with the crime committed. Our policies must also seek to eliminate unfair sentencing disparities.

Civil Rights

The Department of Justice (DOJ) under Obama and Attorneys General Eric Holder and Loretta Lynch has been relentlessly aggressive on civil rights. Holder, the first African American attorney general, held the position for six years before resigning and returning to the law firm where he worked before joining the cabinet. Lynch, the first black woman to hold the post, succeeded him. Holder announced his desire to retire in September 2014, but Lynch was not confirmed until April 23, 2015.

Holder's legacy on civil rights includes the work to stop defending the Defense of Marriage Act and fight for same-sex marriage (see chapter 4) and investigations into police departments like that in Ferguson, Missouri, in the aftermath of the Michael Brown killing by an officer. (See chapter 3.)

Holder also worked to protect voting rights, challenging state laws that negatively affected minority groups, such as voter-identification requirements and shortened voting hours. He was a staunch advocate for the rights of African Americans. He did not mince words, and he backed them up with actions, which often made him enemies.

He set off a storm of controversy when he made remarks to DOJ employees for Black History Month in 2009. "Though this nation has proudly thought of itself as an ethnic melting pot in things racial, we have always been, and we, I believe, continue to be, in too many ways, essentially a nation of cowards," said Holder. "Though race-related issues continue to occupy a significant portion of our political discussion, and though there remain many unresolved racial issues in this nation, we, average Americans, simply do not talk enough with each other about things racial... Through its work and through its example this Department of Justice, as long as I am here, must—and will—lead the nation to the 'new birth of freedom' so long ago promised by our greatest President" (a reference to Lincoln).

Gun Control

Surrounded by survivors of shootings and relatives of people lost to gun violence, President Obama choked up and wiped away tears at a live address from the White House on January 5, 2016. He had started to mention the twenty children, along with six adults, who were killed in a mass shooting at Sandy Hook Elementary School in Newtown, Connecticut, on December 14, 2012. "First-graders... Every time I think about those kids, it gets me mad, and by the way, it happens on the streets of Chicago every day," he said.

The president, speaking from the East Room, continued, letting the tears roll down, as he outlined a number of executive actions he had announced the previous day to tighten restrictions on gun purchases. Primarily, the actions target unlicensed dealers who sell at gun shows, exploiting the "gun show loophole" meant for hobbyists and collectors, or sell online to avoid conducting criminal background checks on purchasers.

"Every single year, more than 30,000 Americans have their lives cut short by guns—30,000. Suicides. Domestic violence. Gang shootouts. Accidents... The United States of America is not the only country on Earth with violent or dangerous people. We are not inherently more prone to violence. But we are the only advanced country on Earth that sees this kind of mass violence erupt with this kind of frequency. It doesn't happen in other advanced countries. It's not even close. And as I've said before, somehow we've become numb to it, and we start thinking that this is normal," he said.

Indeed, mass shootings—with four or more people wounded or dead—were happening at a rate of more than one a day, based on data derived from news accounts, the *New York Times* reported on December 2, 2015, the day fourteen people were gunned down in California.

"Including the worst mass shooting of the year, which unfolded horrifically on Wednesday in San Bernardino, Calif., a total of 462 people have died and 1,314 have been wounded in such attacks this year, many of which occurred on streets or in public settings, the databases indicate," the *Times* said. The newspaper said it was impossible to know whether such shootings were on the rise because the databases did not go back more than a couple of years.

Obama announced that his executive actions would:

- Require all gun sellers to have a license and perform background checks.
- Direct the Federal Bureau of Investigation to overhaul the existing background check system.
- Improve enforcement of existing gun laws.
- Add two hundred new agents to the Bureau of Alcohol, Tobacco, Firearms, and Explosives.
- Make it easier for states to report and share information about people barred from owning guns for mental health reasons.
- Provide $500 million to increase access to mental health care.
- Encourage research in gun-safety technology through the Departments of Defense, Justice, and Homeland Security.

Obama's critics immediately seized upon the plan as an infringement of the Second Amendment right to bear arms and an unlawful expansion of the president's executive powers.

While the actions and responsibilities cut across several departments, Attorney General Loretta Lynch was first up to defend it on Capitol Hill, about two weeks after the announcement. She was there to ask Congress for the funds to beef up FBI enforcement during a Senate Appropriations Committee hearing. The FBI was under her jurisdiction.

Under the White House executive actions, the DOJ planned to hire 200 new FBI agents and investigators, and the Bureau of Alcohol, Tobacco, Firearms, and Explosives (part of the Treasury Department) planned to hire 230 additional employees to help with background checks.

Responding to questions, Lynch argued that the president's proposals merely clarified existing laws and enhanced enforcement and that they were clearly within the president's purview. "I have complete confidence that the common sense steps announced by the president are lawful," Lynch said at the hearing on January 20, 2016. "They are consistent with the Constitution as interpreted by the Supreme Court and the laws passed by Congress . . . The steps that I have outlined—and the actions that President Obama has described—are all well-reasoned measures, well within existing legal authorities."

President Obama will undoubtedly face pushback on his gun policies, but he has shown determination to do something. His words the day he announced them acknowledged those who fear being stripped of their guns, and he framed it as a rights issue, emphasizing the rights of the victims. "Second Amendment rights are important, but there are other rights that we care about as well." Obama said. "And we have to be able to balance them, because our right to worship freely and safely—that right was denied to Christians in Charleston, South Carolina, and that was denied Jews in Kansas City, and that was denied Muslims in Chapel Hill, and Sikhs in Oak Creek. They had rights, too."

CHAPTER 14

Labor

"In this country, a hard day's work deserves a fair day's pay. That's at the heart of what it means to be middle class in America."

President Obama, June 29, 2015

President Obama held a roundtable with students at Lorain County Community College, Elyria, Ohio, about jobs and their futures. From left are David Palmer, Bronson Harwood, and Duane Sutton. All of them had lost jobs and were retraining for new ones. Obama was there to make a speech about the need to prepare more people for the jobs available in an increasingly technical world, April 18, 2012. (Associated Press photo/Carolyn Kaster)

President Obama used executive action and his regulatory authority to enact significant reforms for workers, including extending eligibility for overtime pay to more workers and granting paid family leave to federal workers. He pushed reforms in job training and got a bill for it out of Congress with broad bipartisan support.

The president of the United States used an op-ed article in the *Huffington Post* on June 29, 2015, to announce his proposed rule to extend overtime pay to more workers than previously were covered by the overtime law. "We've got to keep making sure hard work is rewarded," he said. "Right now, too many Americans are working long days for less pay than they deserve. That's partly because we've failed to update overtime regulations for years—and an exemption meant for highly paid, white collar employees now leaves out workers making as little as $23,660 a year—no matter how many hours they work."

Salaried workers who earned less than the $23,660 were automatically entitled to time-and-a-half pay if they worked more than forty hours.

Under new rules, Obama said salaried workers making up to about $50,400 next year would be entitled to overtime pay. The White House estimated that this would increase wages for five million people. The threshold would rise automatically in the future.

"That's good for workers who want fair pay, and it's good for business owners who are already paying their employees what they deserve—since those who are doing right by their employees are undercut by competitors who aren't," he said. "That's how America should do business."

The administration indicated it was hoping to complete a review process of the rule, fend off any challenges, and implement it in 2016 before Obama's term ended, according to *Politico*.

In an interview with the *Huffington Post* in March 2015, Obama said he was ordering the Labor Department to review the rule and propose changes for fair pay for extended hours. "What we've seen is, increasingly, companies skirting basic overtime laws, calling somebody a manager when they're stocking groceries and getting paid $30,000 a year," Obama said. "Those folks are being cheated."

In addition to proposing the overtime rule, signing the Lilly Ledbetter Act (see chapter 2), and granting paid sick leave to employees of federal contractors (see chapter 9), President Obama used his regulatory and executive powers to introduce important reforms for salaried and hourly workers.

Family Leave

President Obama announced in January 2015 that he was granting paid leave after birth or adoption to parents employed by the executive branch, ordering it by way of a presidential memorandum to federal agencies. The program would advance unearned sick time to federal employees and would cost an estimated $250 million a year to implement, White House adviser Valerie Jarrett said.

She announced the details of the plan in a posting to LinkedIn, an employment-related social media site. "The truth is, the success and productivity of our workers is inextricably tied to their ability to care for their families and maintain a stable life at home," she wrote. "The president intends to ensure that the federal government is a model employer."

Obama also called on Congress to extend the same benefit to employees and to pass legislation to allow workers to earn up to seven paid sick days a year, and create a $2 billion incentive fund to help states pay for family leave programs.

While about half of American workers could already take up to twelve weeks' leave under the Family and Medical Leave Act, it was unpaid, and many workers could not afford to take it. Some companies offer paid leave anyway, but the U.S. lags far behind other industrialized countries in the generosity of its parental-leave policies. According to PolitiFact.com, "The United States has the smallest population of women eligible for paid maternity leave among developed countries."

Job Training

On July 22, 2014, President Obama signed legislation providing funding to states and cities for job retraining. Congress passed the Workforce Innovation and Opportunity Act on July 9, 2014, by huge margins, 95-3 in the Senate, and 415-6 in the House.

Noting the rare bipartisan approval of legislation in Congress during his administration, the president told lawmakers, "Let's do this more often. It's so much fun!"

The law reauthorized a program in place since 1998, in the Clinton administration, but it trimmed the bureaucracy behind it and eliminated duplication. The act also included measures to make the training more relevant to the job market.

According to the Government Accountability Office, as of 2011, the federal government was spending $18 billion a year on job training spread over forty-seven programs run by nine agencies. The 2014 law eliminated fifteen of those programs, streamlined others, and gave state and regional officials more flexibility on how to use federal dollars.

> The Workforce Innovation and Opportunity Act, signed July 22, 2014, consolidated federal job-training programs and reauthorized programs for adult education and rehabilitation.

At the signing ceremony, the president said:

In 2011, I called on Congress to reauthorize the Workforce Investment Act, update it for the 21st century. And I want to thank every single lawmaker who is here—lawmakers from both parties—who answered that call. It took some compromising, but, you know what, it turns out compromise sometimes is OK. Folks in Congress got past their differences, and they got a bill to my desk. So this is not a win for Democrats or Republicans. It is a win for American workers. It's a win for the middle class. And it's a win for everybody who is fighting to earn their way into the middle class.

So the bill I'm about to sign will give communities more certainty to invest in job-training programs for the long run. It will help us bring those programs into the 21st century by building on what we know works based on evidence, based on tracking what actually delivers on behalf of folks who enroll in these programs—more partnerships with employers, more tools to measure performance, more flexibilities for states and cities to innovate and to run their workforce programs in ways that are best suited for their particular demographic and their particular industries.

Using the powers available to him through executive action and regulations, President Obama has improved the lives of many workers and set them on a path for greater economic security. His paid family-leave policies will improve the home lives of federal employees, give their children stability, and perhaps ultimately lead to more liberal leave policies in other sectors. The job-training legislation will be important not only to the individuals who benefit but also to the economy as a whole.

CHAPTER 15

Education

"We agree that real opportunity requires every American to get the education and training they need to land a good-paying job. The bipartisan reform of No Child Left Behind was an important start, and together, we've increased early childhood education, lifted high school graduation rates to new highs, and boosted graduates in fields like engineering. In the coming years, we should build on that progress, by providing pre-K for all, offering every student the hands-on computer science and math classes that make them job-ready on day one, and we should recruit and support more great teachers for our kids."

President Obama, January 12, 2016

President Obama visited with children in a pre-kindergarten classroom at Moravia Elementary School in Baltimore, Maryland, during a trip to highlight his initiatives to expand funding for early childhood education, May 17, 2013. (Official White House photo by Pete Souza)

President Obama initiated a public-private sector partnership to fund early childhood education, signed the Every Student Succeeds Act, funded $4.35 billion in K–12 education reforms through the Race to the Top program and funneled more than $77 billion to schools through the Economic Recovery and Reinvestment Act. As part of his plan to make higher education universal and affordable, he increased funding for Pell Grants and made it easier for students to repay student loans.

President Obama pressed for an expansion of early education in his State of the Union addresses in 2013, 2014, and 2015. Having made no headway in Congress, he made the plea again in his 2016 address to lawmakers. As he has on other issues, however, in 2014 he had already teamed up with private-sector allies to get at least some of the work done.

Obama wants to provide daycare and preschool opportunities for every child in the nation. A bipartisan bill to provide grants to states for expansion of early childhood education was introduced in 2013 but had not progressed far as the final year of his term began.

At a summit on early childhood education at the White House on December 10, 2014, President Obama unveiled a $1 billion public-private partnership called Invest in US to expand preschool programs. The White House estimated that sixty-three thousand children would benefit from the funds.

The U.S. Department of Education awarded $250 million in grants to eighteen states to create or expand high-quality preschool programs, and the Department of Health and Human Services gave $500 million to more than forty states to expand Early Head Start and child-care programs for children up to three years old.

In addition, corporations, foundations, and other benefactors gave $330 million for the project led by the First Five Years Fund. Supporters included the Walt Disney Company with $55 million, the LEGO Foundation with $5 million, and the J. B. and M. K. Pritzker Family Foundation with $25 million.

"That's real money," Obama said. "Even in Washington, that's real money."

Obama said that fewer than one-third of the four-year-olds in the United States were in preschool. Those most often left out were children from low-income families. He said studies repeatedy showed that the earlier children are in education programs the more likely they are to graduate, stay out of jail, remain employed, and maintain stable families when they become adults.

A study released the day of the summit by the Council of Economic Advisers found that for every dollar invested in early education, eight dollars could be saved in future funding, as a result of higher graduation rates, increased earnings, and reductions in violent crime. The report also said that providing high-quality, affordable childcare increased rates of employment and incomes for working parents, especially mothers.

Every Student Succeeds

On December 10, 2015, President Obama signed the Every Student Succeeds Act, which swept aside the controversial No Child Left Behind law, which had been in place since 2002. The Every Student Succeeds Act had easily been passed by the Senate, 85-12, the previous day, and the House, 359-64, a week earlier. Obama called it an "example of how bipartisanship should work." He said, "That's something that you don't always see here in Washington. There wasn't a lot of grandstanding, a lot of posturing, just a lot of good, hard work."

The law still requires students nationwide to take annual reading and math exams, but it encourages states to limit the time students spend on testing and returns power to the states for making schools accountable.

"With this bill, we reaffirm that fundamentally American ideal that every child—regardless of race, gender, background, ZIP code—deserves the chance to make out of their lives what they want," Obama said. "This is a big step in the right direction."

No Child Left Behind was intended to make schools more accountable, especially for the education of the poor and disadvantaged, but it became increasingly unpopular. Many educators and parents felt it overemphasized cramming for tests, encouraged schools to eliminate subjects they weren't testing for, and gave the federal government too much control over schools.

Representative John Kline (R-Minn.), chairman of the House Education Committee, who helped push the new bill through Congress, said its enactment meant schools would no longer be micromanaged by the federal government. "Instead, parents, teachers, and state and local education leaders will regain control of their schools," said Kline.

The Every Student Succeeds Act, signed by President Obama on December 10, 2015, reauthorizes school funding under the 1965 Elementary and Secondary Education Act and sets federal funding policy, revising provisions of the No Child Left Behind Act of 2001.

Race to the Top

On July 25, 2009, the Obama administration initiated a $4.35 billion program to award grants to states for innovation and improvements in education. The program, known as Race to the Top, was launched as part of the American Recovery and Reinvestment Act and offered funding for projects in K–12 education.

"The essential idea of Race to the Top was to create incentives for states to continue the good work they had already done to improve education in their states and put forward bold, systemic plans that would lead to, in the President's words, 'Better standards. Better teaching. Better schools,'" said an Education Department report. "Race to the Top empowered states to accelerate the pace and reach of their improvement activities and rewarded states that chose to create and implement comprehensive improvement agendas that they believed would increase student achievement and narrow achievement gaps in their states."

Race to the Top sought reforms in four areas:

- Development of rigorous standards and better assessments
- Adoption of better data systems for monitoring student progress
- Support for educators to become more effective
- Resources to turn around low-performing schools

Forty-six states and the District of Columbia submitted Race to the

Top applications. In 2010, the report said, through the Phase 1 and 2 competitions, eleven states and the District of Columbia received awards ranging from $75 million to $700 million for system-wide improvements. The report assessed the impact of the program on the states that got the first and largest grants.

As examples of how the money was used, the report cited Tennessee and other states that focused on training principals to observe classroom practices and provide teachers with useful feedback, as well as programs in the District of Columbia, Delaware, and Ohio for professional training, in which educators from high-performing schools coached other teachers or principals.

In 2012, the program was expanded to allow school districts, not just statewide systems, to compete for grants.

Even if it did not win, each state or district that applied had to reevaluate its practices, consider where reform might be needed, and decide what approaches might have the most impact. If it won, it would get federal funding to help carry out its own ideas.

The Race to the Top competition had a direct and fast impact on education, according to *Politico*, in a January 2016 article assessing Obama's likely legacy. The program achieved this impact by "inspiring almost every state to embrace at least some of Obama's preferred K-12 reforms—removing caps on charter schools, expanding testing, adopting tougher standards like the Common Core—just to improve their chances for a grant," the article said, and it quoted Education Secretary Arne Duncan as having said, "The Race changed the game in education before the Race even started." In other words, the exercise of having to assess and apply for the grants generated change in education before the money was even dispensed.

Saving Jobs, Building Schools

The American Recovery and Reinvestment Act of 2009 also saved or created hundreds of thousands of jobs in early childhood, K–12, and higher education across America that were at risk because of state and local budget cuts, according to the U.S. Department of Education. It also created thousands of construction jobs for school-modernization projects.

The Recovery Accountability and Transparency Board reported in January 2010 that the Recovery Act education funding that was pumped out quickly to stimulate the economy had played a significant role in averting fiscal crisis by maintaining three hundred thousand education jobs, such as teachers, principals, librarians, and counselors, as of December 31, 2009.

The act included $77 billion in stimulus funding for education, including the following, according to the Department of Education:

- $40 billion to help avert education cuts and fund school modernization, plus up to an additional $33.6 billion for school modernization
- $13 billion for Title I (Education Act funding to close the achievement gap) including $3 billion for school-improvement programs
- $12 billion for Individuals with Disabilities Education Act funding
- $5 billion for Race to the Top grants for states and districts
- $5 billion for early childhood education, including Head Start, Early Head Start, childcare block grants, and programs for infants with disabilities
- $2 billion for other education investments, including pay for performance, data systems, teacher-quality investments, technology grants, vocational rehabilitation, work study, and federal aid to help mitigate the effects of lost property taxes on local school districts

The Recovery Act also increased Pell Grants and tuition tax credits to help more young people attend college with the following allocations:

- $17 billion to close a shortfall in the Pell Grant program and boost grant amounts by $500 to $5,350 in the first year and more in the second year, serving an estimated seven million low- and moderate-income young people and adults. (The Pell program faced significant shortfalls in the amount needed to meet demand in recent years as costs rose dramatically because of a rise in applicants resulting from changes in eligibility rules and a poor economy.)
- $13.8 billion to boost the tuition tax credit from $1,800 to $2,500 for families earning up to $180,000.

Student Loans

President Obama went to the Alexandria campus of Northern Virginia Community College, where Dr. Jill Biden, the wife of the vice president, taught English, to focus attention on sweeping reforms in the student-loan program. In a ceremony at the college on March 30, 2010, he signed the Health Care and Education Reconciliation Act, legislation that he said represented "one of the most significant investments in higher education since the G.I. Bill."

The student-loan overhaul had been included in a bill that was part of the health care package Congress had passed the previous week. "That's two major victories in one week," the president said. "What's gotten overlooked amid all the hoopla, all the drama of last week, is what's happened with education."

The law cut private banks out of the process of making federally insured student loans. It took the program away from Sallie Mae and other private lenders and diverted the savings to Pell Grants for low-income undergraduates.

The law eliminated fees paid to private banks to act as intermediaries in providing loans to college students, freeing up nearly $70 billion over eleven years to expand Pell Grants and make it easier to repay student loans. The law also invested $2 billion in community colleges for retraining of displaced workers.

The law also allowed Pell Grants to increase with inflation, raising the maximum grant to $5,975 from $5,550 by 2017, according to the White House, and provided for 820,000 more grants by 2020.

On June 9, 2014, the president issued an executive order to help more student-loan borrowers repay their debts by capping monthly payments for them at 10 percent of a borrower's income—instead of 15 percent—above a basic living allowance. The order expanded the 2010 law that covered those who started borrowing after October 2007. Obama's order allowed people who borrowed earlier than that to cap their payments. The White House said the order could affect up to five million federal direct student-loan borrowers.

A Congressional Budget Office report released at the time estimated that $1 trillion in federal student loans or loan guarantees and more than $100 billion in private student loans that are not federally guaranteed were outstanding.

Legislation to provide more relief by allowing students to refinance loans and to provide bankruptcy protection for student-loan debtors stalled in Congress.

President Obama visited Georgia Tech on March 10, 2015, to sign a "student aid bill of rights"—as part of a presidential memorandum outlining his directives to make it easier for students to pay back their loans. Addressing a crowd of 9,500 students, he said, "We're going to require that the businesses that service your loans provide clear information about how much you owe, what your options are for repaying it, and if you're falling behind, help you get back in good standing with reasonable fees on a reasonable timeline."

A Student Aid Bill of Rights

1. Every student deserves access to a quality, affordable education at a college that's cutting costs and increasing learning.
2. Every student should be able to access the resources needed to pay for college.
3. Every borrower has the right to an affordable repayment plan.
4. And every borrower has the right to quality customer service, reliable information, and fair treatment, even if they struggle to repay their loans.

The White House said forty million Americans had student loans and that more than 70 percent of bachelor's degree graduates had an average student-loan debt of $28,400.

The presidential memorandum directed the Department of Education and other federal agencies to do more to help borrowers. This included

- Setting up a state-of-the-art complaint system to ensure quality service and accountability for the Department of Education, its contractors, and colleges.
- Helping students set affordable monthly payments and responsibly repay their loans.
- Providing new systems to analyze student-debt trends and recommend legislative and regulatory changes.

These initiatives should go a long way toward improving education from early childhood through college and toward helping more students earn college degrees. The Obama administration's education initiatives push the nation further along toward the goal of graduating more adults with postsecondary-education credentials and creating a workforce ready to compete in the global economy.

CHAPTER 16

Housing and Urban Development

"In some cities, kids living just blocks apart lead incredibly different lives. They go to different schools, play in different parks, shop in different stores, and walk down different streets, and often, the quality of those schools and the safety of those parks and streets are far from equal—which means those kids aren't getting an equal shot in life."

President Obama, July 15, 2013

President Obama met with Julián Castro, secretary of Housing and Urban Development, and members of his staff in the Roosevelt Room of the White House, September 29, 2014. (Official White House photo by Pete Souza)

Under President Obama, the Department of Housing and Urban Development issued regulations to improve enforcement of fair-housing laws and won Supreme Court approval for its concept of challenging disparate impacts on different communities.

Civil rights advocates cheered, but right-wing conservatives nearly lost their minds when the Obama administration issued regulations to diversify neighborhoods and enforce fair-housing laws by encouraging communities using federal funds to build affordable housing in more-affluent areas and upgrade services and amenities in poorer areas. Critics denounced the move as social engineering.

To qualify for certain funds under the regulations, cities were required to examine patterns of segregation in neighborhoods and develop plans to address it. Funds could be withheld for those who failed to show adequate progress. The regulations apply to approximately 1,250 local governments.

The Department of Housing and Urban Development (HUD) regulations in question, known as the Affirmatively Furthering Fair Housing rule and adopted July 16, 2015, were intended to root out discrimination in housing that persists in spite of fair-housing laws and because of government actions that reinforce old patterns of segregated housing.

The Fair Housing Act of 1968, signed into law by President Lyndon B. Johnson, prohibits discrimination based on race, color, religion, gender, or national origin. The law was expanded in 1988 to apply to disability and family status. The Obama administration also changed HUD rules to prohibit discrimination in housing based on gender and sexual orientation.

HUD Secretary Julián Castro said HUD would provide data and other resources to help cities set goals and track progress over time for better enforcement of the Fair Housing Act. "We must give every young person access to a community of opportunity," Castro said. "We can do that by revitalizing struggling communities and by giving people the chance to live in areas where they can thrive; all with local leadership deciding what strategies work best for them and their needs...A zip code should never prevent anyone from reaching their aspirations."

The department said the rule change addressed recommendations from the Government Accountability Office and civil rights activists to improve fair-housing enforcement.

Among the critics was Representative Paul Gosar (R-Ariz.), who said the administration "shouldn't be holding hostage grant monies aimed at community improvement based on its unrealistic utopian ideas of what every community should resemble." Republicans in the House attempted to block adoption of the rule, and Gosar led the effort. "American citizens and communities should be free to choose where they would like to live and not be subject to federal neighborhood engineering at the behest of an overreaching federal government," said Gosar.

The congressman apparently found the specter of urban families moving to affordable housing in the suburbs frightening. "Instead of living with neighbors you like and choose, this breaks up the core fabric of how we start to look at communities," Gosar said. "That just brings unease to everyone in that area. People have to feel comfortable where they live. If I don't feel comfortable in my own backyard, where do I feel comfortable?"

HUD argued that it was obligated to act under the Fair Housing Act prohibiting direct and intentional housing discrimination, but said that it was also looking to curb policies that had disparate impacts on disadvantaged communities.

"This rule is not about forcing anyone to live anywhere they don't want to," said Margery Turner, senior vice president at the Urban Institute. "It's really about addressing long-standing practices that prevent people from living where they want to. In our country, decades of public policies and institutional practices have built deeply segregated and unequal neighborhoods."

Fair-Housing Victory in Court

The Obama administration had increased fair-housing enforcement efforts relying on the disparate-impact theory, winning billions in settlements from lenders like Countrywide, Wells Fargo, and SunTrust Mortgage.

On June 25, 2015, the Supreme Court backed the approach to fair-housing cases, giving the federal government a major victory in its pursuit of lenders who charge members of minority groups more for mortgages than they charge whites with similar credit histories.

"The Supreme Court has made it clear that HUD can continue to use this critical tool to eliminate the unfair barriers that have deferred and derailed too many dreams," HUD Secretary Castro said.

The case before the court involved the Inclusive Communities Project, a Dallas-based nonprofit, which argued that the Texas Department of Housing and Community Affairs concentrated affordable housing in poor neighborhoods instead of spreading it throughout a community as required by law. It presented data showing that the agency had placed 92 percent of the units in predominately minority areas. Texas argued that Inclusive Communities had not proven intent to discriminate.

The Supreme Court ruled that such cases could proceed without proof of intentional bias if the department could show that members of minority groups are negatively affected.

"Bolstered by this important ruling, the Department of Justice will continue to vigorously enforce the Fair Housing Act with every tool at its disposal—including challenges based on unfair and unacceptable discriminatory effects," Attorney General Loretta Lynch said after the ruling.

Writing the majority opinion, Justice Anthony Kennedy referred to "unconscious prejudices and disguised animus"—the kind of bias that has been difficult to prove.

Diane Yentel, vice president of public policy at the advocacy group Enterprise Community Partners, said the ruling could lead to affordable housing's being distributed to more-affluent areas, providing access to better schools, transportation, and health care, as well as to better maintenance of rentals in older neighborhoods.

CHAPTER 17

Transportation

"Today, I'm here [in St. Paul, Minnesota] to launch a new competition for 21st century infrastructure and the jobs that come with it, because any opportunity agenda begins with creating more good jobs. And one of the fastest and best ways to create good jobs is by rebuilding America's infrastructure—our roads, our bridges, our rails, our ports, our airports, our schools, our power grids."

President Obama, February 26, 2014

President Obama rode in a new light rail car at the Metro Transit Light Rail Operations and Maintenance Facility in St. Paul, Minnesota, with Transportation Secretary Anthony Foxx and others, February 26, 2014. (Official White House photo by Pete Souza)

The Obama administration has distributed nearly $5 billion in grants to 381 projects across the country for innovative transportation projects. President Obama signed the first long-term transportation bill passed by Congress in a decade. The administration also pledged resources and removed regulatory roadblocks to accelerate the development of self-driving vehicle systems.

Speaking at the historic Union Depot in St. Paul, Minnesota, on February 26, 2014, President Obama used it as a backdrop to announce a competition for $600 million in transportation funding, the sixth round of grants under a program started as part of the Recovery Act, and to outline his vision for revitalizing America's infrastructure.

He referred to his plan to fix deteriorating roads, bridges, and other facilities related to transit with a $300 billion, four-year program, emphasizing the undertaking as a way to get people still suffering from the Great Recession working again, especially those in the construction industry who had been rendered idle by the collapsed housing market. Obama's plan called for funding the major infrastructure revitalization with $150 billion in new revenue generated through business-tax reform, instead of just relying on the gas tax, but Congress was resistant.

"We've got a lot of work to do out there, and we've got to put folks to work," Obama said in St. Paul.

He pointed out that the Union Depot had been renovated and expanded through the competitive grant program. "This project symbolizes what's possible," he said. "These are competitive grants that we created as part of the Recovery Act, also known as the stimulus, which actually worked despite what everybody claims. So the idea is, if a city or state comes up with a plan to modernize transportation infrastructure that will have a significant impact on economic activity, and if they line up other sources of funding to help pay for it, they can win a TIGER [Transportation Investment Generating Economic Recovery] grant and the federal government becomes a partner with these local communities."

On December 18, 2015, President Obama signed legislation that appropriated $500 million to continue the TIGER competitive grant program for an eighth round.

The program started under the American Recovery and Reinvestment Act of 2009. Since then, TIGER had provided nearly $4.6 billion to 381 projects in all fifty states, the District of Columbia, and Puerto Rico, including 134 projects for rural and tribal communities, according to the Department of Transportation (DOT). The department said it had received more than 6,700 applications with requests that would have added up to more than $134 billion.

Funds were provided for road, rail, transit, and port projects that have significant impact on the nation, a region, or a metropolitan area. The eighth round was funded under the 2016 Omnibus Appropriations Act.

In the selections for the seventh round, announced on October 29, 2015, the DOT said it had provided almost $500 million for thirty-nine projects in thirty-four states or regions. The department said it had given priority to "transportation projects that better connect communities to centers of employment, education, and services, especially in economically distressed areas." According to the DOT, the projects funded included

- $10 million to develop streets and a park trail in Kalispell, Montana, as a catalyst for redevelopment, relocating rails serving an industrial park and removing rails downtown
- $2.9 million for building roads and sidewalks in the Native village of Point Hope, Alaska, and for purchasing transit buses to provide accessible transportation for the disabled
- $20 million for a new fifteen-mile bus rapid transit line in Birmingham, Alabama, connecting residents to employment centers, educational opportunities, and community services
- $15 million to expand the streetcar system in Tacoma, Washington, to improve access to employers, medical services, educational institutions, and other sites

Long-Term Funding

On December 4, 2015 President Obama signed the Fixing America's Surface Transportation (FAST) Act, the first long-term transportation bill passed by Congress in a decade.

Transportation Secretary Anthony Foxx said the law would allow states and local governments to proceed with critical transportation projects, such as highways and transit lines. The Obama administration had lobbied hard for the bill. The $305 billion, five-year funding and authorization bill, paid for primarily by taxes on gas, passed the House 359-65 and the Senate, 83-16.

"After hundreds of Congressional meetings, two bus tours, visits to 43 states, and so much uncertainty—and 36 short term extensions—it has been a long and bumpy ride to a long-term transportation bill," the Transportation secretary said. "It's not perfect, and there is still more left to do, but it reflects a bipartisan compromise I always knew was possible."

The FAST Act increased funding by 11 percent over five years. An administration proposal had sought an increase of 45 percent over that period, according to the department.

The law also streamlined approval processes to speed up new transportation projects, established grant programs for projects to improve freight transit, established a bureau to distribute federal funding and technical assistance to the states and localities, and created improved financing mechanisms.

Specifically, the FAST Act

- Granted authority to prohibit the rental of vehicles that are subject to safety recalls and to increase maximum fines against noncompliant auto manufacturers from $35 million to $105 million.
- Strengthened Buy America requirements (requirements to purchase products made in America) for vehicle and track purchases.
- Made transit-oriented-development (TOD) expenses eligible for funding under highway and rail credit programs. TOD promotes development near transit hubs.

(As part of a compromise in a House-Senate conference, the final bill also reauthorized the Export-Import Bank through September 30, 2019.)

The Fixing America's Surface Transportation Act (FAST Act), signed by President Obama on December 4, 2015, authorized spending for surface transportation programs through fiscal year 2020, reauthorized taxes that support the Highway Trust Fund through 2022, and improved the federal permit review process for major infrastructure projects.

Self-Driving Vehicles

At the North American International Auto Show in Detroit on January 14, 2016, Transportation Secretary Foxx revealed part of a presidential proposal for a ten-year, $4 billion investment to accelerate the development and adoption of safe vehicle automation through pilot projects and to remove regulatory roadblocks to creating the technology.

"We are on the cusp of a new era in automotive technology with enormous potential to save lives, reduce greenhouse gas emissions, and transform mobility for the American people," said Secretary Foxx. "Today's actions and those we will pursue in the coming months will provide the foundation and the path forward for manufacturers, state officials, and consumers to use new technologies and achieve their full safety potential."

President Obama's budget proposal for fiscal year 2017 called for funds for pilot programs to test vehicle systems and work with industry leaders to coordinate efforts to create the self-driving vehicles.

Secretary Foxx also unveiled a policy update for the National Highway Traffic Safety Administration (NHTSA) reflecting that the widespread use of fully automated vehicles was now feasible.

"NHTSA is using all of its available tools to accelerate the deployment of technologies that can eliminate 94 percent of fatal crashes involving human error," said NHTSA administrator Mark Rosekind. "We will work with state partners toward creating a consistent national policy on these innovations, provide options now and into the future for manufacturers seeking to deploy autonomous vehicles, and keep our safety mission paramount at every stage."

Secretary Foxx encouraged manufacturers to submit requests for rule interpretations as needed to enable innovation. For example, NHTSA said it had confirmed for BMW that its remote self-parking system met federal safety standards.

While it might still be years before driverless automobiles and transit systems are in use, these measures are a step forward.

By encouraging and funding innovation in transportation projects and accelerating the development of self-driving vehicle systems, the Obama administration has contributed greatly to reducing energy use and dependence on foreign energy, while creating construction jobs. These measures will also help reduce carbon emissions and contribute to economic growth by making commerce easier and faster.

CHAPTER 18

Homeland Security

"When I took office, I committed to fixing this broken immigration system. And I began by doing what I could to secure our borders. Today, we have more agents and technology deployed to secure our southern border than at any time in our history. And over the past six years, illegal border crossings have been cut by more than half... Overall, the number of people trying to cross our border illegally is at its lowest level since the 1970s."

President Obama, November 20, 2014

President Obama urged Congress to pass cyber-security legislation during a speech at the National Cybersecurity and Communications Integration Center in Arlington, Virginia. He was greeted by Jeh Johnson, secretary of Homeland Security, afterward, January 13, 2015. (Associated Press photo/Evan Vucci)

The number of undocumented immigrants in the country has fallen every year since 2008, to fewer than ten million—in part because of beefed-up border security under the Obama administration. Obama approved raids to deport people who have migrated illegally from Central America, and the administration for the first time compiled data on visitors who overstay their visas.

<hr>

Anyone listening to the rhetoric on the campaign trail leading up to the 2016 presidential race, especially the arguments spewing from Republicans, would think that illegal immigration was on the rise and the country was running over with undesirable foreigners surging over the borders. In fact, the undocumented immigrant population has fallen every year since 2008, according to the Center for Migration Studies (CMS), which issued a report on January 20, 2016. At 10.9 million, the number of people in the U.S. without proper documentation was at its lowest since 2003. The center is a New York–based institution that studies trends in international migration.

"Despite the claims of an ever-rising, out-of-control US undocumented population," said Donald Kerwin, CMS's executive director, "the number of undocumented has fallen each year since 2008. In addition, the number and percentage of foreign-born persons with legal status has increased. These trends should be applauded by partisans on all sides of the immigration debate."

The center's report, based on 2014 census data, showed declines in unauthorized migration from Mexico (9 percent), South America (22 percent), and Europe (18 percent), while illegal immigration from Central America was on the rise (up 5 percent). The report said the Mexican-born undocumented population had declined by more than six hundred thousand since 2010.

Similarly, in 2015, the Pew Research Center estimated that the number of undocumented immigrants—which more than tripled, to 12.2 million from 1990 to 2007—had since dropped to 11.3 million.

At least one candidate for the Republican nomination in 2016, Donald

Trump, proposed building a massive, miles-long wall at the nation's southern border, suggesting that the neighbors to the south were the worst contributors to unauthorized immigration. However, President Obama has argued that the border has never been more secure, and experts have cited tighter border security as one of the reasons for the shifting patterns of immigration. According to the White House, three thousand agents have been added to the border patrol in the Southwest since 2008. The White House said border fencing and unmanned aircraft and ground surveillance systems have more than doubled during Obama's tenure.

"The facts of the report tell a different story than what you might hear on the campaign trail or in the halls of Congress, where many send a message that we're being overrun by undocumented immigrants," said Kevin Appleby, the center's senior director of international migration policy, according to a *Washington Post* report. "The facts and the data show that's just not true."

While calling for comprehensive immigration reform and issuing executive orders to provide relief to some immigrants (see chapter 5), Obama has also approved raids to deport people who have migrated illegally from Central America since 2014. The raids, which have been controversial among Democrats and immigrant-rights groups, focus on people who have remained in the country after immigration judges have denied their petitions for asylum or other forms of relief. The administration has defended the raids as a deterrent to others who might attempt to enter the country without going through proper channels.

Data on Overstays

The day before the CMS released its report, the Department of Homeland Security (DHS) released long-awaited data on people who overstay their visas. In a report that was the first of its kind, DHS said that nearly half a million people who entered the country legally remained after their visas expired in fiscal year 2015.

The data indicates that the visitors who overstay visas are a little more than 1 percent of about forty-five million people who came in 2015 from other countries. However, such visitors who stay on after their visas lapse—as opposed to people who actually slip across borders—are believed to make up a large percentage of the unauthorized immigrants in the country. Congress has been trying to get data on this since 1997, and DHS had insisted it couldn't be done.

DHS said it had produced the January 2016 report "by examining arrival, departure and immigration status information, which is consolidated to generate a complete picture of an individual's travel to the United States." The department said it had identified individuals with no recorded departure and those whose departure was recorded later than the date permitted by their visas.

It appears that far from letting our borders be overrun, the Obama administration has toughened border security, taken measures to deport illegal immigrants, and created a system to compile data on those who overstay their visas. Accordingly, data indicate that illegal immigration is on the decline.

CHAPTER 19

Agriculture

"What we grow here and what we sell is a huge boost to the entire economy, but particularly the rural economy."

President Obama, February 7, 2014

President Obama and Agriculture Secretary Tom Vilsack, right, looked at drought-damaged corn at the McIntosh farm in Missouri Valley, Iowa, and talked with the owners about agricultural issues, August 13, 2012. (Associated Press photo/Carolyn Kaster)

The president signed a $956 billion farm bill that ended the system of subsidies, replacing it with a crop-insurance plan.

President Obama went to the University of Michigan to sign a $956 billion bipartisan farm bill on February 7, 2014. With a horse barn at the university's equine performance center as his backdrop, he said, "We've had the strongest stretch of farm exports in our history. We are selling more stuff to more people than ever before."

Passage of the Agriculture Act of 2014 represented the culmination of four years of arguments over farming subsidies and food stamps. The act eliminated $5 billion in direct crop payments to farmers and replaced them with an insurance program. The act also cut $8 billion over a decade for food stamps, which was a much smaller reduction than the $40 billion some Republicans advocated.

A statement from the Senate Committee on Agriculture, Nutrition, and Forestry described the act as a major reform of agriculture policy, and said:

> After nearly three years of working to create a 5-year Farm Bill that will reform agriculture policy, end unnecessary subsidies, save billions of taxpayer dollars, and help create American agriculture jobs, Members of Congress in the Senate and House have an agreement on a final bipartisan Farm Bill. Members of both parties have been trying to end direct payment subsidies for decades—and with the 2014 Farm Bill, the era of direct payments will finally come to an end.
>
> Despite years of criticism and bipartisan demand that Congress end the wasteful direct payment subsidy program, they have continued to live on—at the expense of taxpayers. The 2014 Farm Bill ends these subsidies once and for all.
>
> By ending direct payment and other unnecessary subsidies, which pay farmers even in good times when there is no actual need for assistance, the Farm Bill cuts farm subsidy spending by billions

of dollars and creates more accountability in agriculture programs. This effort represents a landmark shift in federal agriculture policy.

The committee statement noted that the direct subsidies were paid to farmers "every year whether they need it or not." Under the 2014 law, farmers would buy crop insurance with government help, but would be paid only for actual losses from disaster. "It means farmers are not paid in good times but are protected in the case of disaster, and that also means there is less need for Congress to pass ad hoc disaster relief after disasters strike," the statement explained. "It also means consumers are protected from spikes in food prices that widespread farmer bankruptcy could create."

In spite of this bipartisan achievement, none of the Republicans invited to the signing ceremony in Michigan elected to attend, according to the White House.

At the signing, the president also announced a "Made in Rural America" initiative to help rural businesses market their goods abroad and a number of other related measures. Obama directed the White House Rural Council to host sessions in all fifty states to train Department of Agriculture staff members on how to promote rural exports, and White House officials announced five regional forums on rural exports and a conference on investing in rural America.

The Agriculture Act of 2014, signed by President Obama on February 7, 2014, authorizes $956 billion in spending over the next ten years for agriculture and nutrition programs.

PART III

A MAN OF CONVICTION

★ ★ ★

The president demonstrated repeatedly that he was not afraid to take positions that he felt were right for the nation as a whole and to follow through on establishing policies to support those positions.

He's been an advocate for emissions control and rejected the Keystone XL oil pipeline largely because of the environmental impact. The president also has been a staunch advocate of Internet privacy and openness, stem cell research, and forestalling climate change, among other issues.

Yet, it is the Affordable Care Act, often referred to as Obamacare and reforming health insurance coverage, that is the signature achievement of Obama's administration. Some have pointed out that seven presidents before Obama, dating back to President Harry Truman in 1945, believed that the country should be an active partner in its citizens' health care. Truman called for "the creation of a national health insurance fund to be run by the federal government. This fund would be open to all Americans, but would remain optional. Participants would pay monthly fees into the plan, which would cover the cost of any and all medical expenses that arose in a time of need. The government would pay for the cost of services rendered by any doctor who chose to join the program."

Since then presidents Kennedy, Johnson, Nixon, Ford, Carter, and, of course, Clinton, sought to legislate some form of mandated national health insurance.

It has only been under President Obama, supported by the U.S. Supreme Court, that health care has begun to be accepted as a right, an obligation of this country, as opposed to a privilege of the well educated and well funded.

Despite the protestations of many on the right, the facts and the data suggest that the health care reform was on the way to being a smashing success. More than eleven million previously uninsured Americans were insured in the first five years. Perhaps just as important is this wonderful fact: The health act forbids employers and other entities from banning health coverage because of preexisting medical conditions. That had scared aging employees before and kept workers from venturing on to new opportunities.

This section will look at Obama's approach to some of the larger issues of our day, using his power and often his influence in the world to keep Americans healthy, to preserve the environment, and to open new frontiers in technology.

CHAPTER 20

Health

"Everyone understands the extraordinary hardships that are placed on the uninsured, who live every day just one accident or illness away from bankruptcy."

President Obama, September 9, 2009

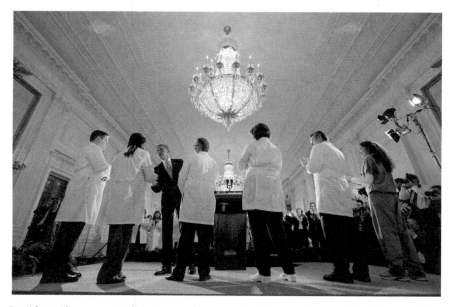

President Obama greeted doctors and nurses after his remarks about health care reform at the White House, March 3, 2010. (Official White House photo by Chuck Kennedy)

President Obama pushed through and signed a groundbreaking reform of the health care system. Within five years, the number of uninsured people in the U.S. had fallen by more than eleven million. Medicaid enrollment grew by nearly 20 percent. He vetoed legislation to repeal the act on January 8, 2016. The president lifted a ban on embryonic stem cell research. He signed legislation allowing the Food and Drug Administration to regulate tobacco.

Before President Obama signed the health care reform act on March 23, 2010, he said, "Today, I'm signing this reform bill into law on behalf of my mother, who argued with insurance companies even as she battled cancer in her final days." He went on to list some other people he was signing it for, too, but those words painted a picture of the millions of uninsured and underinsured people who struggle to pay medical bills at a time when they are most vulnerable.

The forty-fourth president's single most important legacy may be the expansion of affordable health care to millions who would not otherwise have it, reducing risk to their well-being and their lives.

Obama entered office with a promise to create a health care plan that strengthened coverage by employers, made insurance companies accountable, and ensured patient choice of doctor and care without government interference.

Discussing his proposals at a joint session of Congress on September 9, 2009, he said, "I understand how difficult this health care debate has been. I know that many in this country are deeply skeptical that government is looking out for them. I understand that the politically safe move would be to kick the can further down the road—to defer reform one more year, or one more election, or one more term. But that's not what the moment calls for. That's not what we came here to do. We did not come to fear the future. We came here to shape it."

In an effusive introduction of the president on the day of the signing of the bill, Vice President Joe Biden said:

You've made history. History is made when a leader steps up, stays true to his values, and charts a fundamentally different course for the country. History is made when a leader's passion—passion—is matched with principle to set a new course...Mr. President, you are that leader. Your fierce advocacy, the clarity of purpose that you showed, your perseverance—these are in fact—it is not hyperbole to say—these are the reasons why we're assembled in this room together, today...All of us, press and elected officials, assembled in this town over the years, we've seen some incredible things happen. But you know, Mr. President, you've done what generations of not just ordinary, but great men and women, have attempted to do. Republicans as well as Democrats, they've tried before....They've tried. They were real bold leaders. But, Mr. President, they fell short. You have turned, Mr. President, the right of every American to have access to decent health care into reality for the first time in American history.

Among the act's most important provisions are that it

- Bans insurers from denying coverage to those with preexisting conditions.
- Allows adult children to stay on their parents' insurance plan until age twenty-six.
- Requires coverage of preventative care such as wellness exams, screenings, physicals, mammograms, and tests for cholesterol and diabetes.

Once the act became law, President Obama's next major challenge would be defending it from challenges in court and attempts to repeal it. On June 28, 2012, the U.S. Supreme Court upheld the health care law by 5-4, with Chief Justice John Roberts joining four liberals in the majority. The court, ruling in *National Federation of Independent Business v. Sebelius*, found that the requirement that people obtain insurance or pay a penalty was authorized by the power Congress has to levy taxes. "The Affordable Care Act's requirement that certain individuals pay a financial penalty for not obtaining health insurance may reasonably be characterized as a tax," Chief Justice Roberts wrote in the majority opinion. "Because the Constitution permits such a tax, it is not our role to forbid it, or to pass upon its wisdom or fairness."

However, the court rejected the administration's argument that the individual insurance mandate was justified by the power Congress has to regulate interstate commerce. The court also limited the Medicaid expansion, ruling that Congress had exceeded its constitutional authority by threatening states with the loss of federal payments if they did not participate.

Millions Benefit

Five years after Obama signed the health care overhaul, the number of uninsured U.S. residents had fallen by more than eleven million, according to the Centers for Disease Control and Prevention (CDC). While thirty-seven million people remained uninsured, that was the lowest level of uninsured measured in more than fifteen years, the CDC said.

Nearly 11.7 million people signed up for health care through the Obamacare exchange for 2015, according to data from the Department of Health and Human Services (HHS), and the growth in health care spending slowed to record lows. National health spending grew by 3.8 percent each year from 2009 to 2010, and 3.6 percent in 2011, based on federal government data, the lowest rate of growth since it began keeping

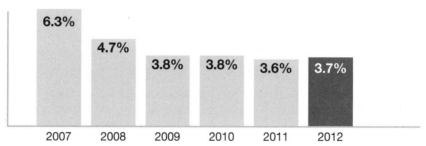

Health care spending

Year	Spending growth
2007	6.3%
2008	4.7%
2009	3.8%
2010	3.8%
2011	3.6%
2012	3.7%

Source: Centers for Medicare and Medicaid Services

The growth in health care spending slowed to record lows—3.8 percent each year from 2009 to 2010 and 3.6 percent in 2011—the lowest rate of growth since the government began keeping such statistics in 1960, and the slowdown continued in 2012 with growth at 3.7 percent.

such statistics in 1960, according to the Kaiser Family Foundation, and the slowdown was continuing in 2012 with growth at 3.7 percent.

The Affordable Care Act allowed states to receive federal matching funds to cover 100 percent of the cost of expanding Medicaid coverage to non-elderly, non-disabled adults up to 133 percent of the federal poverty level, until 2016. After 2016, states must begin contributing to the costs.

Growth in Medicaid enrollment under the Affordable Care Act

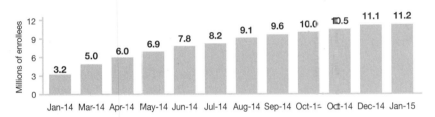

As of February 2016, 32 states, including the District of Columbia, had expanded Medicaid coverage, according to an analysis of U.S. census data by Families USA.

Medicaid enrollment increased in states that expanded coverage, as compared to those that had not (26 percent versus 8 percent). Medicaid enrollment grew from 57.8 million enrollees in the baseline period (July to September 2013) to 70 million enrollees in January 2015, a 19.3 percent growth rate. This chart shows the monthly changes in enrollment, compared to the baseline period.

Source: Center for Medicaid and CHIP Services Monthly Enrollment Reports

Enrollment grew in spite of the fact that Republican governors of some states declined to expand Medicaid to cover more people as provided for in the act. The Obama administration has fended off endless criticism from Republican opponents, threats of repeal, actual legislation to repeal the act, and court challenges to keep the hard-won reforms in place. President Obama vetoed legislation on January 8, 2016, that would have repealed the health care plan. (See chapter 2.) Congress did not have enough votes to attempt to override the veto.

According to the *New York Times*, the vote on the bill "was the 62nd to fully or partly repeal the health law but only the first that sent legislation to the president's desk."

The U.S. Supreme Court ruled 6-3 on June 25, 2015, that the health care act allowed the federal government to provide nationwide tax subsidies to poor and middle-class people so they could buy health insurance.

The case, *King v. Burwell*, hinged on an interpretation of whether such subsidies should apply in states that had elected to let the federal government run the exchanges that the law established to let individuals buy insurance, as opposed to the states' running their own.

On January 19, 2016, the Supreme Court declined to take up a new challenge to the act in the form of a lawsuit to invalidate the law arguing that it violated a constitutional mandate that tax laws originate in the House. The new challenge argued that the act had originated in the Senate, making it unconstitutional. A lower court had found that it did originate in the House.

Stem Cell Research

By executive order, President Obama lifted a ban on embryonic stem cell research that had been in place since 2001. Before signing the order on March 9, 2009, Obama said,

> We will vigorously support scientists who pursue this research. And we will aim for America to lead the world in the discoveries it one day may yield. At this moment, the full promise of stem cell research remains unknown ... but scientists believe these tiny cells may have the potential to help us understand, and possibly cure, some of our most devastating diseases and conditions ... But that potential will not reveal itself on its own. Medical miracles do not happen simply by accident. They result from painstaking and costly research—from years of lonely trial and error, much of which never bears fruit—and from a government willing to support that work.

President George W. Bush had issued the order that banned federal funding for research into stem cell lines, except for those lines that had been created before his decision. He argued that human lives were being destroyed to create the stem cells. He twice vetoed legislation to expand the research. Stem cells typically come from donated frozen embryos destined for destruction in fertility clinics.

Obama acknowledged that many people remained conflicted about or strongly opposed to the use of embryonic stem cells. While their feelings should be taken into account, he said, the work needed to go on. "Rather than furthering discovery, our government has forced what I believe is a false choice between sound science and moral values," Obama said. "In this case, I believe the two are not inconsistent. As a person of faith, I believe we are called to care for each other and work to ease human suffering. I believe we have been given the capacity and will to pursue this research—and the humanity and conscience to do so responsibly. It is a difficult and delicate balance."

Tobacco Regulation

Alluding to his own experience with smoking, on June 22, 2009, President Obama signed the Family Smoking Prevention and Tobacco Control Act (FSPTCA), granting authority to the U.S. Food and Drug Administration (FDA) to regulate tobacco products. The House had passed the bill 298-112 on April 2, 2009, and the Senate, 79-17, on June 11 (with changes that were later accepted by the House, 307-97).

"The decades-long effort to protect our children from the harmful effects of smoking has finally emerged victorious," Obama said at a Rose Garden ceremony for the signing. "It is a law that will save American lives."

President George W. Bush had opposed tobacco-control measures and threatened to veto a version of the bill passed by the House the previous year, but President Obama, who confessed his struggles to quit smoking, had long supported such legislation.

Criticizing the tobacco industry for heavily targeting young people in its marketing, he said, "I know—I was one of these teenagers. I know how difficult it is to break this habit."

Notably, the act restricted marketing and sales to youth, required warning labels on smokeless tobacco products, and required disclosure of ingredients in tobacco products. Under the provisions to protect youth, the act outlawed sales to minors, vending-machine sales except in adult-only facilities, sales of packages of fewer than twenty cigarettes, tobacco-brand sponsorships at sports or other events, and giveaways of cigarettes and tobacco-branded promotional items. It also banned flavored cigarettes (clove, cinnamon, fruit, etc.), except menthol. Smokeless-tobacco product packages and ads for such products as snuff and chewing tobacco were required to carry larger and more visible warning labels with statements such as "WARNING: This product can cause mouth cancer."

The law also prohibited tobacco companies from using terms like "light," "low," or "mild," which imply a product is a less-harmful version, unless they filed an application for a "modified risk" tobacco product and obtained an order to market as such. The act also granted the FDA the authority to regulate levels of nicotine and other ingredients.

Tobacco company owners and operators were required to register annually and open their manufacturing and processing facilities to inspection by the FDA every two years. Funds to regulate tobacco products are raised through a user fee on the manufacturers, based on their U.S. market share.

Some tobacco companies challenged the warning-label provisions as a violation of their First Amendment rights. The Sixth Circuit Court of Appeals rejected their arguments in 2012, ruling the labels a disclaimer about legitimate public-health risks, and on April 22, 2013, the U.S. Supreme Court declined to take up the case. This was a tremendous victory for the Obama administration, one that will save many lives.

The Family Smoking Prevention and Tobacco Control Act, signed by President Obama on June 22, 2009, gave the FDA authority to regulate the manufacture, distribution, and marketing of tobacco products.

CHAPTER 21

Energy and the Environment

"We've got to preserve this beautiful planet of ours for our kids and grandkids. And that means taking serious steps to address climate change once and for all. Now, we've made a lot of progress to cut carbon pollution here at home, and we're leading the world to take action as well. But we've got to do more."

President Obama, October 9, 2015

President Obama spoke at the largest photovoltaic solar plant in the United States, the Sempra U.S. Gas & Power's Copper Mountain Solar 1 facility in Boulder City, Nevada, during a four-state tour to promote his energy policies, March 21, 2012. (Ethan Miller/Getty Images)

President Obama played a leading role in reaching a global agreement on climate change. His administration set standards to cut carbon pollution from power plants and to move the nation toward the development and use of clean energy. He rejected a permit for the Keystone XL oil pipeline, which he said would have set back efforts to mitigate climate change. The administration set new fuel-efficiency standards for vehicles and energy-efficiency standards for household appliances. In his first year in office, President Obama doubled funding for research on clean energy.

When President Obama launched a page on Facebook, on November 9, 2015, the first thing on his mind was climate change. His first posting was a video in which he announced he would be attending a meeting to discuss a global agreement on climate change. "In a few weeks, I'm heading to Paris to meet with world leaders about a global agreement to meet this challenge," the president posted. "I hope you'll join me in speaking out on climate change and educating your friends about why this issue is so important...If we're all in this together, I'm confident we can solve this and do right by future generations."

The meeting in Paris opened on November 30, 2015, just a little over two weeks after coordinated terrorist attacks by Islamic State militants killed 130 people at different sites in that city.

Obama led the charge on combating climate change. In an address to the conference he said, "I come here personally as the leader of the world's biggest economy and second-biggest emitter to say that America not only acknowledges its role in climate change but embraces doing something about it."

The leaders emerged on December 14, 2015, with a landmark agreement among nations to take concrete steps to reduce carbon emissions. A similar effort had failed in 2009.

According to a White House statement, more than 190 countries signed on to the Paris Agreement, committing "to putting forward successive and ambitious, nationally determined climate targets and reporting on their progress towards them using a rigorous, standardized process of review . . . This new global framework lays the foundation for countries to work together to put the world on a path to keeping global temperature rise well below 2 degrees Celsius and sets an ambitious vision to go even farther than that," the statement said. "This Agreement sends a strong signal to the private sector that the global economy is moving towards clean energy, and that through innovation and ingenuity, we can achieve our climate objectives while creating new jobs, raising standards of living and lifting millions out of poverty."

Under the agreement, the countries that ratify the agreement commit to beginning to reduce greenhouse-gas emissions "as soon as possible" and continue reducing them. The goal is to keep global temperatures from rising more than 2 degrees Celsius (3.6 degrees Fahrenheit) by 2100 (a level that scientists warn could still cause catastrophic damage) and ideally 1.5 degrees Celsius (2.7 Fahrenheit).

The agreement also encourages spending for projects to deal with the effects of climate change, such as rising sea levels, and to develop renewable energy sources such as solar or wind-generated power. The agreement left up to each country how to cut its own emissions but requires all countries to report on their efforts and to assess their progress every five years and submit new plans to renew efforts.

Time magazine reported that delegates from most of the countries that agreed to the deal, as well as environmental activists, were generally pleased with the deal. John Coequyt, the Sierra Club's director of federal and international climate campaigns, said the agreement included "all the core elements that the environmental community wanted," *Time* reported.

The agreement did not require approval by Congress. Some of its conservative members have questioned the science behind climate change and the need for action.

In his 2016 State of the Union address, the president said:

Look, if anybody still wants to dispute the science around climate change, have at it. You'll be pretty lonely, because you'll be debating our military, most of America's business leaders, the majority of the American people, almost the entire scientific community, and 200 nations around the world who agree it's a problem and intend to solve it. But even if the planet wasn't at stake; even if 2014 wasn't the warmest year on record—until 2015 turned out even hotter—why would we want to pass up the chance for American businesses to produce and sell the energy of the future?

Reducing Emissions in the U.S.

In June 2013, more than two years before the Paris agreement, President Obama outlined his plan to reduce carbon pollution, which creates the conditions responsible for climate change, to prepare the nation for the effects of climate change, and to encourage other nations to address conditions contributing to global climate change.

"We have a moral obligation to leave our children a planet that's not polluted or damaged, and by taking an all-of-the-above approach to develop homegrown energy and steady, responsible steps to cut carbon pollution, we can protect our kids' health and begin to slow the effects of climate change so we leave a cleaner, more stable environment for future generations," a White House statement said.

The U.S. plan sets standards to reduce emissions of carbon and greenhouse gases and to "move our economy toward American-made clean energy sources that will create good jobs and lower home energy bills," it said.

The White House announced that it was putting in place new rules to cut carbon pollution, and Obama outlined the plans in a speech at Georgetown University in Washington, D.C., on June 25, 2013. The speech was live-streamed on the university's website.

The strategy focused on three key areas: preparing the country for the short- and long-term effects of climate change, cutting the amount of carbon pollution in the United States, and leading global efforts to combat climate change. Obama also outlined efforts to develop and deploy clean energy technologies, with particular focus on wind, solar, and geothermal alternatives.

The president's plan directed the Environmental Protection Agency (EPA) to establish standards for greenhouse-gas emissions for new and existing power plants. At the time, existing plants contributed about 40 percent of carbon emissions in the United States. On June 2, 2014, the EPA proposed rules to carry out his plan. The Obama administration reiterated a goal of reducing overall greenhouse-gas emissions below 2005 levels by the year 2020. The rules would also cut carbon dioxide emissions from existing coal plants up to 30 percent by 2030, compared with 2005 levels, with most of the cuts to be made by 2020.

The EPA proposed a flexible plan to let states and utilities meet the new standard. The EPA's plan offered the states four options: increasing energy efficiency, shifting from coal to natural gas, investing in renewable energy, and upgrading power plants. Utilities could also offer discounts to encourage less use of electricity in peak hours.

EPA administrator Gina McCarthy emphasized the flexibility of the plan. "That's what makes it ambitious, but achievable," she said at a ceremony announcing the rules. "For the sake of our families' health and our kids' future, we have a moral obligation to act on climate."

But the plan was met with opposition. As of early February 2016, more than two dozen states had joined an action attempting to keep the rules from going into effect, according to Reuters. The states, led by West Virginia, a leading coal producer, and Texas, a major oil producer, asked the U.S. Supreme Court for an almost unprecedented stay to keep the regulations from going into effect. The states filed the application for a stay with U.S. Chief Justice John Roberts after an appeals court declined to block the rules while litigation challenging them proceeded. On February 9, 2016, the Supreme Court granted a stay, blocking the regulations, until the U.S. Court of Appeals for the District of Columbia Circuit makes a ruling. The D.C. court was due to hear oral arguments in the case on June 2, 2016.

"If this court does not enter a stay, the plan will continue to unlawfully impose massive and irreparable harms upon the sovereign states, as well as irreversible changes in the energy markets," lawyers for the states said in the filing.

Reuters said more than a dozen other states and the National League of Cities, representing nineteen thousand municipalities, favored the EPA rule.

In another move related to climate change, the Obama administration announced on January 14, 2016, that it was putting a moratorium on new leases for coal mining on federal lands, in effect freezing new coal production on those lands. About 40 percent of coal produced in the U.S. has been mined on federal land. Interior Secretary Sally Jewell said companies could continue production on coal already under lease.

Stopping the Pipeline

In what *Politico* called "the defining environmental controversy of his tenure" up to then, President Obama rejected a permit for the Keystone XL oil pipeline that would run from Alberta, Canada, to Nebraska, on November 6, 2015, saying it would set back efforts to forestall climate change without a significant economic return. "America is now a global leader when it comes to taking serious action to fight climate change," Obama said. "And frankly, approving this project would have undercut that global leadership."

Supporters said the pipeline would have created jobs, but environmentalists said it would have exacerbated climate change.

A few days earlier, the Obama administration had rejected the developer's attempt to stop the clock on consideration, a move that would have stalled action until after the president left office.

Combating climate change had been a major goal of the Obama administration, and Obama had already vetoed legislation to approve the Keystone XL pipeline.

"Shipping dirtier crude oil into our country would not increase America's energy security," Obama said. "What has increased America's energy security is our strategy over the past several years to reduce our reliance on dirty fossil fuels from unstable parts of the world."

Fuel Efficiency

The Obama administration issued final regulations on August 28, 2012, that, combined with previous standards set by the administration, would nearly double the average fuel efficiency of new cars and trucks by the 2025 model year. The standards set by the U.S. DOT and the EPA mandated an average fuel economy of 54.5 miles per gallon for 2025 cars.

The White House said the requirements would "nearly double the fuel efficiency of those vehicles compared to new vehicles currently on our roads. In total, the administration's national program to improve fuel economy and reduce greenhouse gas emissions will save consumers more than $1.7 trillion at the gas pump and reduce U.S. oil consumption by 12 billion barrels." The administration said the efficiencies would reduce greenhouse-gas emissions by half by 2025.

"These fuel standards represent the single most important step we've ever taken to reduce our dependence on foreign oil," said President Obama. "This historic agreement builds on the progress we've already made to save families money at the pump and cut our oil consumption... It'll strengthen our nation's energy security, it's good for middle class families and it will help create an economy built to last."

To meet the standards, auto manufacturers would have to speed up the development of electrified vehicles, engineer more-efficient engines, and build lighter vehicles.

At the time the rules were announced, the Corporate Average Fuel Economy (CAFE) standards mandated that cars and light trucks get about twenty-nine miles per gallon on average with gradual increases to 35.5 miles per gallon by 2016.

The announcement came during President Obama's bid for reelection and on the day the Republican National Convention opened. The campaign of Mitt Romney, the presumptive nominee for the party, immediately attacked the new standards as "extreme," saying they would limit consumer choices and raise costs.

Obama's Transportation secretary, Ray LaHood, said the standards would save consumers more than $8,000 per vehicle by 2025, with fuel savings far exceeding higher costs for the vehicles. The administration and proponents of the changes also said the push for more-efficient vehicles using new technologies would generate hundreds of thousands of jobs.

As part of the economic-stimulus package, Obama also pushed through tax credits to help consumers buy fuel-efficient, plug-in hybrid or all-electric cars as they became available.

Appliance Standards

A little more than two weeks after taking office, President Obama issued a memorandum ordering the U.S. Department of Energy (DOE) to set new energy-efficiency standards for household appliances to lower energy costs by an estimated $500 billion over thirty years and reduce greenhouse-gas emissions by cutting consumption of power. The standards were to cover more than two dozen appliances from big-ticket items, such as refrigerators, to smaller items, such as lamps.

In a speech at the DOE on February 5, 2009, the president said, "This will save consumers money, this will spur innovation, and this will conserve tremendous amounts of energy."

Previous legislation, including the Energy Policy and Conservation Act of 1975, set deadlines for improving appliance efficiency, but previous administrations had not adhered to them even after reaching a consent decree with some states over enforcement.

Obama instructed the DOE to prioritize standards that promised the biggest savings. The department issued final rules on June 29, 2009.

Energy Research

President Obama had campaigned on a promise to double funding for research on clean energy. Not only did he achieve that goal, but he also surpassed it within his first year in office, according to *PolitiFact*, a fact-checking website on which reporters and editors rate the accuracy of political claims. It frequently does "Obameter" fact checks.

As a candidate for the 2008 presidential election, Obama's Plan to Make America a Global Energy Leader said, "At present, the federal government spends over $3 billion per year on all energy innovation efforts," which, it also pointed out, was less than the nation had spent in the late 1970s, adjusted for inflation.

The economic-stimulus package Obama signed not long after being inaugurated included $2.5 billion for applied research, development, and production of geothermal energy, solar energy, wind energy, and other renewable sources under the Office of Energy Efficiency and Renewable Energy. That office also received $2.2 billion in additional appropriations later. The stimulus bill also included $1.2 billion to the DOE Office of Science for construction, laboratory infrastructure, and research. That office also received $4.9 billion in other appropriations.

The grand total came to $10.8 billion for research on clean energy, more than double the earlier allocations of $3 billion for such research, according to *PolitiFact*.

CHAPTER 22

Technology

"In this digital age when you can apply for a job, take a course, pay your bills, order pizza, even find a date [online], the Internet is not a luxury, it's a necessity."

President Obama, July 15, 2015

President Obama talked with Mark Zuckerberg, Facebook founder and CEO, before a dinner with technology business leaders in Woodside, California. Also pictured, from left, are Carol Bartz, Yahoo! president and CEO; Art Levinson, Genentech chairman and former CEO; Steve Westly, founder and managing partner of the Westly Group; and Eric Schmidt, executive chairman and CEO of Google, February 17, 2011. (Official White House photo by Pete Souza)

President Obama nudged the Federal Communications Commission (FCC) to adopt rules to protect the openness of the Internet. The president expanded Internet access to low-income families to close the "homework gap." He initiated action to expand broadband access and computer-science education in grades K–12. He has been a pioneer in the use of social media, live-streaming, and websites to communicate with the public. The president created the U.S. Digital Service to bring leading experts in information technology into the federal government.

President Obama is likely to be remembered for his embrace and sophisticated use of the Internet, social media, and technology as communications tools and social equalizers. He has made expanding access to the Internet a priority.

Significantly, prodded by the president, the FCC adopted strong "net neutrality" rules on January 25, 2015, to protect the openness of the Internet.

President Obama had called for tough new rules in a statement in November 2014. "The time has come for the FCC to recognize that broadband service is of the same importance and must carry the same obligations as so many of the other vital services do," he said. "This is a basic acknowledgment of the services ISPs [Internet service providers] provide to American homes and businesses, and the straightforward obligations necessary to ensure the network works for everyone—not just one or two companies."

Obama, while acknowledging the independence of the FCC, called for reclassifying broadband as a utility under the Telecommunications Act and banning so-called paid fast lanes for some users. The FCC was in the process of drafting new rules after courts twice struck down previous regulations.

In a news release explaining its order, the FCC noted that the U.S. Court of Appeals for the District of Columbia "observed that nearly 15 years ago, the Commission constrained its ability to protect against threats to the open Internet by a regulatory classification of broadband" that did not allow it to apply standards related to telephone networks. In the interim, the nature of broadband access changed and the threats to Internet openness had increased, the court had said.

"The new Open Internet Order restores the FCC's legal authority to fully address threats to openness on today's networks by following a template for sustainability laid out in the D.C. Circuit opinion itself, including reclassification of broadband Internet access as a telecommunications service under Title II of the Communications Act," the FCC said.

The rules say that broadband providers may not

- "Block access to legal content, applications, services, or non-harmful devices."
- "Impair or degrade lawful Internet traffic on the basis of content, applications, services, or non-harmful devices."
- "Favor some lawful Internet traffic over other lawful traffic in exchange for consideration of any kind—in other words, no 'fast lanes.' This rule also bans ISPs from prioritizing content and services of their affiliates."

The president praised the ruling, saying, "This FCC decision will protect innovation and create a level playing field for the next generation of entrepreneurs."

Access at Home

In a speech to members of the Choctaw Nation on July 15, 2015, the president announced a new Housing and Urban Development program, the Connect Home program, to provide low-cost or free Internet to thousands of people in twenty-seven communities. The program also subsidizes the purchase of tablets and digital literacy training.

"You cannot connect with today's economy without having access to the Internet," the president said in the speech in Durant, Oklahoma, headquarters of the Choctaw Nation.

Funding for the program, with the exception of a grant from the U.S. Department of Agriculture, came from foundations and other private-sector commitments. Among the corporate partners was Google, which had also launched a program to provide free Internet service to public-housing residents.

The Council of Economic Advisers reported that 55 percent of low-income children under ten in the United States had no Internet access at home, creating what the White House called "the homework gap": Children lacking easy access cannot perform the same work or benefit from the same information as those who have in-home Internet service.

Delton Cox, a tribal council member, noted that it was the first time a U.S. president had visited Choctaw land since Teddy Roosevelt stopped there in 1905. "This president has done more for our native people than any other president I can remember," Cox said. "That's something we need to recognize him for—everything he's done for our Indian people, all the various tribes he's worked with. We need to thank him for that."

Josh Riley, a Choctaw Nation policy worker, said nearly everyone in the community in rural southeast Oklahoma lacked access to the Internet. "It's tough out here growing up," he said. "You might grow up in a community where the closest grocery store is 45 miles away. The closest Wal-Mart is 60 miles away... Internet has been an issue down here for a long time."

Expanding Computer Education

The Obama administration has also created initiatives to expand broadband availability to K–12 schools and improve computer-science education in schools. In the president's budget proposals for fiscal year 2017, he called for $4.1 billion in spending over three years toward that goal.

On January 30, 2016, in his weekly radio address, he said that in addition to asking Congress for that funding, the administration was "leveraging existing resources [$135 million] at the National Science Foundation and the Corporation for National and Community Service to train more great teachers for these courses." He also said he would ask governors, mayors, business leaders, and technology entrepreneurs to join a bipartisan movement to expand computer-science training in schools.

"In the new economy, computer science isn't an optional skill," the president said. "It's a basic skill, right along with the three 'Rs'... Yet right now, only about a quarter of our K through 12 schools offer computer science... I've got a plan to help make sure all our kids get an opportunity to learn computer science, especially girls and minorities. It's called Computer Science For All. And it means just what it says—giving every student in America an early start at learning the skills they'll need to get ahead in the new economy."

Social Media Strategy

The president's enthusiastic use of social media, including the addition of a Facebook page on November 9, 2015, which was announced on Twitter, have set examples for the rest of the nation to use emerging media technology.

As the *New York Times* reported, Obama set up an Office of Digital Strategy, which employs about twenty aides to manage his social media accounts on Twitter, Facebook, Instagram, and YouTube. The president and his family members have some personal pages, and the White House has official pages. Under the direction of Jason Goldman, a thirty-nine-year-old former executive at Twitter and other sites, the team posts to the accounts, live-tweets speeches, tracks analytics, produces videos or graphics as needed, and lets the president know what issues are trending. The White House also live-streams events and posts official photos daily. A team of bloggers writes for WhiteHouse.gov regularly about events and issues.

Aides said they had to use social media to communicate effectively in a changing world. "Our office is very much tasked and looking for ways to bring his voice directly to people," Kori Schulman, Goldman's deputy, told the *Times*.

The president's innovative reliance on web pages like WhiteHouse .gov, Benefits.VA.gov/GIBill/, and SBA.gov to communicate what his administration is up to on a daily basis demonstrates leadership in using new communications technologies.

President Obama has also initiated a number of other actions related to cybertechnology and communications, including the following:

- He announced shortly after taking office that he would become the first president to use email regularly.
- He became the first president ever to hold an online town hall from the White House, via Twitter, on July 6, 2011.
- He signed an executive order February 12, 2013, to coordinate efforts to improve cybersecurity.
- He directed the director of national intelligence to establish the Cyber Threat Intelligence Integration Center to focus on identifying and protecting against malicious cyberthreats to the nation.

Even the launching of the website for Obamacare, despite its infamous glitches, led to innovation. The administration hired some of the digital and technology experts from the private sector who fixed the Obamacare site, officially HealthCare.gov, to stay on to fix other things in information technology for the federal government and to bring new approaches to access and convenience for site users.

On August 11, 2014, the White House announced it was launching the U.S. Digital Service, described as "a small team made up of our country's brightest digital talent that will work with agencies to remove barriers to exceptional service delivery and help remake the digital experience that people and businesses have with their government."

The team was headed by Mikey Dickerson, formerly a site-reliability engineer for Google who helped solve the HealthCare.gov bottleneck. The IT guru stayed on to become the administrator of the U.S. Digital Service and the deputy federal chief information officer. The announcement said the administration would use existing funds in the 2014 budget to start up the service and would seek funding in future budgets.

In an interview with *Fast Company*, President Obama recalled that after running campaigns in 2008 and 2012 that were on the cutting edge of technology, he had found the state of the federal IT apparatus frustrating. He said he had created the U.S. Digital Service because the crisis with getting HealthCare.gov up and running properly had brought the issues into focus.

"If we are able through the U.S. digital team to recruit a baseline of talent and create a pipeline—on a regular basis, top technology folks are cycling in for a one- or two-year stint, making a difference and improving the lives of veterans or improving our education system, or just making sure that the Social Security network is operating efficiently," the president said, "and if we build that culture of service...that can be transformative."

President Obama met with (from left) Secretary of State John Kerry; National Security Adviser Susan E. Rice; Phil Gordon, White House Coordinator for the Middle East, North Africa, and the Gulf Region; and Ben Rhodes, deputy national security adviser for strategic communications, in his office aboard Air Force One during a flight to Riyadh, Saudi Arabia, on March 28, 2014, at a time when relations between the two countries were strained. (Official White House Photo by Pete Souza)

Seeds of Change

A prayer attributed to the theologian Reinhold Niebuhr is one of my favorites. It is most commonly called the Serenity Prayer, but it could just as well be called the Courage Prayer or the Wisdom Prayer.

> *God, grant me the serenity to accept the things I cannot change,*
> *The courage to change the things I can,*
> *And the wisdom to know the difference.*

The latter two lines succinctly capture President Obama's approach to getting things done. He could easily have accepted that the Republican-controlled, unyielding Congress was a formidable obstacle. He could have accepted that this meant he would not be able to accomplish many of the things he wanted to.

Instead, as I hope this book has made apparent, he has courageously soldiered on to press for changes, and wisely discerned how to leverage the power of the chief executive. He often resorted to executive actions, presidential memorandums, regulations, or short-term pilot programs permitted under law. Some of his detractors have complained that he overused his executive powers, but history will show he used executive actions less than many other presidents have. He has also managed to sign a surprising number of bills with bipartisan support, such as the Farm Bill and the Every Student Succeeds Act, and he frequently brokered public-private partnerships to initiate programs. When necessary, he has used the veto.

In many cases, where he did not manage to get Congress to act, he planted "seeds" by establishing policy for the federal government, federal contractors, or federal prisons—changing the things he could change—such as expanding overtime pay and parental leave. Sometimes he also seems to have planted seeds of federal reforms to get the states to follow suit and bring about change on a much larger scale, as in the efforts to end mass incarceration or curb the use of solitary confinement. These actions set new benchmarks of expectations, which could lead to broader reforms for workers, prisoners, and others. And indeed, over the final weeks I spent putting this book together, he seems to have been quickening the pace of change through such actions. These policies could have implications long after he has left office, no matter who follows him.

It cannot be denied that he has done much to change the landscape of this country.

Certainly, we are all better off having avoided another Great Depression. The lives that have been saved because of the Affordable Care Act and will be saved if no one dismantles it in the next administration are incalculable. We cannot calculate either the value of the minds of young people who will get a better education and in turn be assets to our country because of his efforts to see that we start educating children earlier, improve their schools, and make it possible for more of them to go to college. Our planet, we trust, will be spared disasters brought on by climate change because of the work he has done domestically and globally to set new carbon-emission standards. We enjoy some measure of peace in the world because of the treaties he has reached with Russia and Iran and the normalizing of relations with Cuba.

Perhaps his legacy will be that he just kept moving forward, in spite of the naysayers, and did the things he could, which turned out to be a lot. As he said in his speech about health care reform to a joint session of Congress on September 9, 2009,

> I still believe we can act even when it's hard. I still believe we can replace acrimony with civility, and gridlock with progress. I still believe we can do great things and that here and now we will meet history's test. Because that is who we are. That is our calling. That is our character.

It was finally sinking in. A little girl from Birmingham, Alabama, led the way. We were all treated to a video that went viral that showed first grader Kameria Crayton in a puddle of tears after she learned that the only president she had known would be moving on. She shares the same birthday as the president, August 4, and they are both left-handed, she told him in a letter. He was leaving, and she was having a bit of a meltdown.

She got to go to the White House to meet him at Easter, but I don't think she was alone in her feelings about his departure.

On the last day of April 2016, all kinds of high-profile folks were arriving at a Washington, D.C., hotel for what has become a remarkable annual gathering, the White House Correspondents' Dinner. President Barack Obama had literally been the evening's star attraction for each of the previous seven years. Some of it, obviously, had to do with the fact that he was the most important person on the planet. But most of it had to do with his comedic timing, his ability to be self-effacing, and, no doubt, his use of the element of surprise. Also, he's just laugh-out-loud funny.

And there was this: There was a lot of talk, admittedly among celebrities who were interviewed that night, that the last few months of Obama's presidency were going to be "bittersweet," as iconic songstress Aretha Franklin put it. "He represented the USA well," she said.

Reporters noted that many of those arriving seemed emotional about his waning days. Even Obama noted during his remarks, tongue-in-cheek, that his approval ratings "keep going up" and he was not doing anything different. At that moment, photos of grumpy-looking Republican presidential primary contenders Donald Trump and Ted Cruz flashed across the monitors through the cavernous Washington Hilton ballroom. The audience roared. The suggestion of course, was that Obama's approval rating had risen above 50 percent because much of America was taking another look at his legacy, now that they had some tangible individuals with whom to compare him.

Obama seemed quite upbeat the night of the dinner, joking that if his routine was well received he was going to take it on the road to Goldman Sachs and "earn some serious Tubmans," both a reference to what Hillary Clinton had been raking in for speeches to Goldman Sachs and to the U.S. Treasury Department's decision to put the legendary Harriet Tubman, who led hundreds of enslaved people to freedom, on the $20 bill.

He more than suggested that his former secretary of state would follow him into the White House. If Hillary Clinton defeated Bernie Sanders for the Democratic nomination, and if she were able to put together the same coalition that elected Obama twice—almost all of the African American voters, the majority of Asians and Hispanics, and 39 percent of white Americans—in time for the November 8, 2016, election, recent history suggests that she will be America's first female president in 2017. Already, blacks had proven to be her firewall in primaries throughout the South.

Yet this election season had been different from any other, with Donald Trump, the billionaire real estate mogul and reality star, beating out fifteen more traditional rivals by early May 2016 to become the presumptive Republican nominee in contention to become the country's forty-fifth president. Despite his polarizing rhetoric, voters in the Republican primaries had been steadfast in picking Trump over contenders who had held state and federal office. And, while not always the case, history suggests that after eight years of a Democratic president, Americans could choose a Republican to lead them for at least the next four years.

What was clear was that if Trump emerged as the winner in November, he might work mightily to erase much of the Obama legacy, including his landmark Affordable Care Act. What was equally clear was that Obama was prepared to work mightily to see that his legacy would not be dismantled. Maybe more important, he made clear his belief that the country would not be well served with a Trump presidency.

"I just want to emphasize the degree to which we are in serious times and this is a serious job," Obama told reporters shortly after the Indiana primary in early May, when it was clear that Trump would be his party's presumptive nominee. "This is not entertainment. This is not a reality show."

During spring graduation season in 2016, at Howard University, the country's premier historically black college, he sought to galvanize the graduates to get beyond the progressive rhetoric and the hashtags of social media. "When we don't vote, we give away our power," Obama said. And he made it quite clear that he believed the country was in a better place than it was when he graduated college in 1982 and than it was when he took office.

Still, the president noted that there was still a lot at stake in the waning months of his historic presidency—and beyond.

No doubt, his legacy will include the warming of relationships between the United States and Cuba. Before Obama set foot on the island in late March 2016, the last standing president to visit Cuba was Calvin Coolidge in 1928. Not long after Obama's visit, Carnival's 704-passenger *Adonia* cruise ship sailed there from Miami, becoming the first leisure ship to travel to Cuba in more than fifty years. In addition, Western Union now transferred cash, mostly from the States, to Cuba. It's hard to imagine that capitalism, America style, can be curtailed in Cuba despite the rhetoric that the United States continues to be the evil empire.

It's more than a little remarkable to see Obama in these last few months of his presidency: loose, candid, with sleeves rolled up to defend his legacy. He had joked at the White House Correspondents' Dinner in 2015 that he had taken on a new stance, with something that rhymed with "bucket list." That year he was thinking more than a little about immigration reform and issued executive actions on the matter. Same thing on new climate regulations.

Diving into his last year in office, he ignored the Senate Republican leadership's admonishment that he need not bother to nominate a replacement for Supreme Court Justice Antonin Scalia, who died suddenly from a heart attack in February 2016. Obama nominated Merrick Garland, a federal Court of Appeals judge who was widely respected in the Senate, among his peers, and by civil rights groups such as the NAACP Legal Defense and Educational Fund and the Lawyers' Committee for Civil Rights Under Law.

Though Senate Republicans vowed not to even consider action on the nomination, some pundits argued that if a Democrat were elected president in November, the Senate would approve Garland's nomination, fearing that the new Democratic president would push through a nominee who is much more progressive than Garland, who is known as a moderate.

In his final months, Obama also doubled down on his initiatives for clemency, commuting the sentences of more nonviolent prisoners, raising his total to 306, more than the last six presidents combined and more than any since Franklin Roosevelt.

There was still a great deal to be discussed, argued, negotiated, and even debated before Obama would "drop the mic" and say farewell, officially, to the American public. I would argue that ultimately, historians will portray him favorably, well beyond that obvious citation that he broke the color line.

Maybe actress Cicely Tyson summed it up best when she talked about the president before he addressed the Howard graduates. Obama, she said, "will walk out of the White House leaving a legacy of character, integrity, and resilience."

Chronology

Actions by President Barack Obama

2008

November 4 Won election to the presidency with 53.3 percent of popular vote

2009

January 20 Inaugurated as president of the United States
January 29 Signed the Lilly Ledbetter Fair Pay Act
February 4 Signed the Children's Health Insurance Program Reauthorization Act
February 5 Ordered new energy-efficiency standards for appliances
February 17 Signed the American Recovery and Reinvestment Act
March 9 Lifted the ban on embryonic stem cell research
May 20 Signed the Helping Families Save Their Homes/Fraud Enforcement and Recovery Acts
May 26 Announced nomination of Sonia Sotomayor to the U.S. Supreme Court
June 22 Signed the Family Smoking Prevention and Tobacco Control Act
July 25 Launched Race to the Top, a $4.35 billion grant program for education reforms
July 30 Hosted the "beer summit" with Henry Louis Gates Jr. and the arresting officer, Sergeant James Crowley
September 9 Addressed joint session of Congress about health care reform
October 9 Won the Nobel Peace Prize
October 28 Signed the Matthew Shepard and James Byrd, Jr., Hate Crimes Prevention Act

2010

February 26 Renewed initiative on Historically Black Colleges and Universities and announced new funding

March 23 Signed the Patient Protection and Affordable Care Act

March 30 Signed legislation to reform the student-loan program

April 8 Signed agreement with Russia to reduce nuclear stockpiles

May 10 Nominated Elena Kagan to the U.S. Supreme Court

July 21 Signed the Dodd-Frank Wall Street Reform and Consumer Protection Act

July 26 Issued an order establishing the U.S. government as a model employer for the disabled

August 3 Signed a bipartisan bill reducing disparities in cocaine sentencing

December 13 Signed the Healthy, Hunger-Free Kids Act of 2010

2011

February 23 Informed Congress the administration would no longer defend the Defense of Marriage Act

March 19 Joined the international military action to topple the Qaddafi regime in Libya

May 1–2 Ordered the raid that killed Osama bin Laden

September 20 Ended the Pentagon's Don't Ask, Don't Tell policy

September 21 Addressed the U.N. General Assembly on gay rights

2012

March 23 Commented on the controversy over the killing of Trayvon Martin as the FBI investigated

April 27 Signed an order to protect veterans from unscrupulous practices by colleges

June 15 Announced the Deferred Action for Childhood Arrivals policy

August 28 Issued final rules to double fuel efficiency of automobiles

November 6 Won reelection with 51.1 percent of the popular vote

2013

January 20 Was sworn in for a second term in a private ceremony

January 21 Celebrated his inauguration in a public ceremony

March 7 Signed reauthorization of the Violence against Women Act

June 25 Outlined plans to reduce carbon emissions

October 9 Named Janet Yellen chairman of the Federal Reserve

2014

February 7 Signed a $956 billion, bipartisan farm bill

February 27 Established the My Brother's Keeper Task Force

May 25 Made a surprise visit to U.S. troops in Afghanistan

June 9 Issued an order to cap monthly payments for student loans

July 22 Signed the Workforce Innovation and Opportunity Act

August 11 Launched the U.S. Digital Service to improve government IT

December 10 Unveiled a $1 billion public-private partnership to expand preschool programs

December 17 Ordered the restoration of full diplomatic relations with Cuba

December 18 Established the President's Task Force on 21st Century Policing

December 19 Signed the Stephen Beck Jr. Achieving a Better Life Experience Act

2015

January 15 Extended paid family leave to employees of the executive branch

January 25 Achieved "net neutrality" goal as the Federal Communications Commission adopted strong rules

February 11 Asked Congress for authorization to use military force against the Islamic State in the Levant

March 31 Rejected a congressional resolution to block National Labor Relations Board unionizing reforms

May 18 Banned transfer of certain military equipment to local police agencies

June 25 Won Supreme Court backing in the disparate-impact issue in fair-housing cases

June 26 Delivered a eulogy for a shooting victim at a Charleston, South Carolina, church

June 29 Announced executive action to extend coverage of overtime pay

July 13 Commuted the sentences of forty-six nonviolent drug offenders

July 15 Announced a program for low-cost or free home Internet service

July 16 Adopted final Housing and Urban Development Affirmatively Furthering Fair Housing regulations

July 16 Became the first sitting president to visit a federal prison

September 7 Ordered federal contractors to provide paid sick leave

October 5 Reached agreement on the Trans-Pacific Partnership treaty with Pacific Rim nations

October 15 Announced an end to the withdrawal of forces from Afghanistan

October 22 Vetoed the National Defense Authorization Act over a slush fund issue

November 6 Denied a permit for the Keystone XL oil pipeline

November 25 Signed a revised defense authorization that omitted the provisions he previously rejected

December 4 Signed the Fixing America's Surface Transportation Act

December 4 Opened military combat roles to women

December 7 Opened an investigation into Chicago police force

December 10 Signed the Every Student Succeeds Act, ending No Child Left Behind

December 14 Reached global agreement to reduce carbon emissions

December 18 Commuted the sentences of ninety-five people and pardoned two

2016

January 5 Took executive action to strengthen enforcement of gun laws

January 8 Vetoed a bill that would have repealed the Affordable Care Act and blocked Planned Parenthood funds

January 19 Avoided a new challenge to the Affordable Care Act when the Supreme Court declined to hear the case

January 25 Restricted the use of solitary confinement for federal prisoners

Acknowledgments

First, I thank God for the opportunity to write this book. I would like to express my gratitude to my wife, Angela P. Dodson, CEO of Editors-oncall LLC., for her immeasurable contributions to the research and writing of this book, as well as her encouragement and patience. Being married to an experienced journalist, copy editor, and manager has its advantages.

I also would like to thank Adrienne Ingrum of Hachette Book Group for extending the challenge to explore the accompl shments of the Obama presidency and for her wise guidance throughout this project. I am grateful to Carolyn Kurek, expert production editor, who fit together the many elements of this book.

Finally, I am grateful to my attorney, Lynne Suzette Price, for her assistance in interpreting and negotiating the contract for the book; Michele Y. Washington of Washington Design for her expertise as photo editor for this project; Charles Morris, president/owner of SKM Business Solutions, for coordinating permissions; and Amy Raudenbush for creating graphics.

Without this team, I would not have been able to produce this book.

The Obamas posed for an Easter Sunday portrait with their daughters, Malia and Sasha, and their dogs, Bo and Sunny, in the Rose Garden of the White House on April 5, 2015. (Official White House Photo by Pete Souza)

Notes

Introduction

Rich Karlgaard, "Does the Bradley Effect Overrate Obama in the Polls?" *Forbes*, September 16, 2012, accessed March 30, 2016, http://www.forbes.com/sites/richkarlgaard/2012/09/16/does-the-bradley-effect-overrate-obama-in-the-polls/#239cf9d60736.

Bill Peterson, "For Jackson, a Potential Breakthrough; On Eve of Primary, Support From White Officials and Wisconsin Voters Appears Strong," *Washington Post*, April 4, 1988, accessed March 30, 2016, http://pqasb.pqarchiver.com/washingtonpost/doc/307038519.html?FMT=ABS&FMTS=ABS:FT&type=current&date=Apr%204,%201988&author=Bill%20Peterson&pub=The%20Washington%20Post%20(pre-1997%20Fulltext)&edition=&startpage=a.10&desc=For%20Jackson,%20a%20Potential%20Breakthrough;On%20Eve%20of%20Primary,%20Support%20From%20White%20Officials%20and%20Wisconsin%20Voters%20Appears%20Strong.

White House, Office of the Press Secretary, "Remarks of President Barack Obama—State of the Union Address as Delivered," White House, January 13, 2016, accessed February 8, 2016, https://www.whitehouse.gov/the-press-office/2016/01/12/remarks-president-barack-obama-%E2%80%93-prepared-delivery-state-union-address.

Dick Polman, Facebook, January 13, 2016, accessed January 13, 2016, https://www.facebook.com/dick.polman.3.

Paul Krugman, "In Defense of Obama: The Nobel Prize–Winning Economist, Once One of the President's Most Notable Critics, on Why Obama Is a Historic Success," *Rolling Stone*, October 8, 2014, accessed December 30, 2015, http://www.rollingstone.com/politics/news/in-defense-of-obama-20141008#ixzz3vrKs5bbB.

Chapter 1 *The Young*

White House, "Issues: Education/Higher Education," White House, undated, accessed November 23, 2015, https://www.whitehouse.gov/issues/education/higher-education.

Arne Duncan, "Obama's Goal for Higher Education," *Forbes*, August 1, 2010, accessed November 23, 2015, http://www.forbes.com/2010/08/01/america-education-reform-opinions-best-colleges-10-duncan.html.

U.S. Department of Education, "College Affordability and Completion: Ensuring a Pathway to Opportunity," U.S. Department of Education, undated, accessed November 23, 2015, http://www.ed.gov/college.

Charles Huckabee, "Obama Calls for Pell Grant Changes to Accelerate Progress toward Degrees," *Chronicle of Higher Education*, January 19, 2016, accessed January 19, 2016, http://chronicle.com/blogs/ticker/obama-calls-for-pell-grant -changes-to-accelerate-progress-toward-degrees/107943.

Allie Grasgreen, "Obama Poised to Give Financial Aid to Federal, State Prisoners," *Politico*, July 27, 2016, accessed January 19, 2016, http://www.politico .com/story/2015/07/barack-obama-financial-aid-college-federal-state-prisoners -pell-grant-120680#ixzz3xjaPB584.

U.S. Department of Education, "Obama Administration Announces Final Rules to Protect Students from Poor-Performing Career College Programs," U.S. Department of Education, October 30, 2014, accessed November 23, 2015, http://www.ed.gov/news/press-releases/obama-administration-announces -final-rules-protect-students-poor-performing-career-college-programs.

Stephanie Marken, "U.S. Uninsured Rate at 11.4% in Second Quarter," Gallup .com, July 10, 2015, accessed November 24, 2015, http://www.gallup.com/ poll/184064/uninsured-rate-second-quarter.aspx.

White House, "Family," White House, undated, accessed December 10, 2015, https://www.whitehouse.gov/issues/family/.

Sidebar: Marcelas Owens

Kyung M. Song, "Boy Who Lost Mom Takes Health-Care Story to D.C.," *Seattle Times*, March 9, 2010, accessed November 24, 2015, http://www.seattletimes .com/seattle-news/boy-who-lost-mom-takes-health-care-story-to-dc/.

Louise Radnofsky, "Boy at Obama's Side Now in High School," Washington Wire blog, *Wall Street Journal*, October 1, 2013, accessed December 10, 2015, http:// blogs.wsj.com/washwire/2013/10/01/boy-at-obamas-side-now-in-high-school/.

Chapter 2 Women

White House, Office of the Press Secretary, "Remarks by the President and the First Lady at International Women's Day Reception," White House, March 8, 2010, accessed November 30, 2015, https://www.whitehouse.gov/the-press -office/remarks-president-and-first-lady-international-womens-day-reception.

Deborah L. Brake and Joanna L. Grossman, "Title VII's Protection against Pay Discrimination: The Impact of *Ledbetter v. Goodyear Tire & Rubber Co.*," *Regional Labor Review*, fall 2007, accessed November 30, 2015, http://www .hofstra.edu/pdf/academics/colleges/hclas/cld/cld_rlr_fall07_title7 _grossman.pdf.

Ledbetter v. Goodyear Tire & Rubber Co., Dissent, 550 U.S. 1, at 2, 3 (2007), accessed November 30, 2015, http://www.supremecourt.gov/opinions/06pdf/ 05-1074.pdf.

White House, Office of the Press Secretary, "Fact Sheet: Obama Administration Record for Women and Girls," White House, August 26, 2014, accessed November 30, 2015, https://www.whitehouse.gov/the-press-office/2014/08/26/fact-sheet-obama-administration-record-women-and-girls.

Jeffrey Toobin, "The Obama Brief: The President Considers His Judicial Legacy," *New Yorker*, October 27, 2014, accessed December 1, 2015, http://www.newyorker.com/magazine/2014/10/27/obama-brief.

Peter Baker and Helene Cooper, "Clinton Is Said to Accept Offer of Secretary of State Position," *New York Times*, November 22, 2008, accessed December 1, 2015, http://www.nytimes.com/2008/11/22/us/politics/22obama.html?pagewanted=all.

Cheyenne Hopkins and Joshua Zumbrun, "Yellen to Be Named Fed Chairman, First Female Chief," *Bloomberg News*, October 9, 2013, accessed February 2, 2016, http://www.bloomberg.com/news/articles/2013-10-08/yellen-to-be-named-fed-chairman-as-obama-taps-first-female-chief.

Jonathan Cohn, "Obama Tweaks the Birth Control Mandate—and the Right Is Still Angry," *New Republic*, August 22, 2014, accessed February 4, 2016, https://newrepublic.com/article/119183/hhs-adapts-obamacare-birth-control-rule-hobby-lobby-wheaton.

Nora V. Becker and Daniel Polsky, "Women Saw Large Decrease in Out-Of-Pocket Spending for Contraceptives after ACA Mandate Removed Cost Sharing Health Affairs," *Health Affairs* 34, no. 7 (July 2015: 1204–11), accessed December 2, 2015, http://content.healthaffairs.org/content/34/7/1204.abstract.

Sabrina Tavernise, "Rise in Early Cervical Cancer Detection Is Linked to Affordable Care Act," *New York Times*, November 24, 2015, accessed December 1, 2015, http://www.nytimes.com/2015/11/25/health/rise-in-early-cervical-cancer-detection-is-linked-to-affordable-care-act.html.

Mike DeBonis, "Obama Vetoes Republican Repeal of Health-Care Law, *Washington Post*, January 8, 2016, accessed January 19, 2016, https://www.washingtonpost.com/news/powerpost/wp/2016/01/08/obama-vetoes-republican-repeal-of-health-care-law/.

Juliet Eilperin, "Obama Vows to Defend Abortion Rights," *Washington Post*, April 26, 2013, accessed December 1, 2015, https://www.washingtonpost.com/politics/obama-vows-to-defend-abortion-rights/2013/04/26/c5cae81e-ae80-11e2-8bf6-e70cb6ae056e_story.html.

H.R. 36—Pain-Capable Unborn Child Protection Act, 114th Congress (2015–2016), accessed December 2, 2015, https://www.congress.gov/bill/114th-congress/house-bill/36.

Mollie Reilly, "Obama Praises 'Historic Step Forward' of Allowing Women in All Combat Roles," *Huffington Post*, December 3, 2015, accessed February 3, 2016, http://www.huffingtonpost.com/entry/obama-women-in-military_us_5660be3ae4b08e945feec39e.

David Alexander and Phil Stewart, "U.S. Military Opens All Combat Roles to Women," Reuters, December 4, 2015, accessed February 3, 2016, http://www .reuters.com/article/us-usa-military-women-combat-idUSKBN0TM28520151204.

David Alexander, "Two Women Have Completed 'The Army's Toughest Training.' Here's What That Means for the Military," *Huffington Post*, August 8, 2015, accessed February 3, 2016, http://www.huffingtonpost.com/entry/women -army-rangers_us_55d607fbe4b055a6dab33fc1.

Sidebar: Lilly Ledbetter

Barbara A. Baker, "Lilly Ledbetter," *Encyclopedia of Alabama*, August 16, 2011, last updated May 13, 2014, accessed November 30, 2015, http://www .encyclopediaofalabama.org/article/h-3130.

Glenn Kessler, "Lilly Ledbetter, Barack Obama, and the Famous 'Anonymous Note,'" Fact Checker, *Washington Post*, May 14, 2015, accessed November 30, 2015, https://www.washingtonpost.com/news/fact-checker/wp/2015/05/14/ lilly-ledbetter-barack-obama-and-the-famous-anonymous-note/.

Sidebar: Sonia Sotomayor

Robert Barnes and Michael A. Fletcher, "Sotomayor Embodies Obama's Criteria for the Court," *Washington Post*, May 26, 2009, accessed November 30, 2015, http://www.washingtonpost.com/wp-dyn/content/article/2009/05/26/ AR2009052600889.html.

U.S. Supreme Court, "Biographies of Current Justices of the Supreme Court," U.S. Supreme Court, undated, accessed November 30, 2015, http://www .supremecourt.gov/about/biographies.aspx.

CNN, "Sotomayor's 'Wise Latina' Comment a Staple of Her Speeches," CNN, June 8, 2009, accessed November 30, 2015, http://www.cnn.com/2009/ POLITICS/06/05/sotomayor.speeches/.

Sidebar: Elena Kagan

CNN, "Obama Chooses Kagan for Supreme Court," CNN, May 10, 2010, accessed November 30, 2015, http://www.cnn.com/2010/POLITICS/05/10/scotus.kagan.

U.S. Supreme Court, "Biographies of Current Justices of the Supreme Court," U.S. Supreme Court, undated, accessed November 30, 2015, http://www .supremecourt.gov/about/biographies.aspx.

Sidebar: Vetoes

American Presidency Project, "Presidential Vetoes: Washington-Obama," accessed March 23, 2016, http://www.presidency.ucsb.edu/data/vetoes.php.

U.S. House of Representatives, "Presidential Vetoes," accessed March 23, 2016, http://history.house.gov/Institution/Presidential-Vetoes/Presidential-Vetoes/.

White House, Office of Press Secretary, "Vetoed Legislation," accessed March 23, 2016, https://www.whitehouse.gov/briefing-room/vetoed-legislation.

Chapter 3 *African Americans*

Rebecca Baker Bafford, "The Story of Amazing Grace," Hymns, *Music Is Worship*, January 20, 2014, accessed December 3, 2015, http://rebeccabakerbafford.com/?s=amazing+grace.

Paige Lavender, "You Absolutely Have to Watch and Read Obama's Full Eulogy for Rev. Clementa Pinckney," *Huffington Post*, June 26, 2015, accessed December 3, 2015, http://www.huffingtonpost.com/2015/06/26/obama-eulogy-full-text_n_7674406.html.

Nick Corasaniti, Richard Pérez-Peña, and Lizette Alvarez, "Church Massacre Suspect Held as Charleston Grieves," *New York Times*, June 18, 2015, accessed December 7, 2015, http //www.nytimes.com/2015/06/19/us/charleston-church-shooting.html.

George E. Curry, "White House Aide: Obama Hasn't Abandoned Blacks," Afro .com, February 16, 2013, accessed December 7, 2015, http://www.afro.com/sections/news/national/story.htm/?storyid=77521#sthash.z3U4oQgI.dpuf.

Byron Tau, "Obama: 'If I Had a Son He Would Look Like Trayvon,'" *Politico*, March 23, 2012, accessed December 7, 2015, http://www.politico .com/blogs/politico44/2012/03/obama-if-i-had-a-son-hed-look-like -trayvon-118439#ixzz3tLAsuXOd.

Krissah Thompson and Scott Wilson, "Obama on Trayvon Martin: 'If I had a son, he'd look like Trayvon,'" *Washington Post*, March 23, 2012, accessed December 9, 2015, https://www.washingtonpost.com/politics/obama-if-i-had-a-son -hed-look-like-trayvon/2012/03/23/gIQApKPpVS_story.html.

White House, Office of Press Secretary, "Remarks by the President on Trayvon Martin," White House, July 19, 2013, accessed December 3, 2015, https://www .whitehouse.gov/the-press-office/2013/07/19/remarks-president-trayvon -martin.

U.S. Department of Justice, Office of Public Affairs, "Federal Officials Close Investigation into Death of Trayvon Martin," U.S. Department of Justice, February 24, 2015, accessed December 9, 2015, http://www.justice.gov/opa/ pr/federal-officials-close-investigation-death-trayvon-martin.

Eliott C. McLaughlin, "AG: Justice Department Investigating Whether Chicago Police Broke Law," CNN, December 7, 2015, accessed December 7, 2015, http://www.cnn.com/2015/12/07/us/chicago-police-justice-department -laquan-mcdonald-investigation/.

Federal Bureau of Investigation, U.S. Attorney's Office, Northern District of Illinois, "United States Attorney's Office Provides Update on Investigation into the Shooting Death of Laquan McDonald," Federal Bureau of Investigation, November 24, 2015, accessed December 3, 2015, https://www .fbi.gov/chicago/press-releases/2015/united-states-attorneys-office-provides -update-on-investigation-into-the-shooting-death-of-laquan-mcdonald.

U.S. Department of Justice Office of Public Affairs, "Justice Department Opens Pattern or Practice Investigation into the Chicago Police Department," U.S. Department of Justice, December 7, 2015, accessed December 7, 2015,

http://www.justice.gov/opa/pr/justice-department-opens-pattern-or-practice
-investigation-chicago-police-department.

Frederick H. Lowe, "Justice Department Launches Investigation into the Chicago Police Department," *North Star News Today*, December 8, 2015, accessed December 8, 2015 http://www.northstarnewstoday.com/news/justice -department-launches-investigation-into-the-chicago-police-department/.

Steve Levine, "Chicago Police Really Didn't Want to Release Video of a Cop Shooting Laquan McDonald 16 Times," *Huffington Post*, November 25, 2015, accessed December 8, 2015, http://www.huffingtonpost.com/ entry/chicago-laquan-mcdonald-video_565603e0e4b079b2818a06f6.

Sari Horwitz, Ellen Nakashima, and Wesley Lowery, "Justice Department Will Investigate Practices of Chicago Police," *Washington Post*, December 6, 2015, accessed December 8, 2015, https://www.washingtonpost.com/news/post -nation/wp/2015/12/06/justice-department-will-launch-investigation-into -practices-of-chicago-police/.

U.S. Department of Justice, Office of Public Affairs, "Justice Department Announces Findings of Two Civil Rights Investigations in Ferguson, Missouri: Justice Department Finds a Pattern of Civil Rights Violations by the Ferguson Police Department," U.S. Department of Justice, March 4, 2015, accessed December 8, 2015, http://www.justice.gov/opa/pr/justice-department -announces-findings-two-civil-rights-investigations-ferguson-missouri.

Matt Apuzzo, "Department of Justice Sues Ferguson, Which Reversed Course on Agreement," *New York Times*, February 10, 2016, accessed February 21, 2016, http://www.nytimes.com/2016/02/11/us/politics/justice-department -sues-ferguson-over-police-deal.html.

President's Task Force on 21st Century Policing, *Final Report of the President's Task Force on 21st Century Policing*, Washington, D.C.: Office of Community Oriented Policing Services, 2015, accessed December 8, 2015, http://www .cops.usdoj.gov/pdf/taskforce/taskforce_finalreport.pdf.

Gregory Korte, "Obama Bans Some Military Equipment Sales to Police," *USA Today*, May 18, 2015, accessed December 8, 2015, http://www.usatoday.com/ story/news/politics/2015/05/18/obama-police-military-equipment-sales-new -jersey/27521793/.

Ben Feller, "Beer Summit Begins: Obama Sits Down with Crowley, Gates," Associated Press/*Huffington Post*, August 30, 2009, accessed December 10, 2015, http://www.huffingtonpost.com/2009/07/30/beer-summit-begins-obama -_n_248254.html.

CNN, "Obama: Police Who Arrested Professor 'Acted Stupidly,'" CNN, July 22, 2009, updated July 23, 2009, http://www.cnn.com/2009/US/07/22/harvard .gates.interview/.

White House, Office of the Press Secretary, "Statement by the President in the James S. Brady Briefing Room," White House, July 24, 2009, accessed December 7, 2015, https://www.whitehouse.gov/the-press-office/ statement-president-james-s-brady-briefing-room.

Emily Guskin, Mahvish Shahid Khan, and Amy Mitchell, "The Arrest of Henry Louis Gates, Jr.," Journalism and Media, Pew Research Center, July 26, 2010, accessed December 7, 2015, http://www.journalism.org/2010/07/26/arrest-henry-louis-gates-jr/?utm_expid=53098246-2.Lly4CFSVQG2lphsg-KopIg.0&utm_referrer=http%3A%2F%2Fsearch.aol.com%2Faol%2Fsearch%3Fenabled_terms%3D%26s_it%3Dclient97_searchbox%26q%3DObama%2BLouis%2BGates.

White House, Office of the Press Secretary, "President Obama Signs Executive Order Promoting Excellence, Innovation and Sustainability at Historically Black Colleges and Universities," White House, February 26, 2010, accessed February 3, 2016, https://www.whitehouse.gov/the-press-office/president-obama-signs-executive-order-promoting-e.

U.S. Department of Education, "White House Initiative on Historically Black Colleges and Universities," U.S. Department of Education, undated, accessed February 3, 2016, http://sites.ed.gov/whhbcu/about-us/.

News One, "President Obama's Remarks about HBCUs Spark Controversy," News One, January 15, 2016, accessed February 3, 2016, http://newsone.com/3327953/president-obamas-remarks-about-hbcus/.

"Black Student College Graduation Rates Remain Low, but Modest Progress Begins to Show," *Journal of Blacks in Higher Education*, no. 50 (winter 2005–6), accessed February 3, 2016, http://www.jbhe.com/features/50_blackstudent_gradrates.html.

White House, Office of the Press Secretary, "Fact Sheet: Opportunity for All—President Obama Launches My Brother's Keeper Initiative to Build Ladders of Opportunity for Boys and Young Men of Color," White House, February 27, 2014, accessed December 7, 2015, http://sites.ed.gov/hispanic-initiative/files/2014/05/FACT-SHEET_Opportunity-for-all_President-Obama-Launches-My-Brother%E2%80%99s-Keeper-Initiative-to-Build-Ladders-of-Opportunity-For-Boys-and-Young-Men-of-Color.pdf. Foundations participating in the My Brother's Keeper initiative included the Annie E. Casey Foundation, Atlantic Philanthropies, Bloomberg Philanthropies, the California Endowment, the Ford Foundation, the John S. and James L. Knight Foundation, the Open Society Foundations, the Robert Wood Johnson Foundation, the W. K. Kellogg Foundation, and the Kapor Center for Social Impact.

White House, Office of the Press Secretary, "Remarks by the President at Launch of the My Brother's Keeper Alliance, Lehman College, West Bronx, New York," White House, May 4, 2015, accessed December 7, 2015, https://www.whitehouse.gov/the-press-office/2015/05/04/remarks-president-launch-my-brothers-keeper-alliance.

David Jackson, "Obama Promotes 'My Brother's Keeper' Program," *USA Today*, May 4, 2015, accessed December 7, 2015, http://www.usatoday.com/story/news/nation/2015/05/04/obama-baltimore-new-york-city-my-brothers-keeper-alliance/26869779/.

Jennifer Senior, "The Paradox of the First Black President," *New York*, October 2015, accessed December 7, 2015, http://nymag.com/daily/intelligencer/2015/10/paradox-of-the-first-black-president.html#.

Amy Walter and David Wasserman, "African American Voters: The Overlooked Key to 2016," *Cook Political Report*, July 10, 2015. Accessed February 21, 2016, http://cookpolitical.com/story/8666.

Jonathan Capehart, "How Cornel West Hurts Bernie Sanders," *Washington Post*, January 22, 2016, accessed February 21, 2016, https://www.washingtonpost.com/blogs/post-partisan/wp/2016/01/22/how-cornel-west-hurts-bernie-sanders/.

Sidebar: Trayvon Martin

Charles M. Blow, "A Mother's Grace and Grieving," *New York Times*, March 25, 2012, accessed December 9, 2015, http://www.nytimes.com/2012/03/26/opinion/blow-a-mothers-grace-and-grieving.html.

Nadra Kareem Little, "The Real Trayvon Martin: Facts about the Slain Youth's Life," About.com, updated June 1, 2015, accessed December 9, 2015, http://racerelations.about.com/od/thelegalsystem/a/The-Real-Trayvon-Martin-Facts-About-The-Slain-Youths-Life.htm.

Chapter 4 *LGBT*

Aaron Hicklin, "Out100: President Barack Obama, Ally of the Year," *Out*, November 24, 2015, accessed December 10, 2015, http://www.out.com/out100-2015/2015/11/10/out100-president-barack-obama-ally-year.

Daniel Victor, "Out Magazine Names Obama Its Ally of the Year," *New York Times*, November 13, 2015, accessed December 10, 2015, http://www.nytimes.com/2015/11/13/us/politics/out-magazine-names-obama-its-ally-of-the-year.html.

Ethan Klapper, "On This Day in 1993, Bill Clinton Announced 'Don't Ask, Don't Tell,'" *Huffington Post*, July 19, 2013, accessed December 10, 2015, http://www.huffingtonpost.com/2013/07/19/bill-clinton-dont-ask-dont-tell_n_3623245.html.

U.S. Department of Defense, American Forces Press Service, "Obama: Americans No Longer Have to Lie to Serve," U.S. Department of Defense, accessed December 10, 2015, http://archive.defense.gov/news/newsarticle.aspx?id=65381.

Aaron Belkin, Morton Ender, Nathaniel Frank, Stacie Furia, George R. Lucas, Gary Packard Jr., Tammy S. Schultz, Steven M. Samuels, and David R. Segal, *One Year Out: An Assessment of DADT Repeal's Impact on Military Readiness*, Los Angeles: Palm Center, University of California, Los Angeles, September 20, 2012, accessed December 10, 2015, http://www.palmcenter.org/files/One%20Year%20Out_0.pdf.

Palm Center, Press Room, "First Study of Openly Gay Military Service Finds 'Non-Event' at One-Year Mark," Palm Center, September 10, 2012, accessed December 10, 2015, http://www.palmcenter.org/press/dadt/releases/first_study_openly_gay_military_service_finds_nonevent_oneyear_mark.

U.S. Department of Defense, "Statement by Secretary of Defense Ash Carter on DOD Transgender Policy," U.S. Department of Defense, July 13, 2010, accessed December 10, 2015, http://www.defense.gov/News/News-Releases/News-Release-View/Article/612778.

Ernesto Londoño, "Pentagon to Extend Certain Benefits to Same Sex Couples," *Washington Post*, February 5, 2013, accessed December 10, 2015, https://www.washingtonpost.com/world/national-security/2013/02/05/3f68a638-6fc6-11e2-ac36-3d8d9dcaa2e2_story.html?wpisrc=al_national.

U.S. Department of Defense, "DOD Announces Same-Sex Spouse Benefits," U.S. Department of Defense, August 14, 2013, accessed December 10, 2015, http://archive.defense.gov/releases/release.aspx?releaseid=16203.

White House, Office of the Press Secretary, "Remarks by the President on the Supreme Court Decision on Marriage Equality," White House, June 26, 2015, accessed December 10, 2015, https://www.whitehouse.gov/the-press-office/2015/06/26/remarks-president-supreme-court-decision-marriage-equality.

ABC News, "Transcript: Robin Roberts ABC News Interview with President Obama," ABC News, May 9, 2012, accessed December 11, 2015, http://abcnews.go.com/Politics/transcript-robin-roberts-abc-news-interview-president-obama/story?id=16316043.

Charlie Savage and Sheryl Gay Stolberg, "In Shift, U.S. Says Marriage Act Blocks Gay Rights," *New York Times*, February 23, 2011, accessed December 13, 2015, http://www.nytimes.com/2011/02/24/us/24marriage.html?pagewanted=all&_r=0.

U.S. Department of Justice Office of Public Affairs, "Letter from the Attorney General to Congress on Litigation Involving the Defense of Marriage Act," U.S. Department of Justice, February 23, 2011, accessed December 13, 2015, http://www.justice.gov/opa/pr/letter-attorney-general-congress-litigation-involving-defense-marriage-act.

White House, "Statement by the President on the Supreme Court Ruling on the Defense of Marriage Act," White House, June 26, 2013, accessed December 13, 2015, https://www.whitehouse.gov/doma-statement.

Obergefell et al. v. Hodges, Director, Ohio Department of Health, et al., 576 U.S. 1 (2015), accessed December 12, 2015, http://www.supremecourt.gov/opinions/14pdf/14-556_3204.pdf.

Sam Hananel, "Obama's Gay Appointees Smash Record," Associated Press/*Huffington Post*, October 26, 2010, accessed December 11, 2015, http://www.huffingtonpost.com/2010/10/26/obamas-gay-appointees-sma_n_773898.html.

Kristen Holmes, "Obama Appoints First Transgender White House Staff Member," CNN, August 19, 2015, accessed December 11, 2015, http://www.cnn.com/2015/08/18/politics/transgender-white-house-obama-first-staff/.

Jeffrey Toobin, "The Obama Brief: The President Considers His Judicial Legacy," *New Yorker*, October 27, 2014, accessed December 1, 2015, http://www.newyorker.com/magazine/2014/10/27/obama-brief.

Todd Larson, "President Obama and the Global Fight for LGBT Rights," *Huffington Post*, November 5, 2012, accessed December 11, 2015, http://www.huffingtonpost.com/todd-larson/president-obama-and-the-global-fight-for-lgbt-rights_b_2060883.html.

"A Dozen UN Agencies Issue Unprecedented Call for LGBT Rights," *LGBTQ Nation*, September 29, 2015, accessed December 1, 2015, http://www.lgbtqnation.com/2015/09/a-dozen-un-agencies-issue-unprecedented-call-for-lgbt-rights/.

Sue Pleming, "In Turnaround, U.S. Signs U.N. Gay Rights Document," Reuters, March 18, 2009, accessed December 11, 2015, http://www.reuters.com/article/us-rights-gay-usa-idUSTRE52H5CK20090318#Bg.

White House, Office of the Press Secretary, "Presidential Memorandum—International Initiatives to Advance the Human Rights of Lesbian, Gay, Bisexual, and Transgender Persons, Memorandum for the Heads of Executive Departments and Agencies," White House, December 6, 2011, accessed December 11, 2015, https://www.whitehouse.gov/the-press-office/2011/12/06/presidential-memorandum-international-initiatives-advance-human-rights-l.

Matt Schiavenza, "Why Obama Pushed for Gay Rights in Kenya," *Atlantic*, July 26, 2015, accessed December 11, 2015, http://www.theatlantic.com/international/archive/2015/07/why-obama-pushed-for-gay-rights-in-kenya/399635/.

Aryn Baker, "Obama Defends Gay Rights on Kenya Trip," *Time*, July 26, 2015, accessed December 11, 2015, http://time.com/3972445/obama-kenyatta-gay-rights/.

Jeff Zeleny, "Obama Signs Hate Crimes Bill," Caucus blog, *New York Times*, October 28, 2009, accessed December 13, 2015, http://thecaucus.blogs.nytimes.com/2009/10/28/obama-signs-hate-crimes-bill/.

Sidebar: James Obergefell

Chris Geidner, "Two Years after His Husband's Death, Jim Obergefell Is Still Fighting for the Right to Be Married," *BuzzFeed*, March 22, 2015, accessed December 12, 2015, http://www.buzzfeed.com/chrisgeidner/his-husband-died-in-2013-but-jim-obergefell-is-still-fighting#.tpqV66AzDe.

Chapter 5 *Immigrants*

U.S. Department of Homeland Security, "Deferred Action for Childhood Arrivals: Who Can Be Considered?" U.S. Department of Homeland Security, August 14, 2013, accessed December 13, 2015, http://www.dhs.gov/blog/2012/08/15/deferred-action-childhood-arrivals-who-can-be-considered.

White House, Office of the Press Secretary, "Remarks by the President on Immigration," White House, June 15, 2012, accessed December 13, 2015, https://www.whitehouse.gov/the-press-office/2012/06/15/remarks-president-immigration.

Audrey Singer and Nicole Prchal Svajlenka, "Immigration Facts: Deferred Action for Childhood Arrivals," Brookings Institution, August 14, 2008, accessed December 13, 2015, http://www.brookings.edu/research/reports/2013/08/14-daca-immigration-singer.

Mark Hugo Lopez and Jens Manuel Krogstad, "5 Facts about the Deferred Action for Childhood Arrivals Program," FactTank, Pew Research Center, August 15, 2014, accessed December 13, 2015, http://www.pewresearch.org/fact-tank/2014/08/15/5-facts-about-the-deferred-action-for-childhood-arrivals-program/.

U.S. Citizenship and Immigration Services, "Executive Actions on Immigration," U.S. Citizenship and Immigration Services, updated April 15, 2015, accessed December 14, 2015, http://www.uscis.gov/immigrationaction.

White House, Office of the Press Secretary, "Remarks by the President in Address to the Nation on Immigration," White House, November 20, 2014, accessed December 14, 2015, https://www.whitehouse.gov/the-press-office/2014/11/20/remarks-president-address-nation-immigration.

Adam Liptak and Michael D. Shearjan, "Supreme Court to Hear Challenge to Obama Immigration Actions," *New York Times*, January 19, 2016, accessed January 19, 2016, http://www.nytimes.com/2016/01/20/us/politics/supreme-court-to-hear-challenge-to-obama-immigration-actions.html.

Cristian Farias and Elise Foley, "Supreme Court Will Rule on Obama's Immigration Policy before 2016 Election," *Huffington Post*, January 19, 2016, accessed February 14, 2016, http://www.huffingtonpost.com/entry/supreme-court-immigration-obama-executive-actions_us_56991e9ee4b0b4eb759e1e7e.

Sidebar: Astrid Silva

White House, Office of the Press Secretary, "Remarks by the President in Address to the Nation on Immigration," White House, November 20, 2014, accessed December 14, 2015, https://www.whitehouse.gov/the-press-office/2014/11/20/remarks-president-address-nation-immigration.

Astrid Silva, "Thank You, Mr. President: A Young Immigrant Tells Her Own Story about the New Chance President Obama Has Given Her Family," *USA Today*, November 22, 2014, accessed March 20, 2016, http://www.usatoday.com/story/opinion/2014/11/21/astrid-silva-immigration-obama-amnesty-column/19357475/.

Chapter 6 *The Disabled and the Elderly*

White House, Office of the Press Secretary, "Remarks by the President on the Americans with Disabilities Act," White House, July 20, 2015, accessed

December 16, 2015, https://www.whitehouse.gov/the-press-office/2015/07/20/ remarks-president-americans-disabilities-act.

Michelle Diament, "Obama: ADA 'Fight Is Not Over,'" *Disability Scoop*, July 21, 2015, accessed December 16, 2015, https://www.disabilityscoop .com/2015/07/21/obama-ada-fight-is-not-over/20450/.

White House, "The Affordable Care Act Helps Americans with Disabilities," White House, undated, accessed December 14, 2015, https://www .whitehouse.gov/sites/default/files/docs/the_aca_helps_americans_with _disabilities.pdf.

Kimberly Leonard, "How Obamacare Changes Senior Care: Provisions in the Affordable Care Act Affect Elder Benefits and Cost," *U.S. News and World Report*, February 26, 2014, accessed December 16, 2015, http:// health.usnews.com/health-news/best-nursing-homes/articles/2014/02/26/ how-obamacare-changes-senior-care.

Paula Span, "What the Health Care Ruling Means for Medicare," New Old Age blog, *New York Times*, June 28, 2012, accessed December 16, 2015, http:// newoldage.blogs.nytimes.com/2012/06/28/what-the-health-care-ruling -means-for-medicare/.

Shaun Heasley, "Obama Budget Calls for Boost to Disability Programs," *Disability Scoop*, February 3, 2015, accessed December 15, 2015, https://www .disabilityscoop.com/2015/02/03/obama-budget-disability/20023/.

Executive Order 13548 of July 26, 2010, "Increasing Federal Employment of Individuals with Disabilities," *Federal Register* 75, no. 146 (July 30, 2010), Presidential Documents, 45039, accessed December 15, 2015, https://www .gpo.gov/fdsys/pkg/FR-2010-07-30/pdf/2010-18988.pdf.

Sidebar: Stephen Beck Jr.

"Down Syndrome Advocate Dies amid ABLE Act Action: Stephen Beck Jr. Was a National and Regional Leader," *Record Herald*, December 10, 2015, accessed December 14, 2015, http://www.therecordherald.com/article/20141210/news/ 141219981.

"Crenshaw Moves to Rename ABLE Act in Honor of Stephen Beck, Jr., Long-Time Champion of the Disabled," U.S. Representative Ander Crenshaw press release, December 10, 2014, accessed December 15, 2015, http://crenshaw.house.gov/ index.cfm/pressreleases?ID=8455E842-ECF6-4C0E-80AB-CE6C46BED81C.

Chapter 7 *Veterans*

"Military Personnel Education Fraud Protection," video transcript, C-Span, April 27, 2012, accessed December 19, 2015, http://www.c-span.org/video/?305701-1/ military-personnel-education-fraud-protection&start=1290.

White House, Office of the Press Secretary, "We Can't Wait: President Obama Takes Action to Stop Deceptive and Misleading Practices by Educational Institutions That Target Veterans, Service Members, and Their Families,"

White House, April 26, 2012, accessed December 16, 2015, https://www
.whitehouse.gov/the-press-office/2012/04/26/we-can-t-wait-president
-obama-takes-action-step-deceptive-and-misleading.

Carrie Wofford, "Veterans Benefit from the 'Power of the Pen': The VA Just
Unveiled Brand New Websites for Vets—Thanks to an Obama Executive
Order," *U.S. News and World Report*, February 7, 2014, accessed March 20, 2016,
http://www.usnews.com/opinion/blogs/carrie-wofford/2014/02/07/obama
-executive-orders-have-already-helped-veterans.

Veterans of Foreign Wars, "VFW Salutes New GI Bill Protections: Executive
Order Better Protects Military and Veterans' Communities from Predatory
Practices," Veterans of Foreign Wars, April 27, 2012, accessed December 21,
2015, https://www.vfw.org/News-and-Events/Articles/2012-Articles/VFW
-SALUTES-NEW-GI-BILL-PROTECTIONS/.

White House, Office of the Press Secretary, "Remarks by the President at the
Signing of the Veterans Access, Choice, and Accountability Act," White
House, August 7, 2014, accessed December 19, 2015, https://www.whitehouse
.gov/the-press-office/2014/08/07/remarks-president-signing-veterans-access
-choice-and-accountability-act.

White House, "Veterans and Military Families: Improving Access to Care," White
House, undated, accessed December 19, 2015, https://www.whitehouse.gov/
issues/veterans/health-care.

Sidebar: Mental Health Services for Military and Veterans

U.S. Departments of Defense and Veterans Affairs, "Joint Fact Sheet: DoD and
VA Take New Steps to Support the Mental Health Needs of Service Members
and Veterans," U.S. Department of Veterans Affairs, undated, accessed February 16, 2016, http://www.va.gov/opa/docs/26-AUG-JOINT-FACT-SHEET
-FINAL.pdf.

Chapter 8 *Prisoners*

Peter Baker, "Obama, in Oklahoma, Takes Reform Message to the Prison Cell
Block," *New York Times*, July 16, 2015, accessed December 21, 2015, http://
www.nytimes.com/2015/07/17/us/obama-el-reno-oklahoma-prison.html.

ABC News, "President Obama's Historic Prison Visit," video, ABC News, July
16, 2015, accessed December 21, 2015, http://abcnews.go.com/Politics/video/
president-obamas-historic-prison-visit-32503409.

Tom LoBianco, "President Barack Obama Makes Historic Trip to Prison, Pushes
Reform, CNN, July 17, 2015, accessed December 21, 2015, http://www.cnn
.com/2015/07/16/politics/obama-oklahoma-federal-prison-visit/.

VICE, "Watch 'Fixing the System,' Our HBO Special Report about America's
Broken Criminal Justice System," *VICE*, September 28, 2015, accessed
December 22, 2015, http://www.vice.com/read/watch-fixing-the-system-our
-hbo-special-report-about-americas-broken-criminal-justice-system-985.

Alex Altman and Maya Rhodan, "Senate Introduces 'Gamechanger' Criminal Justice Reform Bill," *Time*, October 1, 2015, accessed December 22, 2015, http://time.com/4057740/criminal-justice-reform-bill/.

Roy Walmsley, "World Prison Population List," 10th edition, London: International Centre for Prison Studies, undated, accessed December 21, 2015, http://www.prisonstudies.org/sites/default/files/resources/downloads/wppl_10.pdf.

Michelle Ye Hee Lee, "Does the United States Really Have 5 Percent of the World's Population and One Quarter of the World's Prisoners?" Fact Checker, *Washington Post*, April 30, 2015, accessed December 21, 2015, https://www.washingtonpost.com/news/fact-checker/wp/2015/04/30/does-the-united-states-really-have-five-percent-of-worlds-population-and-one-quarter-of-the-worlds-prisoners/.

Jeremy Diamond, "Bill Clinton Concedes Role in Mass Incarceration," CNN, May 7, 2015, accessed December 21, 20015, http://www.cnn.com/2015/05/06/politics/bill-clinton-crime-prisons-hillary-clinton/.

Lauren Carroll, "Federal Prison Population Drops for First Time in 3 Decades, Eric Holder Says," *PolitiFact*, February 23, 2015, accessed December 21, 2015, http://www.politifact.com/truth-o-meter/statements/2015/feb/23/eric-holder/federal-prison-population-drops-first-time-3-decad/.

Barack Obama, "Why We Must Rethink Solitary Confinement," *Washington Post*, January 25, 2016, accessed March 20, 2016, https://www.washingtonpost.com/opinions/barack-obama-why-we-must-rethink-solitary-confinement/2016/01/25/29a361f2-c384-11e5-8965-0607e0e265ce_story.html?tid=a_inl.

Chapter 9 *Workers*

White House, Office of the Press Secretary, "Executive Order—Establishing Paid Sick Leave for Federal Contractors," White House, September 7, 2015, accessed December 22, 2015, https://www.whitehouse.gov/the-press-office/2015/09/08/executive-order-establishing-paid-sick-leave-federal-contractors.

White House, Office of the Press Secretary, "Remarks by the President at Greater Boston Labor Council Labor Day Breakfast," White House, September 8, 2015, accessed December 23, 2015, https://www.whitehouse.gov/the-press-office/2015/09/08/remarks-president-greater-boston-labor-council-labor-day-breakfast.

Kevin Liptak, "New Obama Order Requires Contractors to Pay for Sick Leave," CNN, September 8, 2015, accessed December 22, 2015, http://www.cnn.com/2015/09/07/politics/obama-mandatory-sick-leave/.

Gregory Korte, "Through Executive Orders, Obama Tests Power as Purchaser-In-Chief," *USA Today*, October 11, 2015, accessed December 23, 2015, http://www.usatoday.com/story/news/politics/2015/10/11/obama-executive-orders-federal-contractors/22466397/obama-executive-orders.

Dave Boyer, "Obama Vetoes NLRB Legislation," *Washington Times*, March 31, 2015, accessed December 26, 2015, http://www.washingtontimes.com/news/2015/mar/31/obama-veto-nlrb-legislation/.

Timothy Noah and Brian Mahoney, "Obama Labor Board Flexes Its Muscles: Organized Labor Will Have More to Celebrate This Labor Day Than in Decades Thanks to a String of Recent Victories," *Politico*, September 1, 2015, accessed December 26. 2015, http://www.politico.com/story/2015/09/unions-barack-obama-labor-board-victories-213204#ixzz3vTWuIb3S.

Chapter 10 *The Economy*

"Treasury Department Confirms President Obama Has Fully Turned Around the U.S. Economy," DailyNewsBin.com, December 27, 2015. accessed December 28, 2015, http://www.dailynewsbin.com/news/treasury-department-confirms-president-obama-has-fully-turned-around-the-u-s-economy/23369/.

Naomi Jagoda, "Treasury Head: US Economy Better Now Than When Obama Took Office," *Hill*, December 24, 2015, accessed December 28, 2015, http://thehill.com/policy/finance/264205-treasury-head-us-economy-better-now-than-when-obama-took-office.

Julia Limitone, "Jack Lew: U.S. Ending the Year Well Positioned," FOX Business News, December 24, 2015, accessed December 24, 2015, http://www.foxbusiness.com/economy-policy/2015/12/24/jack-lew-us-ending-year-well-positioned/?intcmp=bigtopmarketfeatures.

FOX Business News, Maria Bartiromo interview with U.S. Treasury Secretary Jack Lew, video, FOX Business News. December 24, 2015, accessed December 24, 2015, http://www.foxbusiness.com/economy-policy/2015/12/24/jack-lew-us-ending-year-well-positioned/?intcmp=bigtopmarket features.

Paul Krugman, "In Defense of Obama: The Nobel Prize–Winning Economist, Once One of the President's Most Notable Critics, on Why Obama Is a Historic Success," *Rolling Stone*, October 8, 2014, accessed December 30, 2015, http://www.rollingstone.com/politics/news/in-defense-of-obama-20141008#ixzz3vrKs5bbB.

White House, "Remarks of President Barack Obama—Address to Joint Session of Congress," White House, February 24, 2009, accessed December 27, 2015, https://www.whitehouse.gov/video/EVR022409#transcript.

Congressional Budget Office, *Estimated Impact of the American Recovery and Reinvestment Act on Employment and Economic Output from October 2011 through December 2011*, Washington, D.C.: Congressional Budget Office, February 2012, accessed December 27, 2015, http://www.cbo.gov/sites/default/files/cbofiles/attachments/02-22-ARRA.pdf.

Sarah Jones, "Obama's Winning Streak Continues: Strongest Three Years of Job Creation since 2000," *Politicus usa*, November 6, 2015, accessed February 6, 2016, http://www.politicususa.com/2015/11/06/obama-economy-sets-record-job-growth-streak-surges.html.

White House, Office of the Press Secretary, "Remarks by the President at Greater Boston Labor Council Labor Day Breakfast," White House, September 8, 2015, accessed December 23, 2015, https://www.whitehouse.gov/the-press-office/2015/09/08/remarks-president-greater-boston-labor-council-labor-day-breakfast.

Jason Furman, "The Employment Situation in August," White House blogs, September 4, 2015, accessed December 27, 2015, https://www.whitehouse.gov/blog/2015/09/04/employment-situation-august.

Catherine Rampell, "The Recession Has (Officially) Ended," Economix blog, *New York Times*, September 20, 2010, accessed December 28, 2015, http://economix.blogs.nytimes.com/2010/09/20/the-recession-has-officially-ended/?_r=0.

U.S. Department of the Treasury, "Joint Statement of Jacob J. Lew, Secretary of the Treasury, and Shaun Donovan, Director of the Office of Management and Budget, on Budget Results for Fiscal Year 2015," U.S. Department of the Treasury, October 15, 2015, accessed December 28, 2015, https://www.treasury.gov/press-center/press-releases/Pages/jl0213.aspx.

David E. Sanger, David M. Herszenhorn, and Bill Vlasic, "Bush Aids Detroit, but Hard Choices Wait for Obama," *New York Times*, December 19, 2008, accessed December 28, 2015, http://www.nytimes.com/2008/12/20/business/20auto.html?_r=2&hp.

Jon Greenberg, "Did President Obama Save the Auto Industry?" *PolitiFact*, September 6, 2012, accessed December 28, 2015, http://www.politifact.com/truth-o-meter/article/2012/sep/06/did-obama-save-us-automobile-industry/.

Brent Snavely, "Final Tally: Taxpayers Auto Bailout Loss $9.3B," *Detroit Free Press*, December 30, 2014, accessed December 30, 2015, http://www.usatoday.com/story/money/cars/2014/12/30/auto-bailout-tarp-gm-chrysler/21061251/.

Sean McAlinden and Debra Menk, "CAR Research Memorandum: The Effect on the U.S. Economy of the Successful Restructuring of General Motors," Center for Automotive Research, Industry and Labor Group, and Economic Development and Strategies Group, December 9, 2013, accessed December 31, 2015, http://www.cargroup.org/?module=Publications&event=View&pubID=102.

Robert J. Samuelson, "Celebrating the Auto Bailout's Success, *Washington Post*, April 1, 2015, accessed December 28, 2015, https://www.washingtonpost.com/opinions/celebrating-the-auto-bailouts-success/2015/04/01/67f3f208-d881-11e4-8103-fa84725dbf9d_story.html.

Library of Congress, THOMAS, Bill Summary and Status, 111th Congress (2009–2010), H.R. 4173, Library of Congress, July 21, 2010, accessed December 28, 2015, http://thomas.loc.gov/cgi-bin/bdquery/z?d111:HR04173:@@@L&summ2=m&#major%20actions.

Helene Cooper, "Obama Signs Overhaul of Financial System," *New York Times*, July 21, 2010, accessed December 28, 2015, http://www.nytimes.com/2010/07/22/business/22regulate.html?_r=0.

"Stock Market Analysis." DayTradingStockBlog.Blogspot.com, January 20, 2009, accessed December 29, 2015, http://daytradingstockblog.blogspot .com/2009/01/dow-jones-close-12009-stock-market.html.

"Where Was the Dow Jones When Obama Took Office?" *Investopedia*, October 13, 2014, accessed December 29, 2015, http://www.investopedia .com/ask/answers/101314/where-was-dow-jones-when-obama-took-office .asp#ixzz3vlO267ER.

Kevin Drum, "Obama's Economic Performance Is Even Better Than It Looks," *Mother Jones*, December 28, 2015, accessed December 31, 2015. http://www .motherjones.com/kevin-drum/2015/12/obamas-economic-performance -even-better-it-looks.

Paul Krugman, "Obama: The Job-Killer," Conscience of a Liberal blog, *New York Times*, December 27, 2015, accessed March 20, 2016, http://krugman .blogs.nytimes.com/2015/12/27/obama-the-job-killer/.

U.S. Department of Labor, Bureau of Labor Statistics, "The Employment Situation: January 2009," Bureau of Labor Statistics, February 5, 2009, accessed December 31, 2015, http://www.bls.gov/news.release/archives/ empsit_02062009.pdf.

U.S. Department of Labor, Bureau of Labor Statistics, "Unemployment in October 2009," *TED: The Economics Daily*, Bureau of Labor Statistics, November 10, 2009, accessed December 31, 2015, http://www.bls.gov/opub/ted/2009/ ted_20091110.htm.

Peter S. Goodman, "U.S. Unemployment Rate Hits 10.2%, Highest in 26 Years," *New York Times*, November 6, 2009, accessed December 31, 2015, http://www .nytimes.com/2009/11/07/business/economy/07jobs.html.

U.S. Department of Labor, Bureau of Labor Statistics, "The Employment Situation—November 2015," Bureau of Labor Statistics, December 4, 2015, accessed December 31, 2015, http://www.bls.gov/news.release/pdf/ empsit.pdf.

U.S. Department of Labor, Bureau of Labor Statistics, "The Employment Situation—January 2015," Bureau of Labor Statistics, February 5, 2016, accessed February 6, 2016, http://www.bls.gov/news.release/pdf/empsit.pdf.

Patrick Gillespie, "Black Unemployment Falls to Lowest Since 2007," Money, CNN, January 8, 2016, accessed February 7, 2016, http://money.cnn .com/2016/01/08/news/economy/black-unemployment-falls-hits-8-year-low/ index.html.

Jesse Lee, "Protecting Homeowners, Protecting the Economy," White House blogs, May 20, 2009, accessed January 19, 2016, https://www.whitehouse.gov/ blog/2009/05/20/protecting-homeowners-protecting-economy.

White House, Office of the Press Secretary, "Remarks by the President at Signing of the Helping Families Save Their Homes Act and the Fraud Enforcement and Recovery Act," White House, May 20, 2009, accessed January 17, 2016, https://www.whitehouse.gov/the-press-office/remarks-president-signing -helping-families-save-their-homes-act-and-fraud-enforceme.

Chapter 11 *Defense*

"We Will Kill Bin Laden, We Will Crush Al-Qaeda: Obama," *Nation*, October 8, 2008, accessed January 1, 2016, http://nation.com.pk/Politics/08-Oct-2008/We-will-kill-bin-Laden-we-will-crush-AlQaeda-Obama.

Macon Phillips, "Osama Bin Laden Dead," White House blogs, May 2, 2011, accessed January 1, 2016, https://www.whitehouse.gov/blog/2011/05/02/osama-bin-laden-dead.

Louis Charbonneau, "U.N. Chief Ban Hails Bin Laden Death as 'Watershed,'" Reuters, May 2, 2011, accessed January 1, 2016, http://www.reuters.com/article/us-binladen-un-idUSTRE7414W720110502.

Pew Research Center, "Public 'Relieved' by bin Laden's Death, Obama's Job Approval Rises," Pew Research Center, May 3, 2011, accessed January 1, 2016, http://www.people-press.org/2011/05/03/public-relieved-by-bin-ladens-death-obamas-job-approval-rises/.

Kate Zernike and Michael T. Kaufman, "The Most Wanted Face of Terrorism," *New York Times*, May 2, 2011, accessed January 1, 2016, http://www.nytimes.com/2011/05/02/world/02osama-bin-laden-obituary.html.

"President Obama's Remarks on the Death of Muammar el-Qaddafi," White House blogs, October 20, 2011, accessed February 2, 2016, https://www.whitehouse.gov/blog/2011/10/20/president-obamas-remarks-death-muammar-el-qaddafi.

CNN, "Protesters Attack U.S. Diplomatic Compounds in Egypt, Libya," CNN, September 12, 2012, accessed March 30, 2016, http://www.cnn.com/2012/09/11/world/meast/egpyt-us-embassy-protests/index.html.

Brian Montopoli, "Obama Announces End of Iraq War, Troops to Return Home by Year End," CBS News, October 21, 2011, accessed January 1, 2016, http://www.cbsnews.com/news/obama-announces-end-of-iraq-war-troops-to-return-home-by-year-end/.

BBC News, "Saddam Hussein Executed in Iraq," BBC News, December 30, 2006, accessed January 3, 2016, http://news.bbc.co.uk/2/hi/middle_east/6218485.stm.

Helene Cooper, Mark Landler, and Alissa J. Rubinaug., "Obama Allows Limited Airstrikes on ISIS," *New York Times*, August 7, 2014, accessed January 1, 2016, http://www.nytimes.com/2014/08/08/world/middleeast/obama-weighs-military-strikes-to-aid-trapped-iraqis-officials-say.html#addendums.

White House, Office of the Press Secretary, "Statement by the President," White House, August 7, 2014, accessed January 2, 2016, https://www.whitehouse.gov/the-press-office/2014/08/07/statement-president.

Associated Press, "U.S. May Send More Troops to Train Iraqi Forces," Associated Press, June 10, 2015, accessed January 3, 2016, http://www.cbc.ca/news/u-s-may-send-more-troops-to-train-iraqi-forces-1.3107257.

Nahlah Ayed, "ISIS Poses Bigger Threat after Nearly a Year of Coalition Bombing," CBC News, May 26, 2015, accessed January 3, 2016, http://www.cbc.ca/news/u-s-may-send-more-troops-to-train-iraqi-forces-1.3107257.

White House, Office of the Press Secretary, "Statement by the President on Afghanistan," White House, October 15, 2015, accessed January 4, 2016, https://www.whitehouse.gov/the-press-office/2015/10/15/statement-president-afghanistan.

Scott Wilson, "Obama Makes Surprise Visit to Afghanistan," *Washington Post*, May 25, 2014, accessed January 4, 2016, https://www.washingtonpost.com/politics/obama-arrives-in-afghanistan-on-surprise-visit/2014/05/25/7df61452-e41f-11e3-8f90-73e071f3d637_story.html.

Greg Jaffe, "The War in Afghanistan Follows Obama to His Vacation in Hawaii," *Washington Post*, December 21, 2015, accessed January 4, 2016, https://www.washingtonpost.com/politics/the-war-in-afghanistan-follows-obama-to-his-vacation-in-hawaii/2015/12/21/54a80e9c-a814-11e5-9b92-dea7cd4b1a4d_story.html.

Robert Burns, "1 US Soldier Killed, 2 Wounded in Fighting in Afghanistan," Associated Press, January 5, 2016, accessed January 5, 2016, http://www.msn.com/en-us/news/world/1-us-soldier-killed-2-wounded-in-fighting-in-afghanistan/ar-BBo9qdi?ocid=ansmsnnews11.

Julie Hirschfeld Davis, "In Wielding Rarely Used Veto, President Obama Puts Budget Heat on Republicans," *New York Times*, October 22, 2015, accessed January 4, 2016, http://www.nytimes.com/2015/10/23/us/politics/obama-vetoes-defense-bill-deepening-budget-fight-with-gop.html?smtyp=cur&_r=0.

White House, Office of the Press Secretary, "Statement by the President," White House, November 25, 2015, accessed January 4, 2015, https://www.whitehouse.gov/the-press-office/2015/11/25/statement-president.

CNN, "Obama, Russian President Sign Arms Treaty," CNN, April 8, 2010, accessed January 5, 2016, http://www.cnn.com/2010/POLITICS/04/08/obama.russia.treaty/index.html.

Mary Beth Sheridan and William Branigin, "Senate Ratifies New U.S.-Russia Nuclear Weapons Treaty," *Washington Post*, December 22, 2010, accessed January 5, 2016, http://www.washingtonpost.com/wp-dyn/content/article/2010/12/21/AR2010122104371.html.

Chapter 12 *Diplomacy*

"Global Views of United States Improve While Other Countries Decline," WorldPublicOpinion.org, April 18, 2010, accessed February 4, 2016, http://www.worldpublicopinion.org/pipa/articles/views_on_countriesregions_bt/660.php.

CBS News, "President Obama Wins Nobel Peace Prize," CBS News, October 9, 2009, accessed January 5, 2016, http://www.cbsnews.com/news/president-obama-wins-nobel-peace-prize/.

Timothy Egan, "Obama Can Still Earn His Nobel," *New York Times*, September 25, 2014, accessed January 5, 2016, http://www.nytimes.com/2014/09/26/opinion/obama-can-still-earn-his-nobel.html.

"Archives: Obama Wins Nobel Peace Prize," Reuters/*Chicago Tribune*, May 15, 2014, accessed January 5, 2016, http://articles.chicagotribune.com/2014-05-15/

news/chi-archives-obama-wins-nobel-peace-prize-20140515_1_president
-obama-nobel-peace-prize-major-foreign-policy-success.

Barack H. Obama, "A Just and Lasting Peace," Nobel lecture, Nobelprize.org, December 10, 2009, accessed January 5, 2016, http://www.nobelprize.org/ nobel_prizes/peace/laureates/2009/obama-lecture_en.html.

Peter Baker, "U.S. to Restore Full Relations With Cuba, Erasing a Last Trace of Cold War Hostility," *New York Times*, December 17, 2014, accessed January 5, 2016, http://www.nytimes.com/2014/12/18/world/americas/us-cuba-relations .html.

Tom McCarthy, "US Embassy on Cuba Formally Reopens: 'A Day For Pushing Aside Old Barriers,'" *Guardian*, August 14, 2015, accessed January 5, 2016, http://www.theguardian.com/world/2015/aug/14/us-embassy -cuba-formally-reopens

Dan Lamothe, "These Marines Took Down the U.S. Flag in Cuba in 1961. Today, They Watched It Rise Again," *Washington Post*, August 14, 2015, accessed January 6, 2016, https://www.washingtonpost.com/news/checkpoint/ wp/2015/08/14/these-marines-took-down-the-u-s-flag-in-cuba-in-1961-today -theyll-raise-it-again/.

Michael R. Gordon and David E. Sanger, "Deal Reached on Iran Nuclear Program; Limits on Fuel Would Lessen with Time," *New York Times*, July 14, 2015, accessed January 6, 2016, http://www.nytimes.com/2015/07/15/world/ middleeast/iran-nuclear-deal-is-reached-after-long-negotiations.html.

CNN, "Obama, Russian President Sign Arms Treaty," CNN, April 8, 2010, accessed January 5, 2016, http://www.cnn.com/2010/POLITICS/04/08/ obama.russia.treaty/index.html.

Ted Barrett, Manu Raju, Deirdre Walsh, and Tom LoBianco, "Senate Democrats Protect Obama on Iran Vote," CNN, September 10, 2015, accessed January 6, 2016, http://www.cnn.com/2015/09/10/politics/iran-nuclear-deal-vote -congress/.

Julian Hattem, "Pope Praises Iran Deal before UN," *Hill*, September 25, 2015, accessed January 6, 2016, http://thehill.com/policy/national-security/254934 -pope-praises-iran-deal-before-un.

Thomas Erdbrink and Rick Gladstone, "Iran Frees Americans, Including Jason Rezaian, in Prisoner Swap," *New York Times*, January 16, 2016, accessed January 19, 2016, http://www.nytimes.com/2016/01/17/world/middleeast/iran -releases-washington-post-reporter-jason-rezaian.html?_r=0.

John Parkinson, "Freed American Nosratollah Khosravi-Roodsari Remains a Mystery," ABC News, January 18, 2016, accessed January 19, 2016, http://abcnews .go.com/Politics/freed-american-nosratollah-khosravi-roodsari-remains-mystery/ story?id=36358599.

Reza Marashi, "The U.S.-Iran Prisoner Swap Is Yet Another Victory for Diplomacy and Human Rights," *Huffington Post*, January 16, 2016, accessed January 19, 2016, http://www.huffingtonpost.com/reza-marashi/us-iran -prisoner-swap_b_8989970.html.

White House, Office of the Press Secretary, "Statement by the President on the Trans-Pacific Partnership," White House, October 5, 2015, accessed January 6, 2016, https://www.whitehouse.gov/the-press-office/2015/10/05/statement-president-trans-pacific-partnership.

Kevin Granville, "The Trans-Pacific Partnership Trade Accord Explained," *New York Times*, October 5, 2015, accessed January 6, 2016, http://www.nytimes.com/2015/10/06/business/international/the-trans-pacific-partnership-trade-deal-explained.html?_r=0.

David Nakamura, "U.S. Chamber of Commerce Endorses Obama's Pacific Rim Trade Pact," *Washington Post*, January 6, 2016, accessed January 6, 2016, https://www.washingtonpost.com/news/post-politics/wp/2016/01/06/u-s-chamber-of-commerce-endorses-obamas-pacific-rim-trade-pact/.

Sidebar: Trade Initiatives

White House, Office of the Press Secretary, "Fact Sheet on New Initiatives," White House, November 12, 2010, accessed March 28, 2016, https://www.whitehouse.gov/the-press-office/2010/11/12/fact-sheet-new-initiatives.

Chapter 13 *Justice*

Melanie Garunay, "President Obama Has Shortened the Sentences of More People Than the Last 5 Presidents Combined," White House blogs, December 18, 2015, accessed January 9, 2016, https://www.whitehouse.gov/blog/2015/12/18/president-obama-has-shortened-sentences-more-people-last-5-presidents-combined.

Editorial Board, "Mr. Obama's Trickle of Mercy," *New York Times*, December 31, 2015, accessed January 10, 2016, http://www.nytimes.com/2015/12/31/opinion/mr-obamas-trickle-of-mercy.html?_r=0.

Gregory Korte, "'The Clock Is Running' on Obama Clemency Initiative," *USA Today*, June 24, 2015, accessed January 7, 2016, http://www.usatoday.com/story/news/politics/2015/06/24/clemency-initiative-clock-is-running/29128091/.

Chuck Ross, "Justice Department Plans Attorney Hiring Spree to Keep Pace with Obama's Pardon Push," *Daily Caller*, January 6. 2016, accessed January 8, 2016, http://dailycaller.com/2016/01/06/justice-department-plans-attorney-hiring-spree-to-keep-pace-with-obamas-pardon-push/.

Ryan J. Reilly, "Obama: I'll Use Clemency Power 'More Aggressively,'" *Huffington Post*, March 31, 2015, accessed January 8, 2015, http://www.huffingtonpost.com/2015/03/21/obama-clemency-pardon_n_6911784.html.

Gregory Korte, "U.S. Pardon Attorney to Resign Amid Obama's Last-Year Clemency Push," *USA Today*, January 15, 2016, accessed January 19, 2016, http://www.usatoday.com/story/news/politics/2016/01/15/us-pardon-attorney-deborah-leff-resignation/78877552/#cx_ab_test_id=21&cx_ab_test_variant=cx_advanced_v1&cx_art_pos=1&cx_navSource=arttop&cx_tag=collabctx&cx_rec_type=collabctx&cx_ctrl_comp_grp=false&cxrecs_s.

Josh Gerstein, "Obama Drug Clemency Guidelines Issued," *Politico*, April 23, 2014, accessed January 8, 2016, http://www.politico.com/blogs/under-the -radar/2014/04/obama-drug-clemency-guidelines-issued-187266.

American Civil Liberties Union, "Fair Sentencing Act," American Civil Liberties Union, undated, accessed January 9, 2016, https://www.aclu.org/node/17576.

Gary G. Grindler,"Memorandum for All Federal Prosecutors: The Fair Sentencing Act of 2010," U.S. Department of Justice, Office of the Deputy Attorney General, August 5, 2010, accessed January 9, 2016, http://www.justice.gov/ sites/default/files/oip/legacy/2014/07/23/fair-sentencing-act-memo.pdf.

National Association for the Advancement of Colored People (NAACP), "U.S. Sentencing Commission Votes to Apply New Crack Cocaine Sentencing Guidelines Retroactively," NAACP, undated, accessed January 9, 2016, http:// www.naacp.org/news/entry/u.s.-sentencing-commission-votes-to-apply-new -crack-cocaine-sentencing-guid/.

American Civil Liberties Union, "Cracks in the System: Twenty Years of the Unjust Federal Crack Cocaine Law," American Civil Liberties Union, October 2006, accessed January 9, 2016, https://www.aclu.org/cracks-system -twenty-years-unjust-federal-crack-cocaine-law?redirect=criminal-law-reform /cracks-system-twenty-years-unjust-federal-crack-cocaine-law.

Lauren Carroll, "Federal Prison Population Drops for First Time in 3 Decades, Eric Holder Says," *PolitiFact*, February 23, 2015, accessed December 21, 2015, http://www.politifact.com/truth-o-meter/statements/2015/ feb/23/eric-holder/federal-prison-population-drops-first-time-3-decad/.

U.S. Department of Justice, "Smart on Crime: Reforming the Criminal Justice System for the 21st Century," U.S. Department of Justice, August 2013, accessed January 9, 2016, http://www.justice.gov/sites/default/files/ag/legacy/ 2013/08/12/smart-on-crime.pdf.

Michael Scherer, "Eric Holder Will Leave a Legacy of Civil Rights Activism," *Time*, September 25, 2014, accessed January 10, 2016, http://time .com/3430623/eric-holder-civil-rights/.

U.S. Department of Justice, "Remarks as Prepared for Delivery by Attorney General Eric Holder at the Department of Justice African American History Month Program," U.S. Department of Justice, February 18, 2009, accessed January 10, 2016, https://www.justice.gov/opa/speech/attorney-general-eric -holder-department-justice-african-american-history-month-program.

Gregory Korte, "Obama Announces Gun Actions in Emotional Plea for Congressional Action," *USA Today*, January 5, 2016, accessed January 26, 2016, http://www.usatoday.com/story/news/politics/2016/01/05/obama-announces -gun-actions/78302832/.

Bill Chappell, "In Live Address, Obama Takes His Plan for Gun Control to the Public," NPR, January 5, 2016, accessed January 26, 2016, http://www.npr .org/sections/thetwo-way/2016/01/05/462020685/obama-seeks -commonsense-gun-control-through-executive-actions.

White House, Office of the Press Secretary, "Remarks by the President on Common-Sense Gun Safety Reform," White House, January 5, 2016, accessed January 26, 2016, https://www.whitehouse.gov/the-press-office/2016/01/05/remarks-president-common-sense-gun-safety-reform.

Sharon Lafraniere, Sarah Cohen, and Richard A. Oppel Jr., "How Often Do Mass Shootings Occur? On Average, Every Day, Records Show," *New York Times*, December 2, 2015, accessed January 26, 2016, http://www.nytimes.com/2015/12/03/us/how-often-do-mass-shootings-occur-on-average-every-day-records-show.htm.

Kelsey Snell, "Lynch: Obama Gun Control Actions Are Legal, Plans Underway to Hire Background Check Agents," *Washington Post*, January 20, 2016, accessed January 26, 2016, https://www.washingtonpost.com/news/powerpost/wp/2016/01/20/lynch-obama-gun-control-actions-are-legal-plans-underway-to-hire-background-check-agents/.

Chapter 14 *Labor*

President Barack Obama, "A Hard Day's Work Deserves a Fair Day's Pay," *Huffington Post*, June 29, 2015, accessed January 11, 2016, http://www.huffingtonpost.com/barack-obama/a-hard-days-work-deserves-a-fair-days-pay_b_7691922.html.

Edward-Isaac Dovere and Marianne LeVine, "Obama Overtime Rule Could Raise Wages for 5 Million: The Threshold to Qualify for Overtime Pay, Now $23,660, Will Rise to $50,440," *Politico*, June 29, 2015, accessed January 11, 2016, http://www.politico.com/story/2015/06/obama-overtime-rule-wage-raise-119566.

Dave Jamieson, "Obama Says Workers Are Being 'Cheated' out of Overtime Pay," *Huffington Post*, March 21, 2015, accessed January 11, 2016, http://www.huffingtonpost.com/2015/03/21/obama-overtime-pay_n_6911808.html.

Julie Hirschfeld Davis, "Obama Plans to Push Paid Family and Sick Leave for Workers," *New York Times*, January 14, 2015, accessed January 11, 2016, http://www.nytimes.com/2015/01/15/us/politics/obama-plans-to-push-bill-for-providing-paid-leave-to-workers-.html?_r=0.

Gregory Korte, "Obama to Propose Paid Sick Leave for American Workers," *USA Today*, January 15, 2015, accessed January 11, 2016, http://www.usatoday.com/story/news/politics/2015/01/14/obama-child-care-paid-leave/21768969/.

Steve Contorno, "Barack Obama Says United States Only Developed Country without Paid Maternity Leave, *PolitiFact*, January 21, 2015, accessed January 11, 2016, http://www.politifact.com/truth-o-meter/statements/2015/jan/21/barack-obama/barack-obama-says-united-states-only-developed-cou/.

David S. Joachim, "Obama Signs New Job-Training Law," *New York Times*, July 22, 2014, accessed January 11, 2016, http://www.nytimes.com/2014/07/23/us/obama-signs-new-job-training-law.html.

White House, Office of the Press Secretary, "Remarks by the President and Vice President at Bill Signing of the Workforce Innovation and Opportunity Act,"

White House, July 22, 2014, accessed March 20, 2016, https://www.whitehouse
.gov/the-press-office/2014/07/22/remarks-president-and-vice-president-bill
-signing-workforce-innovation-a.

Gregory Korte, "Obama Signs Bill to Overhaul Job Training Programs," *USA
Today,* July 22, 2014, accessed January 11, 2015, http://www.usatoday.com/
story/news/politics/2014/07/22/obama-job-training-bill/12987339/.

Chapter 15 *Education*

Michael Grunwald, "The Nation He Built: A Politico Review of Barack Obama's
Domestic Policy Legacy—and the Changes He Made While Nobody Was
Paying Attention," *Politico,* vol. 3, no. 2, January 6, 2016, http://www.politico
.com/magazine/story/2016/01/obama-biggest-achievements-213487.

U.S. Department of Education, "Recovery Act Recipients Report Funding Continues to Support over 300,000 Education Jobs," U.S. Department of Education, February 1, 2010, accessed January 13, 2016, http://www2.ed.gov/news/
pressreleases/2010/02/02012010a.html.

U.S. Department of Education, "The American Recovery and Reinvestment Act
of 2009: Education Jobs and Reform," U.S. Department of Education, February 18, 2009, accessed January 13, 2016, http://www2.ed.gov/policy/gen/leg/
recovery/factsheet/overview.html.

Megan McClean, Policy & Federal Relations Staff, "Pell Funding Strain Eases:
No Shortfall Until 2017," National Association of Student Financial Aid
Administrators, April 23, 2014, accessed March 28, 2016, https://www.nasfaa
.org/news-item/1347/Pell_Funding_Strain_Eases_No_Shortfall_Until_2017.

Sam Dillon and Tamar Lewin, "Pell Grants Said to Face a Shortfall of $6 Bil-
lion," *New York Times,* September 17, 2008, accessed March 29, 2016, http://
www.nytimes.com/2008/09/18/education/18grant.html?_r=0.

David Hudson, "Invest in US: President Obama Convenes the White House
Summit on Early Education, White House blogs, December 10, 2014,
accessed January 13, 2016, https://www.whitehouse.gov/blog/2014/12/10/
invest-us-president-obama-convenes-white-house-summit-early-education.

Jennifer C. Kerr, "Obama Announces $1 Billion Investment for Early Child-
hood Education," Associated Press, December 10, 2014, accessed January 13,
2016, http://www.pbs.org/newshour/rundown/obama-announcing-1-billion
-investment-early-childhood-education/.

Jennifer C. Kerr, "Obama Signs the Every Student Succeeds Act; Law Overhauls
'No Child,'" Associated Press, December 10, 2015, accessed January 14, 2016,
http://www.wschronicle.com/2016/01/obama-signs-every-student-succeeds
-act-law-overhauls-no-child/.

"Senate Overwhelmingly Passes Every Student Succeeds Act," *Education World,*
December 10, 2016, accessed January 14, 2016, http://www.educationworld
.com/a_news/senate-passes-every-student-succeeds-act-327497444#sthash
.LScJZ1HZ.dpuf.

White House, "Race to the Top," White House, undated, accessed January 12, 2016, https://www.whitehouse.gov/issues/education/k-12/race-to-the-top.

U.S. Department of Education, Office of State Support, "Fundamental Change, Innovation in America's schools under Race to the Top," U.S. Department of Education, November 2015, accessed January 13, 2016, http://www2.ed.gov/programs/racetothetop/rttfinalrpt1115.pdf.

Roberta Rampton, "Obama Announces Changes for Student Loan Repayment," Reuters, March 10, 2015, accessed January 14, 2016, http://news.yahoo.com/obama-announce-charges-student-loan-repayment-131450580—sector.html.

Peter Baker and David M. Herszenhorn, "Obama Signs Overhaul of Student Loan Program," *New York Times*, March 30, 2010, accessed January 14, 2016, http://www.nytimes.com/2010/03/31/us/politics/31obama.html.

Congressional Budget Office, "S. 2432, Bank on Students Emergency Loan Refinancing Act: Cost Estimate," letter to Elizabeth Warren, Congressional Budget Office, June 6, 2014, accessed January 15, 2016, https://www.cbo.gov/publication/45433.

David Jackson, "Obama's Day: Student Loans," Oval, *USA Today*, June 9, 2014, accessed January 14, 2016, http://www.usatoday.com/story/theoval/2014/06/09/obama-student-loans/10220809/.

Sidebar: A Student Aid Bill of Rights

White House, Office of the Press Secretary, "Fact Sheet: A Student Aid Bill of Rights: Taking Action to Ensure Strong Consumer Protections for Student Loan Borrowers," White House, March 10, 2015, accessed January 14, 2016, https://www.whitehouse.gov/the-press-office/2015/03/10/fact-sheet-student-aid-bill-rights-taking-action-ensure-strong-consumer-.

Chapter 16 *Housing and Urban Development*

Glynn a. Hill, "New Rule Aims to Diversify Neighborhoods, Federal Agency Seeks to Reduce Segregation in Housing Patterns across US," Associated Press, July 8, 2015, accessed January 17, 2016, http://finance.yahoo.com/news/rule-aims-diversify-neighborhoods-231851933.html.

Tim Devaney, "Obama Making Bid to Diversify Wealthy Neighborhoods," *Hill*, June 11, 2015, accessed January 16, 2015, http://thehill.com/regulation/244620-obamas-bid-to-diversify-wealthy-neighborhoods.

Jon Prior, "SCOTUS Upholds Obama Legal Tactic in Fair Housing Cases," *Politico*, June 25, 2015, accessed January 19, 2016, http://www.politico.com/story/2015/06/supreme-court-fair-housing-upholds-119418#ixzz3xjjRRyfQ.

Chapter 17 *Transportation*

"President Obama Speech on the Economy," C-Span, February 26, 2014, accessed January 20, 2016, http://www.c-span.org/video/?318005-1/president-obamas-speech-economy.

Justin Sink, "Obama's $300B Infrastructure Plan," *Hill*, February 26, 2014, accessed January 21, 2016, http://thehill.com/blogs/blog-briefing-room/news/199275-obamas-300b-infrastructure-plan.

U.S. Department of Transportation, "TIGER Discretionary Grants," U.S. Department of Transportation, January 6, 2016, accessed January 16, 2016, https://www.transportation.gov/tiger.

U.S. Department of Transportation, "U.S. Transportation Secretary Foxx Announces $500 Million in TIGER Grants Awarded to 39 Projects: Projects Target Future Needs in Rural and Urban Communities," U.S, Department of Transportation, undated, accessed January 20, 2016, https://www.transportation.gov/briefing-room/secretary-foxx-announces-500-million-in-39-tiger-grants.

U.S. Department of Transportation, "The Fixing America's Surface Transportation Act or 'FAST Act,'" U.S. Department of Transportation, undated, accessed January 20, 2016, https://www.transportation.gov/fastact.

Keith Laing and Jordain Carney, "Senate Sends $305B Highway Bill to Obama," *Hill*, December 3, 2015, accessed January 20, 2016, http://thehill.com/policy/finance/262049-senate-sends-highway-bill-to-obama.

U.S. Department of Transportation, "Secretary Foxx Unveils President Obama's FY17 Budget Proposal of Nearly $4 Billion for Automated Vehicles and Announces DOT Initiatives to Accelerate Vehicle Safety Innovations: DOT Actions Revise Existing Guidance and Clear Administrative Hurdles for New Automotive Technology," U.S. Department of Transportation, January 14, 2016, accessed January 20, 2016, https://www.transportation.gov/briefing-room/secretary-foxx-unveils-president-obama%E2%80%99s-fy17-budget-proposal-nearly-4-billion.

Chapter 18 *Homeland Security*

Jerry Markon, "Federal Eye: U.S. Illegal Immigrant Population Falls below 11 Million, Continuing Nearly Decade-Long Decline, Report Says," *Washington Post*, January 20, 2016, accessed January 22, 2016, https://www.washingtonpost.com/news/federal-eye/wp/2016/01/20/u-s-illegal-immigrant-population-falls-below-11-million-continuing-nearly-decade-long-decline-report-says/.

Center for Migration Studies, "Center for Migration Studies Reports Decline of the US Undocumented Population," Center for Migration Studies, January 20, 2016, accessed January 22, 2016, http://cmsny.org/press-release-undocumented-decline/.

White House, "Continuing to Strengthen Border Security," White House, undated, accessed January 23, 2016, https://www.whitehouse.gov/issues/immigration/border-security.

U.S. Department of Homeland Security, Press Office, "DHS Releases Entry/Exit Overstay Report For Fiscal Year 2015," U.S. Department of Homeland Security, January 19, 2016, accessed January 20, 2016, http://www.dhs.gov/news/2016/01/19/dhs-releases-entryexit-overstay-report-fiscal-year-2015.

Chapter 19 *Agriculture*

Michael D. Shear, "In Signing Farm Bill, Obama Extols Rural Growth," *New York Times*, February 7, 2014, accessed January 21, 2016, http://www.nytimes .com/2014/02/08/us/politics/farm-bill.html?_r=0.

U.S. Senate Committee on Agriculture, Nutrition, and Forestry, "Farm Bill Ends Direct Payment Subsidies," Senate Committee on Agriculture, Nutrition and Forestry, January 28, 2014, accessed January 21, 2016, http://www.agriculture .senate.gov/newsroom/press/release/farm-bill-ends-direct-payment-subsidies.

Part III A Man of Conviction

Harry S. Truman Library and Museum, "This Day in Truman History, November 19, 1945, President Truman's Proposed Health Program," Harry S. Truman Library and Museum, undated, accessed February 9, 2016, http://www .trumanlibrary.org/anniversaries/healthprogram.htm.

Chapter 20 *Health*

White House, Office of the Press Secretary, "Remarks by the President to a Joint Session of Congress on Health Care," White House, September 9, 2009, accessed January 23, 2016, https://www.whitehouse.gov/the-press-office/ remarks-president-a-joint-session-congress-health-care.

Adam Liptak, "Supreme Court Allows Nationwide Health Care Subsidies," *New York Times*, June 25, 2015, accessed March 29, 2016, http://www.nytimes .com/2015/06/26/us/obamacare-supreme-court.html.

Associated Press, "Number of Uninsured Fell by More Than 11 Million Since Passage of Obamacare, CDC Reports," Associated Press, *Huffington Post*, March 24, 2015, accessed January 23, 2016, http://www.huffingtonpost .com/2015/03/24/obamacare-uninsured-americans_n_6929310.html.

Henry J. Kaiser Family Foundation, "Assessing the Effects of the Economy on the Recent Slowdown in Health Spending," Henry J. Kaiser Family Foundation, April 22, 2013, accessed January 24, 2016, http://kff.org/health-costs/issue -brief/assessing-the-effects-of-the-economy-on-the-recent-slowdown-in -health-spending-2/.

U.S. Department of Health and Human Services, "Medicaid Enrollment and the Affordable Care Act," U.S. Department of Health and Human Services, March 20, 2015, accessed January 24, 2016, https://aspe.hhs.gov/sites/default/ files/pdf/139236/ib_MedicaidEnrollment.pdf.

Robin A. Cohen, and Michael E. Martinez, *Health Insurance Coverage: Early Release of Estimates From the National Health Interview Survey, January– March 2015*, U.S. Department of Health and Human Services, Centers for Disease Control, National Center for Health Statistics, August 2015, accessed January 23, 2016, http://www.cdc.gov/nchs/data/nhis/earlyrelease/ insur201508.pdf.

Lena H. Sun, "More Than 11.3 Million Americans Signed Up for Obamacare, HHS Says," *Washington Post*, January 7, 2016, accessed January 23, 2016, https://www.washingtonpost.com/news/to-your-health/wp/2016/01/07/more -than-11-3-million-americans-signed-up-for-obamacare-report-says/.

U.S. Department of Health and Human Services, Office of the Assistant Secretary for Planning and Evaluation (ASPE), "Health Insurance Marketplaces 2016 Open Enrollment Period: January Enrollment Report for the Period: November 1–December 26, 2015," ASPE, January 7, 2016, accessed January 23, 2016, https://aspe.hhs.gov/sites/default/files/pdf/167981/MarketPlace EnrollJan2016.pdf.

White House, "Remarks by the President and Vice President at Signing of the Health Insurance Reform Bill," White House, March 23, 2010, accessed January 23, 2016, https://www.whitehouse.gov/photos-and-video/ video/president-obama-signs-health-reform-law#transcript.

Adam Liptak, "Supreme Court Upholds Health Care Law, 5-4, in Victory for Obama," New York Times, June 28, 2012, accessed March 29, 2015, http://www .nytimes.com/2012/06/29/us/supreme-court-lets-health-law-largely-stand.html.

Mike DeBonis, "Obama Vetoes Republican Repeal of Health-Care Law," *Washington Post*, January 8, 2016, accessed January 27, 2016, https:// www.washingtonpost.com/news/powerpost/wp/2016/01/08/obama-vetoes -republican-repeal-of-health-care-law/.

Cristian Farias, "Supreme Court Trashes Latest Legal Attack on Obamacare: The Justices Already Ruled the Law Constitutional. They're Done for Now," *Huffington Post*, January 19, 2016, accessed January 27, 2016, http://www.huffingtonpost.com/ entry/supreme-court-obamacare_us_569e765ce4b0cd99679b7e00.

White House, "Remarks of the President—as Prepared for Delivery—Signing of Stem Cell Executive Order and Scientific Integrity Presidential Memorandum," White House, March 9, 2009, accessed January 27, 2016, https://www .whitehouse.gov/the-press-office/remarks-president-prepared-delivery -signing-stem-cell-executive-order-and-scientifi.

CBS News/Associated Press, "Obama Ends Stem Cell Research Ban," Associated Press/CBS News, March 9, 2009, accessed January 27, 2016, http://www .cbsnews.com/news/obama-ends-stem-cell-research-ban/.

U.S. Food and Drug Administration, "Tobacco Control Act," U.S. Food and Drug Administration, November 13, 2015, accessed January 28, 2016, http:// www.fda.gov/TobaccoProducts/GuidanceComplianceRegulatoryInformation/ ucm246129.htm.

H.R. 1256 (111th): Family Smoking Prevention and Tobacco Control Act, Govtrack.us, accessed January 28, 2016, https://www.govtrack.us/congress/ bills/111/hr1256.

Associated Press, "Obama Signs Sweeping Anti-Smoking Bill," Associated Press/ NBC News, June 22, 2009, accessed January 28, 2016, http://www.nbcnews .com/id/31481823/ns/politics-white_house/t/obama-signs-sweeping-anti -smoking-bill/#.VqqQIcywVHA.

Sam Baker, "Supreme Court Rejects Challenge to Tobacco Warnings," *Hill*, April 22, 2013, accessed January 28, 2016, http://thehill.com/policy/healthcare/295255-supreme-court-rejects-challenge-to-tobacco-warnings.

Chapter 21 *Energy and the Environment*

President Obama Facebook page, November 9, 2015, accessed January 30, 2016, https://www.facebook.com/potus/.

Kim Hjelmgaard, "Obama Urges Climate Deal as U.N. Summit Opens in Tense Paris," *USA Today*, November 30, 2015, accessed January 30, 2016, http://www.usatoday.com/story/news/world/2015/11/30/climate-talks -kick-off-france/76551062/.

White House, Office of the Press Secretary, "U.S. Leadership and the Historic Paris Agreement to Combat Climate Change," White House, December 12, 2015, accessed January 28, 2016, https://www.whitehouse.gov/the-press -office/2015/12/12/us-leadership-and-historic-paris-agreement-combat -climate-change.

Justin Worland, "What to Know about the Historic 'Paris Agreement' on Climate Change," *Time*, December 12, 2015, accessed January 30, 2016, http://time .com/4146764/paris-agreement-climate-cop-21/.

White House, Office of the Press Secretary, "Remarks of President Barack Obama—State of the Union Address as Delivered," White House, January 13, 2016, accessed February 8, 2016, https://www.whitehouse.gov/the-press -office/2016/01/12/remarks-president-barack-obama-%E2%80%93-prepared -delivery-state-union-address.

Denise Chow, "President Obama to Announce Climate Change Plan Today," LiveScience.com/Yahoo.com, June 25, 2013, accessed January 28, 2016, http://news.yahoo.com/president-obama-announce-climate-change-plan -today-120624144.html.

White House, Office of the Press Secretary, "Fact Sheet: President Obama's Cli- mate Action Plan: President Obama's Plan to Cut Carbon Pollution—Taking Action for Our Kids," White House, June 25, 2013, accessed January 28, 2016, https://www.whitehouse.gov/the-press-office/2013/06/25/fact-sheet-president -obama-s-climate-action-plan.

Alan Neuhauser, "EPA Chief: Carbon Regs Fulfill 'Moral Obligation' to Act," *U.S. News and World Report*, June 2, 2014, accessed March 29, 2016, http:// www.usnews.com/news/articles/2014/06/02/carbon-limits-fulfill-moral -obligation-to-act-on-global-warming-epa-chief-says.

Juliet Eilperin and Steven Mufson, "EPA Proposes Cutting Carbon Dioxide Emissions from Coal Plants 30% by 2030," *Washington Post*, June 2, 2014, accessed March 29, 2016, https://www.washingtonpost.com/national/health -science/epa-to-propose-cutting-carbon-dioxide-emissions-from-coal-plants -30percent-by-2030/2014/06/01/f5055d94-e9a8-11e3-9f5c-9075d5508f0a_story .html.

Lawrence Hurley, "States Ask U.S. Top Court to Block Obama Carbon Emissions Plan," Reuters, January 26, 2016, accessed January 28, 2016, http://news.yahoo .com/states-ask-u-top-court-block-obama-carbon-220655438—finance.html.

Adam Liptak and Coral Davenport, "Supreme Court Deals Blow to Obama's Efforts to Regulate Coal Emissions," *New York Times*, February 9, 2016, accessed February 21, 2016, http://www.nytimes.com/2016/02/10/us/politics/ supreme-court-blocks-obama-epa-coal-emissions-regulations.html.

Coral Davenport, "In Climate Move, Obama Halts New Coal Mining Leases on Public Lands," January 14, 2016, accessed February 6, 2016, http://www .nytimes.com/2016/01/15/us/politics/in-climate-move-obama-to-halt-new -coal-mining-leases-on-public-lands.html?_r=.

Elana Schor, "Obama Rejects Keystone XL Pipeline: The Long-Awaited Decision Is a Huge Loss for the Oil Industry, the Canadian Government and Republicans in Congress," *Politico*, November 6, 2015, accessed January 28, 2016, http://www.politico.com/story/2015/11/obama-administration -expected-to-reject-keystone-xl-pipeline-215597.

Bill Vlasic, "U.S. Sets Higher Fuel Efficiency Standards," *New York Times*, August 28, 2012, accessed January 30, 2016, http://www.nytimes.com/2012/08/29/business/ energy-environment/obama-unveils-tighter-fuel-efficiency-standards.html.

White House, Office of the Press Secretary, "Obama Administration Finalizes Historic 54.5 MPG Fuel Efficiency Standards: Consumer Savings Comparable to Lowering Price of Gasoline by $1 Per Gallon by 2025," White House, August 28, 2012, accessed January 30, 2016, https://www.whitehouse.gov/the -press-office/2012/08/28/obama-administration-finalizes-historic-545-mpg -fuel-efficiency-standard.

Robert Farley, "Stimulus Includes Tax Credit for Plug-in Hybrids," *PolitiFact*, March 23, 2009, accessed January 30, 2016, http://www.politifact .com/truth-o-meter/promises/obameter/promise/459/enact-tax-credit -for-consumers-for-hybrid-cars/.

Ian Talley, "Obama Mandates New Appliance-Efficiency Standards," *Wall Street Journal*, February 5, 2009, accessed January 30, 2016, http://www.wsj.com/ articles/SB123387168605454125.

White House, Office of the Press Secretary, "Obama Administration Launches New Energy Efficiency Efforts," White House, June 29, 2009, accessed January 30, 2016, https://www.whitehouse.gov/the-press-office/ obama-administration-launches-new-energy-efficiency-efforts.

Catharine Richert, "Research Money Has More Than Doubled," *PolitiFact*, January 8, 2010, accessed January 30, 2016, http://www.politifact.com/ truth-o-meter/promises/obameter/promise/495/double-federal-spending -for-research-on-clean-fuel/.

Chapter 22 *Technology*

Federal Communications Commission, "FCC Adopts Strong, Sustainable Rules to Protect the Open Internet," Federal Communications Commission, January 26, 2015, accessed February 1, 2016, https://www.fcc.gov/document/fcc-adopts-strong-sustainable-rules-protect-open-internet.

Alex Byers and Brooks Boliek, "Obama Endorses Tough Net Neutrality Rules, *Politico*, November 10, 2014, accessed February 1, 2016, Http://www.politico.com/story/2014/11/obama-net-neutrality-rules-112741.

White House, "Net Neutrality: President Obama's Plan for a Free and Open Internet," White House, undated, accessed February 1, 2016, https://www.whitehouse.gov/net-neutrality.

Brady Vardeman, "Choctaw Nation Embraces Durant Visit," *OU Daily*, July 15, 2015, accessed March 20, 2016, http://www.oudaily.com/news/choctaw-nation-embraces-obama-s-durant-visit/article_42c11f4e-2b57-11e5-bad4-87aaea9fe138.html.

Alexander Howard, "White House Wants to Close Homework Gap," *Huffington Post*, July 16, 2015, accessed February 1, 2016, http://www.huffingtonpost.com/entry/connect-home-program_us_55a7b846e4b0896514d066b6.

White House, Office of the Press Secretary, "Weekly Address: Giving Every Student an Opportunity to Learn through Computer Science For All," White House, January 30, 2016, accessed February 1, 2016, https://www.whitehouse.gov/the-press-office/2016/01/30/weekly-address-giving-every-student-opportunity-learn-through-computer.

Julie Hirschfeld Davis, "A Digital Team Is Helping Obama Find His Voice Online," *New York Times*, November 8, 2015, accessed February 1, 2016, http://www.nytimes.com/2015/11/09/us/politics/a-digital-team-is-helping-obama-find-his-voice-online.html.

Kori Schulman, "#AskObama at the First Ever Twitter @Townhall at the White House," June 30, 2011, accessed February 2, 2016, https://www.whitehouse.gov/blog/2011/06/30/askobama-first-ever-twitter-townhall-white-house.

Guinness World Records, "First President with Regular Email Access," Guinness World Records, accessed Feb. 1, 2016, http://www.guinnessworldrecords.com/world-records/first-president-with-regular-email-access/.

White House, Office of the Press Secretary, "Fact Sheet: Cyber Threat Intelligence Integration Center," White House, February 25, 2015, accessed February 2, 2016, https //www.whitehouse.gov/the-press-office/2015/02/25/fact-sheet-cyber-threat-intelligence-integration-center.

Beth Cobert, Steve Vanroekel, and Todd Park, "Delivering a Customer-Focused Government through Smarter IT," White House, August 11, 2014, accessed February 2, 2016, https://www.whitehouse.gov/blog/2014/08/11/delivering-customer-focused-government-through-smarter-it.

Robert Safian, "President Obama: The Fast Company Interview," *Fast Company*, June 15, 2015, accessed February 2, 2016, http://www.fastcompany.com/3046757/innovation-agents/president-barack-obama-on-what-we-the-people-means-in-the-21st-century.

President Obama talked with a World War II veteran, Kenneth "Rock" Merritt, aboard Marine One on a flight from France after attending a ceremony marking the seventieth anniversary of D-Day on June 6, 2014. (Official White House Photo by Pete Souza)

Bibliography

ABC News. "President Obama's Historic Prison Visit." Video. July 16, 2015. Accessed December 21, 2015. http://abcnews.go.com/Politics/video/president-obamas-historic-prison-visit-32503409.

ABC News. "Transcript: Robin Roberts ABC News Interview with President Obama." ABC News. May 9, 2012. Accessed December 11, 2015. http://abcnews.go.com/Politics/transcript-robin-roberts-abc-news-interview-president-obama/story?id=16316043.

Alexander, David. "Two Women Have Completed 'The Army's Toughest Training.' Here's What That Means for the Military." *Huffington Post.* August 8, 2015. Accessed February 3, 2016. http://www.huffingtonpost.com/entry/women-army-rangers_us_55d607fbe4b055a6dab33fc1.

Alexander, David, and Phil Stewart. "U.S. Military Opens All Combat Roles to Women." Reuters. December 4, 2015. Accessed February 3, 2016. http://www.reuters.com/article/us-usa-military-women-combat-idUSKBN0TM28520151204.

Altman, Alex, and Maya Rhodan. "Senate Introduces 'Gamechanger' Criminal Justice Reform Bill." *Time.* October 1, 2015. Accessed December 22, 2015. http://time.com/4057740/criminal-justice-reform-bill/.

American Civil Liberties Union. "Cracks in the System: Twenty Years of the Unjust Federal Crack Cocaine Law." October 2006. Accessed January 9, 2016. https://www.aclu.org/cracks-system-twenty-years-unjust-federal-crack-cocaine-law?redirect=criminal-law-reform/cracks-system-twenty-years-unjust-federal-crack-cocaine-law.

American Civil Liberties Union. "Fair Sentencing Act." American Civil Liberties Union. Accessed January 9, 2016. https://www.aclu.org/node/17576.

American Presidency Project. "Presidential Vetoes: Washington-Obama." Accessed March 23, 2016. http://www.presidency.ucsb.edu/data/vetoes.php.

Appuzzo, Matt. "Department of Justice Sues Ferguson, Which Reversed Course on Agreement." *New York Times.* February 10, 2016. Accessed February 21, 2016. http://www.nytimes.com/2016/02/11/us/politics/justice-department-sues-ferguson-over-police-deal.html.

"Archives: Obama Wins Nobel Peace Prize." Reuters/*Chicago Tribune.* May 15, 2014. Accessed January 5, 2016. http://articles.chicagotribune.com/2014-05-15/news/chi-archives-obama-wins-nobel-peace-prize-20140515_1_president-obama-nobel-peace-prize-major-foreign-policy-success.

Associated Press. "Number of Uninsured Fell by More Than 11 Million Since Passage of Obamacare, CDC Reports." Associated Press/*Huffington Post.*

March 24, 2015. Accessed January 23, 2016. http://www.huffingtonpost
.com/2015/03/24/obamacare-uninsured-americans_n_6929310.html.

Associated Press. "Obama Ends Stem Cell Research Ban." March 9, 2009. Associated Press/CBS News. Accessed January 27, 2016. http://www.cbsnews.com/ news/obama-ends-stem-cell-research-ban/.

Associated Press. "Obama Signs Sweeping Anti-Smoking Bill." June 22, 2009. Associated Press/NBC News. Accessed January 28, 2016. http://www.nbcnews .com/id/31481823/ns/politics-white_house/t/obama-signs-sweeping-anti -smoking-bill/#.VqqQIcywVHA.

Associated Press. "U.S. May Send More Troops to Train Iraqi Forces." Associated Press. June 10, 2015. Accessed January 3, 2016. http://www.cbc.ca/ news/u-s-may-send-more-troops-to-train-iraqi-forces-1.3107257.

Ayed, Nahlah. "ISIS Poses Bigger Threat after Nearly a Year of Coalition Bombing." CBC News. May 26, 2015. Accessed January 3, 2016. http://www.cbc.ca/ news/u-s-may-send-more-troops-to-train-iraqi-forces-1.3107257.

Bafford, Rebecca Baker. "The Story of Amazing Grace." Hymns, *Music is Worship*. Accessed December 3, 2015. http://rebeccabakerbafford.com/tag/hymns/.

Baker, Arynr. "Obama Defends Gay Rights on Kenya Trip." *Time*. July 26, 2015. Accessed December 11, 2015. http://time.com/3972445/obama-kenyatta -gay-rights/.

Baker, Barbara A. "Lilly Ledbetter." *Encyclopedia of Alabama*. August 16, 2011. Last updated May 13, 2014. Accessed November 30, 2015. http://www .encyclopediaofalabama.org/article/h-3130.

Baker, Peter. "Obama, in Oklahoma, Takes Reform Message to the Prison Cell Block." *New York Times*. July 16, 2015. Accessed December 21, 2015. http:// www.nytimes.com/2015/07/17/us/obama-el-reno-oklahoma-prison.html.

Baker, Peter. "U.S. to Restore Full Relations With Cuba. Erasing a Last Trace of Cold War Hostility." *New York Times*. December 17, 2014. Accessed January 5, 2016. http://www.nytimes.com/2014/12/18/world/americas/us-cuba-relations .html.

Baker, Peter, and Helene Cooper. "Clinton Is Said to Accept Offer of Secretary of State Position." *New York Times*. November 22, 2008. Accessed December 1, 2015. http://www.nytimes.com/2008/11/22/us/politics/22obama.html?pagewanted=all.

Baker, Peter, and David M. Herszenhorn. "Obama Signs Overhaul of Student Loan Program." *New York Times*. March 30, 2010. Accessed January 14, 2016. http://www.nytimes.com/2010/03/31/us/politics/31obama.html.

Baker, Sam. "Supreme Court Rejects Challenge to Tobacco Warnings." *Hill*. April 22, 2013. Accessed January 28, 2016. http://thehill.com/policy/ healthcare/295255-supreme-court-rejects-challenge-to-tobacco-warnings.

Barnes, Robert, and Michael A. Fletcher. "Sotomayor Embodies Obama's Criteria for the Court." *Washington Post*. May 26, 2009. Accessed November 30, 2015. http://www.washingtonpost.com/wp-dyn/content/article/2009/05/26/ AR2009052600889.html.

Barrett, Ted, Manu Raju Deirdre Walsh, and Tom LoBianco. "Senate Democrats Protect Obama on Iran Vote." CNN. September 10, 2015. Accessed January 6, 2016. http://www.cnn.com/2015/09/10/politics/iran-nuclear-deal-vote-congress/.

BBC News. "Saddam Hussein Executed in Iraq." BBC News. December 30, 2006. Accessed January 3, 2016. http://news.bbc.co.uk/2/hi/middle_east/6218485.stm.

Becker, Nora V., and Daniel Polsky. "Women Saw Large Decrease in Out-of-Pocket Spending for Contraceptives after ACA Mandate Removed Cost Sharing." *Health Affairs* 34, no. 7 (July 2015): 1204–11. Accessed December 2, 2015. http://content.healthaffairs.org/content/34/7/1204.abstract.

Belkin, Aaron, Morton Ender, Nathaniel Frank, Stacie Furia, George R. Lucas, Gary Packard Jr., Tammy S. Schultz, Steven M. Samuels, and David R. Segal. *One Year Out: An Assessment of DADT Repeal's Impact on Military Readiness.* Los Angeles: Palm Center, University of California, Los Angeles, September 20, 2012. Accessed December 10, 2015. http://www.palmcenter.org/files/One%20Year%20Out_0.pdf.

"Black Student College Graduation Rates Remain Low, but Modest Progress Begins to Show." *Journal of Blacks in Higher Education.* No. 50 (Winter 2005–6). Accessed February 3, 2016. http://www.jbhe.com/features/50_blackstudent_gradrates.html.

Blow, Charles M. "A Mother's Grace and Grieving." *New York Times.* March 25, 2012. Accessed December 9, 2015. http://www.nytimes.com/2012/03/26/opinion/blow-a-mothers-grace-and-grieving.html.

Boyer, Dave. "Obama Vetoes NLRB Legislation." *Washington Times.* March 31, 2015. Accessed December 26, 2015. http://www.washingtontimes.com/news/2015/mar/31/obama-veto-nlrb-legislation/.

Brake, Deborah L., and Joanna L. Grossman. "Title VII's Protection against Pay Discrimination: The Impact of *Ledbetter v. Goodyear Tire & Rubber Co.*" *Regional Labor Review.* Fall 2007. Accessed November 30, 2015. http://www.hofstra.edu/pdf/academics/colleges/hclas/cld/cld_rlr_fall07_title7_grossman.pdf.

Burns, Robert. "1 US Soldier Killed, 2 Wounded in Fighting in Afghanistan." Associated Press. January 5, 2016. Accessed January 5, 2016 http://www.msn.com/en-us/news/world/1-us-soldier-killed-2-wounded-in-fighting-in-afghanistan/ar-BBo9qdi?ocid=ansmsnnews11.

Byers, Alex, and Brooks Boliek. "Obama Endorses Tough Net Neutrality Rules." *Politico.* November 10, 2014. Accessed February 1, 2016. http://www.politico.com/story/2014/11/obama-net-neutrality-rules-112741.

Capehart, Jonathan. "How Cornel West Hurts Bernie Sanders." *Washington Post,* January 22, 2016. Accessed February 21, 2016. https://www.washingtonpost.com/blogs/post-partisan/wp/2016/01/22/how-cornel-west-hurts-bernie-sanders/.

Carroll, Lauren. "Federal Prison Population Drops for First Time in 3 Decades, Eric Holder Says." *PolitiFact.* February 23, 2015. Accessed December 21, 2015. http://www.politifact.com/truth-o-meter/statements/2015/feb/23/eric-holder/federal-prison-population-drops-first-time-3-decad/.

CBS News. "President Obama Wins Nobel Peace Prize." CBS News. October 9, 2009. Accessed January 5, 2016. http://www.cbsnews.com/news/president-obama-wins-nobel-peace-prize/.

Center for Migration Studies. "Center for Migration Studies Reports Decline of the US Undocumented Population." Center for Migration Studies. January 20, 2016. Accessed January 22, 2016. http://cmsny.org/press-release-undocumented-decline/.

Chappell, Bill. "In Live Address, Obama Takes His Plan for Gun Control to the Public." January 5, 2016. Accessed January 26, 2016. http://www.npr.org/sections/thetwo-way/2016/01/05/462020685/obama-seeks-commonsense-gun-control-through-executive-actions.

Charbonneau, Louis. "U.N. Chief Ban Hails Bin Laden Death as 'Watershed.'" Reuters. May 2, 2011. Accessed January 1, 2016. http://www.reuters.com/article/us-binladen-un-idUSTRE7414W720110502.

Chow, Denise. "President Obama to Announce Climate Change Plan Today." LiveScience.com/Yahoo.com. June 25. 2013. Accessed January 28, 2016. http://news.yahoo.com/president-obama-announce-climate-change-plan-today-120624144.html.

CNN. "Obama: Police Who Arrested Professor Acted Stupidly." July 23, 2009. Accessed December 10, 2015. http://www.cnn.com/2009/US/07/22/harvard.gates.interview/.

CNN. "Obama Chooses Kagan for Supreme Court." CNN. May 10, 2010. Accessed November 30, 2015. http://www.cnn.com/2010/POLITICS/05/10/scotus.kagan/.

CNN. "Obama, Russian President Sign Arms Treaty." CNN. April 8, 2010. Accessed January 5, 2016. http://www.cnn.com/2010/POLITICS/04/08/obama.russia.treaty/index.html.

CNN. "Protesters Attack U.S. Diplomatic Compounds in Egypt, Libya." CNN. September 12, 2012. Accessed March 30, 2016. http://www.cnn.com/2012/09/11/world/meast/egypt-us-embassy-protests/index.html.

CNN. "Sotomayor's 'Wise Latina' Comment a Staple of Her Speeches." CNN. June 8, 2009. Accessed November 30, 2015. http://www.cnn.com/2009/POLITICS/06/05/sotomayor.speeches/.

Cobert, Beth, Steve Vanroekel, and Todd Park. "Delivering a Customer-Focused Government through Smarter IT." White House. August 11, 2014. Accessed February 2, 2016. https://www.whitehouse.gov/blog/2014/08/11/delivering-customer-focused-government-through-smarter-it.

Cohen, Robin A., and Michael E. Martinez. *Health Insurance Coverage: Early Release of Estimates From the National Health Interview Survey, January–March 2015.* U.S. Department of Health and Human Services. Centers for Disease

Control. National Center for Health Statistics. August 2015. Accessed January 23, 2016. http://www.cdc.gov/nchs/data/nhis/earlyrelease/insur201508.pdf.

Cohn, Jonathan. "Obama Tweaks the Birth Control Mandate—and the Right Is Still Angry." *New Republic.* August 22, 2014. Accessed February 4, 2016. https://newrepublic.com/article/119183/hhs-adapts-obamacare-birth-control-rule-hobby-lobby-wheaton.

Congressional Budget Office. *Estimated Impact of the American Recovery and Reinvestment Act on Employment and Economic Output from October 2011 through December 2011.* Washington, D.C.: Congressional Budget Office, February 2012. Accessed December 27, 2015. http://www.cbo.gov/sites/default/files/cbofiles/attachments/02-22-ARRA.pdf.

Congressional Budget Office. "S. 2432. Bank on Students Emergency Loan Refinancing Act: Cost Estimate." Letter to the Honorable Elizabeth Warren. Congressional Budget Office. June 6, 2014. Accessed January 15, 2016. https://www.cbo.gov/publication/45433.

Contorno, Steve. "Barack Obama Says United States Only Developed Country without Paid Maternity Leave." *PolitiFact.* January 21, 2015. Accessed January 11, 2016. http //www.politifact.com/truth-o-meter/statements/2015/jan/21/barack-obama/barack-obama-says-united-states-only-developed-cou/.

Cooper, Helene. "Obama Signs Overhaul of Financial System." *New York Times.* July 21, 2010. Accessed December 28, 2015. http://www.nytimes.com/2010/07/22/business/22regulate.html?_r=0.

Cooper, Helene, Mark Landler, and Alissa J. Rubinaug. "Obama Allows Limited Airstrikes on ISIS." *New York Times.* August 7, 2014. Accessed January 1, 2016. http://www.nytimes.com/2014/08/08/world/middleeast/obama-weighs-military-strikes-to-aid-trapped-iraqis-officials-say.html#addendums.

Corasaniti, Nick, Richard Pérez-Peña, and Lizette Alvarez. "Church Massacre Suspect Held as Charleston Grieves." *New York Times.* June 18, 2015. Accessed December 7, 2015. http://www.nytimes.com/2015/06/19/us/charleston-church-shooting.html.

"Crenshaw Moves to Rename ABLE Act in Honor of Stephen Beck, Jr., Long-Time Champion of the Disabled." U.S. Representative Ander Crenshaw press release. December 10, 2014. Accessed December 15, 2015. http://crenshaw.house.gov/index.cfm/pressreleases?ID=8455E842-ECF6-4C0E-80AB-CE6C46BED81C.

Curry, George E. "White House Aide: Obama Hasn't Abandoned Blacks." Afro.com. Feb 16, 2013. Accessed December 7, 2015. http://www.afro.com/sections/news/national/story.htm/?storyid=77521#sthash.c3L4oQgI.dpuf.

DailyNewsBin.com. "Treasury Department Confirms President Obama Has Fully Turned Around the U.S. Economy." December 27, 2015. Accessed December 28, 2015. http://www.dailynewsbin.com/news/treasury-department-confirms-president-obama-has-fully-turned-around-the-u-s-economy/23369/.

Davenport, Coral. "In Climate Move, Obama Halts New Coal Mining Leases on Public Lands." January 14, 2016. Accessed February 6, 2016. http://www

.nytimes.com/2016/01/15/us/politics/in-climate-move-obama-to-halt-new
-coal-mining-leases-on-public-lands.html?_r=.

Davis, Julie Hirschfeld. "A Digital Team Is Helping Obama Find His Voice Online." *New York Times.* November 8, 2015. Accessed February 1, 2016. http://www.nytimes.com/2015/11/09/us/politics/a-digital-team-is-helping -obama-find-his-voice-online.html.

Davis, Julie Hirschfeld. "In Wielding Rarely Used Veto President Obama Puts Budget Heat on Republicans." *New York Times.* October 22, 2015. Accessed January 4, 2016. http://www.nytimes.com/2015/10/23/us/politics/obama-vetoes -defense-bill-deepening-budget-fight-with-gop.html?smtyp=cur&_r=0.

Davis, Julie Hirschfeld. "Obama Plans to Push Paid Family and Sick Leave for Workers." *New York Times.* January 14, 2015. Accessed January 11, 2016. http://www.nytimes.com/2015/01/15/us/politics/obama-plans-to-push-bill-for -providing-paid-leave-to-workers-.html?_r=0.

DeBonis, Mike. "Obama Vetoes Republican Repeal of Health Care Law." *Washington Post.* January 8, 2016. Accessed January 19, 2016. https:// www.washingtonpost.com/news/powerpost/wp/2016/01/08/obama -vetoes-republican-repeal-of-health-care-law/.

Devaney, Tim. "Obama Making Bid to Diversify Wealthy Neighbor-hoods." *Hill.* June 11, 2015. Accessed January 16, 2016. http://thehill.com/ regulation/244620-obamas-bid-to-diversify-wealthy-neighborhoods.

Diament, Michelle. "Obama: ADA 'Fight Is Not Over." *Disability Scoop.* July 21, 2015. Accessed December 16, 2015. https://www.disabilityscoop .com/2015/07/21/obama-ada-fight-is-not-over/20450/.

Diamond, Jeremy. "Bill Clinton Concedes Role in Mass Incarceration." CNN. May 7, 2015. Accessed December 21, 2015. http://www.cnn.com/2015/05/06/ politics/bill-clinton-crime-prisons-hillary-clinton/.

Dillon, Sam, and Tamar Lewin. "Pell Grants Said to Face a Shortfall of $6 Bil-lion." *New York Times.* September 17, 2008. Accessed March 29, 2016. http:// www.nytimes.com/2008/09/18/education/18grant.html?_r=0.

Dovere, Edward-Isaac, and Marianne LeVine. "Obama Overtime Rule Could Raise Wages for 5 Million." *Politico.* June 29, 2015. Accessed January 11, 2016. http:// www.politico.com/story/2015/06/obama-overtime-rule-wage-raise-119566.

"Down Syndrome Advocate Dies amid ABLE Act Action: Stephen Beck Jr. Was a National and Regional Leader." *Record Herald.* December 10, 2015. Accessed December 14, 2015. http://www.therecordherald.com/article/20141210/news/ 141219981.

"A Dozen UN Agencies Issue Unprecedented Call for LGBT Rights." *LGBTQ Nation.* September 29, 2015. Accessed December 1, 2015. http://www.lgbtqnation .com/2015/09/a-dozen-un-agencies-issue-unprecedented-call-for-lgbt-rights/.

Drum, Kevin. "Obama's Economic Performance Is Even Better Than It Looks." *Mother Jones.* December 28, 2015. Accessed December 31, 2015. http://www .motherjones.com/kevin-drum/2015/12/obamas-economic-performance -even-better-it-looks.

Duncan, Arne. "Obama's Goal for Higher Education." *Forbes*. Accessed November 23, 2015. http://www.forbes.com/2010/08/01/america-education-reform-opinions-best-colleges-10-duncan.html.

Editorial Board. "Mr. Obama's Trickle of Mercy." *New York Times*. December 31, 2015. Accessed January 10, 2016. http://www.nytimes.com/2015/12/31/opinion/mr-obamas-trickle-of-mercy.html?_r=0.

Egan, Timothy. "Obama Can Still Earn His Nobel." *New York Times*, September 25, 2014. Accessed January 5, 2016. http://www.nytimes.com/2014/09/26/opinion/obama-can-still-earn-his-nobel.html.

Eilperin, Juliet. "Obama Vows to Defend Abortion Rights." *Washington Post*. April 26, 2013. Accessed December 1, 2015. https://www.washingtonpost.com/politics/obama-vows-to-defend-abortion-rights/2013/04/26/c5cae81e-ae80-11e2-8bf6-e70cb6ae066e_story.html.

Eilperin, Juliet, and Steven Mufson. "EPA Proposes Cutting Carbon Dioxide Emissions from Coal Plants 30% by 2030." *Washington Post*. June 2, 2014. Accessed March 29, 2016. https://www.washingtonpost.com/national/health-science/epa-to-propose-cutting-carbon-dioxide-emissions-from-coal-plants-30percent-by-2030/2014/06/01/f5055d94-e9a8-11e3-9f5c-9075d5508f0a_story.html.

Erdbrink, Thomas, and Rick Gladstone. "Iran Frees Americans, Including Jason Rezaian, in Prisoner Swap." *New York Times*. January 16, 2016. Accessed January 19, 2016. http://www.nytimes.com/2016/01/17/world/middleeast/iran-releases-washington-post-reporter-jason-rezaian.html?_r=0.

Executive Order 13548 of July 26, 2010. "Increasing Federal Employment of Individuals with Disabilities." *Federal Register* 75, no. 146 (July 30, 2010). Presidential Documents, 45039. Accessed December 15, 2015. https://www.gpo.gov/fdsys/pkg/FR-2010-07-30/pdf/2010-18988.pdf.

Farias, Cristian. "Supreme Court Trashes Latest Legal Attack on Obamacare: The Justices Already Ruled the Law Constitutional. They're Done for Now." *Huffington Post*. January 19, 2016. Accessed January 27, 2016. http://www.huffingtonpost.com/entry/supreme-court-obamacare_us_569e765ce4b0cd99679b7e00.

Farias, Cristian, and Elise Foley. "Supreme Court Will Rule On Obama's Immigration Policy before 2016 Election." *Huffington Post*. January 19, 2016. Accessed February 14, 2016. http://www.huffingtonpost.com/entry/supreme-court-immigration-obama-executive-.

Farley, Robert. "Stimulus Includes Tax Credit for Plug-in Hybrids." *PolitiFact*. March 23, 2009. Accessed January 30, 2016. http://www.politifact.com/truth-o-meter/promises/obameter/promise/459/enact-tax-credit-for-consumers-for-hybrid-cars/.

Federal Bureau of Investigation. U.S. Attorney's Office. Northern District of Illinois. "United States Attorney's Office Provides Update on Investigation into the Shooting Death of Laquan McDonald." Federal Bureau of Investigation. November 24, 2015. Accessed December 8, 2015. https://www.fbi.gov/chicago/press-releases/2015/united-states-attorneys-office-provides-update-on-investigation-into-the-shooting-death-of-laquan-mcdonald.

Federal Communications Commission. "FCC Adopts Strong, Sustainable Rules to Protect the Open Internet." January 26, 2015. Accessed February 1, 2016. https://www.fcc.gov/document/fcc-adopts-strong-sustainable-rules-protect -open-internet.

Feller, Ben. "Beer Summit Begins: Obama Sits Down with Crowley, Gates." Associated Press/*Huffington Post*. August 30, 2009. Accessed December 10, 2015. http://www.huffingtonpost.com/2009/07/30/beer-summit-begins-obama -_n_248254.html.

FOX Business News. Maria Bartiromo interview with U.S. Treasury Secretary Jack Lew. Video. FOX Business News. December 24, 2015. Accessed December 24, 2015. http://www.foxbusiness.com/economy-policy/2015/12/24/jack-lew-us -ending-year-well-positioned/?intcmp=bigtopmarketfeatures.

Furman, Jason. "The Employment Situation in August." White House blogs. September 4, 2015. Accessed December 27, 2015. https://www.whitehouse .gov/blog/2015/09/04/employment-situation-august.

Garunay, Melanie. "President Obama Has Shortened the Sentences of More People Than the Last 5 Presidents Combined." White House blogs. December 18, 2015. Accessed January 9, 2016. https://www.whitehouse.gov/blog/2015/12/18/president -obama-has-shortened-sentences-more-people-last-5-presidents-combined.

Geidner, Chris. "Two Years after His Husband's Death, Jim Obergefell Is Still Fighting for the Right to Be Married." *BuzzFeed*. March 22, 2015. Accessed December 12, 2015. http://www.buzzfeed.com/chrisgeidner/his-husband-died -in-2013-but-jim-obergefell-is-still-fighting#.tpqV66AzDe.

Gerstein, Josh. "Obama Drug Clemency Guidelines Issued." *Politico*. April 23, 2014. Accessed January 8, 2016. http://www.politico.com/blogs/under-the -radar/2014/04/obama-drug-clemency-guidelines-issued-187266.

Gillespie, Patrick. "Black Unemployment Falls to Lowest Since 2007." Money. CNN. January 8, 2016. Accessed February 7, 2016. http://money.cnn .com/2016/01/08/news/economy/black-unemployment-falls-hits-8-year-low/ index.html.

"Global Views of United States Improve While Other Countries Decline." WorldPublicOpinion.org. April 18, 2010. Accessed February 4, 2016. http:// www.worldpublicopinion.org/pipa/articles/views_on_countriesregions _bt/660.php.

Goodman, Peter S. "U.S. Unemployment Rate Hits 10.2%. Highest in 26 Years." *New York Times*. November 6, 2009. Accessed December 31, 2015. http:// www.nytimes.com/2009/11/07/business/economy/07jobs.html.

Gordon, Michael R., and David E. Sanger. "Deal Reached on Iran Nuclear Program; Limits on Fuel Would Lessen with Time." *New York Times*. July 14, 2015. Accessed January 6, 2016. http://www.nytimes.com/2015/07/15/world/ middleeast/iran-nuclear-deal-is-reached-after-long-negotiations.html.

Govtrack.us. H.R. 1256 (111th): Family Smoking Prevention and Tobacco Control Act. Accessed January 28, 2016. https://www.govtrack.us/congress/ bills/111/hr1256.

Granville, Kevin. "The Trans-Pacific Partnership Trade Accord Explained." *New York Times*. October 5, 2015. Accessed January 6, 2016. http://www.nytimes.com/2015/10/06/business/international/the-trans-pacific-partnership-trade-deal-explained.html?_r=0.

Grasgreen, Allie. "Obama Poised to Give Financial Aid to Federal, State Prisoners." *Politico*. July 27, 2016. Accessed January 19, 2016. http://www.politico.com/story/2015/07/barack-obama-financial-aid-college-federal-state-prisoners-pell-grant-120680#ixzz3xjaPB584.

Greenberg, Jon. "Did President Obama Save the Auto Industry?" *PolitiFact*. September 6, 2012. Accessed December 28, 2015. http://www.politifact.com/truth-o-meter/article/2012/sep/06/did-obama-save-us-automobile-industry/.

Grindler, Gary G. "Memorandum for All Federal Prosecutors: The Fair Sentencing Act of 2010." U.S. Department of Justice. Office of the Deputy Attorney General. Washington, D.C. August 5, 2010. Accessed January 9, 2016. http://www.justice.gov/sites/default/files/oip/legacy/2014/07/23/fair-sentencing-act-memo.pdf.

Grunwald, Michael. "The Nation He Built: A Politico Review of Barack Obama's Domestic Policy Legacy—and the Changes He Made While Nobody Was Paying Attention." *Politico*. Vol. 3. No. 2. January 6, 2016. http://www.politico.com/magazine/story/2016/01/obama-biggest-achievements-213487.

Guinness World Records. "First President with Regular Email Access." Guinness World Records. Accessed February 1, 2016. http://www.guinnessworldrecords.com/world-records/first-president-with-regular-email-access/.

Guskin, Emily, Mahvish Shahid Khan, and Amy Mitchell. "The Arrest of Henry Louis Gates, Jr." Journalism and Media. Pew Research Center. July 26, 2010. Accessed December 7, 2015. http://www.journalism.org/2010/07/26/arrest-henry-louis-gates-jr/?utm_expid=53098246-2.Lly4CFSVQG2lphsg-KopIg.0&utm_referrer=http%3A%2F%2Fsearch.aol.com%2Faol%2Fsearch%3Fenabled_terms%3D%26s_it%3Dclient97_searchbox%26q%3DObama%2BLouis%2BGates.

Hananel, Sam. "Obama's Gay Appointees Smash Record." Associated Press/*Huffington Post*. October 26, 2010. Accessed December 11, 2015. http://www.huffingtonpost.com/2010/10/26/obamas-gay-appointees-sma_n_773898.html.

Harry S. Truman Library and Museum. "This Day in Truman History. November 19, 1945. President Truman's Proposed Health Program." Harry S. Truman Library and Museum. Undated. Accessed February 9, 2016. http://www.trumanlibrary.org/anniversaries/healthprogram.htm.

Hattem, Julian. "Pope Praises Iran Deal before UN." *Hill*. September 25, 2015. Accessed January 6, 2016. http://thehill.com/policy/national-security/254934-pope-praises-iran-deal-before-un.

Heasley, Shaun. "Obama Budget Calls for Boost to Disability Programs." *Disability Scoop*. February 3, 2015. Accessed December 15, 2015. https://www.disabilityscoop.com/2015/02/03/obama-budget-disability/20023/.

Henry J. Kaiser Family Foundation. "Assessing the Effects of the Economy on the Recent Slowdown in Health Spending." Henry J. Kaiser Family Foundation. April 22, 2013. Accessed January 24, 2016. http://kff.org/health-costs/issue-brief/assessing-the-effects-of-the-economy-on-the-recent-slowdown-in-health-spending-2/.

Hicklin, Aaron. "Out100: President Barack Obama. Ally of the Year." *Out.* November 24, 2015. Accessed December 10, 2015. http://www.out.com/out100-2015/2015/11/10/out100-president-barack-obama-ally-year.

Hill, Glynn a. "New Rule Aims to Diversify Neighborhoods. Federal Agency Seeks to Reduce Segregation in Housing Patterns across US." Associated Press. July 8, 2015. Accessed January 17, 2016. http://finance.yahoo.com/news/rule-aims-diversify-neighborhoods-231851933.html.

Hjelmgaard, Kim. "Obama Urges Climate Deal as U.N. Summit Opens in Tense Paris." *USA Today.* November 30, 2015. Accessed January 30, 2016. http://www.usatoday.com/story/news/world/2015/11/30/climate-talks-kick-off-france/76551062/.

Holmes, Kristen. "Obama Appoints First Transgender White House Staff Member." CNN. August 19, 2015. Accessed December 11, 2015. http://www.cnn.com/2015/08/18/politics/transgender-white-house-obama-first-staff/.

Hopkins, Cheyenne, and Joshua Zumbrun. "Yellen to Be Named Fed Chairman, First Female Chief." *Bloomberg News.* October 9, 2013. Accessed February 2, 2016. http://www.bloomberg.com/news/articles/2013-10-08/yellen-to-be-named-fed-chairman-as-obama-taps-first-female-chief.

Horwitz, Sari, Ellen Nakashima, and Wesley Lowery. "Justice Department Will Investigate Practices of Chicago Police." *Washington Post.* December 6, 2015. Accessed December 8, 2015. https://www.washingtonpost.com/news/post-nation/wp/2015/12/06/justice-department-will-launch-investigation-into-practices-of-chicago-police/.

Howard, Alexander. "White House Wants to Close Homework Gap." *Huffington Post.* July 16, 2015. Accessed February 1, 2016. http://www.huffingtonpost.com/entry/connect-home-program_us_55a7b846e4b0896514d066b6.

H.R. 36—Pain-Capable Unborn Child Protection Act, 114th Congress (2015–2016). Accessed December 2, 2015. https://www.congress.gov/bill/114th-congress/house-bill/36.

Huckabee, Charles. "Obama Calls for Pell Grant Changes to Accelerate Progress toward Degrees." January 19, 2016. Accessed January 19, 2016. http://chronicle.com/blogs/ticker/obama-calls-for-pell-grant-changes-to-accelerate-progress-toward-degrees/107943.

Hudson, David. "Invest in US: President Obama Convenes the White House Summit on Early Education." White House blogs. December 10, 2014. Accessed January 13, 2016. https://www.whitehouse.gov/blog/2014/12/10/invest-us-president-obama-convenes-white-house-summit-early-education.

Hurley, Lawrence. "States Ask U.S. Top Court to Block Obama Carbon Emissions Plan." Reuters. January 26, 2016. Accessed January 28, 2016. http://news

.yahoo.com/states-ask-u-top-court-block-obama-carbon-220655438—finance
.html.

Jackson, David. "Obama Promotes 'My Brother's Keeper' Program." *USA Today.*
May 4, 2015. Accessed December 7, 2015. http://www.usatoday.com/story/
news/nation/2015/05/04/obama-baltimore-new-york-city-my-brothers-keeper
-alliance/26869779/.

Jackson, David. "Obama's Day: Student Loans." Oval. *USA Today.* June 9,
2014. Accessed January 14, 2016. http://www.usatoday.com/story/theoval/
2014/06/09/obama-student-loans/10220809/.

Jaffe, Greg. "The War in Afghanistan Follows Obama to His Vacation in Hawaii."
Washington Post. December 21, 2015. Accessed January 4, 2016. https://www
.washingtonpost.com/politics/the-war-in-afghanistan-follows-obama-to-his
-vacation-in-hawaii/2015/12/21/54a80e9c-a814-11e5-9b92-dea7cd4b1a4d
_story.html.

Jagoda, Naomi. "Treasury Head: US Economy Better Now Than When Obama
Took Office." *Hill.* December 24, 2015. Accessed December 28, 2015. http://
thehill.com/policy/finance/264205-treasury-head-us-economy-better-now
-than-when-obama-took-office.

Jamieson, Dave. "Obama Says Workers Are Being 'Cheated' Out Of Overtime
Pay." *Huffington Post.* March 21, 2015. Accessed January 11, 2016. http://www
.huffingtonpost.com/2015/03/21/obama-overtime-pay_n_6911808.html.

Joachim, David S. "Obama Signs New Job-Training Law." *New York Times.* July
22, 2014. Accessed January 11, 2016. http://www.nytimes com/2014/07/23/us/
obama-signs-new-job-training-law.html.

Jones, Sarah. "Obama's Winning Streak Continues: Strongest Three Years of Job
Creation since 2000." *Politicus usa.* November 6, 2015. Accessed February 6,
2016. http://www.bls.gov/news.release/empsit.nr0.html.

Karlgaard, Rich. "Does the Bradley Effect Overrate Obama in the Polls?" *Forbes.*
September 16, 2012. Accessed March 30, 2016. http://www.forbes.com/sites/
richkarlgaard/2012/09/16/does-the-bradley-effect-overrate-obama-in-the
-polls/#289cf9d60736.

Kerr, Jennifer C. "Obama Announces $1 Billion Investment for Early Child-
hood Education." Associated Press. December 10, 2014. Accessed January 13,
2016.   http://www.pbs.org/newshour/rundown/obama-announcing-1-billion
-investment-early-childhood-education/.

Kerr, Jennifer C. "Obama Signs the Every Student Succeeds Act; Law Overhauls
'No Child.'" Associated Press. December 10, 2015. Accessed January 14, 2016.
http://www.wschronicle.com/2016/01/obama-signs-every-student-succeeds
-act-law-overhauls-no-child/.

Kessler, Glenn. "Lilly Ledbetter, Barack Obama, and the Famous 'Anonymous
Note.'" Fact Checker. *Washington Post.* Accessed November 30, 2015. https://
www.washingtonpost.com/news/fact-checker/wp/2015/05/14/lilly-ledbetter
-barack-obama-and-the-famous-anonymous-note/.

Klapper, Ethan. "On This Day in 1993, Bill Clinton Announced 'Don't Ask,

Don't Tell.'" *Huffington Post.* July 19, 2013. Accessed December 10, 2015. http://www.huffingtonpost.com/2013/07/19/bill-clinton-dont-ask-dont -tell_n_3623245.html.

Korte, Gregory. "'The Clock Is Running' on Obama Clemency Initiative." *USA Today.* June 24, 2015. Accessed January 7, 2016. http://www.usatoday.com/story/ news/politics/2015/06/24/clemency-initiative-clock-is-running/29128091/.

Korte, Gregory. "Obama Announces Gun Actions in Emotional Plea for Congressional Action." *USA Today.* January 5, 2016. Accessed January 26, 2016. http://www.usatoday.com/story/news/politics/2016/01/05/obama-announces -gun-actions/78302832/.

Korte, Gregory. "Obama Bans Some Military Equipment Sales to Police." *USA Today.* May 18, 2015. Accessed December 8, 2015. http://www.usatoday.com/ story/news/politics/2015/05/18/obama-police-military-equipment-sales-new -jersey/27521793/.

Korte, Gregory. "Obama Signs Bill to Overhaul Job Training Programs." *USA Today.* July 22, 2014. Accessed January 11, 2015. http://www.usatoday.com/ story/news/politics/2014/07/22/obama-job-training-bill/12987339/.

Korte, Gregory. "Obama to Propose Paid Sick Leave for American Workers." *USA Today.* January 15, 2015. Accessed January 11, 2016. http://www.usatoday .com/story/news/politics/2015/01/14/obama-child-care-paid-leave/21768969/.

Korte, Gregory. "Through Executive Orders, Obama Tests Power as Purchaser-in-Chief." *USA Today.* October 11, 2015. Accessed December 23, 2015. http://www.usatoday.com/story/news/politics/2015/10/11/obama-executive -orders-federal-contractors/22466397/obama-executive-orders.

Korte, Gregory. "U.S. Pardon Attorney to Resign Amid Obama's Last-Year Clemency Push." *USA Today.* January 15, 2016. Accessed January 19, 2016. http://www.usatoday.com/story/news/politics/2016/01/15/us-pardon -attorney-deborah-leff-resignation/78877552/#cx_ab_test_id=21&cx_ab _test_variant=cx_advanced_v1&cx_art_pos=1&cx_navSource=arttop&cx _tag=collabctx&cx_rec_type=collabctx&cx_ctrl_comp_grp=false&cxrecs_s.

Krugman, Paul. "In Defense of Obama: The Nobel Prize–Winning Economist, Once One of the President's Most Notable Critics, on Why Obama Is a Historic Success." *Rolling Stone.* October 8, 2014. Accessed December 30, 2015. http://www.rollingstone.com/politics/news/in-defense-of-obama -20141008#ixzz3vrKs5bbB.

Krugman, Paul. "Obama: The Job-Killer." Conscience of a Liberal blog. *New York Times.* December 27, 2015. Accessed March 20, 2016. http://krugman .blogs.nytimes.com/2015/12/27/obama-the-job-killer/.

Lafraniere, Sharon, Sarah Cohen, and Richard A. Oppel Jr. "How Often Do Mass Shootings Occur? On Average, Every Day, Records Show." *New York Times.* December 2, 2015. Accessed January 26, 2016. http://www.nytimes .com/2015/12/03/us/how-often-do-mass-shootings-occur-on-average-every -day-records-show.html.

Laing, Keith, and Jordain Carney. "Senate Sends $305B Highway Bill to Obama." *Hill*. December 3, 2015. Accessed January 20, 2016. http://thehill.com/policy/finance/262049-senate-sends-highway-bill-to-obama.

Lamothe, Dan. "These Marines Took Down the U.S. Flag in Cuba in 1961. Today, They Watched It Rise Again." *Washington Post*. August 14, 2015. Accessed January 6, 2016. https://www.washingtonpost.com/news/checkpoint/wp/2015/08/14/these-marines-took-down-the-u-s-flag-in-cuba-in-1961-today -theyll-raise-it-again/.

Larson, Todd. "President Obama and the Global Fight for LGBT Rights." *Huffington Post*. November 5, 2012. Accessed December 11, 2015. http://www .huffingtonpost.com/todd-larson/president-obama-and-the-global-fight-for -lgbt-rights_b_2060883.html.

Lavender, Paige. "You Absolutely Have to Watch and Read Obama's Full Eulogy for Rev. Clementa Pinckney." *Huffington Post*. June 26, 2015. Accessed December 3, 2015. http://www.huffingtonpost.com/2015/06/26/obama-eulogy-full -text_n_7674406.html.

Ledbetter v. Goodyear Tire & Rubber Co. Dissent, 550 U.S. 1 (2007). Accessed November 30, 2015. http://www.supremecourt.gov/opinions/06pdf/05 -1074.pdf.

Lee, Jesse. "Protecting Homeowners, Protecting the Economy." White House blogs. May 20, 2009. Accessed January 19, 2016. https://www.whitehouse.gov/ blog/2009/05/20/protecting-homeowners-protecting-economy.

Lee, Michelle Ye Hee. "Does the United States Really Have 5 Percent of the World's Population and One Quarter of the World's Prisoners?" Fact Checker. *Washington Post*. April 30, 2015. Accessed December 21, 2015. https://www .washingtonpost.com/news/fact-checker/wp/2015/04/30/does-the-united -states-really-have-five-percent-of-worlds-population-and-one-quarter-of-the -worlds-prisoners/.

Leonard, Kimberly. "How Obamacare Changes Senior Care: Provisions in the Affordable Care Act Affect Elder Benefits And Cost." *U.S. News and World Report*. February 26, 2014. Accessed December 16, 2015. http:// health.usnews.com/health-news/best-nursing-homes/articles/2014/02/26/ how-obamacare-changes-senior-care.

Levine, Steve. "Chicago Police Really Didn't Want to Release Video of a Cop Shooting Laquan McDonald 16 Times." *Huffington Post*. November 25, 2015. Accessed December 8, 2015. http://www.huffingtonpost.com/ entry/chicago-laquan-mcdonald-video_565603e0e4b079b2818a06f6.

Library of Congress. THOMAS. Bill Summary and Status, 111th Congress (2009-2010). H.R. 4173. Library of Congress. July 21, 2010. Accessed December 28, 2015. http://thomas.loc.gov/cgi-bin/bdquery/z?d111:HR04173:@@@ L&summ2=m&#major%20actions.

Limitone, Julia. "Jack Lew: U.S. Ending the Year Well Positioned." FOX Business News. December 24, 2015. Accessed December 24, 2015. http://www

.foxbusiness.com/economy-policy/2015/12/24/jack-lew-us-ending-year-well-positioned/?intcmp=bigtopmarketfeatures.

Liptak, Adam. "Supreme Court Allows Nationwide Health Care Subsidies." *New York Times.* June 25, 2015. Accessed March 29, 2016. http://www.nytimes.com/2015/06/26/us/obamacare-supreme-court.html.

Liptak, Adam. "Supreme Court Upholds Health Care Law, 5-4, in Victory for Obama." *New York Times.* June 28, 2012. Accessed March 29, 2015. http://www.nytimes.com/2012/06/29/us/supreme-court-lets-health-law-largely-stand.html

Liptak, Adam, and Coral Davenport. "Supreme Court Deals Blow to Obama's Efforts to Regulate Coal Emissions." *New York Times.* February 9, 2016. Accessed February 21, 2016. http://www.nytimes.com/2016/02/10/us/politics/supreme-court-blocks-obama-epa-coal-emissions-regulations.html.

Liptak, Adam, and Michael D. Shearjan. "Supreme Court to Hear Challenge to Obama Immigration Actions." *New York Times.* January 19, 2016. Accessed January 19, 2016. http://www.nytimes.com/2016/01/20/us/politics/supreme-court-to-hear-challenge-to-obama-immigration-actions.html.

Liptak, Kevin. "New Obama Order Requires Contractors to Pay for Sick Leave." CNN. September 8, 2015. Accessed December 22, 2015. http://www.cnn.com/2015/09/07/politics/obama-mandatory-sick-leave/.

Little, Nadra Kareem. "The Real Trayvon Martin: Facts about the Slain Youth's Life." About.com. Accessed December 9, 2015. http://racerelations.about.com/od/thelegalsystem/a/The-Real-Trayvon-Martin-Facts-About-The-Slain-Youths-Life.htm.

LoBianco, Tom. "President Barack Obama Makes Historic Trip to Prison, Pushes Reform." CNN. July 17, 2015. Accessed December 21, 2015. http://www.cnn.com/2015/07/16/politics/obama-oklahoma-federal-prison-visit/.

Londoño, Ernesto. "Pentagon to Extend Certain Benefits to Same Sex Couples." *Washington Post.* February 5, 2013. Accessed December 10, 2015. https://www.washingtonpost.com/world/national-security/2013/02/05/3f68a638-6fc6-11e2-ac36-3d8d9dcaa2e2_story.html?wpisrc=al_national.

Lowe, Frederick H. "Justice Department Launches Investigation into the Chicago Police Department." *North Star News Today.* December 8, 2015. Accessed December 8, 2015. http://www.northstarnewstoday.com/news/justice-department-launches-investigation-into-the-chicago-police-department/.

Marashi, Reza. "The U.S.-Iran Prisoner Swap Is Yet Another Victory for Diplomacy and Human Rights." *Huffington Post.* January 16, 2016. Accessed January 19, 2016. http://www.huffingtonpost.com/reza-marashi/us-iran-prisoner-swap_b_8989970.html.

Marken, Stephanie. "U.S. Uninsured Rate at 11.4% in Second Quarter." Gallup.com. July 10, 2015. Accessed November 24, 2015. http://www.gallup.com/poll/184064/uninsured-rate-second-quarter.aspx.

Markon, Jerry. "Federal Eye: U.S. Illegal Immigrant Population Falls below 11 Million, Continuing Nearly Decade-Long Decline, Report Says." *Washington*

Post. January 20, 2016. Accessed January 22, 2016. https://www.washingtonpost .com/news/federal-eye/wp/2016/01/20/u-s-illegal-immigrant-population -falls-below-11-million-continuing-nearly-decade-long-decline-report-says/.

McAlinden, Sean, and Debra Menk. "CAR Research Memorandum: The Effect on the U.S. Economy of the Successful Restructuring of General Motors." Center for Automotive Research. Industry and Labor Group, and Economic Development and Strategies Group. December 9, 2013. Accessed December 31, 2015. http://www.cargroup.org/?module=Publications&event=View& pubID=102.

McCarthy, Tom. "US Embassy on Cuba Formally Reopens: 'A Day For Pushing Aside Old Barriers.'" *Guardian.* August 14, 2015. Accessed January 5, 2016. http://www.theguardian.com/world/2015/aug/14/us-embassy-cuba-formally -reopens.

McClean, Megan. "Pell Funding Strain Eases: No Shortfall Until 2017." National Association of Student Financial Aid Administrators, Policy & Federal Relations Staff. April 23, 2014. Accessed March 28, 2016. https://www.nasfaa .org/news-item/1347/Pell_Funding_Strain_Eases_No_Shortfall_Until_2017.

McLaughlin, Eliott C. "AG: Justice Department Investigating Whether Chicago Police Broke Law." CNN. December 7, 2015. Accessed December 7, 2015. http:// www.cnn.com/2015/12/07/us/chicago-police-justice-department-laquan -mcdonald-investigation/.

"Military Personnel Education Fraud Protection." Video transcript. C-Span. April 27, 2012. Accessed December 19, 2015. http://www.c-span.org/ video/?305701-1/military-personnel-education-fraud-protection&start=1290.

Montopoli, Brian. "Obama Announces End of Iraq War, Troops to Return Home by Year End." CBS News. October 21, 2011. Accessed January 1, 2016. http://www.cbsnews.com/news/obama-announces-end-of-iraq-war-troops -to-return-home-by-year-end/.

Nakamura, David. "U.S. Chamber of Commerce Endorses Obama's Pacific Rim Trade Pact." *Washington Post.* January 6, 2016. Accessed January 6, 2016. https://www.washingtonpost.com/news/post-politics/wp/2016/01/06/ u-s-chamber-of-commerce-endorses-obamas-pacific-rim-trade-pact/.

National Association for the Advancement of Colored People (NAACP). "U.S. Sentencing Commission Votes to Apply New Crack Cocaine Sentencing Guidelines Retroactively." NAACP. Accessed January 9, 2016. http://www .naacp.org/news/entry/u.s.-sentencing-commission-votes-to-apply-new-crack -cocaine-sentencing-guid/.

Neuhauser, Alan. "EPA Chief: Carbon Regs Fulfill 'Moral Obligation' to Act." *U.S. News and World Report.* June 2, 2014. Accessed March 29, 2016. http:// www.usnews.com/news/articles/2014/06/02/carbon-limits-fulfill-moral -obligation-to-act-on-global-warming-epa-chief-says.

News One. "President Obama's Remarks About HBCUs Spark Controversy." News One. January 15, 2016. Accessed February 3, 2016. http://newsone .com/3327953/president-obamas-remarks-about-hbcus/.

Noah, Timothy, and Brian Mahoney. "Obama Labor Board Flexes Its Muscles: Organized Labor Will Have More to Celebrate This Labor Day Than in Decades Thanks to a String of Recent Victories." *Politico.* September 1, 2015. Accessed December 26, 2015. http://www.politico.com/story/2015/09/unions -barack-obama-labor-board-victories-213204#ixzz3vTWuIb3S.

Obama, Barack. "A Hard Day's Work Deserves a Fair Day's Pay." *Huffington Post.* June 29, 2015. Accessed January 11, 2016. http://www.huffingtonpost.com/ barack-obama/a-hard-days-work-deserves-a-fair-days-pay_b_7691922.html.

Obama, Barack H. "A Just and Lasting Peace." Nobel lecture. Nobelprize.org. December 10, 2009. Accessed January 5, 2016. http://www.nobelprize.org/ nobel_prizes/peace/laureates/2009/obama-lecture_en.html.

Obama, Barack. "Why We Must Rethink Solitary Confinement." *Washington Post.* January 25, 2016. Accessed March 20, 2016. https://www .washingtonpost.com/opinions/barack-obama-why-we-must-rethink-solitary -confinement/2016/01/25/29a361f2-c384-11e5-8965-0607e0e265ce_story .html?tid=a_inl.

Obergefell et al. v. Hodges, Director, Ohio Department of Health, et al., 576 U.S. 1 (2015). Accessed December 12, 2015. http://www.supremecourt.gov/ opinions/14pdf/14-556_3204.pdf.

Office of Homeland Security. "Deferred Action for Childhood Arrivals: Who Can Be Considered?" August 14, 2013. Accessed December 13, 2015. http://www.dhs.gov/blog/2012/08/15/deferred-action-childhood-arrivals -who-can-be-considered.

Palm Center. Press Room. "First Study of Openly Gay Military Service Finds 'Non-Event' At One-Year Mark." Palm Center. September 10, 2012. Accessed December 10, 2015. http://www.palmcenter.org/press/dadt/releases/first_study _openly_gay_military_service_finds_nonevent_oneyear_mark.

Parkinson, John. "Freed American Nosratollah Khosravi-Roodsari Remains a Mystery." ABC News. January 18, 2016. Accessed January 19, 2016. http:// abcnews.go.com/Politics/freed-american-nosratollah-khosravi-roodsari -remains-mystery/story?id=36358599.

Peterson, Bill. "For Jackson, a Potential Breakthrough; On Eve of Primary, Support From White Officials and Wisconsin Voters Appears Strong." *Washington Post.* April 4, 1988. Accessed March 30, 2016. http://pqasb.pqarchiver.com/ washingtonpost/doc/307038519.html?FMT=ABS&FMTS=ABS:FT&type= current&date=Apr%204,%201988&author=Bill%20Peterson&pub=The%20 Washington%20Post%20(pre-1997%20Fulltext)&edition=& startpage=a.10&desc=For%20Jackson,%20a%20Potential%20 Breakthrough;On%20Eve%20of%20Primary,%20Support%20From%20 White%20Officials%20and%20Wisconsin%20Voters%20Appears%20Strong.

Pew Research Center. "5 Facts about the Deferred Action for Childhood Arrivals Program." August 15, 2014. Accessed December 13, 2015. http://www .pewresearch.org/fact-tank/2014/08/15/5-facts-about-the-deferred-action-for -childhood-arrivals-program/.

Pew Research Center. "Public 'Relieved' by bin Laden's Death, Obama's Job Approval Rises." Pew Research Center. May 3, 2011. Accessed January 1, 2016. http://www.people-press.org/2011/05/03/public-relieved-by-bin-ladens-death -obamas-job-approval-rises/.

Phillips, Macon. "Osama Bin Laden Dead." White House blogs. May 2, 2011. Accessed January 1, 2016. https://www.whitehouse.gov/blog/2011/05/02/osama -bin-laden-dead.

Pleming, Sue. "In Turnaround, U.S. Signs U.N. Gay Rights Document." Reuters. March 18, 2009. Accessed December 11, 2015. http://www.reuters.com/ article/us-rights-gay-usa-idUSTRE52H5CK20090318#Bg.

Polman, Dick. Facebook. January 13, 2016. Accessed January 13, 2016. https:// www.facebook.com/dick.polman.3.

President Obama Facebook page. November 9, 2015. Accessed January 30, 2016. https://www.facebook.com/potus.

"President Obama Speech on the Economy." C-Span. February 26, 2014. Accessed January 20, 2016. http://www.c-span.org/video/?318005-1/president -obamas-speech-economy.

President's Task Force on 21st Century Policing. *Final Report of the President's Task Force on 21st Century Policing.* Washington, D.C.: Office of Community Oriented Policing Services, 2015. Accessed December 8, 2015. http://www .cops.usdoj.gov/pdf/taskforce/taskforce_finalreport.pdf.

Prior, Jon. "SCOTUS Upholds Obama Legal Tactic in Fair Housing Cases." *Politico.* June 25, 2015. Accessed January 19, 2016. http://www.politico.com/ story/2015/06/supreme-court-fair-housing-upholds-119413#ixzz3xjjRRyfQ.

Radnofsky, Louise. "Boy at Obama's Side Now in High School." Washington Wire. *Wall Street Journal.* October 1, 2013. Accessed December 10, 2015. http:// blogs.wsj.com/washwire/2013/10/01/boy-at-obamas-side-now-in-high-school/.

Rampell, Catherine. "The Recession Has (Officially) Ended." Economix blog. *New York Times.* September 20, 2010. Accessed December 28, 2015. http://economix .blogs.nytimes.com/2010/09/20/the-recession-has-officially-ended/?_r=0.

Rampton, Roberta. "Obama Announces Changes for Student Loan Repayment." Reuters. March 10, 2015. Accessed January 14, 2016. http://news.yahoo.com/ obama-announce-changes-student-loan-repayment-131450680—sector.html.

Reilly, Mollie. "Obama Praises 'Historic Step Forward' of Allowing Women in All Combat Roles." *Huffington Post.* December 3, 2015. Accessed February 3, 2016. http://www.huffingtonpost.com/entry/obama-women-in-military_us _5660be3ae4b08e945feec39e.

Reilly, Ryan J. "Obama: I'll Use Clemency Power 'More Aggressively.'" *Huffington Post.* March 31, 2015. Accessed January 8, 2015. http://www.huffingtonpost .com/2015/03/21/obama-clemency-pardon_n_6911784.html.

Richert, Catharine. "Research Money Has More Than Doubled." *PolitiFact.* January 8, 2010. Accessed January 30, 2016. http://www.politifact.com/ truth-o-meter/promises/obameter/promise/495/double-federal-spending -for-research-on-clean-fuel/.

Ross, Chuck. "Justice Department Plans Attorney Hiring Spree to Keep Pace with Obama's Pardon Push." *Daily Caller.* January 6, 2016. Accessed January 8, 2016. http://dailycaller.com/2016/01/06/justice-department-plans-attorney-hiring-spree-to-keep-pace-with-obamas-pardon-push/.

Safian, Robert. "President Obama: The Fast Company Interview." *Fast Company.* June 15, 2015. Accessed February 2, 2016. http://www.fastcompany.com/3046757/innovation-agents/president-barack-obama-on-what-we-the-people-means-in-the-21st-century.

Samuelson, Robert J. "Celebrating the Auto Bailout's Success. *Washington Post.* April 1, 2015. Accessed December 28, 2015. https://www.washingtonpost.com/opinions/celebrating-the-auto-bailouts-success/2015/04/01/67f3f208-d881-11e4-8103-fa84725dbf9d_story.html.

Sanger, David E., David M. Herszenhorn, and Bill Vlasic. "Bush Aids Detroit, but Hard Choices Wait for Obama." *New York Times.* December 19, 2008. Accessed December 28, 2015. http://www.nytimes.com/2008/12/20/business/20auto.html?_r=2&hp.

Savage, Charlie, and Sheryl Gay Stolberg. "In Shift, U.S. Says Marriage Act Blocks Gay Rights." *New York Times.* February 23, 2011. Accessed December 13, 2015. http://www.nytimes.com/2011/02/24/us/24marriage.html?pagewanted=all&_r=0.

Scherer, Michael. "Eric Holder Will Leave a Legacy of Civil Rights Activism." *Time.* September 25, 2014. Accessed January 10, 2016. http://time.com/3430623/eric-holder-civil-rights/.

Schiavenza, Matt. "Why Obama Pushed for Gay Rights in Kenya." *Atlantic.* July 26, 2015. Accessed December 11, 2015. http://www.theatlantic.com/international/archive/2015/07/why-obama-pushed-for-gay-rights-in-kenya/399635/.

Schor, Elana. "Obama Rejects Keystone XL Pipeline: The Long-Awaited Decision Is a Huge Loss for the Oil Industry, the Canadian Government, and Republicans in Congress." *Politico.* November 6, 2015. Accessed January 28, 2016. http://www.politico.com/story/2015/11/obama-administration-expected-to-reject-keystone-xl-pipeline-215597.

Schulman, Kori. "#AskObama at the First Ever Twitter @Townhall at the White House." June 30, 2011. Accessed February 2, 2016. https://www.whitehouse.gov/blog/2011/06/30/askobama-first-ever-twitter-townhall-white-house.

"Senate Overwhelmingly Passes Every Student Succeeds Act." *Education World.* December 10, 2016. Accessed January 14, 2016. http://www.educationworld.com/a_news/senate-passes-every-student-succeeds-act-327497444#sthash.LScJZ1HZ.dpuf.

Senior, Jennifer. "The Paradox of the First Black President." *New York.* October 2015. Accessed December 7, 2015. http://nymag.com/daily/intelligencer/2015/10/paradox-of-the-first-black-president.html#.

Shear, Michael D. "In Signing Farm Bill, Obama Extols Rural Growth." *New York Times.* February 7, 2014. Accessed January 21, 2016. http://www.nytimes.com/2014/02/08/us/politics/farm-bill.html?_r=0.

Sheridan, Mary Beth, and William Branigin. "Senate Ratifies New U.S.-Russia Nuclear Weapons Treaty." *Washington Post*. December 22, 2010. Accessed January 5, 2016. http://www.washingtonpost.com/wp-dyn/content/article/2010/12/21/AR2010122104371.html.

Silva, Astrid. "Thank You, Mr. President: A Young Immigrant Tells Her Own Story about the New Chance President Obama Has Given Her Family." *USA Today*. November 22, 2014. Accessed March 20, 2016. http://www.usatoday.com/story/opinion/2014/11/21/astrid-silva-immigration-obama-amnesty-column/19357475/.

Singer, Audrey, and Nicole Prchal Svajlenka. "Immigration Facts: Deferred Action for Childhood Arrivals." Brookings Institution. Accessed December 13, 2015. http://www.brookings.edu/research/reports/2013/08/14-daca-immigration-singer.

Sink, Justin. "Obama's $300B Infrastructure Plan." *Hill*. February 26, 2014. Accessed January 21 2016. http://thehill.com/blogs/blog-briefing-room/news/199275-obamas-300b-infrastructure-plan.

Snavely, Brent. "Final Tally: Taxpayers Auto Bailout Loss $9.3B." *Detroit Free Press*. December 30, 2014. Accessed December 30, 2015. http://www.usatoday.com/story/money/cars/2014/12/30/auto-bailout-tarp-gm-chrysler/21061251/.

Snell, Kelsey. "Lynch: Obama Gun Control Actions Are Legal, Plans Underway to Hire Background Check Agents." *Washington Post*. January 20, 2016. Accessed January 26, 2016. https://www.washingtonpost.com/news/powerpost/wp/2016/01/20/lynch-obama-gun-control-actions-are-legal-plans-underway-to-hire-background-check-agents/.

Song, Kyung M. "Boy Who Lost Mom Takes Health-Care Story to D.C." *Seattle Times*. March 9, 2010. Accessed November 24, 2015. http://www.seattletimes.com/seattle-news/boy-who-lost-mom-takes-health-care-story-to-dc/.

Span, Paula. "What the Health Care Ruling Means for Medicare." New Old Age blog. *New York Times*. June 28, 2012. Accessed December 16, 2015. http://newoldage.blogs.nytimes.com/2012/06/28/what-the-health-care-ruling-means-for-medicare/.

"Stock Market Analysis." DayTradingStockBlog.Blogspot.com. January 20, 2009. Accessed December 29, 2015. http://daytradingstockblog.blogspot.com/2009/01/dow-jones-close-12009-stock-market.html.

Sun, Lena H. "More Than 11.3 Million Americans Signed Up for Obamacare, HHS says." *Washington Post*. January 7, 2016. Accessed January 23, 2016. https://www.washingtonpost.com/news/to-your-health/wp/2016/01/07/more-than-11-3-million-americans-signed-up-for-obamacare-report-says/.

Talley, Ian. "Obama Mandates New Appliance-Efficiency Standards." *Wall Street Journal*. February 5, 2009. Accessed January 30, 2016. http://www.wsj.com/articles/SB123387168605454125.

Tau, Byron. "Obama: If I Had a Son He Would Look Like Trayvon." *Politico*. March 23, 2012. Accessed December 7, 2015. http://www.politico.com/

blogs/politico44/2012/03/obama-if-i-had-a-son-hed-look-like-trayvon
-118439#ixzz3tIAsuXOd.

Tavernise, Sabrina. "Rise in Early Cervical Cancer Detection Is Linked to Affordable Care Act." *New York Times.* November 24, 2015. Accessed December 1, 2015. http://www.nytimes.com/2015/11/25/health/rise-in-early-cervical -cancer-detection-is-linked-to-affordable-care-act.html.

Thompson, Krissah, and Scott Wilson. "Obama on Trayvon Martin: 'If I Had a Son, He'd Look Like Trayvon.'" *Washington Post.* March 23, 2012. Accessed December 9, 2015. https://www.washingtonpost.com/politics/obama-if-i-had-a -son-hed-look-like-trayvon/2012/03/23/gIQApKPpVS_story.html.

Toobin, Jeffrey. "The Obama Brief: The President Considers His Judicial Legacy." *New Yorker.* October 27, 2014. Accessed December 11, 2015. http://www .newyorker.com/magazine/2014/10/27/obama-brief.

U.S. Citizenship and Immigration Services. "Executive Actions on Immigration." U.S. Citizenship and Immigration Services. Updated April 15, 2015. Accessed December 14, 2015. http://www.uscis.gov/immigrationaction.

U.S. Department of Defense. American Forces Press Service. "Obama: Americans No Longer Have to Lie to Serve." U.S. Department of Defense. Accessed December 10, 2015. http://archive.defense.gov/news/newsarticle .aspx?id=65381.

U.S. Department of Defense. "DOD Announces Same-Sex Spouse Benefits." U.S. Department of Defense. August 14, 2013. Accessed December 10, 2015. http://archive.defense.gov/releases/release.aspx?releaseid=16203.

U.S. Department of Defense. "Statement by Secretary of Defense Ash Carter on DOD Transgender Policy." U.S. Department of Defense. July 13, 2010. Accessed December 10, 2015. http://www.defense.gov/News/News-Releases/ News-Release-View/Article/612778.

U.S. Department of Education. "The American Recovery and Reinvestment Act of 2009: Education Jobs and Reform." U.S. Department of Education. February 18, 2009. Accessed January 13, 2016. http://www2.ed.gov/policy/gen/leg/ recovery/factsheet/overview.html.

U.S. Department of Education. "College Affordability and Completion: Ensuring a Pathway to Opportunity." U.S. Department of Education. Undated. Accessed November 23, 2015. http://www.ed.gov/college.

U.S. Department of Education. "Fundamental Change, Innovation in America's Schools Under Race to the Top." U.S. Department of Education. November 2015. Accessed January 13, 2016. http://www2.ed.gov/programs/racetothetop/ rttfinalrpt1115.pdf.

U.S. Department of Education. "Obama Administration Announces Final Rules to Protect Students from Poor Performing Career College Programs." U.S. Department of Education. October 30, 2014. Accessed November 23, 2015. http://www.ed.gov/news/press-releases/obama-administration-announces -final-rules-protect-students-poor-performing-career-college-programs.

U.S. Department of Education. "Recovery Act Recipients Report Funding Continues to Support over 300,000 Education Jobs." U.S. Department of Education. February 1, 2010. Accessed January 13, 2016. http://www2.ed.gov/news/pressreleases/2010/02/02012010a.html.

U.S. Department of Education. "White House Initiative on Historically Black Colleges and Universities." U.S. Department of Education. Undated. Accessed February 3, 2016. http://sites.ed.gov/whhbcu/about-us/.

U.S. Department of Health and Human Services. "Medicac Enrollment and the Affordable Care Act." U.S. Department of Health and Human Services. March 20, 2015. Accessed January 24, 2016. https://aspe.hhs.gov/sites/default/files/pdf/139236/ib_MedicaidEnrollment.pdf.

U.S. Department of Health and Human Services. Office of the Assistant Secretary for Planning and Evaluation (ASPE). "Health Insurance Marketplace's 2016 Open Enrollment Period: January Enrollment Report for the Period: November 1–December 26, 2015." ASPE. January 7, 2016. Accessed January 23, 2016. https://aspe.hhs.gov/sites/default/files/pdf/167981/MarketPlace EnrollJan2016.pdf.

U.S. Department of Homeland Security. Press Office. "DHS Releases Entry/Exit Overstay Report for Fiscal Year 2015." U.S. Department of Homeland Security. January 19, 2016. Accessed January 20, 2016. http://www.dhs.gov/news/2016/01/19/dhs-releases-entryexit-overstay-report-fiscal-year-2015.

U.S. Department of Justice. "Remarks as Prepared for Delivery by Attorney General Eric Holder at the Department of Justice African American History Month Program." U.S. Department of Justice. February 13, 2009. Accessed January 10, 2016. http://www.justice.gov/opa/speech/attorney-general-eric-holder-department-justice-african-american-history-month-program.

U.S. Department of Justice. "Smart on Crime: Reforming the Criminal Justice System for the 21st Century." U.S. Department of Justice. August 2013. Accessed January 9, 2016. http://www.justice.gov/sites/default/files/ag/legacy/2013/08/12/smart-on-crime.pdf.

U.S. Department of Justice. Office of Public Affairs. "Federal Officials Close Investigation into Death of Trayvon Martin." U.S. Department of Justice. February 24, 2015. Accessed December 9, 2015. http://www.justice.gov/opa/pr/federal-officials-close-investigation-death-trayvon-martin

U.S. Department of Justice. Office of Public Affairs. "Justice Department Announces Findings of Two Civil Rights Investigations in Ferguson, Missouri: Justice Department Finds a Pattern of Civil Rights Violations by the Ferguson Police Department." U.S. Department of Justice. March 4, 2015. Accessed December 8, 2015. http://www.justice.gov/opa/pr/justice-department-announces-findings-two-civil-rights-investigations-ferguson-missouri.

U.S. Department of Justice. Office of Public Affairs. "Justice Department Opens Pattern or Practice Investigation into the Chicago Police Department." U.S. Department of Justice. December 7, 2015. Accessed December 7, 2015.

http://www.justice.gov/opa/pr/justice-department-opens-pattern-or-practice -investigation-chicago-police-department.

U.S. Department of Justice. Office of Public Affairs. "Letter from the Attorney General to Congress on Litigation Involving the Defense of Marriage Act." U.S. Department of Justice. February 23, 2011. Accessed December 13, 2015. http://www.justice.gov/opa/pr/letter-attorney-general-congress-litigation -involving-defense-marriage-act.

U.S. Department of Labor. Bureau of Labor Statistics. "The Employment Situation: January 2009." Bureau of Labor Statistics. February 5, 2009. Accessed December 31, 2015. http://www.bls.gov/news.release/archives/ empsit_02062009.pdf.

U.S. Department of Labor. Bureau of Labor Statistics. "The Employment Situation: January 2016." Bureau of Labor Statistics. February 5, 2016. Accessed February 6, 2016. http://www.bls.gov/news.release/pdf/empsit.pdf.

U.S. Department of Labor. Bureau of Labor Statistics. "Unemployment in October 2009." *TED: The Economics Daily.* Bureau of Labor Statistics. November 10, 2009. Accessed December 31, 2015. http://www.bls.gov/opub/ted/2009/ ted_20091110.htm.

U.S. Department of Labor. Bureau of Labor Statistics. "The Employment Situation: November 2015." Bureau of Labor Statistics. December 4, 2015. Accessed December 31, 2015. http://www.bls.gov/news.release/pdf/ empsit.pdf.

U.S. Department of Labor. Bureau of Labor Statistics. "Labor Force Statistics from the Current Population Survey." Bureau of Labor Statistics. Accessed December 31, 2015. http://data.bls.gov/timeseries/LNS14000000.

U.S. Department of the Treasury. "Joint Statement of Jacob J. Lew, Secretary of the Treasury, and Shaun Donovan, Director of the Office of Management and Budget, on Budget Results for Fiscal Year 2015." U.S. Department of the Treasury. October 15, 2015. Accessed December 28, 2015. https://www .treasury.gov/press-center/press-releases/Pages/jl0213.aspx.

U.S. Department of Transportation. "The Fixing America's Surface Transportation Act or 'FAST Act.'" U.S. Department of Transportation. Undated. Accessed January 20, 2016. https://www.transportation.gov/fastact.

U.S. Department of Transportation. "Secretary Foxx Unveils President Obama's FY17 Budget Proposal of Nearly $4 Billion for Automated Vehicles and Announces DOT Initiatives to Accelerate Vehicle Safety Innovations: DOT Actions Revise Existing Guidance and Clear Administrative Hurdles for New Automotive Technology." U.S. Department of Transportation. January 14, 2016. Accessed January 20, 2016. https://www.transportation.gov/briefing -room/secretary-foxx-unveils-president-obama%E2%80%99s-fy17-budget -proposal-nearly-4-billion.

U.S. Department of Transportation. "TIGER Discretionary Grants." U.S. Department of Transportation. January 6, 2016. Accessed January 16, 2016. https://www.transportation.gov/tiger.

U.S. Department of Transportation. "U.S. Transportation Secretary Foxx Announces $500 Million in TIGER Grants Awarded to 39 Projects: Projects Target Future Needs in Rural and Urban Communities. U.S. Department of Transportation. Undated. Accessed January 20, 2016. https://www.transportation.gov/briefing-room/secretary-foxx-announces-500-million-39-tiger-grants.

U.S. Departments of Defense and Veterans Affairs. "Joint Fact Sheet: DoD and VA Take New Steps to Support the Mental Health Needs of Service Members and Veterans." U.S. Department of Veterans Affairs. Undated. Accessed February 16, 2016. http://www.va.gov/opa/docs/26-AUG-JOINT-FACT-SHEET -FINAL.pdf.

U.S. Food and Drug Administration. "Tobacco Control Act." U.S. Food and Drug Administration. November 13, 2015. Accessed January 28, 2016. http://www .fda.gov/TobaccoProducts/GuidanceComplianceRegulatoryInformation/ ucm246129.htm.

U.S. House of Representatives. "Presidential Vetoes." History, Art & Archives. U.S. House of Representatives. Accessed March 23, 2016. http://history.house .gov/Institution/Presidential-Vetoes/Presidential-Vetoes/.

U.S. Senate Committee on Agriculture, Nutrition, and Forestry. "Farm Bill Ends Direct Payment Subsidies." U.S. Senate Committee on Agriculture, Nutrition, and Forestry. January 28, 2014. Accessed January 21, 2016. http://www .agriculture.senate.gov/newsroom/press/release/farm-bill-ends-direct-payment -subsidies.

U.S. Supreme Court. "Biographies of Current Justices of the Supreme Court." U.S. Supreme Court. Undated. Accessed November 30, 2015. http://www .supremecourt.gov/about/biographies.aspx.

Vardeman, Brady. "Choctaw Nation Embraces Durant Visit." OU Daily. July 15, 2015. http://www.oudaily.com/news/choctaw-nation-embraces-obama-s -durant-visit/article_42c11f46-2b57-11e5-bad4-87aaea9fe138.html.

Veterans of Foreign Wars. "VFW Salutes New GI Bill Protections: Executive Order Better Protects Military and Veterans' Communities from Predatory Practices." Veterans of Foreign Wars. April 27, 2012. Accessed December 21, 2015. https://www.vfw.org/News-and-Events/Articles/2012-Articles/ VFW-SALUTES-NEW-GI-BILL-PROTECTIONS/.

VICE. "Watch 'Fixing the System,' Our HBO Special Report about America's Broken Criminal Justice System." VICE. September 28, 2015. Accessed December 22, 2015. http://www.vice.com/read/watch-fixing-the-system-our -hbo-special-report-about-americas-broken-criminal-justice-system-985.

Victor, Daniel. "Out Magazine Names Obama Its Ally of the Year." New York Times. November 13, 2015. Accessed December 10, 2015. http://www.nytimes .com/2015/11/13/us/politics/out-magazine-names-obama-its-ally-of-the-year.html.

Vlasic, Bill. "U.S. Sets Higher Fuel Efficiency Standards." New York Times. August 28, 2012. Accessed January 30, 2016. http://www.nytimes.com/2012/08/29/ business/energy-environment/obama-unveils-tighter-fuel-efficiency -standards.html.

Walmsley, Roy. "World Prison Population List." 10th edition. London: International Centre for Prison Studies. Undated. Accessed December 21, 2015. http://www.prisonstudies.org/sites/default/files/resources/downloads/wppl_10.pdf.

Walter, Amy, and David Wasserman. "African American Voters: The Overlooked Key to 2016." *Cook Political Report.* July 10, 2015. Accessed February 21, 2016. http://cookpolitical.com/story/8666.

"We Will Kill Bin Laden, We Will Crush Al-Qaeda: Obama." *Nation.* October 8, 2008. Accessed January 1, 2016. http://nation.com.pk/Politics/08-Oct-2008/We-will-kill-bin-Laden-we-will-crush-AlQaeda-Obama.

"Where Was the Dow Jones When Obama Took Office?" *Investopedia.* October 13, 2014. Accessed December 29, 2015. http://www.investopedia.com/ask/answers/101314/where-was-dow-jones-when-obama-took-office.asp#ixzz3vlO267ER.

White House. "Continuing to Strengthen Border Security." White House. Undated. Accessed January 23, 2016. https://www.whitehouse.gov/issues/immigration/border-security.

White House. "Family." White House. Undated. Accessed December 10, 2015. https://www.whitehouse.gov/issues/family/.

White House. "Issues: Education/Higher Education." White House. Undated. Accessed November 23, 2015. https://www.whitehouse.gov/issues/education/higher-education.

White House. "Net Neutrality: President Obama's Plan for a Free and Open Internet." White House. Undated. Accessed February 1, 2016. https://www.whitehouse.gov/net-neutrality.

White House. "Remarks of President Barack Obama—Address to Joint Session of Congress." White House. February 24, 2009. Accessed December 27, 2015. https://www.whitehouse.gov/video/EVR022409#transcript.

White House. "Veterans and Military Families: Improving Access to Care." White House. Undated. Accessed December 19, 2015. https://www.whitehouse.gov/issues/veterans/health-care.

White House. Office of the Press Secretary. "The Affordable Care Act Helps Americans with Disabilities." White House. Undated. Accessed December 14, 2015. https://www.whitehouse.gov/sites/default/files/docs/the_aca_helps_americans_with_disabilities.pdf.

White House. Office of the Press Secretary. "Executive Order—Establishing Paid Sick Leave for Federal Contractors." White House. September 7, 2015. Accessed December 22, 2015. https://www.whitehouse.gov/the-press-office/2015/09/08/executive-order-establishing-paid-sick-leave-federal-contractors.

White House. Office of the Press Secretary. "Fact Sheet: A Student Aid Bill of Rights: Taking Action to Ensure Strong Consumer Protections for Student Loan Borrowers." White House. March 10, 2015. Accessed January 14, 2016.

https://www.whitehouse.gov/the-press-office/2015/03/1C.Fact-sheet-student
-aid-bill-rights-taking-action-ensure-strong-consumer-.

White House. Office of the Press Secretary. "Fact Sheet: Cyber Threat Intelligence Integration Center." White House. February 25, 2015. Accessed
February 2, 2016. https://www.whitehouse.gov/the-press-office/2015/02/25/
fact-sheet-cyber-threat-intelligence-integration-center.

White House. Office of the Press Secretary. "Fact Sheet on New Initiatives."
White House. November 12, 2010. Accessed March 28, 2016. https://www
.whitehouse.gov/the-press-office/2010/11/12/fact-sheet-new-nitiatives.

White House. Office of the Press Secretary. "Fact Sheet: Obama Administration Record for Women and Girls." White House. August 26, 2014. Accessed
November 30, 2015. https://www.whitehouse.gov/the-press-office/2014/08/26/
fact-sheet-obama-administration-record-women-and-girls.

White House. Office of the Press Secretary. "Fact Shee- Opportunity for
All—President Obama Launches My Brother's Keeper Initiative to Build
Ladders of Opportunity for Boys and Young Men of Color." February 27,
2014. Accessed December 7, 2015. http://sites.ed.gov/hispanic-initiative/
files/2014/05/FACT-SHEET_Opportunity-for-all_President-Obama
-Launches-My-Brother%E2%80%99s-Keeper-Initiative-to-Build-Ladders-of
-Opportunity-For-Boys-and-Young-Men-of-Color.pdf.

White House. Office of the Press Secretary. "Fact Sheet: President Obama's Climate Action Plan: President Obama's Plan to Cut Carbon Pollution—Taking
Action for Our Kids." White House. June 25, 2013. Accessed January 28, 2016.
https://www.whitehouse.gov/the-press-office/2013/06/25/fact-sheet-president
-obama-s-climate-action-plan.

White House. Office of the Press Secretary. "Obama Administration Finalizes Historic
54.5 MPG Fuel Efficiency Standards: Consumer Savings Comparable to Lowering Price of Gasoline by $1 Per Gallon by 2025." White House. August 28, 2012.
Accessed January 30, 2016. https://www.whitehouse.gov/the-press-office/2012/
08/28/obama-administration-finalizes-historic-545-mpg-fuel-efficiency-standard.

White House. Office of the Press Secretary. "Obama Administration Launches
New Energy Efficiency Efforts." White House. June 29, 2009 Accessed January
30, 2016. https://www.whitehouse.gov/the-press-office/obama-administration
-launches-new-energy-efficiency-efforts.

White House. Office of the Press Secretary. "Presidential Memorandum—
International Initiatives to Advance the Human Rights of Lesbian, Gay,
Bisexual, and Transgender Persons. Memorandum for the Heads of Execu-
tive Departments and Agencies." White House. December 5, 2011. Accessed
December 11, 2015. https://www.whitehouse.gov/the-press-office/2011/12/06/
presidential-memorandum-international-initiatives-advance-human-rights-l.

White House. Office of the Press Secretary. "President Obama Signs Executive
Order Promoting Excellence, Innovation, and Sustainability at Historically
Black Colleges and Universities." White House. February 26, 2010. Accessed

February 3, 2016. https://www.whitehouse.gov/the-press-office/president-obama
-signs-executive-order-promoting-e.

White House. Office of the Press Secretary. "President Obama's Remarks
on the Death of Muammar el-Qaddafi." White House. October 20, 2011.
Accessed February 2, 2016. https://www.whitehouse.gov/blog/2011/10/20/
president-obamas-remarks-death-muammar-el-qaddafi.

White House. Office of the Press Secretary. "Race to the Top." White House.
Undated. Accessed January 12, 2016. https://www.whitehouse.gov/issues/
education/k-12/race-to-the-top.

White House. Office of the Press Secretary. "Remarks by the President and the First
Lady at International Women's Day Reception." White House. March 8, 2010.
Accessed November 30, 2015. https://www.whitehouse.gov/the-press-office/
remarks-president-and-first-lady-international-womens-day-reception.

White House. Office of the Press Secretary. "Remarks by the President and Vice
President at Bill Signing of the Workforce Innovation and Opportunity Act."
White House. July 22, 2014. Accessed March 20, 2016. https://www.whitehouse
.gov/the-press-office/2014/07/22/remarks-president-and-vice-president-bill
-signing-workforce-innovation-a.

White House. Office of the Press Secretary. "Remarks by the President and Vice
President at Signing of the Health Insurance Reform Bill." White House.
March 23, 2010. Accessed January 23, 2016. https://www.whitehouse.gov/
photos-and-video/video/president-obama-signs-health-reform-law#transcript.

White House. Office of the Press Secretary. "Remarks by the President at Greater
Boston Labor Council Labor Day Breakfast." White House. September 8,
2015. Accessed December 23, 2015. https://www.whitehouse.gov/the-press
-office/2015/09/08/remarks-president-greater-boston-labor-council-labor-day
-breakfast.

White House. Office of the Press Secretary. "Remarks by the President at Launch
of the My Brother's Keeper Alliance, Lehman College, West Bronx, New
York." May 4, 2015. Accessed December 7, 2015. https://www.whitehouse.gov/
the-press-office/2015/05/04/remarks-president-launch-my-brothers-keeper-
alliance.

White House. Office of the Press Secretary. "Remarks by the President at Signing of the Helping Families Save Their Homes Act and the Fraud Enforcement and Recovery Act." White House. May 20, 2009. Accessed January 17,
2016. https://www.whitehouse.gov/the-press-office/remarks-president-signing
-helping-families-save-their-homes-act-and-fraud-enforceme.

White House. Office of the Press Secretary. "Remarks by the President at the
Signing of the Veterans Access, Choice, and Accountability Act." White
House. August 7, 2014. Accessed December 19, 2015. https://www.whitehouse
.gov/the-press-office/2014/08/07/remarks-president-signing-veterans-access
-choice-and-accountability-act.

White House. Office of the Press Secretary. "Remarks by the President in Address
to the Nation on Immigration." White House. November 20, 2014. Accessed

December 14, 2015. https://www.whitehouse.gov/the-press-office/2014/11/20/remarks-president-address-nation-immigration.

White House. Office of the Press Secretary. "Remarks by the President on Common-Sense Gun Safety Reform." White House. January 5, 2016. Accessed January 26, 2016. https://www.whitehouse.gov/the-press-office/2016/01/05/remarks-president-common-sense-gun-safety-reform.

White House. Office of the Press Secretary. "Remarks by the President on Immigration." White House. June 15, 2012. Accessed December 13, 2015. https://www.whitehouse.gov/the-press-office/2012/06/15/remarks-president-immigration.

White House. Office of the Press Secretary. "Remarks by the President on the Americans with Disabilities Act." White House. July 20, 2015. Accessed December 16, 2015. https://www.whitehouse.gov/the-press-office/2015/07/20/remarks-president-americans-disabilities-act.

White House. Office of the Press Secretary. "Remarks by the President on the Supreme Court Decision on Marriage Equality." White House. June 26, 2015. Accessed December 10, 2015. https://www.whitehouse.gov/the-press-office/2015/06/26/remarks-president-supreme-court-decision-marriage-equality.

White House. Office of the Press Secretary. "Remarks by the President on Trayvon Martin." White House. July 19, 2013. Accessed December 3, 2015. https://www.whitehouse.gov/the-press-office/2013/07/19/remarks-president-trayvon-martin.

White House. Office of the Press Secretary. "Remarks by the President to a Joint Session of Congress on Health Care." White House. September 9, 2009. Accessed January 23, 2016. https://www.whitehouse.gov/the-press-office/remarks-president-a-joint-session-congress-health-care.

White House. Office of the Press Secretary. "Remarks of President Barack Obama—State of the Union Address as Delivered." White House. January 13, 2016. Accessed February 8, 2016. https://www.whitehouse.gov/the-press-office/2016/01/12/remarks-president-barack-obama-%E2%80%93-prepared-delivery-state-union-address.

White House. Office of the Press Secretary. "Remarks of the President—as Prepared for Delivery—Signing of Stem Cell Executive Order and Scientific Integrity Presidential Memorandum." White House. March 9, 2009. Accessed January 27, 2016. https://www.whitehouse.gov/the-press-office/remarks-president-prepared-delivery-signing-stem-cell-executive-order-and-scientifi.

White House. Office of the Press Secretary. "Statement by the President." White House. November 25, 2015. Accessed January 4, 2015. https://www.whitehouse.gov/the-press-office/2015/11/25/statement-president.

White House. Office of the Press Secretary. "Statement by the President in the James S. Brady Briefing Room." White House. July 24, 2009. Accessed December 7, 2015. https://www.whitehouse.gov/the-press-office/statement-president-james-s-brady-briefing-room.

White House. Office of the Press Secretary, "Statement by the President on Afghanistan." White House. October 15, 2015. Accessed January 4, 2016. https://

www.whitehouse.gov/the-press-office/2015/10/15/statement-president
-afghanistan.

White House. Office of the Press Secretary. "Statement by the President on the Supreme Court Ruling on the Defense of Marriage Act." White House. June 26, 2013. Accessed December 13, 2015. https://www.whitehouse.gov/doma-statement.

White House. Office of the Press Secretary. "Statement by the President on the Trans-Pacific Partnership." White House. October 5, 2015. Accessed January 6, 2016. https://www.whitehouse.gov/the-press-office/2015/10/05/statement-president-trans-pacific-partnership.

White House. Office of the Press Secretary. "Statement by the President [Regarding air strikes on Iraq]." August 7, 2014. Accessed January 2, 2016. https://www.whitehouse.gov/the-press-office/2014/08/07/statement-president.

White House. Office of the Press Secretary. "U.S. Leadership and the Historic Paris Agreement to Combat Climate Change." White House. December 12, 2015. Accessed January 28, 2016. https://www.whitehouse.gov/the-press-office/2015/12/12/us-leadership-and-historic-paris-agreement-combat-climate-change.

White House. Office of the Press Secretary. "We Can't Wait: President Obama Takes Action to Stop Deceptive and Misleading Practices by Educational Institutions That Target Veterans, Service Members and Their Families." White House. April 26, 2012. Accessed December 16, 2015. https://www.whitehouse.gov/the-press-office/2012/04/26/we-can-t-wait-president-obama-takes-action-stop-deceptive-and-misleading.

White House. Office of the Press Secretary. "Weekly Address: Giving Every Student an Opportunity to Learn through Computer Science for All." White House. January 30, 2016. Accessed February 1, 2016. https://www.whitehouse.gov/the-press-office/2016/01/30/weekly-address-giving-every-student-opportunity-learn-through-computer.

White House. Office of the Press Secretary. "Vetoed Legislation." White House. Accessed March 23, 2016. https://www.whitehouse.gov/briefing-room/vetoed-legislation.

Wilson, Scott. "Obama Makes Surprise Visit to Afghanistan." *Washington Post*, May 25, 2014. Accessed January 4, 2016. https://www.washingtonpost.com/politics/obama-arrives-in-afghanistan-on-surprise-visit/2014/05/25/7df61452-e41f-11e3-8f90-73e071f3d637_story.html.

Wofford, Carrie. "Veterans Benefit from the 'Power of the Pen': The VA Just Unveiled Brand New Websites for Vets—Thanks to an Obama Executive Order." *U.S. News and World Report*. February 7, 2014. Accessed March 20, 2016. http://www.usnews.com/opinion/blogs/carrie-wofford/2014/02/07/obama-executive-orders-have-already-helped-veterans.

Worland, Justin. "What to Know about the Historic 'Paris Agreement' on Climate Change." *Time*. December 12, 2015. Accessed January 30, 2016. http://time.com/4146764/paris-agreement-climate-cop-21/.

Zeleny, Jeff. "Obama Signs Hate Crimes Bill." Caucus blog. *New York Times*. October 28, 2009. Accessed December 13, 2015. http //thecaucus.blogs .nytimes.com/2009/10/28/obama-signs-hate-crimes-bill/

Zernike, Kate, and Michael T. Kaufman. "The Most Wanted Face of Terrorism." *New York Times*. May 2, 2011. Accessed January 1, 2016. http://www.nytimes .com/2011/05/02/world/02osama-bin-laden-obituary.html.

The Obamas visited with 106-year-old Virginia McLaurin of Washington, D.C., in the Blue Room of the White House before a reception celebrating African American History Month on February 18, 2016. She petitioned for months to get an invitation to meet them. "I didn't think I would live to see a colored president, because I was born in the South and didn't think it would happen," she wrote. (Official White House Photo by Lawrence Jackson)

Index

Page numbers in italics refer to photographs and illustrations.

ABC News (television network), 62
Abedini, Saeed, 131
Achieving a Better Life Experience
    Act (ABLE), 79–80
Adonia (cruise ship), 209
Affordable Care Act (ACA), 4, 15–17,
    19, 30–31, 30–35, 77–78, 103,
    179–180, 181–188, 206, 208
Afghanistan, 122–123, 127–128
African American community
    and civil rights, 144–145
    and Fair Sentencing Act (FSA),
        140–144, *141*
    and higher education, 48–51
    My Brother's Keeper, 51–53
    and racial profiling, 40–48
    and support for Obama, 56–57
    voting power of, 208
Afro.com (website), 39
agriculture, 176–178
    Agriculture Act of 2014, 177
    Farm Bill, 177–178, 205
Alcoa Davenport Works, *101*
Alexander, Elizabeth, 6
Alphonse Fletcher Jr. University, 46
Al Qaeda, 117–119, 120, 123
Amazing Grace (Traditional), 6
AARP (American Association of
    Retired Persons), 78
American Cancer Society, 31
ACLU (American Civil Liberties
    Union)
    Fair Sentencing Act (FSA), 141–144

American Opportunity Tax Credit, 14
American Recovery and Reinvestment
    Act of 2009, 14–15, 17, 79,
    98–99, 103–105, 156–161,
    167–168
    Child Care and Development Block
        Grant, 17
    Child tax credit, 17
    Make Work Pay tax credit, 17
Americans with Disabilities Act
    (ADA), 76
Appleby, Kevin, 174
Arthur, John, 64
Associated Press, 122
automobile industry, 107–108, 167–171
    fuel efficiency, 194–195
    self-driving vehicles, 170–171

Baer, John, 1
Barnes, Melody, 56
Bartiromo, Maria, 102
Bartz, Carol, 197
BBC World Service, 126
Beck, Stephen, Jr., 79–80
Benefits.VA.gov (website), 201
Bernanke, Ben S., 23
Berry, John, 66
Biden, Jill, 158–159
Biden, Joe, 18, 19, 48, 59, 182–183
bin Laden, Osama, 4, 59, 117–119
Blow, Charles M., 54, 55
Booker, Cory, 57
Bradley, Tom, 2

Bradley Effect, 2
Breckenridge, Anita, 29
Brookings Institution, 71
Browder, Kalief, 92
Brown, Michael, 43
Burton, Bill, 56
Burwell, Sylvia Mathews, 29
Bush, George H. W., 26, 31, 76, 137
Bush, George W., 17, 26, 31, 107, 112,
    137, 187
BuzzFeed (website), 64
Byrd, James, Jr., 59, 65

Cambridge, Massachusetts
    police department and racial
        profiling, 46–48
Caparella, Kitty, 3
Capehart, Jonathan, 57
Carnes, Julie E., 29
Carney, Jay, 40
Carney, Susan L., 29
Carter, Ash, 34–35, 61
Carter, Jimmy, 48, 127, 137, 179
Castro, Fidel, 129
Castro, Julián, 162, 163–164
Castro, Raúl, 125, 129
Center for Automotive Research
    (CAR), 108
CDC (Centers for Disease Control
    and Prevention), 184
CIA (Central Intelligence Agency), 117
Chicago, Illinois
    police department and racial
        profiling, 41–42
Choctaw Nation, 199
Christen, Morgan, 29
Chrysler, 107–108
civil rights, 144–145
    Civil Rights Act of 1964, 21, 23
    Defense of Marriage Act, 59,
        62–64, 144
    fair housing initiatives, 163–165
    Fair Sentencing Act (FSA),
        140–144, *141*

and racial profiling within police
    departments, 40–48, 144
same-sex marriage, 4, 59,
    62–64, 144
Clinton, Bill, 24, 26, 31, 61, 66, 91,
    137, 179
Clinton, Hillary, x, 27–28, 129, 208
CNN (television network), 4, 91
CNN.com (website), 42
Coequyt, John, 191
Cohen, Larry, 97
Cole, James, 139
Colin, Diana, 69
Common Core, 157
Congress, 4, 12, 14–15, 17, 21, 30–33,
    43, 60, 63, 65, 70, 74, 79,
    82–84, 86, 95–96, 103–106,
    109, 114, 122, 127, 129–130,
    133–134, 146–147, 149–151,
    154, 156, 159, 167, 169, 174–
    175, 177–178, 182–185, 192,
    200, 205–206
consumer advocacy groups
    Enterprise Community
        Partners, 165
    Washington Community Action
        Network, 18
Contreras-Sweet, Maria, 29
Cook Political Report, 56–57
Coolidge, Calvin, 209
correctional facilities. *See* prisons
Council of Economic Advisers, 155
Cox, Delton, 200
Crayton, Kameria, 207
Crenshaw, Ander, 79
Crowley, James, 46–48
Cruz, Ted, 207
Cuba, 128–129, 206, 209
Curry, George E., 39

DailyNewsBin.com (website), 102
Defense of Marriage Act, 59,
    62–64, 144
Dempsey, Martin E., *116*

DeNoyer, Richard L., 84
Dickerson, Mikey, 202
Dinkins, David, 1–2
disabilities
    Americans with Disabilities Act
        (ADA), 76–77
    and FEMA (the Federal Emergency
        Management Agency), 77
    Stephen Beck Jr. Achieving a Better
        Life Experience Act (ABLE),
        79–80
DisabilityScoop.com (website), 78
Dodd, Chris, 109
Dodd-Frank Wall Street Reform and
        Consumer Protection Act of
        2010, 103, 108–111
Donohue, Thomas J., 135
Don't Ask, Don't Tell (DADT) policy,
        35, 59–62
Drum, Kevin, 111–112
Dukakis, Michael, 1
Duncan, Arne, 13–15, 157

East, Francis, 129
Ebola, 4
economy, 5, 98–99, 101–115
    agriculture, 176–178
    American Opportunity Tax
        Credit, 14
    American Recovery and
        Reinvestment Act of 2009,
        14–15, 17, 79, 98–99, 103–105,
        156–161, 167–168
    Council of Economic Advisers, 155
    Dodd-Frank Wall Street Reform
        and Consumer Protection Act
        of 2010, 103, 108–111
    and employment, 111–114, 150–152
    financial reforms of banking
        industry and Wall Street, 103,
        108–111
    Fixing America's Surface
        Transportation (FAST) Act,
        169–170

Great Recession, 5, 102, 105–106,
        108–109, 114, 206
    and the housing market, 114–115,
        162–165
    and technology, 198–203
    TIGER (Transportation Investment
        Generating Economic
        Recovery), 167–168
education initiatives, 11–19, 153–161
    America's College Promise, 15
    Common Core, 157
    and the disabled, 78–79
    Every Student Succeeds Act, 154–
        156, 205
    Head Start, 17, 153–155
    Health Care and Education
        Reconciliation Act of 2010,
        13–14, 159–161
    Healthy, Hunger-Free Kids Act of
        2010, 17
    higher education and career
        training, 12–14
    Historically Black Colleges and
        Universities (HBCUs) and
        funding, 48–51
    Individuals with Disabilities
        Education Act, 78–79
    Invest in US, 154
    My Brother's Keeper Task Force and
        Alliance, 51–53
    No Child Left Behind (NCLB), 155
    Pell Grants, 13–14, 49, 159–161
    Race to the Top program, 13,
        156–157
    Student Aid and Fiscal
        Responsibility Act, 49
    and technology, 200–201
    and U.S. veterans, 82–84
Edwards, Donna, 14
Egan, Timothy, 127
Eisenhower, Dwight D., 129
Emanuel African Methodist
        Episcopal Church, 37–38
Encyclopedia of Alabama, 23

environment, 189–196
    climate change, 189–196
    Environmental Protection Agency
        (EPA), 192–196
    Keystone XL pipeline, 179, 190, 194
Environmental Protection Agency
    (EPA), 192–196

Facebook, 190, 201
fair housing initiatives, 163–165
fair pay
    Equal Employment Opportunity
        Commission (EEOC), 22, 23
    Family and Medical Leave Act
        (FMLA), 150
    Lilly Ledbetter Fair Pay Act, 21–23,
        149–150
Fair Sentencing Act (FSA),
    140–144, *141*
Family and Medical Leave Act
    (FMLA), 150
Fanning, Eric K., 59
Fast Company (magazine), 202–203
FBI (Federal Bureau of Investigation),
    40, 42, 115, 146
Ferguson, Missouri, 45
    police department and racial
        profiling, 43–44
Fisk College, 51
Florida
    Stand Your Ground law, 55
Forbes (magazine), 13
Ford, 107–108
Ford, Gerald, 179
FOX Business (television network), 102
FOX News (television network), 4
Foxx, Anthony, 56, *165*, 169–171
Frank, Barney, 109
Franklin, Aretha, 207
Fraud Enforcement and Recovery Act,
    114–115
FOIA (Freedom of Information Act), 42
Freedman-Gurspan, Raffi, 66
Fulton, Sybrina, 54–55

Gallup organization, 16
Garland, Merrick B., 26, 209–210
Gaspard, Patrick, 56
Gates, Henry Louis, Jr., 46–48
Gates, Robert, *x*
General Motors, 107–108
George Mason University, 44
Georgetown University, 192
Georgia Tech, 160
Gillion, Daniel Q., 38
Ginsburg, Ruth Bader, 22, 24
Goldman, Jason, 201
Goodyear Tire and Rubber Company,
    21–22, 23
Google, 202
Gordon, Phil, *204*
Gosar, Paul, 164
Government Accountability Office,
    151, 164
Green, Brandy, 54
Griest, Kristen, 35
Guantánamo Bay, 124
gun control, 145–147

Harkin, Tom, 75
Harris, Pamela, 29
Harvard University
    Hutchins Center for African and
        African American
        Research, 46
    Law School, 25, 27
Harwood, Bronson, *148*
hate crimes, 38–39, 64–65
    and gun control initiatives,
        145–147
    Matthew Shepard and James Byrd,
        Jr., Hate Crimes Prevention
        Act, 59
Haver, Shaye, 35
HBO (television network), 90
Head Start, 17, 154–155
Health Affairs (journal), 30
HealthCare.gov (website), 202
health care initiatives

Affordable Care Act (ACA), 4,
    15–17, 19, 30–35, 77–78, 103,
    179–180, 181–188, 206, 208
Children's Health Insurance
    Program Reauthorization Act,
    16–17
and the disabled, 77–78
and the elderly, 77–78
Family Smoking Prevention
    and Tobacco Control Act
    (FSPTCA), 187–188
HealthCare.gov (website), 202
Healthy, Hunger-Free Kids Act of
    2010, 17
and Medicare and Medicaid, 4, 18,
    30, 77–78
spending, *184*
stem cell research, 186–187
and U.S. veterans, 84–88
Veterans' Access to Care through
    Choice, Accountability, and
    Transparency Act of 2014,
    84–85
Hekmati, Amir, 131
Helping Families Save Their Homes
    Act, 114
Hochberg, Fred, 66
Holder, Eric, 43, 56, 63, 91,
    143, 144
Holmes, Oliver Wendell, 24–25
Howard University, 209, 210
Hoyer, Steny, 75
H&R Block, 23
Huebner, David, 66
Huffington Post, 65, 131, 139–140, 149
Human Rights Campaign, 65
Hussein, Saddam, 120

immigration issues, 69–74,
    172–175
Center for Migration Studies
    (CMS), 173–174
Deferred Action for Childhood
    Arrivals (DACA) policy, 70–72

DREAM (Development, Relief,
    and Education for Alien
    Minors) Act, 70–74
Instagram, 201
IRS (Internal Revenue Service), 17
International Centre for Prison
    Studies, 91
international trade
    relations with Asia, 134–135
    Trans-Pacific Partnership (TPP),
    132–134
Investopedia (website), 110–111
Iran, 130–131
Iraq, 120–122, 127–128
Islamic State
    ISIL (Islamic State in the Levant),
    120–123, 190
    ISIS (Islamic State of Iraq and
    Syria), 122

Jack in the Box restaurant, 18
Jackson, Jesse, 1
Jackson, Lisa, 29
Jacksonville State University, 23
Jagland, Thorbjøern, 127
Jarrett, Valerie, 29, 39, 56, 69, 150
J. B. and M. K. Pritzker Family
    Foundation, 154
Jewell, Sally, 29, 193
Johnson, Broderick, 56
Johnson, Jeh, 56, 172
Johnson, Lyndon B., 31, 163, 179
Johnson, Ronald, 42
Jones, Cory L., 5–6
Jones, Van, 56
Journal of Blacks in Higher Education
    (journal), 50

Kagan, Elena, 20, 24–25, 27, 29
Kahan, Kate, 69
Keenan, Barbara Milano, 29
Kelly, Jane Louise, 29
Kennedy, Anthony, 165
Kennedy, Caroline, 29

Kennedy, Edward M., 65
Kennedy, John F., 39, 129, 179
Kennedy, Vicki, *18*
Kenya, 67–68, 117
Kenyatta, Uhuru, 67
Kerry, John, 129, 132, *204*
Kerwin, Donald, 173
Key, Keegan-Michael, 4
Khosravi-Roodsari, Nosratollah, 131
Kim, Angie, *69*
Ki-moon, Ban, 118
King, Martin Luther, Jr., 127
King, Rodney, 43
Kleinfeld, Klaus, *101*
Kline, John, 156
Krause, Cheryl Ann, 29
Krugman, Paul, 4, 102–103, 111–112

labor initiatives and reforms, 148–152
    Family and Medical Leave Act
        (FMLA), 150
    Healthy Families Act, 95–97
    National Labor Relations Board
        (NLRB), 96–97
    Workforce Innovation and
        Opportunity Act, 150–152
LaHood, Ray, 195
Langevin, James, 75
Larson, Todd, 67
League of Nations, 127
Leal, Miguel, *69*
Ledbetter, Charles, 23
Ledbetter, Lilly, 21–23
Lee, Kevin, *69*
Leff, Deborah, 139
LEGO Foundation, 154
Lehman College, 52
LGBT (Lesbian, Gay, Bisexual and
        Transgender) community
    and global issues, 66–68
    and hate crimes, 64–65
    National Center for Transgender
        Equality, 66
    and Obama Administration, 58–68

same-sex marriage, 4, 62–64, 144
    and U.S. Military and Don't Ask,
        Don't Tell (DADT) policy, 35,
        59–62
Levinson, Art, *197*
Lew, Jacob J., 102, 108
Libya, 119
LinkedIn (website), 150
lobbying groups
    Health Care for America Now, 19
Lorain County Community
    College, *148*
Lotito, Michael, 97
Love, Reggie, 56
Lynch, Loretta, 28, 29, 41–44, 56, 144,
    146–147, 165

Mahraoui, Mehdi, *69*
Mandela, Nelson, 127
Marashi, Reza, 131
Marshall, George C., 127
Marshall, Marlon, 56
Marshall, Thurgood, 27
Martin, Beverly B., 29
Martin, Tracy, 54–55
Martin, Trayvon, 40–41, 46, 52, 54–55
mass shootings, 6–7, 38–39, 145–147
    and gun control, 145–147
    Sandy Hook Elementary
        School, 145
McCain, John, 111, 117
McCarthy, Gina, 29, 193
McDaniel, Edna Smith, 23
McDaniel, J. C., 23
McDonald, Laquan, 41–42
McGill, Charles, *101*
McGuire-Maniau, Melissa, *69*
McHugh, Carolyn B., 29
McLaurin, Virginia, 278
Medicare and Medicaid, 4, 18, 30,
    77–78, 184–186
    enrollment, *185*
Medvedev, Dmitry, 131–132
Merritt, Kenneth, 248

Mikva, Abner, 27
Millett, Patricia Ann, 29
Mills, Karen, 29
Mora, Justino, 69
Morehouse College, 50, 51
Moritz, Nancy, 29
Morris, Larry, 129
Mother Jones (magazine), 111
Mullen, Mike, *x*, 60
Muñoz, Cecilia, 29, 69
Murguia, Mary H., 29
Murphy, Malcolm, *101*
Murray, Patricia Lynn, 18–19
Murray, Shailagh, 29
My Brother's Keeper Task Force and
    Alliance, 51–53

Napolitano, Janet, 24, 28
Nathanson, Paul, 78
NAACP (National Association for
    the Advancement of Colored
    People), 90, 209
  and Fair Sentencing Act (FSA),
    142–143
National Highway Traffic Safety
    Administration (NHTSA),
    170–171
National Science Foundation (NSF),
    49, 200–201
National Senior Citizens Law
    Center, 78
New York (magazine), 39
New Yorker (magazine), 25–26, 66
New York Times, 27–28, 54, 55, 78,
    109, 112, 117, 124, 127, 129,
    130, 132, 137–138, 145–146,
    185, 201
  Economix (blog), 105
  NYTimes.com (website), 111
Nguyen, Jacqueline, 29
Niebuhr, Reinhold, 205
9/11, 82, 84, 117, 123
Nixon, Richard, 179
Nobel Prize, 99, 102, 126–128

Northern Virginia Community
    College, Alexandria campus,
    158–159
Nuclear Non-Proliferation Treaty,
    131–132

Obama, Barack, *ii*, *vi*, *x*, 8, *11*, *18*, *20*,
    36, 58, 69, 75, 81, 89, 94, 98,
    101, 116, 125, 136, 148, 153,
    162, 166, 172, 176, 181, 189,
    197, 204, 216, 248, 278
  and African Americans, 37–57
  chronology of actions while in
    office, 211–214
  and diplomatic relations with Cuba,
    128–129, 206, 209
  and diplomatic relations with
    Middle East, 120–124, 127–
    128, 130–131
  economic initiatives and reforms of,
    101–115
  education initiatives of, 11–15,
    48–53, 78–79, 153–161,
    200–201
  election of, 1–2
  and environmental initiatives,
    189–196
  health initiatives of, 15–19, 30–35,
    150, 179–180, 181–188
  and homeland security,
    172–175, 202
  immigration initiatives of, 69–74,
    172–175
  and infrastructure initiatives,
    162–178, 198–203
  initiatives and policies for the
    people, 9–103, 148–152,
    198–203
  initiatives and policies for veterans,
    81–88
  initiatives and reforms of police
    departments 40–48, 144
  initiatives for the disabled and
    elderly, 76–80, 150

Obama, Barack, (*cont.*)
  initiatives for the LGBT
      community, 58–68, 144
  initiatives for women and women's
      rights, 21–35
  international diplomatic relations,
      120–124, 125–135
  and Kenya, 67–68
  labor initiatives and reforms of,
      94–97, 148–152
  legacy of, 205–210
  Nobel Peace Prize, 99, 126–128
  presidential vetoes of, 30–33, 96,
      124, 130, 185, 205
  prison reforms, clemency and
      sentencing, 89–93, 137–140,
      138, 140–144, *141*
  State of the Union addresses, 3, 17,
      64, 83, 154, 191–192
  and trade relations with Asia,
      134–135
Obama, Malia, *ii*, 38, *216*
Obama, Michelle, *ii*, 17, 38, 53, 58, 64,
      82, *216*, 278
Obama, Sasha, *ii*, 38, *216*
Obamacare. *See* Affordable Care Act
Obergefell, James, 64
O'Connor, Sandra Day, 24
O'Malley, Kathleen M., 29
Out (magazine), 59
Owens, Gina, 18
Owens, Marcelas, 15, *18*, 18–19
Owens, Tifanny, 18–19

Pakistan, 117–118, 123
Palmer, David, *148*
Panetta, Leon, 60, *116*, 118
*The Paradox of the First Black
      President* (Senior), 39
Pew Research Center, 48, 71, 119,
      173–174
Philadelphia, Jacob, 9
Philadelphia Daily News, 1
Pierson, Julia, 29

Pillard, Nina, 29
Pinckney, Clementa C., 6
  funeral of, *36*, 37–38
Planned Parenthood, 30, 33–34
police departments
  and military equipment, 45–46
  and racial profiling, 40–48
  Task Force on 21st Century
      Policing, 44–46
Politico, 97, 149, 157
PoliticusUSA (website), 106
PolitiFact.com (website), 150, 196
Polman, Dick, 3–4
Pope Francis, *vi*, 129, 130
Power, Samantha, 29
Praise Song for the Day
      (Alexander), 6
Princeton University, 27
Prindiville, Kevin, 78
prisons
  and abuse of solitary confinement,
      92–93
  and clemency initiative,
      137–140, *138*
  El Reno Correctional Institution,
      89, 90
  Fair Sentencing Act (FSA),
      140–144, *141*
  and prisoners, 89–93
  reforms of, 89–93
  Rikers Island, 92
  and sentencing, 140–144, *141*
Pritzker, Penny, 29
Pryor, Jill A., 29
PBS (Public Broadcasting Service),
      46, 47, 72
Puhl, Jennifer Klemetsrud, 29

Qaddafi, Muammar, 119

Ramsey, Charles H., 44
Rand Corporation, 14
Reagan, Ronald, 24, 31, 137
Reid, Harry, 73

Reuters, 126–127, 193
Rezaian, Jason, 131
Rhodes, Ben, 11, *204*
Rhodes, Ella, *11*
Rice, Susan E., 29, 56, *204*
Richtman, Max, 78
Riley, Josh, 200
Roberts, John, *20*, 183–184, 193
Roberts, Robin, 62
Robinson, Laurie, 44
Robinson, Marian Shields, *ii*, 38
Rodriguez, Julie Chavez, 69
Rolling Stone (magazine),
    4, 102–103
Romney, Mitt, 195
Roof, Dylann Storm, 38
Roosevelt, Theodore, 127, 200
Rosekind, Mark, 170
Rosenbaum, Robin S., 29
Rung, Anne, 96
Russia, 131–132
Russo-Japanese war, 127

same-sex marriage, 4, 59, 62–64, 144
Samuels, Charles, 89
Samuelson, Robert J., 108
Sanders, Bernie, 208
SBA.gov (website), 201
Scalia, Antonin, 26, 209
Schmidt, Eric, *197*
Schulman, Kori, 201
Schweitzer, Albert, 127
Scott, Bobby, 14
Seattle Times, 18
Sebelius, Kathleen, 28
Selby, Myra C., 29
Sensenbrenner, Cheryl, 75
Sensenbrenner, James, 75
September 11th. *See* 9/11
Serenity Prayer (Niebuhr) 205
Shea, Sandra, 2
Shepard, Dennis, 65
Shepard, Judy, 65
Shepard, Matthew, 59, 65

Shwartz, Patty, 29
Sierra Club, 191
Silva, Astrid, 72–73
Simpson, Amanda, 66
Smart on Crime Initiative, 143–144
Social Security, 203
    National Committee to Preserve
        Social Security and
        Medicare, 78
Solis, Hilda, 28
Solmonese, Joe, 65
Sotomayor, Sonia, 24–25, 26–27, 29
Souter, David H., 24
Southern University, 49
Spelman College, 50, 51
Stevens, John Paul, 24
Stoll, Kara Farnandez, 29
Stranch, Jane Branstetter, 29
Strategic Arms Reduction Treaty
    (START), 131–132
SNAP (Supplemental Nutrition
    Assistance Program), 17
Sutley, Nancy, 66
Sutton, Duane, *148*

Taliban, 122–123
Tanzania, 117
Task Force on 21st Century Policing,
    44–46
technology industry, 197–203
    Federal Communications
        Commission (FCC) and
        internet access, 198–199
Thompson, O. Rogeriee, 29
Time (magazine), 191
Toobin, Jeffrey, 25–26
Tracy, Jim, 129
Trans-Pacific Partnership (TPP),
    132–135
transportation, 166–171
    fuel efficiency, 194–195
    self-driving vehicles, 170–171
Truman, Harry, 179
Trump, Donald, 173–174, 207–208

Tubman, Harriet, 208
Turner, Margery, 164
Twitter, 201
Tyson, Cicely, 210

United Nations, 118, 130
  and global LGBT (Lesbian, Gay,
    Bisexual and Transgender)
    issues, 66–68
  nuclear disarmament, 127
University of California, Santa
  Barbara
  Palm Center, 60–61
University of Chicago
  Law School, 27
University of Michigan, 177
University of Pennsylvania, 38
University of Wyoming, 65
USA Today, 72, 96
U.S. Census, 91
U.S. Census Bureau, 56
U.S. Chamber of Commerce, 133–134
U.S. Constitution, 42
  Article II, 137
  First Amendment, 43, 188
  Fourteenth Amendment, 43, 63
  Fourth Amendment, 43
  Second Amendment, 146–147
U.S. Court of Appeals, 23, 24, 26, 27,
  29, 189–199, 193, 209
U.S. Department of Defense, 45,
  116–124
  and Don't Ask, Don't Tell (DADT)
    policy, 35, 59–62
  military branches and women in
    combat service, 34–35
  National Defense Authorization Act
    (NDAA), 124
U.S. Department of Education, 12–15,
  17, 154–161
  and Historically Black Colleges and
    Universities (HBCUs), 48–51
U.S. Department of Energy (DOE),
  195–196

U.S. Department of Health and
  Human Services, 17
U.S. Department of Homeland
  Security, 24, 28, 45, 100, 146,
  172–175, 184–185, 202
U.S. Department of Housing and
  Urban Development (HUD),
  163–165
  Connect Home program, 199–200
  Fair Housing Act of 1968, 163–164
U.S. Department of Justice, 14, 27,
  65, 137
  Bureau of Justice Statistics, 91, 143
  and civil rights, 144–145
  and fair housing, 164–165
  Fraud Enforcement and Recovery
    Act, 114–115
  and investigations of racial profiling
    in police departments, 41–44
  and investigations of solitary
    confinement abuse in U.S.
    prisons, 92–93
  Office of Community Oriented
    Policing Services, 45
  and presidential clemency initiative,
    138–140
  U.S. Sentencing Commission, 142
U.S. Department of State, 77
U.S. District Court, 23, 26–27
U.S. Military
  Air Force, 35
  Army
    Army Rangers, 35
    Green Berets, 35
  Don't Ask, Don't Tell (DADT)
    policy, 35, 59–62
  Marine Corps, 35
  military branches and women in
    combat service, 34–35
  Navy
    SEALs, 35, 117
  and veterans, 81–88
  and wars in Iraq and Afghanistan,
    120–124

U.S. News and World Report
    (magazine), 83
U.S. Secretary of State, 27–28, 129
U.S. Supreme Court, 27, 34, 97
    and Affordable Care Act (ACA), 78,
        179–180, 183–184, 186
    DREAM (Development, Relief,
        and Education for Alien
        Minors) Act, 73–74
    and fair housing, 164–165
    and greenhouse-gas emissions
        policy, 193–194
    Hobby Lobby, 30
    King v. Burwell, 186
    Ledbetter v. Goodyear Tire &
        Rubber Co., 21–23
    National Federation of Independent
        Business v. Sebelius, 183–184
    and Obama appointees 24–27
    Obergefell et al. v. Hodges, Director,
        Ohio Department of Health,
        63, 64
    same-sex marriage, 4, 62–64
    United States v. Windsor, 63, 64
U.S. Treasury Department, 208
    and automobile industry, 107–108
    Bureau of Alcohol, Tobacco,
        Firearms, and Explosives, 146
    Federal Reserve, 28
    Helping Families Save Their
        Homes Act, 114–115
    Office of Management and Budget,
        5, 106–107

Van Dyke, Jason, 42
Vatican, 129
Veterans of Foreign Wars (VFW), 84
VICE: Fixing the System (television
    documentary), 90
Vilsack, Tom, 176

Wall Street and stock market, 103,
    108–110
    Dow Jones Industrial Average, *110*
    NASDAQ, 110
Walt Disney Company 154
Warlick, Ronald, 89
Washington, Harold 1
Washington Post, 24, 40, 41–42, 57, 92,
    108, 119, 131, 174
weapons of mass destruction
    (WMDs), 120
Westly, Steve, *197*
White House Correspondents'
    Dinner, 207, 209
WhiteHouse.gov (website), 201
WIC (Special Supplemental Nutrition
    Program for Women, Infants,
    and Children), 17
Wilson, Darren, 43
Wilson, Woodrow, 127
Wise, Terrence, 94
women's rights
    and fair pay, 21–23
    and health concerns, 30–35
    and the Obama administration,
        21–35
    Violence against Women Act, 34
Wood, Diane P., 24
Workforce Innovation and
    Opportunity Act, 150–152

Yale Law Journal (journal), 27
Yale University
    Law School, 27
Yellen, Janet, 28, 29
Yentel, Diane, 165
YouTube, 201

Zimmerman, George, 40–41, 54–55
Zuckerberg, Mark, 197

About the Author

Photo Credit: Arthur Mohead

Michael I. Days is the editor of the *Philadelphia Daily News*. He was first named editor in 2005, becoming the first African American to lead the paper in its ninety-year history. He then served as managing editor, the second-in-command, at the *Philadelphia Inquirer*, for seventeen months, starting in January 2011. He returned to the editor's position at the *Daily News* in June 2012. He remains one of only a handful of African Americans to head newspapers in the United States.

Under his leadership, the *Daily News* has won dozens of national, state, and local awards, including the Pulitzer Prize for investigative reporting in 2010. He also has served as a juror for the Pulitzer Prizes. At the *Philadelphia Daily News*, he previously served as a City Hall reporter, assistant city editor, business editor, deputy managing editor, and managing editor.

He has also worked at the *Wall Street Journal*, the *Louisville (Kentucky) Courier-Journal*, and the *Democrat and Chronicle* in Rochester, New York, in varied reporting positions. He started his professional career with a yearlong internship at the *Minneapolis Tribune*.

Days is a Philadelphia native. He graduated from the College of the Holy Cross in Worcester, Massachusetts, with a degree in philosophy. He earned a master's degree from the University of Missouri School of Journalism. He is a McCormick Fellow and a graduate of the Media Management Center's Advanced Executive Program at Northwestern University.

Days was recently elected to a second stint on the national board of the Associated Press Media Editors and is the former editor of its quarterly magazine, *APME News*. Days is a member of the American Society of News Editors and the National Association of Black Journalists (NABJ). He is a former regional director and national board member of NABJ.

He also serves on the advisory board of the Scripps Howard School of Journalism and Communication at Hampton University and the board of visitors at Temple University's School of Media and Communication. He has served on the advisory board of the Knight Center for Specialized Journalism and as a board member of the Pennsylvania Society of News Editors.

Days has been honored twice by the Philadelphia Association of Black Journalists, receiving the President's Award and the Trailblazer Award. He also was honored with the Lillian Award, for outstanding service to journalism, from the Delta Sigma Theta Sorority, Inc.

Days received the Robert McGruder Award for Diversity Leadership given jointly by the Associated Press Media Editors and the American Society of News Editors. In March 2015, he was selected as one of 125 persons of distinction by his alma mater, Roman Catholic High School, for its 125th anniversary.

He is a member of the Knights of St. John International, a worldwide fraternal service organization of Roman Catholic men.

Michael Days has been a frequent guest and commentator on radio and television in the Philadelphia market and a sought-after speaker, panelist, and moderator in many venues. He most recently moderated a panel on community policing held at Philadelphia's Constitution Center.

GREEK SCULPTURE
The Archaic Period

 W9-BND-783

Calf-bearer from the Acropolis, Athens. See *112*

GREEK SCULPTURE

The Archaic Period

a handbook

JOHN BOARDMAN

NEW YORK AND TORONTO
OXFORD UNIVERSITY PRESS
1978

© 1978 Thames and Hudson Ltd, London
All rights reserved

Library of Congress Cataloging in Publication Data
Boardman, John, 1927–
    Greek sculpture.
    (World of art)
    Bibliography: p.
    Includes index.
    1. Sculpture, Greek. I. Title. II. Series
ND90.B62   733'.3   77–25202
ISBN 0–19–520046–2
ISBN 0–520047–0 pbk.

Printed in Great Britain by Jarrold and Sons Ltd, Norwich

CONTENTS

1   INTRODUCTION   7

2   THE DARK AGES AND GEOMETRIC PERIOD   9

3   THE ORIENTALIZING STYLES   11

Eastern styles in Crete and Greece; The Daedalic style;
Other early Archaic statuary

4   MARBLE AND THE MONUMENTAL   18
    TO ABOUT 570 BC

The first marble sculpture; Kouroi; Korai; Perirrhanteria;
Artists and authors

FIGURES 1–80   28

5   THE MATURING ARCHAIC STYLES   63
    TO ABOUT 530 BC

Sources; Kouroi and realism; Korai; East Greek sculpture
and sculptors; Attic sculpture and sculptors (Phaidimos,
The Rampin Master, Aristion of Paros); Other areas;
Proportions and techniques

6   THE LATER ARCHAIC STYLES TO ABOUT 480 BC   82

Attic sculpture and sculptors (Endoios, Antenor); East
Greek sculpture and sculptors; Other areas

FIGURES 81–186   90

7 ARCHITECTURAL SCULPTURE 151

Placing and character; The beginnings, Corfu; Athens;
Central and south Greece; Treasuries; East Greece

8 RELIEFS 162

Grave reliefs; Votive and other reliefs

9 ANIMALS AND MONSTERS 167

10 CONCLUSION 169

FIGURES 187–271 172

Abbreviations 241

Notes and Bibliographies 242

Index of Illustrations 248

Acknowledgments 249

Index of Artists 250

General Index 250

Chapter One

INTRODUCTION

'A critical history of Greek art would show how late the Greeks commenced to practise the arts. After the Persian war a new world opens at once, and from that time they advanced with great strides. But everything that was produced before the Persian war – a few of those works are still extant – was, if we judge of it without prejudice, altogether barbarous.' When the great historian Niebuhr wrote this, at the beginning of the last century, there were few existing examples of Archaic Greek art from the period before the Persian war, and most were not generally recognized for what they were. It is an art which has been learnt by patient scholarly recognition of the vases and bronzes exported to Italy in antiquity, and for its sculpture mainly from the finds in excavations of the last hundred years. Connoisseurship of style and the evidence of ancient authors combine to map clearly the development of Classical sculpture. For the earlier period, when regional independence in the arts was more marked, it is not surprising that it has proved hard to achieve a scholarly consensus about the development of styles, their origins and dates. This was a period in which the seeds of Classical art were sown, but the growth was not as inexorable or even-paced as the summary art histories might lead us to believe. There could have been no conscious striving towards realism until realism was understood as a possible and desirable goal. And there were many false starts or periods of preoccupation with sterile styles and techniques. The art historian seeks the rationale which will lead to a better understanding of why Greek art took the course it did. The archaeologist puzzles evidence of date, traces the sources and routes of foreign inspiration. The iconographer probes the convention of a narrative style which is to serve western art for centuries. This is hardly the subject for the specialist who cannot see how interdependent these approaches must be.

   This little book attempts to present the evidence fairly, but also to propose a pattern by which the development may be the better understood. If it did not, the undertaking would have proved as boring for the author as the reader. Much is uncontroversial, but in places the manner of presentation is novel. The narrative concentrates on the history of style by period and region, as the material dictates, and it attempts to be as comprehensive as space allows rather than so selective as to exclude even mention of the majority of types, places and names relevant to the subject. As in the companion handbooks to Athenian black figure and Archaic red figure vases, the illustrations are small but numerous, both aides-mémoires to the familiar and glimpses of the uncommon. Drawings have been used where photographs would be obscure or where composition is more important than nuances of style, and several fine new drawings have been made by Marion Cox to offer a fuller view of important complexes of narrative relief than most handbooks, even weighty ones, allow. Captions are fuller too, relieving the text of much discussion of subject matter and technical data. The notes serve to demonstrate sources of further information about all illustrated works (designated by italicized numbers in square brackets), and to list more detailed studies. Dates, of course, are all BC. Where sanctuary sites are named in captions the major deity may be assumed as the object of a dedication unless otherwise stated; and the major museum where a town is named. 'The Acropolis' is the Athenian. The material is always marble unless otherwise indicated and measurements are in metres. I hope that any apparently laconic treatment will be excused: it is in the interests of providing as much illustrative material as possible within the format of the series.

It is only the sculpture of the Greek homeland, islands and the eastern seaboard on the Aegean, 'east Greece', that is studied here. The Greek colonies in South Italy and Sicily, and to a lesser extent in Africa and on the shores of the Black Sea, have also something to contribute to the story, but their studios are derivative and have no important reciprocal effect on homeland styles. Consideration of these must be reserved for inclusion in a proposed sequel to this handbook.

8

Chapter Two

THE DARK AGES AND GEOMETRIC PERIOD

The Greek Bronze Age civilization finally collapsed in the twelfth century and left no heritage in stone sculpture for later centuries, no tradition to foster or revive through the Dark Ages that followed. A few works of Mycenaean Greece, such as the relief on the Lion Gate at Mycenae, stood to be admired, but were not copied. In a period when the technically more demanding arts were forgotten, together with the palace patronage which had encouraged them, the only craft traditions to survive were those dependent on the simplest techniques. At this level we can detect cultural and artistic continuity, and although this held little promise for the future it is worth observing.

In the later Bronze Age it had been a common practice, in Greece and Crete, to fashion figurines of clay, sometimes of considerable size, on the potters' wheel. A cylinder served as the body for a standing figure or an animal, and to it were added, free-hand, head and limbs, all being painted and fired as any painted vase, with the same pigments, the same patterns. Indeed, some of these figures were vases. The tradition in standing figures can be followed readily enough in Crete [1, 2], and the wheel-made animals are to be found in many parts of the Greek world, and in Cyprus, serving as votive offerings or as grave furniture. Illustrated are two of the more elaborate examples which can be placed not only from the circumstances of their finding but also from their decoration, which was applied by the vase painter and matches that on decorated vases. One is from tenth-century Athens, a stag [3], the other, a little later, from Euboea [4]. The latter is what a later Greek would call a centaur, and there are other man-animal monsters, sphinxes or bull-men. The style is pretentious, but most minor sculpture of the Greek Dark Ages is trivial and it required a new impetus, of wealth or foreign example, to engender a demand for a greater range of types, greater sophistication. The results are not startling but they prove decisive for the later history of Greek sculpture.

With the advent of the full Geometric period, and especially in the eighth century, the true renaissance of the arts in Greece begins. The population was growing rapidly and towns were already looking overseas for new resources, new land for their citizens, in the 'colonial' areas of Italy and Sicily; through trade and travel the near east was quickening the appetites and skills of Greek craftsmen. In Greece itself several major sanctuaries were established, some of local (as Athens, Samos), some of national importance (as Olympia, Delphi,

9

Dodona), which provided a market for votives, a focus for the artists' expertise.

The contribution of the east was a special one, as we shall see. Otherwise, sculptural works are small, though plentiful, executed in clay or bronze. The clay is hand-fashioned and fired solid, with far less use now of the potters' wheel. The bronze too is cast solid, in a clay mantle around the modelled wax original which is melted out in the firing. Each work, then, is unique and there can be no re-use of moulds. Many of the figurines or heads, both in clay and bronze, were destined for attachment to vessels, supporting the ring handles of cauldrons [5] which were popular and expensive offerings, or decorating the rims of open vases. The rather soft, plastic forms encouraged by the technique are soon controlled to present alert 'Geometric' features on which more and more detail is admitted, in either the casting or the later chasing of the bronze figures, and through the painting of the clay ones [6].

Other stylistic features are the elongation of necks and limbs and the geometricizing of parts of the body in a manner easily paralleled by the contemporary figures painted on vases. The painter offers strong broad shoulders to make a triangular torso, long strong thighs and tight buttocks, treating each part in its most characteristic 'frontal' view. The coroplast or bronze worker, with an extra dimension, observes the same formula and conceives his figures in parts – the torso may be broad from the front but wafer-thin from the side, the legs well muscled from the side, spindly from the front.

We know the figures principally from the offerings found at the sanctuaries I have named. The free-standing figures may represent deities – the warrior Zeus at Olympia; or animals – memorials or substitutes for sacrifice (often bulls) and thank-offerings for success (the horse was an important status symbol); or the worshipper himself, as warrior [7] or charioteer. The quadrupeds, horses and the occasional stag [8, 9], as well as birds, beetles, hares, are often set on rectangular (or, rarely, round) open-work plaques, which may be decorated in intaglio beneath. It looks very much as though these small offerings were to be suspended in the sanctuary. Like the men, the animals resemble those drawn on vases, with the flat sweep of the horse's strong neck emphasized and the muzzle sometimes stylized into a trumpet form. There are enough of these bronze horses for regional styles to be detected, in the Peloponnese and central Greece.

By the end of the period an inscription may name the donor, recipient and circumstances of the gift [10], if a free-standing figure is involved. By this time too we find more ambitious compositions, either in the pose of a single figure, a bowman or helmet-maker [11], or in groups [12, 13], where the subject is heroic, and we are reminded by them that Greek interest in narrative was beginning to be expressed by Geometric artists other than Homer. The components of these figures and groups obey the same formulae as the simpler figurines, but the freedom in their use is quite new. We might well think that this is an indication of a new and expressive departure in Geometric art which will be the key to dramatic new developments in the seventh century. And we would be wrong.

Chapter Three

THE ORIENTALIZING STYLES

Eastern styles in Crete and Greece

The earliest surviving stone sculpture in Iron Age Greece is from Crete: a fragmentary head [14], and a small relief from a frieze showing a goddess in a shrine helped by bowmen against a chariot [15]. They cannot be dated from their context of discovery but stylistically they belong to a series of objects – gold jewellery, bronze armour and statuary – which re-introduce to the Greek world long-forgotten techniques, apparently from the general area of Syria and the neo-Hittite kingdoms. Finds in tombs indicate that the style was centred on Knossos and flourished from the end of the ninth century, but hardly later than the end of the eighth. Probably the latest examples are the three bronze cult figures found in a small temple of Apollo at Dreros [16], which was built in the second half of the eighth century. These were made of sheets of hammered bronze fastened on to a wooden core, with traced decoration on the dress. Very like the 'Apollo' is a small cast bronze found recently at Afrati in an eighth-century context [17], which proves that the early date for the Dreros figures, suspected on other grounds though they are still often put in the mid-seventh century, is correct. In Knossos at least the explanation for this unusual series of objects seems likely to be an immigrant group or family who plied their craft for a century or more, and practised techniques novel for Geometric Greece but still not learned from them by their Greek neighbours, since their more sophisticated techniques disappear with them (fancy goldsmithing and the working of hard stone). The stone and bronze statuary mentioned, if not theirs, was clearly inspired by their work, and at a lower level we may notice that some of the new, curvilinear, non-Geometric patterns they used were copied by Knossian vase painters in a style we know as Protogeometric B (late ninth century). This represents the first major penetration of Greek lands by oriental art and artists, and it is interesting to note that, despite the quality and variety of the works produced, it had no following, although it may well have established a preference for a plastic style which was to be more enthusiastically adopted from the east in Crete and elsewhere in the seventh century – the 'Daedalic'.

Characteristics of the eighth-century figures are the long oval heads, domed skulls with long hook-locks for the men, pill-box hats for the women (a type of headgear reserved in Greece for priestesses or representations of deities and called a *polos*), rather formless bodies, and for the women the cloak worn symmetrically over the shoulders, open at the front (it was fastened by two pins and a chain worn across the chest, as we see in later views of it).

Another immigrant studio in Crete, which may not have arrived so early as that already discussed, is best known from the bronze shields hammered and traced with concentric friezes of figured scenes and with animal-head bosses in the round, found in the Idaean Cave, at other Cretan sites and at a few Greek mainland ones. The style of the figures is more distinctly oriental, but it seems likely that the workshop was still open to near the middle of the seventh century and its later work betrays more Greek taste in composition, style and subject matter. The only sculptural interest it offers, apart from the shield bosses, is the strange bronze head vase from the Cave [*18*], very oriental in appearance although the concept seems Greek. This must be one of the latest products of the studio.

In Athens and Attica other immigrant goldsmiths worked jewellery related to the Cretan, but there were no sculptural side-effects, unless they are to be detected in the use of a new material, now introduced again to Greece, ivory. Minor worked ivories from the east had arrived earlier, but in an Athenian grave of about 730 is a group of ivory girls, in pose and nakedness copying the eastern Astarte figures, yet without their opulent physique [*19*]. Instead they are pared down to a truly Geometric sleekness, and their polos-hats carry a Greek maeander. Here, then, is a Greek artist who has learned a new technique with a new material, and practises it with distinction.

The only other orientalizing works worth noting in this context are bronze attachments to cauldrons – a function of many of the purely Geometric bronzes. Vessels imported from the east from the later eighth century on carried either cast attachments in the form of what the Greeks would later have called sirens, or lion (and perhaps griffin) heads in hollow hammered bronze. Examples are known with both cast and hammered attachments (in Olympia [*20*] and Cyprus), and the source may be Syria or beyond. What is of interest here is the stylistic change in the Greek copies of these works. The siren heads exchange their plump cheeks for Geometric angularity [*21*], the griffins, soon cast rather than beaten, acquire sinuous and graceful beaks, to become impressive decorative attachments [*22*]. The sirens appear mainly in central and south Greece, the griffins also in east Greece (especially Samos). The translation of these human and animal forms is an important commentary on Greek attitudes to minor sculpture as decoration, but we are still far from 'real' sculpture, or anything even nearly monumental.

The Daedalic style

A description of the Auxerre goddess [28] is our best introduction to the Daedalic style – we shall attempt to meet Daedalus himself later, at the end of the next chapter. The figure is a limestone statuette of a woman dressed in what we have already recognized as a Cretan manner, with cloak covering both shoulders and a broad, probably metallic, belt. The breasts are unusually well shaped over the high waist and the formless skirt covered with incised patterns defining areas of colour [128]. The hand carried across the breast is probably in a gesture of adoration, but may also derive from the eastern breast-holding fertility goddess. The other long-fingered hand is pressed to her side, the feet are big, lumpy. The face is triangular, rounding in the chin, rather flat-topped, the forehead defined by a straight row of curls. The hair is dressed in vertical locks with knob terminals, but also with horizontally ranged crimps. There was a lot of colour, including a scale or feather pattern on the breast.

The dress, shape of head and hair typify the Daedalic style no less than the strict frontality, and a frontal head alone is enough to identify it, either on its own or applied, for instance, to a sphinx or a male figure. The hair is more commonly dressed only with horizontal waves. It is often described as a wig (the *Etagenperücke*) and, although it certainly owes something to eastern and ultimately Egyptian representations of wigs or head-dresses, in Greece the convention is used to indicate long, carefully combed hair. The Daedalic style is expressed in stone, clay, ivory and jewellery, and may be taken to have flourished from the second quarter of the seventh century to its end.

The clues to its origins lie in its favourite figure – the frontal woman, in the medium in which it is most often expressed – clay relief, and, perhaps in the area where it is best represented – Crete. The frontal goddess, naked and with hands pressed to breasts and loins, is familiar in Syria in dozens of mould-made clay plaques representing Astarte. In Corinth such a plaque [23] was imported in the seventh century and at the same site we find a locally made mould for a figure of purely eastern type [24]; cf. [51]. The introduction of the mould to Greece, particularly in association with figures related to the Daedalic, is important. It enabled the mass-production of such figures, which in turn led to a certain stereotyping of the form and must have contributed to its long life. The naked goddess, whom we have met already in ivory in Athens [19], is also copied in Cretan Daedalic plaques [26]; cf. [27], but soon clothed. The female nude is not yet a proper subject for Greek art.

Crete's probable role in the development of the style is further suggested by its superficial similarity to the eighth-century orientalizing works in the island [16, the women], which are often erroneously classed as Daedalic, and by some Cretan clay heads of aggressively triangular outline, which are not mould-made but indicate a preference for this type; compare [25, 44]. Finally, it is a characteristic of Cretan seventh-century figures that while there are several of women or goddesses wholly naked, all the men are clothed, rarely exposing their genitals (in the least 'orientalizing' works). This is virtually the reverse of the practice in the rest of Greece. It is probably another indication of the strong influence in Crete of the east, where the naked goddess was commonplace but male nudity abhorrent; and it also echoes the Minoan practice of semi-nudity for women, covered loins for men.

It may be, then, that the Daedalic style and its propagation owe much to the mould technique for clay reliefs (there are abortive attempts with two-piece moulds), but it is soon translated into stone. The Auxerre statuette [28] may well be Cretan and there are several other figures from the island, standing, seated and in high relief. Illustrated are two fragmentary seated figures (the earliest in stone from Greece) from Astritsi [29] and Gortyn [30], a prolific site. Between them they demonstrate the horizontally waved hair and elaborate painted decoration on the skirt. Each whole figure has been made in two pieces. From Gortyn too comes the relief slab [31] with another triad like the Dreros bronzes, but the girls are naked, in eastern fashion, and their hair more eastern, as [28], springing from high behind the temples. This is from an architectural setting, and so is a later assemblage from Prinias including seated figures, reliefs and relief dado slabs [32]. Finally, there is part of another possibly seated figure from Eleutherna [33]. Of these [29, 30, 33] are lifesize – all are limestone.

Crete is not the only source for the style, nor even Dorian Greece (the Peloponnese, Melos, Thera, Rhodes) although this has often been alleged, and the style is certainly best represented in this area. There is little in stone, however, outside the island. Best known are the reliefs from Mycenae, in the canonic style [35]: odder, in style and function, a relief from Boeotia [36], but from the Ptoon comes a Daedalic woman whose base carries part of what may be our first sculptor's signature (. . .]otos). In clay the style is better represented, especially in the Peloponnese, but the mould is not used only for plaques. In Crete, at Gortyn, we have fine examples of miniature clay sculpture in the round, as with the Athena [34] whose bell skirt follows the older Cretan tradition of wheel-made figurines, which continues, for figures mainly like this, in various parts of Greece through the seventh century. Daedalic and mould-made too are the heads of figures, often sphinxes, on clay relief vases (*pithoi*) mainly from Crete, and the style is represented also in jewellery, in Crete, Rhodes and Melos. In other materials and at greater scale we see it in a hollow cast head from Olympia [37], where a fine incised pattern for the hair answers the bolder rendering in stone. By now too Greek studios for ivories can work in this fully hellenized orientalizing style and the sphinx from Perachora is purely Daedalic [38], while the strange high-relief group of strippers in New York [39] may be an attempt at a myth scene.

It is time to consider dates. Two stumpy figures with Daedalic heads are the earliest examples in stone [40] which are datable, before the middle of the seventh century, from their context with pottery in a grave on Thera. In clay

14

the mould-made heads applied to (Proto-) Corinthian oil flasks are valuable because the vases are painted in a distinctive manner which is quite closely datable. The example [41] shown is of about 650. Some frontal heads painted on Corinthian vases are of less value for close comparison and profile views, notably on Cretan vases (less closely datable), are usually better developed than the profile views of the primarily frontal Daedalic heads. Other moulded heads on Corinthian vases indicate the style of the end of the century. There must have been many regional variations though a good sequence can be observed and has, by some scholars, been rather too elaborately defined. But the trend can be detected both in the datable pieces named and wherever there is a good series of types from a single site, like Gortyn. The tendency is from the angular to the more rounded in features, with a growing sensitivity to the volume and depth of the head (undervalued in the early plaques), and a reduction in the emphasis of certain features – size of eyes, lips, hands. The sequence in the Cretan series may be observed here as follows: [29–28–31–32–33].

The Daedalic was basically a decorative style, which is why it was so often enlisted for small works in ivory or metal, and rarely achieves lifesize in stone, in the second half of the seventh century. We have touched upon the reasons for the stereotyping of the style. In fact it still follows the Geometric formula for figures in the round or in relief, but new and sometimes foreign elements of pattern and detail are added to the conventional rendering of parts, bare or clothed. There is no challenge to nature here, little progress in rendering of anatomy, and the frontal aspect, which often left ears (only shown on later works and perhaps an egyptianizing feature) attached to hair rather than head as [32, 33], hardly encouraged experiment in this direction. It promised only stagnation, and there is no other major genre in Greek art which progressed so slowly in the Archaic period. The east had revitalized most Greek crafts with new techniques, new forms and figures, but it was going to require something more than the east could offer if the plastic arts in Greece were to move forward, or even recapture the vision, flair and freedom of some of the latest Geometric.

Other early Archaic statuary

The Daedalic style, however defined, hardly accounts for all Greek seventh-century statuary, large or small, not executed in marble. Even in limestone there are figures which, in their bulk, display a fine disregard for the rather two-dimensional frontality of the Daedalic – such as the chubby male from Tanagra [42] – although the heads of such figures will probably have roughly resembled the Daedalic in angularity of features and style of hair.

Smaller works display greater variety and differing traditions or sources. They demonstrate the growing command of techniques in bronze and ivory, and often a greater freedom in composition. Despite the differences in scale and material this all contributes to the Greek sculptor's emancipation from the

Daedalic and realization of the monumental, which we study in the next chapter.

Solid cast bronzes remain more informative than terracottas. More of them now are independent figures, with their own bases, not for attachment to a vessel or furniture. Two main sources well illustrate their range. Even in Crete we can find pieces that renounce the Daedalic, but probably because they owe more to rather different eastern traditions. It is hard to say whether the little lyre-player is an easterner or a Cretan [43]. His head resembles the pre-Daedalic, but the free pose reminds us of the latest Geometric bronzes. The little sphinx's snaky locks [44] are almost Minoan, but the one wing carried forward renders in the round an eastern convention more familiar on painted vases in Greece and Crete. And the ram-bearer [45] has the heavy Cretan features and Cretan loin-cloth, but is modelled with a feeling for depth which is foreign to the Daedalic. These two must be from quite late in the seventh century despite the features of [45] which should probably be explained as non-Daedalic rather than pre-Daedalic. They have been called Eteocretan, invoking an indigenous non-Hellenic style which might owe something to the island's Minoan past. The old blood and language may have survived, but it is less easy to discern the necessary continuity in the arts, and probably wrong to try.

In the Peloponnese Olympia remains an important source for bronze votives. The warrior [46] is the seventh-century descendant of the Geometric Zeuses, but with more detailing of features, more volume to limbs and torso and incipient observation of the pattern of flesh and muscle on the body. This is all carried a stage further in the Olympia charioteer [47]. The Boeotian [48] betrays its lateness in details but looks primitive.

Wood must have been a common material for early sculpture but it survives only in conditions of extreme damp or dryness. The waterlogged sanctuary of Hera on Samos has yielded a glimpse of riches lost to us elsewhere. In the smaller works we might expect the style and even subjects to reflect the influence of eastern ivory carving, a cognate art. While the goddess [49] is thoroughly Daedalic the group [50] looks more eastern for the rotundity of features, yet it is to Crete again that we turn for details of the dress – the tunic and shawl. In ivory there are distinguished successors to the Athens girls [19], and in some respects even less hellenized. The head from Perachora [51] is almost certainly an import but what of the god with a lion from Delphi [52]? The highly stylized beast is Assyrian, the fluid treatment of the body non-Greek, yet in the features the flabby oriental is being pared to near-Daedalic alertness, and although the scheme for the group is eastern there are no such ivory statuettes in Syria and beyond, and the theme of god and lion might suit Apollo, while the pattern on the base looks Greek or at least Anatolian. There must have been several ivory workshops in seventh-century Greece, perhaps staffed or instructed by easterners who could transpose something of their style and knowledge of eastern themes. East Greece, in touch with the kingdoms of Phrygia and Lydia, must have been well used to this exchange. Ephesus is an important source of such work, continuing into the sixth century. Closely related to the Ephesian is the ivory fitting from a lyre [53], plumply oriental in concept of body, dress and the supporting monster: in the same tradition, then, as other strongly orientalizing ivories of the seventh century from Greece. Yet the only similar lyre-fitting known, also from East Greece and of about the same date, takes us into a different world. The youth from Samos [54] owes little enough to eastern forms, yet, for all the angularity of his head, is quite free from the restrictions of the Daedalic. He displays a crisp simplicity which the loving detail devoted to hair, hands, belt and features, does nothing to obscure. It is not, I hope, only the optimism of a Hellenist which can see in this tiny and decorative work the qualities of form and even monumentality that we can readily admire in the later, larger works of Greek sculpture. We shall see time and again that unity of form in Greek art, despite the rapid development of the Archaic period and later, transcends scale, material and techniques, leaving always something jewel-like in the colossal, something monumental in the minute.

Chapter Four

MARBLE AND THE MONUMENTAL
to about 570 BC

The first marble sculpture

The impetus for technical and stylistic changes in Greek sculpture in the eighth and first half of the seventh century came, as we have seen, from the near east, from lands whose wealth and expertise the Greeks had begun to seek again in the ninth century. For relations with Egypt in these years the evidence is slight, yet this is to be the source of the next major innovation.

The pharaoh Psammetichos I (664–610) invited east Greek and Carian mercenaries to serve him against his enemies, and this resulted in concessions to Greeks to settle and then to trade in Egypt. By 638 we hear of a Samian captain, Kolaios, already acquainted with the route south. In Egypt the Greeks saw lifesize statuary, and larger, in hard stone, for standing and seated figures, superficially not unlike their own less ambitious statues and statuettes, with some features already familiar to them from the egyptianizing arts of the near east. It would not have required many visits by many craftsmen, being Greeks and imbued with characteristic Greek curiosity and aptitude to learn, for these novel (to them) concepts in statuary and the means of their execution to be introduced to Greece itself. Basic features are size and material. The size appealed to that sense for the monumental which the Iron Age Greeks had so far expressed only in their architecture and pottery. Given that no Greek statuary answering these new concepts can be securely dated before this attested interest in Egypt, given the existence of the models for them in Egypt as well as other details of technique and appearance yet to be mentioned, and the absence of such models in the east where even major statuary is basically decorative or architectural rather than free-standing monumental, it is impossible not to associate this new era in Greek sculpture with influence from Egypt.

Hitherto stone sculpture in Greece had been made of the readily accessible limestone (*poros*) or sandstone which required nothing more complicated than a carpenter's tools and might even betray the woodworker's technique. The harder material, marble, crystalline rather than granular in composition and requiring some new tools and quite different techniques, was no less easy to obtain, with white, grey and bluish varieties accessible to surface quarrying in the islands and many other mainland areas. The islands are the earliest important source, notably the Cyclades. Naxian marble we know from Naxian works and

18

quarries in the island – it is coarse grained, sparkling. Parian marble is more sugary in texture and potentially translucent. In both islands we have Archaic work from the quarries [55], blocked out and left unfinished after accidents in working or transport. The Parian, unlike the Naxian, is often referred to with approval by later authors or named in inscriptions. Pentelic marble from near Athens has a tighter, opaque structure and a distinctive rust-coloured age patina, but is not used much before the mid-sixth century, and then sparingly until the fifth, and there are other varieties to be noticed, such as the bluish neighbouring Hymettan. It is important, however, not to be misled by descriptions of crystal-size and translucency. In early days it was probably the marble's characteristics in working rather than its appearance which determined use, since the finished surface was never highly polished and was in fact often painted – even on the flesh parts where we might have expected the quality of the marble to have been best exploited. So our observations about crystal-size relate to working rather than appearance, and these were the criteria by which the sculptor judged and ordered his stone. The fact that analysis of modern sampling from the sources named shows wide varieties of crystal type in the same area is irrelevant. The sculptor knew what to expect of his 'Parian', 'Naxian' or 'Pentelic' and uncharacteristic stone would not have been acceptable, whatever the label. At any rate, the artist would normally have chosen his stone in the quarry at this period and worked much of it there. We have to judge his choice of material by the standards of antiquity, not of the present day, and the fact that he *could* have got similar material elsewhere does not matter if we have good reason to believe that he *did* not.

In Egypt the hard stones were worked mainly by the laborious process of pounding and abrasion: their copper tools were useless and iron almost unknown. But the Greeks were already using iron for knives and chisels, and this enabled them to make more rapid progress in their carving and in the improvement of techniques and tools to suit the harder material. The iron point, held vertically or at an obtuse angle to the surface, removed quite large flakes of stone. For the early marble statues this is followed by work with a flat chisel, which was especially important in rendering detail, the finish being achieved by abrasive, probably emery (obtainable on Naxos) in the form of powder or rubbers. Drills worked with a bow, and wedges (of dry wood, then swollen with water) were used to split the blocks from the quarry beds, but the drill was also used to render details and help remove chunks or channels of stone by breaking through a line of close-set drilled holes. This must certainly have been the practice from the beginning since only thus could arms be freed from flanks safely, as on [63]. This use of flat chisel and drill has only recently been demonstrated on early Greek marble statues (by Mrs Adam), earlier scholars denying their use so soon.

The Egyptian role in all this has been challenged by some recent writers. Certainly it can be exaggerated, but we may review briefly other apparent links, apart from the purely technical and the example of sheer size. The pose for male figures – the *kouroi*, youths, to give them their familiar title – had been familiar in Greece already. In fact most such stone figures in Egypt stood with the withdrawn leg vertical, not properly balanced. Moreover, they were normally dressed in at least a loin-cloth, while the Greek are naked, but for a number of island figures wearing only a belt. However, the male (and female) figures now stand with clenched fists, like the Egyptian, and not stiff-fingered, and the men may have in the fist an unworked mass which recalls the short baton held by many Egyptian figures. This could easily have been omitted to leave an agreeable, tighter geometric pattern of the fingers. Seated figures, not necessarily themselves inspired by Egyptian art, although this is not impossible, may also now sit with palms outstretched on their thighs, in the Egyptian manner.

In our period Egyptian sculptors laid out preliminary sketches for their figures on the smoothed face of the unworked block according to a grid which determined the placing and size of parts of the body, with twenty-one squares or units from eye line to the soles of the feet. For any figure of lifesize or more some such sketch is an absolute necessity and a grid predetermining proportions was an obvious aid. One Greek kouros may have been laid out in a similar grid (drawing, and [63]), and Diodorus (i, 98) has a story of two mid-sixth-century Samian sculptors, Telekles and Theodoros, making halves of a statue separately by this system (twenty-one units plus one-quarter cubit from eyes to crown: this part being a variable in Egyptian figures, often occupied by a crown or head-dress), and fitting them perfectly. Clearly, the Egyptian practice was known, and could be used, but most other complete Archaic Greek figures appear to obey no such strict scheme, although absolute height was important and proportional changes, tending to the realistic, can be observed (see next chapter). This is hardly surprising, given the Greek genius for learning, adapting and improving foreign techniques. That subtler principles of proportion could and did concern them is clear from the existence of books on the subject written by Classical sculptors such as Polykleitos.

So far as we know, the early monumental statues which have survived were all commemorative – votive or funerary. We do not know whether any were cult statues, yet the need for such works, and the claims of the monumental temples whose members were soon to be executed in stone and rendered into 'orders', again under the probable inspiration of Egyptian practice, could have played an important part in encouraging the new sizes, styles and techniques. Of earlier cult images we know nothing. Descriptions in later authors suggest that they were crude, often wooden and aniconic, deriving their sanctity from legend ('fallen from heaven') or the finery with which they could be decked out: those, for instance, to be clothed in a robe or having one laid on their knees on ceremonial occasions, like Athena at Troy (*Iliad* vi, 302 f.). And it seems that many temples were furnished with these primitive idols well into the Roman

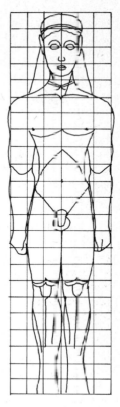

period, so the demand, except for installation in brand-new structures, may have been less than we imagine. If any major new works in wood were executed in the earlier Archaic period we have no reason to believe that they could have been different in appearance from the Daedalic – a style not originally dependent on wood – nor is there any clear evidence for significant influence on seventh-century statuary from any carpentry styles, other than the purely technical. Any early wooden statues might, however, have been large. The probable base for the wooden cult statue of the early Heraion on Samos was a stone cylinder with a sinking o·57 square. The bases for early marble statues are generally shallow blocks with a sinking for the plinth, the marble slab cut with the feet and rounded off close to them, fastened in position with lead. Sphinxes and human figures could also be mounted on columns, Ionic or Doric according to local architectural practice. An exceptional kouros base is boulder-like, with heads at each corner, signed by Euthykartidas of Naxos [16]. It is no later than 600, one of our earliest sculptor's signatures, and important in telling us that the sculptor was also the dedicator, and so a man of substance.

Kouroi

The battered torsos and heads of the early stone kouroi leave us unable to distinguish easily, let alone date closely, the first of this important new series which is to be the yardstick of sculptural progress through the sixth century, and the first realization of true monumental sculpture in Greek lands. It is clear, however, that the type is established from the beginning – an upright stance, with straight or lightly flexed arms at the sides, fists clenched. One leg is slightly advanced, usually the left. We step off naturally with the left foot so this enhances the impression of energy and movement as well as providing a more secure support for the heavy mass of the solid marble body balanced on two slim ankles. Moreover, the Greeks preferred profile figures to the right with the farther leg advanced, and the preliminary sketch on a block for a kouros would dictate this pose. The hands, after the earliest, are empty. The belt worn by the early island figures is the only dress beyond a hair fillet or necklet, and exceptionally the boots for [70], and the belt is the same type as that worn by the Daedalic women. Bronze warriors wore helmet and belt alone, well into the seventh century [46]. The kouroi are not warriors, but this is a closer parallel than remote and irrelevant eastern belt-wrestling practices, which have been mentioned in this context, and we shall shortly remark a possible Cretan connection.

What are the kouroi? They used to be called Apollos but none are cult statues, or even certainly representations of a deity, although the type can be converted to this use by raising the forearms to hold attributes [150]. In sanctuaries of male deities they are dedications offering more permanent and silent service to a god than could mortal flesh. Most of this class are from Apollo sanctuaries, the only notable exceptions being from Sounion (Poseidon), while the very few from sanctuaries of goddesses – Athena (Athens) and Hera (Samos) – do not seriously upset this pattern, and some fragmentary candidates might be from figures of other types or groups. In their other function, as grave markers, the kouroi replace cruder slabs, which may tend to the anthropomorphic (see Chapter Eight). Without pretending to portray the dead they summon up remembrance of the youth and vigour admired by their kin and friends, who are often named as donors of the monument, and now lost to them. So both usages are in a way substitute and commemorative. Only grave kouroi, and a few of them, may acknowledge variations in age, with some barely adolescent, but none more than young-mature, and none admitting by dress their calling – warriors, for instance, although the epitaph may have them 'fallen in battle'. An Archaic cemetery peopled with these intent pale figures must have been an unnerving place.

For the appearance of a complete early kouros from the islands we may turn to the famous bronze statuette from Delphi [57]. In proportion and details of limbs and belt he exactly matches his more battered marble comrades [58, 59], and we may deduce that the earliest of them had Daedalic heads, like the bronze. The head looks very Cretan, and most scholars have taken the bronze to be Cretan. There are no Cretan stone kouroi but the belt is an old Cretan one so the bronze is perhaps a hint that Cretan statuary skills were enrolled in the early island studios, and the belt might then be a concession to that Cretan shyness we have already noted. The Crete-Delphi association was a strong one—in religion (the worship of Apollo Delphinios) and in dedication of statues (Pindar, *Pythian* 5, 39–42, of wood). Crete's devotion to the dressed female type in statuary and her lack of marble may explain the absence of early kouroi in the island. Cretan artists had the tradition in statuary the tools, and the connections with Egypt requisite for the inception of monumental marble sculpture. All they lacked was the material and it may well have been Cretans that manned the early island quarry-studios, since the islanders themselves lacked these prerequisites.

There are several different sources for our early marble kouroi, all, except the Samian and Boeotian, using Cycladic marble. There are regional differences, which probably did not emerge strongly until after 600, when local studios achieve some independence of style though still mainly dependent on island sources of stone.

In the islands the belted fragments from Delos give a fair idea of the new type, slim, small-buttocked, barely modelled, the hair in beaded tresses [53, 59]. The Naxian colossus [60] which stood near four times lifesize, is one of the latest, with the hair spreading in realistic curled locks on to the chest, and the head, to judge from drawings, already a full oval. Thera has also yielded an important early series, from a cemetery rather than a sanctuary [61]. One of these wears a belt, the only marble example outside Delos but proving that the belt is not a peculiarly Apolline feature. In Ionia Samos takes the lead with a number of thrice-lifesize kouroi in local marble, from the Heraion, preserved only in fragments.

Athens enters the story around 600 with the Dipylon head [62] and its companion, the complete but far inferior New York kouros [63] which is probably from a countryside cemetery in Attica. Here we can study in detail some characteristics of the early kouroi, though few others of this date may have been so carefully finished or are so pattern-conscious, and this is the figure whose proportions seem to have been determined by a canon of Egyptian type. Previously, anatomy patterns had been barely observed on figures, whether drawn or in the round, though ribcage, pectorals and shoulder blades were commonly worked on lifesize bronze corselets and hinted at in some figurines [46]. On the New York kouros details are designed almost as independent patterns – volute ears, beaded hair with even the knot of the fillet stylized; the lightly grooved and relief patterns of the front of the body, neck and sinewy legs; the shoulder blades, the hands, wrists, elbows, knee-caps. Individually they are unrealistic but totally effective translations into pure pattern, not of carefully observed anatomy, but of those details and groupings of pattern, each laid out in a rigid frontal view, which the artist conceives to make up the whole man. But their organic interrelation has yet to be understood, and the sum of parts achieves monumentality less by any perceived unity than by the almost spectral hint of life, imparted by the pose and size. In execution the figure has not shrugged free from the rectangular block of stone from which it was hewn. This is clearest in the face, with the broad flat cheek. But the sharply intersecting planes of the face, especially around the eyes, and the linear patterns achieved by neat grooves, sharp or shallow, indicate the many new possibilities in rendering the body. After years of inhibiting convention or trivial though delicate decoration, a first step is taken towards a fully satisfactory expression in stone of the Greek view of man, of his relationship to his fellows and his gods, the acknowledgement of a rightness, restraint and proportion, which are as applicable to conduct as to statuary, the *kalon kai agathon*.

The kouroi from the Poseidon temple at Sounion [*64, 65*] in south Attica are slightly more developed than the New York kouros. The forelocks on the hairband are like shells, the hollow-beaded tresses like wind-rippled sand. Grooved anatomy patterns on back and stomach are more aggressively decorative, chin and forehead more emphatic.

The crude pair on the stele from Boeotia [*66*] show what can happen away from the major marble-working centres, with proportion and pattern badly scaled. And the kouros from Boeotia [*67*] with its comparatively late egg-shaped head and more naturally lobed ears reveals similar faults of design. The head [*68*] is better, a country cousin to [*62*].

The kouros type was adapted for the unfinished ram-bearer from Thasos (a Parian colony), its hair recalling the New York kouros, its sleek figure the earlier island kouroi [*69*]. Another adaptation is the stocky pair, Kleobis and Biton, dedicated by the Argives at Delphi [*70*]. From the front the low brows and hair bunched behind the ears seem sub-Daedalic, but from the side we notice the more natural ears, the extremely thickset bodies and tough flexed arms which, with the traces of the boots they wore, recall the purpose of the dedication, commemorating their strength in pulling a chariot along the Argos road. The slight differences between the twins are trivial yet some have sought to explain the more battered one as the work of an Ionian apprentice. Kleobis and Biton give us, nearly, their sculptor's name – . . .]medes of Argos.

Korai

The marble statues of women served the same purposes as the kouroi. Rather fewer of them are demonstrably funerary (from Attica; possibly Samos, Chios and Thera) and in goddess sanctuaries they may serve Artemis (Delos, Klaros), Hera (Samos), Nymphs (Samos), Athena (Athens, Miletus), Demeter (Eleusis).

Their importance in the development of Archaic Greek sculpture comes only after the period studied in this chapter, since the early marble examples are

24

wholly Daedalic in appearance. The earliest complete statue is Nikandre's dedication on Delos [71, right], but for all the similarity in style we have only to set her beside the Auxerre statuette [28; 71, left] to realize what the increase in size can add in presence and monumentality. Her date, relative to Auxerre, is hard to determine since the raw rectangularity must be in large part due to the difficulty of working the less familiar, harder material. Closer to Auxerre in detail was an even larger kore from Samos, of which only one substantial fragment survives [72]. This and similar early pieces on Samos are in imported marble but after about 600 local sources are used.

For a view of the heads of these figures we turn to other Daedalic work of smaller size, then to the moulded clay heads on Corinthian vases with their more developed features and oval outline. And, since korai are rare in these years, for other female statuary to the lifesize seated figures in soft stone or the smaller figures studied in the next section. When we come to the sixth century a head from Olympia [73], but of limestone, shows us how the female features match in general outline those of the latest kouroi so far considered. It appears to be from the seated Hera which, with a standing Zeus, was the cult group in the Temple of Hera (Pausanias v, 17.1) and probably made for the new temple in the early sixth century. The rather stark features suit its size and function.

Perirrhanteria

Over a dozen seventh-century marble perirrhanteria are known [74–79] – shallow water basins, some with knobbed handles, supported by three or four female figures who, in most cases, stand on or beside lions, holding them by tail and lead. The women are up to one metre high. The type is derived from Syria or Cyprus, where we find dishes carried by figures or sphinxes, and deities standing on lions or lion-bases. In Greece the basins come from sanctuaries and have been found in Laconia (five), Olympia (two or more), Isthmia (near Corinth), Delphi, Rhodes, Samos, the Ptoon (Boeotia). Early dates have been proposed – early enough to make them Greece's first marble sculpture – but this is improbable. The figures are not Daedalic, but the sharp features, smooth and well-modelled bodies, and the pcdgy lion heads seem all characteristic of Laconia where many have been found. The material of many too is a grey marble which can pass as Laconian, but it is commonly held that some were made where they were found (Rhodes, Samos) despite the general unity of style and dissimilarity to other local work. This overall concord of style suggests a short period of production although the general form and style is repeated on some marble lamps with relief heads (which include some Daedalic) and the ensemble is recalled on the Athens Acropolis in the sixth century. The Laconian or laconizing basins need be no earlier than the last third of the seventh century. Sparta may seem a surprising home for this alternative to the Daedalic style, in marble and on such foreign-looking objects, but the concept is borrowed for smaller Daedalic objects in clay and we may take this as further evidence for Laconia's special links with the east and with some Ionians (Samos), otherwise best shown by her ivories. Another Laconian oddity in marble, perhaps also inspired by the east, is the kneeling goddess [80].

Artists and authors

Contemporary texts tell us little or nothing about statuary. Homer has no word for 'statue' (later *andrias*, as on [60]) and *agalma* refers to workmanship on any scale. Later authors like Pausanias comment on the crudity of early wooden figures and have no real conception of the early development. At first there may have been a distinctly magical aspect to major statuary, and the Rhodian Telchines, said to have made the first images of the gods (Diodorus v, 55), were wizards who could also control the weather and change their shapes. The word *kolossos*, which does not necessarily imply 'colossal', could refer to a substitute for men (compare [40]). The figures of Daedalus were said to see and walk, even talk. We have met his name already, applied by modern scholars to the seventh-century orientalizing style. '*Daidalos*' means 'cunningly wrought' and there is a Daedalus creating wonders in the myth history of the Bronze Age (aeronautics with Ikaros, etc.). Many lifelike and Archaic but not primitive works were attributed to Daedalus, and when Diodorus (iv, 76) says his figures have open eyes, separate legs as if walking and arms free of the body, clearly the early stone kouroi are indicated, nothing earlier, although many alleged '*daidala*' are wooden. Diodorus (i, 97) also associated him with Egypt saying that his statues have the *rhythmos* of the Egyptian, which makes sense, and he made a famous folding stool; Egyptian furniture was introduced to Greece around 600. Many make him Cretan, like his Bronze Age predecessor (the two are not distinguished in the sources), which also makes sense in terms of the island's seventh-century record and possible contribution to the island kouroi. Others have him Athenian. A contemporary, Smilis of Aegina (Pausanias vii, 4) was said to have made the cult image of Hera on Samos. Of Daedalus' pupils Dipoinos and Skyllis, said to have been born in Crete, were working in the Peloponnese in the second quarter of the sixth century, and Endoios in Athens in the second half. These were real artists: Daedalus may be a personification of those early monumental styles from which their work derived, or, if the view taken here of the Delphi bronze [57] is correct, a Cretan artist who understandably acquired a reputation as teacher of the first sculptors of truly monumental works in Greece.

We get hardly closer to the anonymous artists of the works which have survived. Homer knows palace craftsmen and itinerant *demioergoi*. In Archaic Greece an important sanctuary like Olympia might attract resident artists, as the Bronze Age palaces did, and some have seen a Laconian Geometric studio for bronzes established there. The guild or family which brought eastern fashions to Crete before 800 was certainly foreign. Within Greece the sources of stone, especially marble, were inevitably at first the homes of the sculptors' studios, but we have already detected independent local styles, as in Attica so it was possible for the individuality of an artist to be stamped on the works of a school, wherever he may have learned his craft or still have to acquire hi material. Euthykartidas signed his work on Delos [56] but primarily perhaps as its dedicator. With . . .]medes' signature at Delphi we meet a proud claim of creation, not gainsaid by the dedicators, and the sixth century will see a growing awareness by artists of the individual quality of their work, perhaps not without some thought for advertisement.

1 Clay figure from a shrine at Karphi (Crete). More probably an adorant than a goddess. She wears a Minoan horns symbol on her cap, and the type is traditional in Crete, including the raised hands gesture. The feet are made separately and hung in the skirt. (Heraklion Mus.; H. 0·67) About 1000

2 Clay janiform head, from Piskokephalo (Crete). The features were painted and the conical lower part was probably for insertion in a wooden body over half lifesize. (Oxford AE 1102; H. 0·295) About 900

3 Clay stag, from a grave in Athens, decorated in the Protogeometric style. (Athens, Kerameikos Mus. 641; H. 0·26) About 925 (dated by context)

4 Clay centaur, found part within a tomb, part over another tomb, at Lefkandi (Euboea). A deliberate painted nick in the right foreleg has been associated with the story that the centaur Chiron was wounded in the leg by Herakles with an arrow, but a myth figure in the round so early is unexpected and we would look for more explicit statement of the action. Eretria; H. 0·36) Before about 900 (dated by context)

6 Clay helmeted head, from the Amyklaion sanctuary (Laconia). (Athens; H. 0·115) About 700

7 Bronze warrior from Karditsa (Thessaly). His spear is missing but he wears helmet, belt and 'Dipylon' shield (a light wicker or hide shield, stylized into this shape by the Geometric artist). (Athens Br. 12831; H. 0·28) About 700

5 Bronze man from Olympia, from the ring handle of a tripod cauldron, on which he stood holding a spear in his right hand, the lead of a horse in his left. (Olympia B 4600; H. 0·144) About 750

8 Bronze horse. The base is an openwork of triangles. (Berlin 31317; H. 0·16) About 750–700

9 Bronze antlered deer with fawn and bird, from the Kabirion sanctuary near Thebes. Greek artists often show deer with antlers, into the classical period. (Boston 98.650, Pierce Fund; H. 0·07) About 750–700

10 Bronze man from Thebes. The dedication by Mantiklos is written in two hexameters on the thighs. 'Mantiklos offers me as a tithe to Apollo of the silver bow; do you, Phoibos, give some pleasing favour in return.' (Boston 3.997; H. 0·20) Early 7th c.

Μαντικλος μ'ανεθεκε ϝεκαβολοι αργυροτοχσοι
τας {δ}δεκατας· τυ δε Φοιβε διδοι χαριϝετταν αμοιϝ[αν]

11 Bronze helmet-maker. This is unusual for this period in having no base or signs of attachment. The subject suggests a craftsman's dedication. (New York 42.11.42, Fletcher Fund; H. 0·052) Early 7th c.

12 Bronze hunter and dog attacking a lion with prey in its mouth, from Samos. The helmet lends a heroic air to a heroic occasion (there were no lions in the Greek islands although Homer knew their behaviour well). Beneath the base is an intaglio swastika. (Once Samos; H. 0·09) About 700

13 Bronze hero fighting a centaur, from Olympia (?). Both are helmeted; he plunges a sword into the monster's flank. Possibly Herakles and Nessos. (New York 17.190.2072, Morgan Gift; H. 0·11) About 750–700

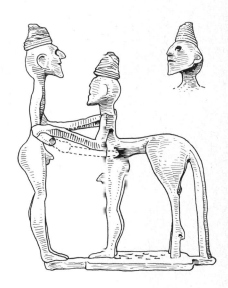

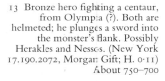

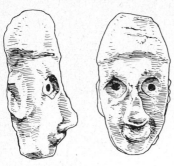

14 Limestone head from Amnisos.
The eyes had been inlaid, probably in
bone. (Heraklion 345; H. 0·16) 8th c.

15 Limestone relief from Chania. A goddess stands frontal in the
gateway of her temple or city. Pairs of archers, one above the
other, protect her. They wear helmets of eastern type and the
horse from the attacking chariot resembles the Assyrian,
somewhat geometricized. The relief may be from a building.
There is a comparable scene on a bronze belt of this style from
Knossos. (Chania 92; H. 0·39) 8th c.

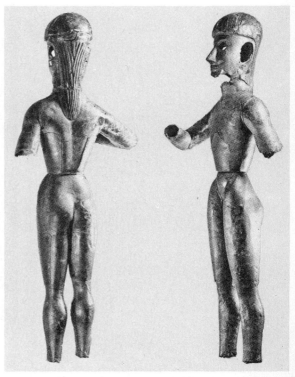

16 Bronze statues (one of two female and the male) from Dreros. Probably cult images
which stood on the corner basis of the 8th-c. temple of Apollo. The god's hair is worked in
long hook-locks; the restoration of his arms is uncertain. The bronze sheets were pinned
together over a wooden core having been hammered into shape, a technique familiar also for
gold figures of this style (called *sphyrelaton*). The eyes had been inlaid. (Heraklion 2445–7; H.
0·40, 0·80) About 700

17 Bronze statuette from Afrati, in a deposit of the second half of the 8th c. Compare the 'Apollo' *16* especially for the head and hair. (Heraklion) Late 8th c.

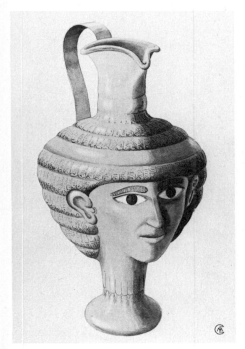

18 Bronze head vase from the Idaean Cave sanctuary of Zeus. The patterned hair, brows and shape of head are eastern. Neck and handle are restored in the drawing. (Oxford AE 211 and Heraklion; W. 0·114) Mid-7th c.

19 Ivory girl from Athens. The largest of five similar figures in a grave dated by its pottery to about 730. It also contained three faience lion figurines and worked bone. The figure may have served as a handle, like eastern counterparts. The proportions resemble the (clothed) Dreros figures *16*. (Athens 776; H. 0·24)

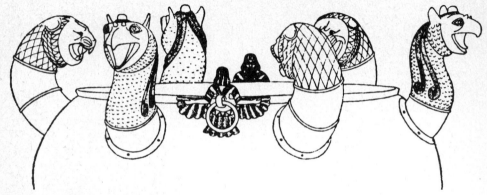

20 Bronze cauldron from Olympia with beaten lion and griffin heads and cast siren attachments. (Olympia; lip diam. about 0·65) Early 7th c.

22 Cast bronze griffin from a cauldron, from Olympia. A later refinement of the hammered griffins. The series continues into the 6th c. (Olympia) Mid-7th c.

21 Heads from bronze siren attachments to cauldrons, from Olympia. The imported eastern type above a Greek version. The series of these figures is of the latest 8th and early 7th c. (Olympia)

23 Clay plaque from
Corinth. Imported from
Syria. Astarte, with
hands to breast and
loins. (Corinth MF 4039;
H. 0·10) 7th c.

24 Clay mould (cast) from Corinth.
Made locally but from an eastern
original. (Corinth KH 1; H. 0·06)
7th c.

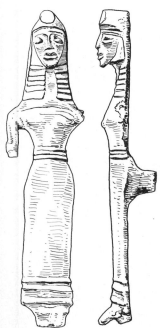

25 Bronze handle from Gortyn,
temple of Apollo.
(Heraklion 2448; H. 0·17)
Early 7th c.

26 Clay plaque from Crete.
The *polos* hat had been squashed
before firing. Aphrodite (?).
(Oxford AE 403; H. 0·14) Mid-7th c.

27 Clay figure (plaque) from
Axos, sanctuary of a goddess
later identified as Athena.
A goddess bares her belly in
a ritual, fertility gesture.
(Chania; H. 0·13) Mid-7th c.

29 Limestone seated figure from
Astritsi. (Heraklion 407; H. 1·04)
About 650–640

28 The 'Auxerre goddess', limestone, formerly
in the Auxerre Museum, originally perhaps from
Crete. Incision and traces of painted lines
indicate a coloured scale pattern on the chest,
squares along the cloak border and concentric
squares on the skirt. (Louvre 3098; H. 0·65)
About 640–630. See also *128*

30 Limestone seated woman from
Gortyn, sanctuary of 'Athena'.
Traces of red paint on the belt
and skirt patterns. (Heraklion
380; H. 0·80) About 650–630

31 Limestone relief from Gortyn temple of Apollo. A god striding between two naked women, wearing *poloi*, his hands on their shoulders. One of two similar slabs which probably stood as dado blocks at the front of the temple where there seem also to have been half-relief sphinxes (another eastern feature) in the doorway. (Heraklion 379; H. 1·50) About 630–620

32.1

32 Sculpture from Prinias See next page

32·3

32·2

32.4 Limestone sculpture from a temple at Prinias. The restoration is highly problematic. The seated women face each other over a lintel carved with animals in front and perhaps behind, with frontal standing women on the underside. The lower parts of the faces of both the seated and relief figures are restored. They were set either on the façade or over the cella door. The riders frieze was more probably a dado in the porch, in the eastern manner, than a crowning frieze, in the later Greek manner. The horses' long legs look primitive but this is a recurrent Cretan feature for the creatures and set low the extra length would be foreshortened. (Heraklion; H. of seated woman (231) 0·82; of frieze (232) 0·84) About 620–600

33 Limestone seated woman from Eleutherna. (Heraklion 47; H. 0·57) About 600

34 Clay 'Athena' from Gortyn. She holds spear and shield, and wears a helmet, made separately. The body is wheel-made, the face moulded. (Heraklion 18502; complete H. 0·36) About 660–650

35 Limestone reliefs from Mycenae acropolis. On one (above) a woman draws cloak over head, a gesture of modesty and rank. The reliefs must be from a building, probably a dado frieze of slabs in the Cretan-eastern manner. Other fragments are from fighting scenes and one (below) is plausibly restored as two sphinxes lifting a body, perhaps the Keres on the battlefield, but there was no certain unity of theme in the frieze. (Athens 2869, H. 0·40 and the restored fragment Athens 2870, H. of slab about 0·90) About 630

36 Limestone relief from Malesina (Boeotia). Provincial Daedalic – the oval face and high forehead indicate a late date. Apparently to be restored as a bust only, like an eastern 'woman in the window', so probably votive. (Louvre MND 910; H. 0·34) About 600–590

46 cm

37 Bronze head from Olympia. Hollow cast, probably from a complete figure which served as a support, perhaps for a bowl (there is a hole at the crown of the head). The hair is shown by incised vertical wavy lines at the back but in horizontal layers at the side. The eyes were inlaid. (Karlsruhe F 1890; H. 0·087) About 640

38 Ivory sphinx from Perachora, sanctuary of Hera Limenia. (Athens 16519; H. 0·08) About 650

39 Ivory group in high relief. Two girls, one tying (or untying) her girdle, baring her upper body, the other with her cloak falling from her. A similar pair, baring themselves, are seen on a contemporary painted metope from Thermon. They may be the daughters of the Argive king Proitos, maddened by Hera. (New York 17.190.73, Morgan Gift; H. 0.137) About 630

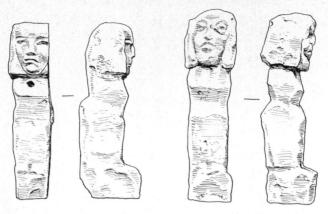

40 Limestone figures from Thera. The bodies are roughly blocked out. They were found in a mass cenotaph ('Schiff's grave') dated by the pottery found in it, and may have been substitutes for bodies lost at sea or in some other disaster. (Thera; H. 0·19, 0·18) About 660–650

41 Protocorinthian oil flask (aryballos) from Thebes. The head is mould-made. The painted decoration, by the Boston Painter, can be closely dated. (Louvre CA 931; H. 0·068) About 650

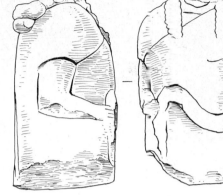

42 Limestone figure from Tanagra (Boeotia). The rounded bell-like treatment of the dress resembles late 7th-c. figures on vases. This is probably a man (inscribed '...imarou' (?)), holding an animal. (Thebes; H. 0·43) Late 7th c.

43 Bronze lyre-player from Crete (?). (Heraklion 2064; H. 0·055) Early 7th c.

44 Bronze sphinx from Crete (?). This was fastened to an object and something is broken away from above the bud-like terminal. One wing is carried forward and turned flat. The raising of the hindquarters is in fact a 6th-c. feature for stone sphinxes, cf. 224. (Berlin 31342; H. 0·078) Late 7th c. or later

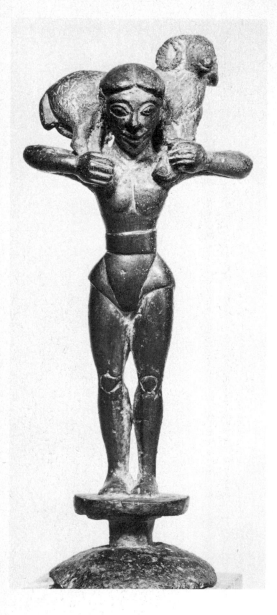

45 Bronze ram-bearer (*kriophoros*) from Crete. For the action, appropriate to Hermes as well as a shepherd, see 69. The stalk and mass below the base are from the casting channel and usually cut away. (Berlin 7477; H. 0·18) About 620

46 Bronze warrior from Olympia. (Olympia B 1701; H. 0·17) About 650

47 Bronze charioteer from Olympia. This has been thought Attic work. (Olympia B 1700; H. 0·23) About 650

48 Bronze woman from Thebes. Said to have been found with *10* but decidedly later, her hair style is Daedalic. The clenched hand had something in it, the other is held open, palm up (Baltimore, Walters Art Gallery 54.773; H. 0·18) Third quarter of the 7th c.

49 Wooden goddess from Samos. The high *polos* is open behind and is perhaps to be taken as Hera's tower-headdress, *pyleon*. The shawl and dress are as the Cretan, also the disposition of the pattern, cf. *28*. The forearms, made separately, were held forward. The tenon below is for fixing into a larger object rather than a base in the later manner of stone statuary. (Samos inv. H 41; H. 0·287) About 630

50 Wooden plaque from Samos. A man embraces a woman, holding her breast. A flying bird (eagle or omen) between their heads. This is often taken for a 'sacred marriage' (*hieros gamos*) scene with Zeus and Hera. Its findplace might support this but the scheme is oriental. (Once Samos, now disintegrated; H. 0·191) About 630–600

51 Ivory head from Perachora, sanctuary of Hera Limenia. Eastern work. (Athens 16520; H. 0·04) About 700

52 Ivory group from Delphi. The scheme resembles eastern reliefs
of a hero with a lion, the long spiral curls, skirt split to the belt and
the style of the lion are also eastern. Apollo's association with lions
is attested later, but would be unusual in this form at this date
unless by reference to his sister Artemis, as Mistress of Animals.
The base carries a pattern met in east Greece and Lydia but not
closely datable. (Delphi; H. 0·24) First half of the 7th c.

53 Ivory woman standing on a sphinx or
siren. From the arm of a lyre, as 54.
(Berlin 1964.36; H. 0·225) About 600

54 Ivory youth from Samos. Eyes, brows, ear lobes (with earrings) and pubic hair were inlaid. The figure was one of a pair set on the corners of a lyre. The head profile is distinctive; cf. 51. (Athens; H. 0·145) Late 7th c.

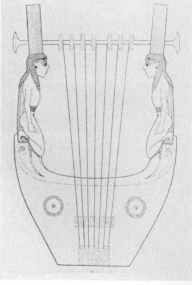

55 Unfinished kouros on the path from the quarries, Naxos

56 Kouros base from Delos. Ram, lion and gorgon head bosses. Signed 'Euthykartidas the Naxian made and dedicated me'. (Delos A 728; H. 0·58) About 600

Εὐθυκαρτίδης :
μ' α{ξ}νεσεκε : ho
Naho̅ιος : πο-
-ιε̄σος

58 Kouros from Delos. (Delos A 334; H. 0·69) About 625–600

57 Bronze kouros from Delphi. (Delphi 2527; H. 0·197) About 630

59 Kouros from Delos. The more advanced anatomical detail (pubic hair, divided scrotum) indicate a later date than the comparatively featureless 58. The penis was made separately, now missing. (Delos A 333; H. 0·85=about 2·80 complete) About 580

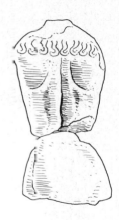

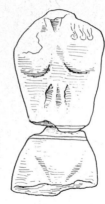

OΛΡΥΤΟΡΙΘΟΕΜΙΑΝΔΡΙΑΞΚΑΙΤΟΣΦΕΓΑS

[τ]ο αϝυτο λιϡο εμι ενϖιας και το σφελας

60 Kouros from Delos. Two fragments and perhaps a hand (on Delos) and the toes (in London) remain. A sketch after Cyriacus of Ancona who saw it in AD 1445, shows the head too. The locks and belt were modelled, the holes are perhaps for later embellishment. The base into which the statue with its plinth was set declares 'I am of the same stone, statue and *sphelas*'. *Sphelas* should mean base: the allusion remains enigmatic but could refer to the monolithic character of *each* colossal part. A later inscription describes it as a dedication of the Naxians. It was knocked over by the bronze palm tree dedicated by Nikias in 417, which stood 27 m away. Its top had perhaps been blown on to the statue in a gale. (Delos; H. 2·20, 1·20= about 10·0 complete) About 580–570

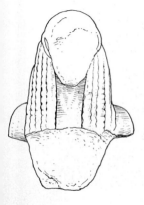

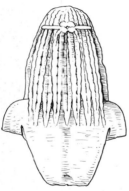

61 Kouros from Thera cemetery (?). The face and most of the chest are broken away. (Thera; H. 1·03=about 2·50 complete) About 625–600

62 Kouros ('Dipylon head') from Athens. From the same workshop as *63* but the hair is gathered at the nape and its beading interlocks instead of lying in horizontal rows. One hand is also preserved and closely comparable fragments from the Agora (*Kouroi* no. 7). (Athens 3372; H. 0·44) About 590

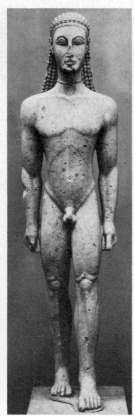

63 Kouros from Attica (?).
(New York 32.11.1; H. 1·8ₘ)
About 600–590

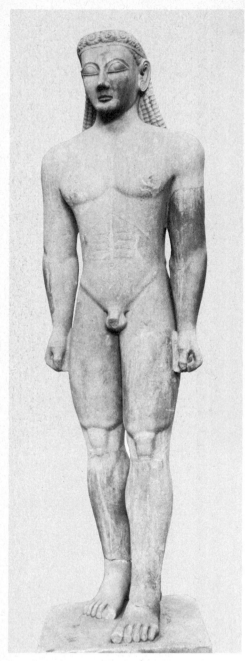

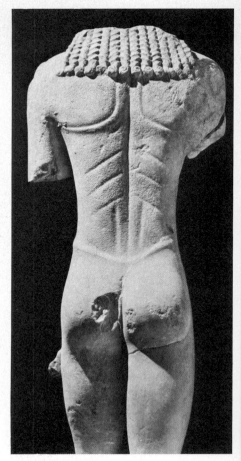

65 Kouros from Sounion. This shows the same elaborate groove and ridge patterning typical of the Sounion figures. (Athens 3645; H. 1·65) About 590–580

64 Kouros from Sounion. Left arm and leg, right shin, most of left eye, nose and mouth restored; the feet may not belong. Closely related to 63 (notice ears, eyes, torso front). Found in a pit in the sanctuary of Poseidon with parts of at least two other kouroi and, in all, four bases. They had presumably been buried after a disaster – perhaps the Persian invasion of 480. (Athens 2720; H. restored 3·05) About 590–580

67 Kouros from Orchomenos (Boeotia). (Athens 9; bluish marble, probably local; H. 1·27=about 2·0 complete) About 580–570

66 Limestone stele from Tanagra. Inscribed by each figure 'Dermys', 'Kitylos', and on the base 'Amphalkes put (this up for D. and K.'. Each has one arm round the other's shoulder, set impossibly high. The gesture appears in sculpture for Egyptian couples. (Athens 56; H. of figures 1·47) About 580

68 Limestone kouros head from the Ptoon
(Boeotia). (Athens 15; H. 0·33) About 580

69 Ram-bearer from Thasos. This identifies more
closely with the dedicator, since the figure carries an
offering. The statue is unfinished, blocked out with the
point and only the hair more fully worked. The
arrangement of the hair and placing of ears look
unskilful rather than primitive. (Thasos; H. 3·5) About
580

70 Kleobis and Biton from Delphi. See next page

70 Kleobis and Biton from Delphi (see previous page). They probably stood side by side.
The young men had taken the place of oxen to pull their priestess-mother's cart from Argos
to the temple of Hera. For their piety and strength she begged from the goddess the greatest
boon for mortals: and they died in their sleep. Herodotus (i, 31) goes on to say that the
Argives sent statues of them to Delphi. We do not know when the alleged feat was
performed, but the pious and uncontroversial dedication was made just after the First Sacred
War when Argos and Dorians in general were unpopular at Delphi. The fate of the brothers
is strangely paralleled by the fate of the brother architects (Agamedes and Trophonios) of the
first stone temple of Apollo, completed about this time. Inscriptions run across the tops of
the plinths naming them, alluding to the story, and naming the artist, Argive Poly?]medes.
The figures are booted. The chunky style is taken by many scholars to be characteristic of the
Peloponnese. (Delphi 467, 1524; H. restored 1·97) About 580

[Πολυ?]μεδες εποιϝε ηοργϵιος   ΜΕΔΕΜΕΓΟΙΕΕΘΑΡΓΕΙΟΜ

72 Kore from Samos. Fragment of neck and upper body.
(Samos I. 95; H. 0·42=about 2·5 complete) About 640–630

71 (right) Kore from Delos, sanctuary
of Artemis. Inscribed along the left of
her skirt. 'Nikandre dedicated me to
the far-shooter of arrows, the excellent
daughter of Deinodikes of Naxos,
sister of Deinomenes, wife of Phraxos
n(ow?)'. She was no doubt a priestess.
The figure is nowhere more than 0·17
deep. The surviving hand is pierced by
a drill hole 0·06 deep, to hold a floral
or possibly the lead of a lion, as 74, 75.
(Athens 1; H. 1·75) About 640–630.
This is the cast in Oxford, set beside
the cast of 28

ΝΙΚΑΝΔΡΒΜΑΜΕΘΕΚΕΜΒΚΕΚΟΓΟΙΙΟΧΕΑΙΡΒΙΡΟΡΒΔΕΙΝ
ΒΤΜΙΛΣΑΗΔΙΧΟΣΤΕΜΟΒΙΑΟΧΟΣΟΙΚΟΑΜΟΤΟΒΧΙΑ
ΦΒΡΑΟΣΟΔΑΛΟΧΟΣΝ

Νικανδρη μ'ανεθεκεν h⟨ε⟩κηβολōι ιοχεαιρηι, θορη Δεινο-
-δικηο το Ναhσιο, εhσοχος αλōν, Δεινομενεος δε κασιγνετη,
Φhραhσο δ'αλοχος ν⟨υν?⟩

73 Limestone head of Hera from Olympia, temple of Hera. There were traces of red on the
hairband, and yellowish red on the hair. The ear and mass beside it suggest that she was
seated on a high-backed throne. A scrap from what may be the base can be restored with a
man between lions, an orientalizing composition seen in the east (with a demon) on a base
from Carchemish. (Olympia; H. 0·52, over twice lifesize) About 580

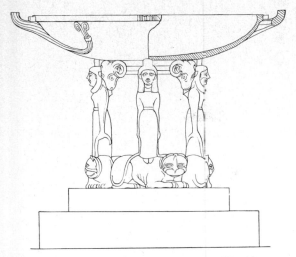

74 Perirrhanterion from Isthmia, sanctuary of Poseidon. The women stood on lions, holding them by lead and tail. Much restored. (Corinth; H. 1·26 without stepped base) Late 7th c.

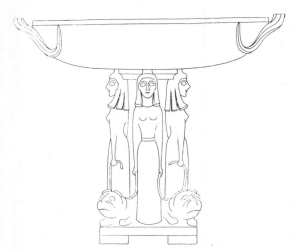

75 Perirrhanterion from Samos. (Berlin 1747; H. restored 0·52) Late 7th c.

76 Perirrhanterion from Olympia, figure support only. The centre support was in the form of a Doric column. (Olympia; H. 0·475). Late 7th c.

79 Perirrhanterion from Sparta. Head and handle attachment from the basin. (Sparta 1658; H. of head 0·105) Late 7th c.

77 Perirrhanterion from Kameiros (Rhodes). (Rhodes; H. 1·0) Late 7th c.

80 Naked goddess kneeling, flanked by a pipes player, and another figure at her other side, from Sparta. Probably a goddess of fertility or childbirth (the piper drowns the cries). (Sparta 364; H. 0·48) About 600

78 Perirrhanterion from Sparta. Only the lions are preserved. (Sparta; W. 0·52) Late 7th c.

Chapter Five

THE MATURING ARCHAIC STYLES
to about 530 BC

Sources

Most major statuary of the Archaic period was intended either for commemoration of the dead or for dedication and decoration in a sanctuary. The grave markers and dedications betoken a degree of personal or family wealth readily comprehensible in states whose agriculture and trade remained largely in the hands of rich families supported by dependents and slaves. The quality of the dedications was partly determined by the splendours of the sanctuary in which they stood and which they had to match. The more grandiose architecture of the national sanctuaries could be financed from offerings of individuals or states, as at Delphi or Olympia. In other cities major works depended on the resources, vision and sometimes the ostentatious pride of their rulers. This is the age of 'tyrants' in many Greek cities. Their wealth and authority enforced by arms provided the impetus for major architecture and other works; and their courts, which complemented rather than suppressed the life-style of aristocratic families, themselves became a focus for the activity of artists of all sorts in a manner recalling the Bronze Age palaces and anticipating the Hellenistic kingdoms.

The two prime sources for sculpture of our period were the seats of two of the most powerful 'tyrannies'. The Hera temple on Samos had already a long and distinguished history, but a new and massive temple was being built in the second quarter of the sixth century, and in the third the tyrant Polycrates commissioned many public works including a rebuilding of the temple. These are years in which the sanctuary, town and cemetery are richest in statuary recovered by excavation.

In Athens the Acropolis had been devoted to religious affairs by the late 560s, a new temple had been built and the state festival of Athens, the Panathenaia, reorganized. The later tyrant Peisistratos had played some part in this, perhaps. He dominates, with his sons, the years down to 510 and this is an extremely rich period for sculpture and architecture on the Acropolis. While Peisistratos was still alive the new glories of the Acropolis were mainly architectural, with their accompanying sculpture, and it seems that for some of the time he and his sons shared the sacred rock with the gods and lived upon it. After his death in 527 the proliferation of dedications begins in earnest. The buildings and statues were

63

overthrown by the Persians in 480/479, but the returning Athenians buried the broken marble statuary and bases on the Acropolis, whence they were recovered by excavation at the end of the last century. It seems to have been an act of tidiness rather than piety on the part of the Athenians since, from the bases found, we know that at least half the dedications were bronze. Virtually no bronze statues of any size were found, nor could Xerxes have taken them all away. Some may have survived undamaged; the broken ones were perhaps melted down – broken marbles are useless.

This is the richest single source for this period and tends to overweight our view of Archaic sculpture in favour of Athens, well supplemented as it is by finds in the city cemetery and in the smaller graveyards in the Attic countryside, where many rich families lived. The Acropolis finds also give us a vital dating point for late Archaic art although it is possible that some of the architectural sculpture found had been already discarded or replaced before the Persians arrived and at least one Archaic marble statue may have survived the Persians [135]. The circumstances of discovery of grave monuments in Attica will be discussed in Chapter Eight.

Elsewhere in Greece finds have been sporadic but plentiful, from cemeteries and sanctuaries: besides Olympia, Delos and Delphi the shrine of Apollo Ptoos should be mentioned, on a high hillside 20 km north of Thebes and the source of nearly 120 fragmentary kouroi, and the great Ionian sanctuary sites at Ephesus and Didyma. But of other cities whose wealth and importance is attested by historians we still lack any significant range of finds (Corinth, Thebes, Sicyon, Argos, Chios), and since our evidence is so partial the attempt to identify local sculptural styles, except through minor arts where they often can be defined, is found to be a highly speculative one.

One phenomenon at least which has a historical context can be detected simply from observation of styles and signatures – the diaspora of east Greek artists from before the middle of the century on. Oppression by Lydia followed by the fall of Sardis (546) and the advance of the Persian empire to the Aegean taught many east Greeks the wisdom of seeking new homes in mainland Greece or farther west. Their influence can be traced where our evidence is fullest, in Athens, and it goes far beyond that dissemination of style which casual itinerant sculptors, commissioned or themselves seeking employment, would have effected.

In this chapter we consider first, generically, the two prime figure types, kouros and kore, then the main regional styles. The architectural sculpture and reliefs are reserved for Chapters Seven and Eight.

Kouroi and realism

In the sixth century the kouros type, with no change of pose and little in proportions, proceeds inexorably towards the more realistic though still immobile creations of the end of the century. The parts of the body become more accurately rendered. Ears are no longer volute patterns but begin to look like ears. The unnatural twist which put the forearms facing forward though the fists were turned in is properly adjusted. Patterns of muscle and sinew which had been rendered by groove and ridge are carved in subtler realistic planes and the patterns themselves take forms closer to life – a double division between ribcage and navel, not triple or more, and over the knee-caps a proper asymmetry of muscles. All this accompanies a growing skill at integrating these pattern elements into a more plausible whole, as the sculptor frees himself from the technical limitations which had imprinted on the finished statue the strictly frontal/ofile aspects in which it had been conceived, and as, in other works of sculpture (relief) and art (drawing), he begins to face the problems of relating figures to each other in action or in the ambience of a narrative.

Stated in these terms sculptural progress can be measured through growing anatomical knowledge, as it is in Miss Richter's book, and it is easy to fall in with the assumption that the sculptors were deliberately striving after realistic effects. But you cannot consciously strive for a goal you do not recognize. An artist who wanted to carve or draw an ear or eye realistically had only to look across the room at his fellows and copy what he saw: he could hardly have been inhibited by the consideration that such realism was not due for another fifty years! Wholly representational art was neither understood nor sought by Archaic Greek artists, who, sculptor and painter, were observing still the old Geometric formula for composition of parts, observed individually and frontally, and were presenting images and compositions to be 'read', not compared with life. They went far along the path to achieving realism, however, not by design, not by accident, but by a sort of Natural Selection. An artist draws or carves as he has been taught. He will introduce varieties of rendering in the interests of better realizing his concept of, in this case, man, through the patterns and conventional forms he has been taught. Thanks to the example of foreign arts his work already bears something of the stamp of realism – far removed, in detail at least, from the near-abstraction of the Geometric age. Those innovations which more closely approximated to nature were instinctively judged, rather than positively identified, as more effective realizations of the desired end, and with a better command of technique and appreciation of mass the product was bound to be more realistic. But the figures are still no more than effectively communicated symbols for life or live action, read part by part, figure by figure, as a poem is line by line, and another century must pass before the artist realizes that he can produce replicas of man and action, so successful as to deceive the eye into confusing art with nature for the first time in western art.

We observe progress, therefore, only partly in terms of anatomical accuracy. Differentiation of age in the forms of the body is only tentatively expressed and relies generally in differences of dress or pose: this is clearest on the grave stelai.

Expression of emotion too relies on complex conventions of gesture, when it comes to the action figures of architectural sculpture or reliefs. In the faces we look for no more than a grimace of lust, pain or terror. The 'Archaic Smile' may have owed something to the difficulties of carving the transition from mouth to cheek (otherwise managed by a straight vertical cut beside the lips) but it was retained not because the expression was recognized as one of good cheer (inappropriate in much funerary art) but because it made the features look more alive, and it was abandoned once technique and observation combined to render the mouth more acceptable – that is, realistic.

If we understand what it was that the artists were trying to achieve, and that realism was almost the accidental by-product of their progress towards the most effective symbols or images of their men and gods, we shall be more patient of their mistakes along the way, and we shall better appreciate the quality of their achievement, especially when it is measured against the record of sculpture in the near east and Egypt, where the break-through from the conceptual to the observed in art never really happened. There was, of course, no particular reason why it should, and we admire it in Greek art for what it enabled the artists to express and what it taught later ages. The Archaic kouroi, many of them dull enough figures in their own right, teach us how the Greek artist made his way to a representational style, based primarily on the male nude, which dominated the visual arts of the western world for nearly two and a half millennia.

Korai

The break with the Daedalic korai and their foldless dress is so complete as to suggest that the sixth-century kore can be regarded as a new sculptural type. An interest in the pattern of drapery we shall see developed first in east Greece, in Chios then Samos and the Cyclades, and the sculptural styles and new modes of dress introduced to Attica to flourish in the great series of Acropolis korai. This too marks the point at which the dress patterning ceases to be mainly surface or two-dimensional decoration and is expressed in depth, making the dress as such a subject of independent interest to the artist, and at the same time leaving him freer to consider more effective modelling of the body apart from the dress, or, eventually, as it is revealed and accentuated by the dress. The progress can easily be grasped by looking at the different treatment of the lower parts of the figures [87—0–1–0].

The story is a comparatively simple one, in these terms, and the sculptural type is rare in Greece outside the areas named, which is not true of the kouroi. Few korai are demonstrably grave markers, none demonstrably deities, and most can be taken as symbols of unwearying service to the goddesses whose sanctuaries they adorn. Few are now made more than lifesize, and many are only a half or less. They stand with their left foot slightly advanced (early ones with toes in line, and in east Greece with the right foot forward first) gathering their skirts in a natural gesture which the sculptor exploits to display folds at first, then folds and the outlines of the limbs beneath. They are often holding an offering – fruit, fowl, hare – in the free hand. In the Attic series there is a marked tendency to favour either the double-diagonal effect of slung mantle and withdrawn skirt, or verticality, with symmetrical mantle and the skirt s folds undisturbed, even when clasped, rather than any combination (odd exceptions occur). The foot plinths are generally oval, set in blocks or occasionally stepped bases, and on the Acropolis there is the clearest evidence for korai mounted on columns, from the mid century on, the columns bearing Ionic or related capitals and at the end of the century hemispherical ones. Dedicatory inscriptions appear on the bases or column shafts, and in east Greece often on the dress of the figures themselves.

The development of the sixth-century korai is expressed more in treatment of drapery than of anatomy, so we must try to understand their dress. This is not always easy since its appeal to a sculptor was the pattern of folds it presented, and pattern was more important than the details of dress-making. There are no fitted garments, only rectangles of cloth, skilfully cut, buttoned or pinned, and the commonest of these for korai (rarely for men in sculpture) is the Ionic *chiton*. Here the cloth is stitched into a cylinder, the top partly closed with two sets of buttons leaving room for head and arms, so that the buttons fall along the upper arm, producing a decorative splay of folds from each. A belt at the waist produces baggy sleeves below the buttons and an overfall (*kolpos*) of material pulled over it and generally obscuring it except on many of the earlier east Greek korai. Sculptors show the upper part of the chiton in rippling creases gathered round shoulders and breasts, the lower part in flat sweeping folds, but it is all one garment. On top may be a small *himation* ('mantle' here), a long rectangle fastened with buttons, not across the short sides but towards the ends of a long edge, and then usually worn like a sash, its upper edge rolled under the left arm and over the right shoulder, so that the buttons overlie the chiton sleeve. Generally it looks as though the sculptor is simply showing the chiton buttons through the mantle, splaying folds and all gradually giving place to the vertical folds of the mantle. Often the distinction in dress is thoroughly confused. Worn thus the longer mantle ends hang from the right arm with another gathering of folds below the left arm, being caught up at the centre. Occasionally (in the pediment of the Apollo temple at Delphi [*142*]) we see the mantle buttoned at both shoulders and this, if real, must be a two-piece; or there may be simply a pin or button at one shoulder leaving a short 'sleeve' at that side. A larger mantle may lie over all (*epiblema*), in east Greece sometimes carried over the back of the head and generally covering only the back and flanks and virtually foldless [*87*], but it can even be worn like a toga, more like a man's himation. The *peplos* is a heavier dress, again a simple rectangle, open or stitched at the side, belted, and folded down from the neckline with a bib-like

67

CHITON

PEPLOS

MANTLE

overfall to about the waist, pinned at the shoulders and so sleeveless. A few mid century and earlier korai wear a peplos *over* the chiton, and in the fifth century it will largely replace the chiton, at least as the sculptor's preferred dress for ladies.

East Greek sculpture and sculptors

There is a deceptive dearth of kouroi from east Greece but Samos has yielded a valuable series, including even some from the sanctuary of the goddess Hera. The artists did not share the mainlanders' preoccupation with pattern-anatomy, and the more fluent forms which long remain characteristic of Ionian figures leave their naked males looking almost self-consciously undressed beside their sinewy cousins from Attica and south Greece. Leukios' dedication is a good example of this [81], followed by others, mainly fragmentary. Several heads, however, have survived, and these display a rather surprising and distinctive spherical form with the hair brushed back in a 'quiff' over the ears [82]. On many of these Ionian heads (mainly south Ionian – Samos, Miletus and down to Dorian Rhodes [83]) the eyes are narrowed, slanting, the eyeball only lightly defined within the lids. Whether the addition of colour would have made the heads more realistic or more other-worldly than mainland kouroi is hard to say. The spherical form is possibly one inspired by eastern sculpture (see below). On more northerly Ionian works the crown of the head is higher, even pointed, but the same hair-style may be seen, as it is on a lifesize kouros from Kyzikos on the Sea of Marmora. This is a head type which was carried into the arts of the western Mediterranean and Etruria, and it is often associated with Phocaea, whose citizens emigrated first to Corsica then Italy (Velia).

If the Ionian artists' interest did not lie in anatomy pattern we would expect to find it occupied with dress. That this was the case is abundantly clear from the kore series, as we shall see – indeed the easterners lead Greece in this. But they even clothe some men, rather unpleasant figures [84] whose pattern of dress resembles that of the seated figures from Didyma [94, 95]. Like them they may be the dedications of dignitaries whom they 'represent', not permanent staff for a sanctuary nor grave markers.

The first intimation of the new dress patterning for korai in east Greece comes with the two large fragments in Chios [85, 86]. The lines are simply incised, radiating from the sleeve buttons in triple wavy lines, crossing decoratively rather than realistically at the back where the belt shows as a recessed rectangle. The next phase is well demonstrated by an important group from Samos which takes us to beyond the mid century. The folds are modelled now, often close-set and contrasted with the broad plain areas of mantle and epiblema to exploit the contrasts of texture. Cheramyes' kore [87] is the prime example, where we have the contrast of plain epiblema, covering the back and tucked in to the belt at the front, striated chiton skirt, and the oblique folds of the mantle countered by short vertical grooves at the lower front edge. Another feature, apparent in varying degrees on other Samian korai, is the cylindrical body, splaying to the plinth where the hem is cut back to show the toes. The form is less likely to be inspired by tree-trunk sculpture than by large wheel-made figures of clay, well known in Ionia, but it is likely that her head was spherical too, like other Samian figures. This combination so closely matches Mesopotamian sculptural types which had persisted into the contemporary neo-Babylonian empire, that it is not easy to escape the conclusion that the sphere-and-cylinder forms were influenced by eastern figures, though thoroughly transformed in Greek hands, the decorative dress attracting interest in its own right while the bodies come to acknowledge the sculptors' success with the naked figures of kouroi. This orientalizing phase was avoided in Attica where the early korai are hardly more than transvestite kouroi.

The Ionian cylindrical forms are well displayed in the famous ivory priestess from Ephesus [88] and the Samian style is represented at Miletus [89] where we are better supplied with heads showing, rather later, refinement of the old spherical forms [90]; in a figure from Erythrae (opposite Chios); and in rather sleeker versions at Cyrene in Libya where the connection is harder to explain unless it is via the patronage of Sparta which was actively interested in both Samos and Cyrene in these years. We shall turn to comparable works in Athens and the islands in a moment. The remarkable group made by Geneleos [91–93] and dedicated in the Samos Heraion includes typical korai, a seated figure and a reclining one (the dedicator) which expresses the soft, boneless quality of much Ionian sixth-century sculpture, with fluent masses on to which the dress is, as it were, poured like chocolate sauce. Remembering the carving technique involved, and that this is not hand-modelled clay but chiselled marble, we can better appreciate the artist's achievement in creating these sinuous forms.

The reclining figure seems a peculiarly east Greek type, represented by votives elsewhere (Myus and Didyma). The seated figure in the Geneleos group, Phileia, is as rigid as her seventh-century predecessors. A notable series of seated figures, perhaps more than fifty originally, of which fifteen have survived, flanked a processional way to the temple of Apollo at Didyma, near Miletus, independent dedications by local rulers and priests (the Branchidai). Most are of men, rather over lifesize, but there are a few women late in the series, which ranges in date from about 570 to about 530. One of the earliest [94] has its head still, the spherical form familiar from Samos and Miletus. The flat overlapping folds of the himation present linear patterns similar to those of the more supple Samian. Later figures develop the dress pattern in a manner analogous to the Samian and the dedication of the Carian ruler Chares [95] is still a very wooden precursor of a finer Samian statue, the famous Aiakes [96]. This was found in the town of Samos, not the Heraion, and if the Aiakes is father of the tyrant Polykrates it is likely to be earlier than his son's 'reign' (from 532 on). If so it shows that the new (for Ionia) observation of anatomy and distinctive corrugation of folds were already well developed in Samian sculpture in the 530s. Here, at last, the figure is conceived and rendered as a separate mass from the throne, but the pose remains static (contrast [135]).

A comparable development in the rendering of dress on korai at this time is shown by a figure from the Heraion [97] who still reveals her belt in the old manner, but whose mantle and bulgy overfall have the new corrugated folds, while the pose (still with right leg forward, however) and dress declare the new generation of Ionian korai whose influence had already been felt in Attica. The very latest of the Didyma seated figures are of just this period, with others, of women, from the cemetery at Miletus.

We revert now to the islands and Attica. Two korai from the Acropolis [98,

99] display a treatment of dress which is quite un-Attic, but very close indeed to the Samian of the Geneleos period. But one has her head, and this is very different from the Samian, being instead a high oval, rather flat-topped and small-featured. The close similarity of this head to that of the Naxian sphinx at Delphi [100], allowing for the creature's rather earlier date and monster eyes, suggests Naxos as the origin for the two Acropolis korai, and indicates that the island workshops at this time shared views on dress with Ionia, but kept to a distinctive local head type which is far closer to the early Attic.

There is something of this style in heads of kouroi from the Cyclades – one from Thera [101], at least for its profile and outline of features, and later even in the kouros from Melos [102] which has a slim grace quite foreign to the east Greek kouroi with which we began this section. Both Thera and Melos are Dorian islands, not Ionian, but by now race counts for nothing in affinities of style. The medial position of the Cyclades, in matters of style as of geography, finds us describing its kouroi in the section on east Greece, its later kora with Attica (below). The studios of the marble islands, Naxos and Paros, were busy still, but it is not clear whether the 'dry, linear style' attributed by scholars to Naxos, the softer 'Ionian' to Paros, is wholly justified by the evidence. Thus, a kouros head from Naxos combines the old horizontally layered hair with forehead ringlets from which the hair is brushed back almost in a Samian manner.

Finally, another dedication in the Cyclades, Delos this time, brings us back to Chios, where our account of Ionian korai began. Pliny knew of a Chian sculptor called Archermos, who was of a family of sculptors – grandfather Melas, father Mikkiades, sons Boupalos and Athenis. Archermos worked on Delos and Lesbos, he tells us, and another ancient scholar says he was the first to make a Nike (Victory) with wings. The earliest free-standing statue of a winged woman (Nike or Artemis) has been excavated on Delos [103]. She is shown in the Archaic kneeling-running pose and is stylistically datable about 550, which chimes with Pliny's suggested date for Archermos. Near it was found a base with an irregular cutting in its top, which could well have taken the drapery mass hanging below the Nike's legs, and with an inscription naming Archermos, Mikkiades and Melas. The figure must go with the base but the tantalizing inscription appears to make Archermos the sculptor, Mikkiades the dedicator (as he is also for a work on Paros) and Melas possibly an ancestor or a founder hero of Chios, a poetic indication of the dedicator's home; and the lettering is of Paros, where no doubt the studio was. Scholars have seen discrepancies between the dates of the base and figure, which are not strictly valid, and have worried that such a sober peplos-wearing figure could be Ionian, or by a hand whose later probable work (or his sons') in Athens seems so different. When the French found the figure's arms after the last war she was revealed as wearing a chiton beneath her peplos, and her peplos was very gaily painted. The head certainly has little in it to match the later Ionian figures, but

71

the difference in date counts for a lot, and it is clear from other evidence (clay figures) that north Ionia (Chios, Clazomenae, Smyrna) did not share Samos' penchant for the spherical cranium. The Delos figure's head is readily related to island korai of 550–540, or the 'ex-Cnidian' caryatid [209] from Delphi (the forehead wavy hair), and seems an acceptable predecessor to later Chian korai. We may rest confident that she is the Nike of Archermos and it is easy to see how Pliny's source created the artist's sculptural ancestry from a misreading of the inscription. There is a head from the Athens Acropolis (Acr. 659) comparable with the Nike, but the base found there and signed by Archermos is later, and the work of Archermos or his sons will engage us again.

Of other named Ionian sculptors Eudemos and Terpsikles are known from the Didyma statues, but the outstanding figure was Theodoros of Samos, a colleague of Rhoikos in the construction of the Hera temple, and named (Pausanias) with him as the first (sic) to cast bronze statues. Diodorus makes him a son of Rhoikos and, with his brother Telekles, the exponent of the Egyptian method in measuring statues (see p. 20). His reputation was in bronze work and this brings home to us just how little we can know of the best sculpture of the period; nor can we tell what of the marble statuary on Samos might be his work or of his studio. The family names are confused but the jeweller and gem-engraver Theodoros who worked for Polykrates is likely to be the same artist.

Attic sculpture and sculptors

This is a particularly rich period for kouroi from Attic cemeteries. The pattern forms of the bodies are no less emphatic for their more skilful modelling. The earlier figures have rather distinctively high, shallow heads in profile view. The hair seems brushed back from the forehead in flame-like locks over the fillet on the Volomandra kouros [104; cf. 105], a style matched in contemporary vase painting, but on the Munich kouros [106] these locks seem part of the fillet's decoration since the spiral forehead curls are also shown. Later the heads are deeper, and on [106] the spirals spread unusually over the crown and the hair is cut short behind. But this figure's stomach has still the unnatural triple division and its back is patterned in grooves in the old manner, while others wear their hair still at shoulder length. The features of the new kouros from Merenda [108a] are exceptional for the impression of youthfulness which the artist has conveyed through the small eyes and lips set in the softly modelled face. The body of this remarkable statue seems also more deliberately adolescent than the generalized young-maturity of most kouroi. The marker for the grave of Kroisos [107] is another exceptional statue, the body more robustly modelled, the face with traits which we shall recognize as most distinctively Attic on attributed works yet to be described.

The korai of Attica in this period are better represented in the cemeteries than on the Acropolis. First come chiton figures with foldless dress: one recent find, from A. Ioannis Rentis, still has wig-like hair and palm flat against her side – a throwback to the seventh century in pose. After these the Berlin kore [108] is generally recognized now as a grave marker, and Phrasikleia, recently found at Merenda, certainly is. They have much in common – jewellery, the elaborate crown and sandals, feet together, simple vertical lines of dress though the former has an over-garment whose close folds are contradicted by the overlapping at the front edges. The Berlin kore's oval head and heavy features, hands and feet look back to earlier Attic kouroi, but she belongs to the 560s. Her counterpart on the Acropolis is [109] Phrasikleia [108a] has the slimmer features and body of kouroi nearer the mid century, like the Volomandra [104] She makes no concession to the bulgy overfalls and fold patterns of Ionian korai, though the new swinging folds are understood in her hem line. (We await definitive publication of her and the kouros found buried in a pit [108a] with her, but her base has been known since 1729: 'Marker of Phrasikleia. I shall ever be called maiden (kore), the gods alloting me this title in place of marriage: [Aris]tion of Paros made me'.)

σε̄μα Φρασικλειας·	ϟΕΜΑΦΡΑϟΙΚΛΕΙΑϟ
κορε̄ κεκλε̄σομαι	ΚΟΡΕΚΕΚΛΕϟΟΜΑΙ
αιει, αντι γομο	ΔΙΕΙΑΜΤΙΛΑΜΟ
παρα ϟεο̄ν τουτο	ΓΑΡΑ⊕ΕΟΜΤΟΥΤΟ
λαχοσ' ονομα.	ΛΑΧΟϟΟΜΟΜΑ

The Lyons kore [110] from the Acropolis is little earlier than Phrasikleia. She wears a crown too, which shows that this is an indicator of date and place, rather than function. But the new dress style is Ionian, with a pure pattern of folds allowed to develop along her left flank and over her bottom, and the grasp of the skirt allowed to display the shape of her legs, while on Phrasikleia it remains a conventional gesture contributing to a display neither of folds nor anatomy. But the dress of the Lyons kore clings to the body still and has no real mass of its own. Her fleshiness is Attic strength rather than Ionian sensuousness, and her honest sonsy face is pure Athenian (cf. [108], and the Rampin Master below).

The sculptors are quicker to adopt new dress and posture for the Acropolis korai than for the grave figures but there is a lingering sobriety seen, for example, in the Peplos kore [115] or [111] which is at or after about 530, and which abjures the cross-slung mantle and splay-folded skirt for a vertical accent, achieved by hanging the mantle symmetrically, like [118].

We have remarked one or two stylistic attributions to single sculptors and shall turn shortly to some whose names and works are known, or whose unsigned works can be assembled. Study of the signatures and names themselves is revealing. A sculptor is not necessarily his own scribe and we can

73

identify single scribes cutting dedications or signatures for several sculptors, possibly in one studio. We have about seventeen Archaic sculptors' names from the Acropolis (in some twenty-five signatures), seven from the Attic cemeteries (in some fifteen signatures), yet only Endoios and Philergos appear in both groups, the latter as collaborator of Endoios both on the Acropolis and on a grave kouros base. At least a third of the named Acropolis sculptors are known to be or strongly suspected of being non-Athenian (e.g., Gorgias of Sparta, Kallon and Onatas of Aegina, Euenor of Ephesus, Bion of Miletus, the Chians); of the cemetery sculptors only Aristion declares himself a Parian. It seems that more 'guest artists' were employed for dedications, and that the student of Attic style might then do well to start with the cemeteries not the Acropolis. Several names are decidedly non-Athenian, several are apparently sobriquets rather than given names – Philergos = 'energetic'; Eleutheros = 'free(d)'; Phaidimos = 'brilliant', etc. – a phenomenon we observe also with the vase painters (*ARFH* 9f.) and which is explained by the strong non-citizen (metic) and non-Athenian element in Athens' artists quarter.

Phaidimos

We have three signatures of Phaidimos: on a stele base for the grave of Chairedemos, to which part of a spearman relief has been doubtfully attributed; on a kore base for the grave of Phile (name or adjective 'dear'?); and on a stele base for the grave of Archias and his sister. On the last two his work is described as 'beautiful' (*kalon*) and on the last the sculptor himself as 'skilful' (*sophos*) – he had no problems of self-confidence, and his assumed name means 'brilliant'. (The sort of man to make his way to the front of any queue? – cf. *ABFH* fig. 46.4.) The bases date from about 560 to 540. 'Phile's' feet are little enough on which to base attributions, but her distinctive square toenails have led scholars on the one hand to the gorgon stele [*231*] and an Acropolis kore (Acr. 582); on the other to the Calf-bearer [*112*]. The latter is the more plausible attribution and the scribe of its dedication served also for two of Phaidimos' bases. This would then be one of his earliest works (560s). The hair and heavy arms recall the earlier Attic kouroi; the dress has no mass but its hem limits a colour area on the naked body; the features depend still on linear effects. The calf's tender, indeed succulent body and its head, brought forward into the plane of the man's head, and providing a brilliant pattern contrast with it, validate the claim in the artist's name.

The Sabouroff head [*113*] has also been associated with the Calf-bearer, but any plausible link with Phaidimos himself must be too tenuous to take seriously. It is a strikingly individual characterization, yet no portrait. The rough-picked hair, moustache and beard, with its original colour, provided a texture contrast with the smooth flesh areas, a technique repeated on a few later works (as [*145*]) and one entailing, though not necessarily dictated by, some economy in

74

carving. It has been thought to be preparation for additions in plaster, which is improbable here and on some other figures impossible.

The Rampin Master

Payne saw that the Rampin head in the Louvre joins the body of an Acropolis horseman [114]. The lace-like carving of hair and beard, the delicacy of the features makes this one of the most memorable and individual of Archaic heads. The face and profile led scholars to attribute to the same hand the famous Peplos kore [115] despite the probability that she is some fifteen years later. The simplicity of her over-garment contrasts with her rich hair and the painting of her dress, just as the plain block-like modelling of the horseman's torso does with his hair and the mane of his mount. One could hardly imagine a more Athenian pair, with that subtlety in contrast of planes around the eyes and mouth which were the hallmark of yet earlier Athenian sculpture. The hint of the kore's girlish body beneath the heavy cloth, her soft arms, head gently inclined towards the side where she holds her offering, these have all to be enjoyed before the statue itself rather than in the most skilful photograph. Another kore head was attributed to the artist by Payne [116]. Its features are most like the horseman's and it may be a little earlier. The famous fragment of a grave stele with a boy shouldering a discus [117] goes with them (notice the profile, ear lobes). Much of the artist's work seems of the mid century or just before, and its Atticness is further demonstrated by similarities even to works like the Berlin kore [108]. But the Peplos kore is later, of the 530s, and the master's influence can be seen in a contemporary kore, no less distinctive in features and dress [118]. The master's real name surely lurks among those we read on bases which lack their stelai or statues, and which so deny us the chance to identify their handiwork elsewhere. He deserves a better fate since he had no equal in mid-century Athens.

Aristion of Paros

Phaidimos shared the services of a scribe for his bases with the sculptor Aristion of Paros and with Aristokles, each known from only one extant signature, the latter's being later in the century [235]. The association could be that of a studio, but might be slighter if such scribes were freelance. Aristion worked in the third quarter of the century and since he signs himself 'Parian' he may have learned his craft on the marble island and plied it in Athens. He signed a base for a column monument, perhaps two others for kouroi, and the famous kore Phrasikleia from Merenda [108a]. Whatever his training or origin his style is purely Attic and the kore has much in common with the Berlin kore in stance and dress, and with the Volomandra kouros in features. The elaboration of jewellery and painted dress pattern is the more effective for the foldless simplicity of the dress and the adolescent body of the girl whom, as her epitaph tells, death took before a husband. To modern eyes she is perhaps the most beautiful of the korai.

Other areas

At the Ptoon sanctuary in Boeotia the rather inorganic local style, executed in local marble, flourished still [*119*] but there is strong island influence too and intermittent arrivals from Attica, including dedications by rival factions: by a son of Alkmaion and later by a son of Peisistratos (the bases only preserved). We may recall the work of Attic vase painters emigrant to Boeotia (*ABFH* 183).

In the Peloponnese there are two important regions yielding sculpture of this period, the north-east and Laconia. Corinth is so far best known for its minor arts in clay [*120*] and bronze, though there are some good stone animals (see Chapter Nine) and the sculpture of Corfu [*187*] is Corinthian in style. The elegant kouros from Tenea [*121*] near by is by the first Archaic sculptor to succeed in creating a lifelike figure within the conventions and patterns of the kouros pose. The understated anatomy, and balance of strength and slimness in this small (five-foot) youth makes it one of the finest of the century.

Nearby Sicyon has, on paper, a more distinguished record. Kleisthenes' tyranny had made the city wealthy and influential. She dedicated treasuries at Olympia and Delphi and we have the sculptures from the latter [*208*]. The Cretan sculptors Dipoinos and Skyllis, 'pupils of Daedalus', worked there in the second quarter of the century, withdrew because of some alleged injustice and returned only after the city had been plagued, and advised by Delphi to bring them back to complete their work – a group which may have shown the struggle between Herakles and Apollo for the tripod, a story which was used to symbolize the First Sacred War at Delphi in which Sicyon was prominent.

Spartan studios seem to have been singularly active in these years, to judge from text references to artists, and especially in bronze work which we can best admire in cast attachments to vases and mirrors, and in statuettes. A large hollow-cast head gives an idea of the quality of larger works [*122*]. In stone the surviving work is distinctly cruder, with the primitive and puzzling pyramidal base and its two-figure groups [*123*], and some other series of reliefs [*253–4*]. There are also, however, scraps of marble relief sculpture which seem Ionian in style or subject, as [*124*], and we know that the Ionian sculptor Bathykles of Magnesia designed the sculptural setting for the cult image of Apollo at Amyklai, near Sparta. The Spartan sculptor Gitiadas made a bronze Athena for her temple (Athena Chalkioikos – 'of the brazen temple'), its dress also apparently covered with bronze plates carrying panels with myth scenes. Pausanias describes the figure and we may get an idea of it from coins [*125*].

Coins also tell us something of a cult statue elsewhere in Greece, the Apollo made by Tektaios and Angelion, pupils of Dipoinos and Skyllis, for Delos [*126*].

It looks like a long-haired kouros flanked by sphinxes (rather than griffins), and we can detect the three Graces and the bow which ancient authors saw in its hands. Later inscriptions suggest it may have been gilt.

By this time there is increasing use made of precious metals in statuary. We learn this mainly from texts, and even in the seventh century the Corinthian tyrant had dedicated a Zeus of beaten gold, 'of good size', at Olympia. But from mid-century Delphi, with debris from a destroyed treasury excavated beneath the Sacred Way, we have pieces of two-thirds life size gold and ivory statues – the flesh parts ivory, gold plates on the dress – of the most refined workmanship, probably Ionian in origin [127], which presage yet more ambitious works in these materials in the following century. From the same find has recently been composed a lifesize silver bull!

Proportions and techniques

Pattern and proportion were of prime importance even in the most fully representational styles of later Greek art. In the Archaic period it is especially the kouros figures that might demonstrate the application of principles of proportion and measurement, as they do the progress in realistic representation of anatomy. The possible debt to the Egyptian grid system of twenty-one units for figure height has already been mentioned. The Greeks came to prefer a statement of proportions in terms of their measuring system, itself appropriately and naturally based on the human body, with a basic unit of a foot. But in the Archaic period Greek mensuration was extremely imprecise. A coherent system could be used for one building or perhaps in one studio but there were as yet no national or city standards. The deduction of a 'long foot' of 32·65 cm and a 'short foot' of 29·4 cm, or of regional variations, over-simplifies the issue, and these rather indicate the range of measures in use, a range properly matched by the variations in the convenient human extremity on which the unit is based. Greater (cubit, fathom) and lesser (palm, finger) units were readily related to the foot, as they were in a far more systematic way in Egypt and the near east. Metrological analysis of kouroi has been hampered by great expectations, while arguments based on careful measurement of minor details projected from the round into two dimensions, never quite persuade. The artist no doubt laid out the figure on the surface of the uncut block, but hardly in great detail, and approaching the final worked surface any such guide had long disappeared and even a guiding sketch would be ignored in favour of the artist's own response to his material and the realization in it of his concept of the finished figure. From unfinished statues it seems clear that he worked in systematically from all sides of the block, and that in the final stages it was a matter of reducing from a larger, roughly detailed mass, rather than exact predetermination of details by measure. Egyptians seem to have worked mainly from one side at a time, re-drawing their guide lines as the work progressed. At

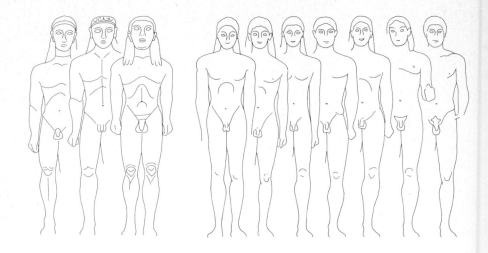

any rate, once the larger figures had been roughed out in the quarries it was perhaps too late for detailed grids and the precisely mathematical placing of parts. So we can only glimpse the principles of measure and proportion which lay behind any statue.

A plot of the relative heights of complete or safely completable kouroi, and of the approximate proportions of head to body produces a fairly simple and intelligible plan of development. It shows that the variety in their heights did not depend on the observable variety in life, or provision for the superhuman for monumental or heroizing effect. Apart from the truly colossal all the complete kouroi are six-, five- or seven-footers, in the vague terms of the Greek foot which I have already explained. On a frontal human body the neatest expression of any basic module is not the length of foot but height of head. An 'ideal' man is and was six feet tall. The earliest complete kouros is a six-footer with a big one-foot head [63]. But in life a man's head is nearer one-seventh of his height, and as the artist's experiments led him closer to the creation of man-symbols realistic in proportions as in details, two solutions were presented: to put the one-foot head in a seven-foot body [102, 106]; or to abandon the foot-head for the 1:7 proportion in a six-footer, and it is this solution which naturally won the day for the majority of figures ([104, 107, 145, 150] and Merenda). Reduce the complete kouroi (five- to seven-footers) to one height and the rapidly achieved standardization of proportions after the early and the outsize is clearly apparent (see drawing).

Outsize kouroi have eccentric head:body proportions – 1:8 for Thasos [69] (12 feet), 1:6·5 for Sounion [64] and 1:9 for Samos/Istanbul [82, head] (both 10 feet).

78

FEET		KOUROI	KORAI	METRES

7 — 2·20

6 — 2·00

— 1·80

5 — 1·60

Kleobis and Biton [70] are seven-footers with residual outsize heads (1:6·5) if this is not rather a result of seeking a deliberate visual impression of strength in the upper body. The five-foot Tenea kouros [121] and the five-and-a-half-foot Calf-bearer have 'normal' heads.

Plausible identification of other significant measurements and proportions is possible, provided that obsession with meaningless or minor measurements is suppressed (there are similar pitfalls in the study of vase shapes). Thus, it seems that in the Aristodikos [145] the head height (0·28) was used as a module for the rest of the body, and there were other basic proportions to observe such as the crotch at half-height. Gradually the ruler is abandoned in favour of more realistic systems of proportion between parts of the body, systems which were to occupy classical sculptors and become subjects for treatises.

Progress in rendering of anatomy and observation of proportions may have gone at a different rate in different cities and studios, but the freedom with which artists travelled, the display of works in the national sanctuaries, and the concentration of expertise in the few sources of marble, mainly the island quarries where the figures were blocked out, probably helped ensure an overall unity of pace; and if they did not, we do not have precise enough dating evidence for individual statues to prove it.

The progress we have considered was accompanied by progress in technique. Woodworking techniques had given place to the use of the point, flat chisel, drill and abrasives for the early marble figures. A heavier broad chisel the drove, could be used for flat areas. In the second quarter of the century the Greeks invented the claw chisel, usually five-toothed and about 1·5 cm wide,

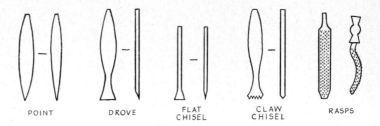

POINT DROVE FLAT CHISEL CLAW CHISEL RASPS

but smaller are known. This could be used at varying angles and its effect was almost to plane away the marble; and held vertically it made a sharp re-entrant edge. The rasp could be used more freely to smooth away the rougher tool marks, and the drill was called on more and more for subtler details of hair and dress or undercutting. The sculptors generally took pains to remove all traces of tool work but it is often apparent in the less accessible or ordinarily invisible parts of many figures.

There was no compunction, as was felt in later periods of western art, to complete a figure from a single block. The seated Daedalic figures were often two-piece, and in the sixth century the projecting arms of korai or even minor parts of limbs, could be made separately and dowelled into place, or even glued (the beard tip of [235]). Nor was there any absolute avoidance of supports or struts, to safeguard arms held away from the body [145] or as pillars below the bellies of horses.

The coarser or shelly limestones were coated with stucco, on which the paint often survives better than on marble, but it is unlikely that parts modelled in stucco were added to marble figures (e.g., hair; see on [113]) though this has been suspected. Materials might be mixed and the Lindos temple chronicle refers to an early fifth-century wooden Gorgon with a marble face. The most lavish technique was the chryselephantine, practised already in the Archaic period [127]. Spears, swords, even helmets might be added in metal and this was the rule for most jewellery and attachments to diadems, while on reliefs, such as that on the Siphnian Treasury at Delphi [212] whole wheels might be made separately and parts receding on to the background were only painted [130], though this is an exceptional technique. Inlaid eyes were made of bone, crystal or glass. On the heads of free-standing statues, especially korai, discs on metal spikes (meniskoi – 'little moons') were fitted to protect the features from being soiled by birds: cf. [129].

The use of colour on Archaic statuary was more general than casual acquaintance with surviving pieces might lead us to believe, more general than we might wish to credit, but the traces left on statues buried soon after completion (as on the Acropolis), the figures of fired clay, and early Archaic vase painting leave us in no doubt. Most clothing was painted though on the

80

later korai we see more often patterns alone added on the pale marble. Male flesh was probably painted red or brown for the earlier figures, including kouroi, and is seen still on the Ephesus column reliefs [217] and the Acropolis scribes [164]. Female flesh was probably whitened and on the later males there was no doubt still some tinting. All this apart from the obvious painting of hair, eyebrows, eyes, lips, nipples, pubic hair. Relief backgrounds were usually dark blue or red. The colours may not have been intense, and in brilliant sunlight would have been muted, but it is hard to say how easily we could have judged subtleties of carving, let alone texture of finish, on the original fully painted works. Modern restoration with colour never quite convinces and it is probably safer to restore in black and white and let the modern eye, used to this convention in photography, make its own adjustment. The results of both methods, and modern paintings, are offered here [128–33].

Turning to metalwork, we found the early bronzes cast solid, the originals being probably of wax, coated with a clay mantle to serve as mould. Early in the seventh century the model may be given a core of other material which can be worked out of the final cast, lightening it and saving bronze. The ultimate refinement is to make the core nearly the size of the desired figure, coat it with wax with finished detail to the required thickness of the bronze, then make the clay mantle, fixing it to the core with rods, melting out the wax, pouring in the bronze. This is the technique, still experimental, of the Piraeus kouros [150] which yet encloses the iron skeleton on which the model was built. Its wrists and hands are solid and there is less use of inlay (as for the eyes, a practice well known in marble) than for most later, large bronzes on which a redder copper might be used for lips and nipples. Later too this *cire-perdue* technique was refined with the use of piece moulds.

The use of hammered-sheet bronze, as in the Dreros figures [16] and some other early orientalizing works [20] was later confined mainly to vessels, the figure attachments to which are cast separately, or to decorative relief plaques, but there are some examples of large figures in this technique at Olympia – a near-lifesize bust of a winged goddess [134] – and we may recall Gitiadas' Athena or the comparable treatment of gold sheet on the chryselephantine figures.

Chapter Six

THE LATER ARCHAIC STYLES
to about 480 BC

Attic sculpture and sculptors

This is a period of stress and change in Athens: harsh tyranny after the death of Peisistratos in 527 until his family was finally expelled in 510, then the construction of a new 'democracy', its success at Marathon in 490, closing with the sack of the city by the Persians in 480. It is tempting to associate sculptors with rival factions (see below) or the overthrow of gravestones and buildings with reverses of political fortunes. This is fair speculation but difficult to carry to proof, and the general dearth of public and private monuments after about 500 is not easy to explain on grounds of politics and only partly explicable in terms of assumed sumptuary legislation. We start with two names, then return to the basic sculptural types.

Endoios

Endoios, another of the alleged pupils of Daedalus, was almost certainly an Athenian. Pausanias says he made seated Athenas for Athens and Erythrae (in Ionia; of wood) and another for Tegea (of ivory); and Pliny, the statue of Artemis at Ephesus (wood or ivory). The Athena is recognized by many in an Acropolis marble [135], so battered that we might well believe that it survived the Persians and was seen by Pausanias (though it is possible that its state is due to re-use as building material in late antiquity). The contrast with the earlier seated figures of Ionia [94–96] is dramatic. Her arms are sharply bent, one leg drawn back, ready to rise from her stool with a realistic air of imminent motion, shared to some degree by the slightly earlier Dionysos [162]. A column shaft from the Acropolis bears a joint signature of Endoios and Philergos, and appears to have carried a kore [136] who holds her dress as does [153]. Another Acropolis dedication, a relief showing a potter holding two cups, may well bear his signature too [137]. The face is sadly damaged but the cap-like treatment of the hair shows that this is appreciably later than the Athena and the kore. The head is enough like those on the famous ball-player base [138] for scholars to attribute this to Endoios too. The base was probably for a grave kouros, and was found near the Piraeus Gate in Athens where another base signed by Endoios was recovered. This carried a lost kouros for Nelonides and the base also bears traces of a painted seated figure. From the same area come pieces of a large kouros to which scholars ascribe the famous 'Rayet head' in Copenhagen [139].The kouros might have stood on an Endoios base, or one signed by Philergos (Endoios' collaborator in the kore) which was also found close by and was made for the Samian Leanax. The general correspondence of the Rayet head with the ball-player basis and potter relief (note, for example, the hair and thick ears) suggests that it is from Endoios' studio if not hand. It is one of the earliest heads to display the trim hair-style of the latest kouroi, here cut in crescent locks, not the combed zigzag coiffure of the potter. The delicately striated hair and Rayet-like features of an exquisite small bronze youth from the Acropolis [140] show that this too belongs stylistically with works executed or influenced by Endoios. Finally, we have the master's signature on a base for a stele commemorating Lampito, who died far from home (presumably Ionia).

The sum of these works helps define a style which is with less certainty traced in architectural sculpture – the marble pediment from the Acropolis [199], and the work of the artist of the north and east friezes of the Siphnian treasury [212.1, 2], the garbled artist's signature on which is now read as Attic. That Endoios helped execute or plan at least the former of these is by no means unlikely.

Antenor

Antenor was remembered in antiquity for executing in bronze the group of Harmodios and Aristogeiton, the tyrant-slayers. The death of the tyrant Hipparchos was in 514, the group erected some time after the tyrant family was expelled in 510, but it was taken to Persia by Xerxes, replaced by one made by Kritios and Nesiotes after the Persian Wars, and returned only after Alexander's conquest of Persia. The surviving fragments of base were probably cut for the replacement and are not from the old base, re-used, which would make Antenor's group very late indeed. Its significance lies in the fact that it is an early example of a civic commemorative group for a very recent event and that it positively identified the two men, though not, of course, in portraits. Antenor's signature appears on an Acropolis base to which the over-lifesize kore [141] almost certainly belongs. This is virtually the last of the truly monumental Attic korai, a seven-footer like many kouroi, wearing her Ionian dress with a near-masculine swagger which contrasts vividly with her contemporary [151]. It is quite the same treatment of body and dress that we see in the female figures of the marble pediment in the temple of Apollo at Delphi [142], which Antenor may have designed. The Webb head in London [143] resembles the kore head: the head is a Roman copy and has been thought a replica of his Harmodios.

Antenor's work on the Delphi pediment, paid for by the exiled Alkmaionids, and then on the tyrant-slayers, seems to indicate some rapport with anti-tyrant patrons. Endoios, on the other hand, is busy in Peisistratid Athens and in Ionia, where the tyrants had close friends, and for Ionians in Athens, perhaps especially Samians. But there is no call to look for more politics than this in the careers of Archaic sculptors, who had far less opportunity and range for free comment about the contemporary scene or even myth than did the vase painters. We shall meet other sculptors' names in a later chapter. Other, anonymous, works must provide the fuller picture of progress in the art in Attica of these years.

Several wholly or nearly complete kouroi well demonstrate the range and quality in the last phase of the type. The Keos figure (from the island off Attica) is old-fashioned still in hair and anatomy but already shows the new confidence in handling the body masses [144]. Aristodikos [145] is near perfect. In balance of limbs and detail of modelling of the figure the artist shows fuller understanding of the structure of the body, but he has yet to learn how it moves, and how the movement of one limb may affect the balance and pose of the whole. It remains almost embarrassingly inert. It is at this point that we might reflect how further progress became possible. Aristodikos is a carefully planned and measured figure, the head height apparently serving as a module for other parts of the body. Sculptors who plan their works thus are also draughtsmen, and it is in the drawing – on vases – of years even earlier than Aristodikos, that we see in Athens that artists, and not necessarily other artists, are experimenting with the expression in two dimensions not only of free action poses but of the balance and stance of individual figures, and we meet deliberate study of accurate anatomical detail. Already they are observing what will inevitably take longer to render plausibly in three dimensions (cf. *ARFH* figs 22–53 *passim*, the Pioneers). Intimations in statuary that this relaxation of frontality was due are slight asymmetries in figures, inclined heads like that of the Rampin horseman [114], and early attempts to correct foreshortening of features.

We see the triumphant expression of the Attic sculptor's solution in a statue of some twenty years later than Aristodikos, the 'Kritian boy' from the Acropolis [147]. He is not so much the last of the kouroi as precursor of the Classical athlete statues. We cannot be quite certain that he was standing when the Persians sacked Athens, and the way the break at the neck is chipped has suggested to some that the head is a replacement, but the probability is that he was made little before 480. The contrast with Aristodikos is striking, yet the change was inevitable, given the success the sculptors of the kouros series had achieved in re-phrasing the theme ever close to life. Not only is the proportion and surface treatment correct, but so is the underlying form and comprehension of the architecture of limb and muscle. From now on a statue can bid not merely to symbolize or stand as substitute for man but to imitate him. The decisive physical changes are slight, but enough to break the rigid vertical axis on which all earlier free-standing statuary had been based. The right knee is flexed with the weight of the body mainly on the left leg; as a result the right hip is lowered, the buttock relaxed; the shoulder slackens to this side too and the head inclines gently in the same direction: like a sigh of relief for the history of western art.

The 'Blond boy' from the Acropolis [148] carries his head even more emphatically tilted and the fragment of his loins displays the tough, muscled patterning of late Archaic art with the new pose, left leg and buttock taut. The pose is similar but the Kritian boy is barely adolescent (like his immediate predecessor [146]), the Blond boy near manhood, and his head and the treatment of hair and plait are even closer to the Classical and the sculptures of Olympia. The head has much in common with that of Euthydikos' kore [160] which is somewhat earlier, and could be by the same artist whom some have thought Peloponnesian by training. This could well be true, given the eclectic character of the Acropolis display. This characterization of different ages in head and body is not entirely new in Archaic art but it is another feature in which the Olympia Master will excel.

For the last of the kouroi from Attica two singletons, the first a kouros translated to a worshipper holding an offering [149]. The almost tailored pleating of his cloak, the emphatic muscles and trim pubic moustache all show how much pure Archaic pattern still meant. And secondly a puzzling bronze. The Piraeus Apollo [150] is lifesize, our first complete example in a technique which we know had been practised already for some years in Greece. The kouros type is adapted here for a cult image as it had been on Delos [126]. The style sits uneasily with the Attic series, and the circumstances of its discovery do not demand Attic origin – with some other pieces in the find it may be from Delos. That scholars have thought it archaizing, or a copy of an earlier Archaic marble, is some indication of the problems it poses and of our continuing ignorance of high quality work in the more precious material.

The record of korai in Attica is far richer, thanks to the Acropolis finds and several fine examples from Eleusis. [151] is generally regarded as one of the most strongly ionicizing although the rather pointed skull is not so much north Ionian (Acropolis examples are discussed in the next section) as a version of the Attic high oval – she might be a daughter of the Volomandra kouros [104] with similar pinched cheeks. The hair is particularly elaborate, folded waves across the crown, scaly at the back, twisted at the front, the forehead with the now familiar flames and ringlets. Observe the varied treatment of the linear wave patterns on dress, differing on each shoulder and on the breast. Moreover, the complexity of the painted decoration on the dress is unrivalled on Acropolis korai. Where the cloth clings the body is positively sensuous. Our korai have hitherto been female, as [108], or at the best ladies, as [115]; this is a real woman. Her dress is disposed in the new conventional manner. The artist of [152] and [153] (surely the same hand) is more enterprising. One is contrary in combining symmetrical mantle with the withdrawn skirt; the other discards mantle and preserves the vertical line by holding her skirt forward, not to the side, despite a certain illogicality in the fall of the skirt from her hand over the unruffled overfall. The facial similarity of these two korai to a kouros [180] and a kore

85

head from the Ptoon suggests that the artist worked also in Boeotia, might even have been Boeotian.

We have seen already how the hair may be gathered in a sweep before the ears, on [*111*] and on the beautiful [*154*] where the ruff of locks spreads like a flower over her cheeks. [*155*], a colourful but dully modelled piece, carries this style further, and on later korai [*158–160*] the hair is brought across the forehead in one mass to dip over each temple. [*156*], an undervalued figure, wears a full himation like a man.

By the end of the century the features, in detail and expression, have become far more natural [*157*] and the decline of the Archaic smile can give place in the fifth century to an expression which can appear calm [*158*], dull or even sulky [*160*]. The last earned the sobriquet 'la Boudeuse', but we are not to impose our recognition of nuances of expression on Archaic Greek art as readily as we try to on, for example, the Mona Lisa. She is Euthydikos' kore, for we have the dedicator's name on the column capital which carried her. She is petite, hardly more than a metre tall – we are far from the eastern colossi of a century before. The body is carefully observed and feminine – narrow rounded shoulders, soft breast, slim legs and feet, and in full colour any air of sobriety would surely have been dispelled – her chiton shoulder was painted (as if embroidered) with racing chariots.

Finally, [*161*]: the absence of immediately post-Persian offerings on the Acropolis rather than its find place show that this was made no later than 480. Hair, features and type of dress are all familiar, but the rendering of the broad soft folds is already early Classical. Her contemporary, the Kritian boy [*147*], heralded what was to follow in his pose and anatomy – features which had kept the kouros type a live interest for sculptors for a century and a half: in korai their interest lay in dress and its pattern, and it is in this kore's dress that the future is as surely prefigured.

The other major figure type of Archaic sculpture is seated, and we have already seen its development in east Greece [*94–96*] as well as Endoios' Athena [*135*]. The type served in Attica as a grave monument from at least the 560s but it is a moot point whether some examples might represent Dionysos. A figure from his sanctuary at Ikaria must surely be the god but a fine statue from Athens [*162*], seated on a panther skin, which could well be a Dionysos, is from a cemetery area. Seated women may also have been set over graves but the example from Rhamnus [*163*] is presumably votive. A special class is the Acropolis 'scribes', which are Egyptian in subject rather than style or pose [*164*].

Riders too could serve as grave monuments, but are more familiar as votives, like the Rampin figure [*114*]. Its successors on the Acropolis include other naked horsemen [*165, 166*] and one wearing archer's dress. There are other Nikai on the Acropolis too, including a Chian (see below). The most interesting, atop an Ionic column, was dedicated for Kallimachos, the general at Marathon, apparently for a victory in games before the battle in which he died, but completed after it and commemorating both successes [*167*].

Unusual and puzzling dedications on the Acropolis are represented by scraps of what seem to be narrative groups in the round which include the heroes Ajax and Achilles playing dice before Athena (cf. *ABFH* figs 100, 227) and Theseus fighting a brigand [*168*]. There is also an Eros.

More specialized religious sculpture from Athens and Attica is represented by herms and masks. The former are pillars topped by the god Hermes' head and with erect genitals on the shaft. We know that many were dedicated in Athens' streets by Hipparchos, son of Peisistratos, and there are Archaic examples from Athens, even on the Acropolis, but I show the best surviving one of this period, from the island of Siphnos [*169*]. The 'masks' are of Dionysos [*170*] and recall the pillars with masks of the god being worshipped on Athenian vases (cf. *ABFH* fig. 178 and the later *ARFH* fig. 31:). One from Marathon [*171*], which appears to have worn horns, has been thought to represent Pan, the rustic deity who was believed to have helped the Athenians at the battle and was subsequently worshipped by them, but other Athenian Pans of these years have goat features while this is Olympian.

Our last Athenian sculptures are Athenas from her Acropolis. Fragments of what seem an Athena [*172*] ('the foot is unsurpassed in all archaic sculpture' – Payne) are associated with a column bearing the signature of Pythis, who must be an Ionian. Another [*173*], the work of Euenor, was also set on a column. In common with other statues we have mentioned doubt must linger whether this is in fact a work of before 480 or a rare survivor from the years immediately following – rare because so little by way of private dedication is likely to have survived many centuries to be seen by Pausanias. The Athena is probably earlier than 480 and it shows the new, early Classical stance with relaxed right leg, and the new preference in dress – the heavy broad folds of the peplos, its overfall belted-in in the Attic manner. With the Blond boy and the Kritian she looks forward across rather empty years for major statuary in Athens, to the great new era of the Periclean rebuilding and the refurnishing of the Acropolis with temples and statues worthy of her.

East Greek sculpture and sculptors

An east Greek world bedevilled by Persians does not seem a promising ground for the development of further sculptural achievements, and our evidence is in fact more sparse, but the major sanctuaries still attract offerings and give employment, especially for architectural sculpture, and the studios trained artists whose services were in demand elsewhere, east and west.

The peculiarly east Greek dressed male type continues, with a fine example now in Paris, a statuette offered by Dionysermos [*174*]. The rotundity of the head is belied somewhat in profile, where we see a more pointed crown, and the figure steps out more realistically than his predecessors. For a naked figure, and late in the series, a tubby kouros from Samos [*175*] presents the rather loose definition of parts apparent in earlier Ionian anatomical studies yet is on the way to the Kritian boy and the right leg seems slack rather than simply advanced. By contrast, but admittedly earlier, the superb warrior from Samos [*176*], with elegantly patterned armour and flowing locks, expresses an Ionian sense of pattern on softly rounded surfaces in a subject better served by the more formal and vigorous styles of mainland Greek schools.

For korai we must return to Athens, to Archermos of Chios whom we have met already [*103*], and his family. A column from the Acropolis carries his signature and a dedication by Iphidike; another has the signature of an unnamed Chian. Scale and material suggest that the columns could have borne two figures, apparently by one artist, a kore [*177*] and a Nike. The quarter century between these and the Delos Nike [*103*] make close stylistic comparison difficult, but in terms of contemporary statuary the Athens figures carry all the pattern characteristics of Ionian work, and the rather pointed crown to the head seems a north Ionian, so Chian, feature, to judge from terracottas, and was current, or at least influential even farther north [*178*]. The sons of Archermos, Boupalos and Athenis, are dated by Pliny to the early 530s and we might have expected their names associated with the Acropolis figures rather than their father's. They were said to have worked at home, in Delos, Lesbos, Iasos and Smyrna (a Tyche with the horn of plenty and three golden Graces) and to have caricatured the poet Hipponax, but they have been better served by ancient authors than by survival of works which can be plausibly attributed to them. An Artemis by them was, says Pliny, set high and her features seemed sad as you approached, joyful as you left, possibly the effect of an Archaic smile viewed close from below and head-on at a distance, respectively (compare [*205.2*]).

Other areas

The last generation of kouroi is represented on a wide range of sites, including the colonial, but outside Athens and Boeotia it is not distinguished. [*179*] is an example of some quality from the Ptoon but it lacks the clear grasp of form and features of its Attic contemporary from Keos [*144*]. Rather later [*180*] is also from the Ptoon, dedicated by a Boeotian but the style is far closer to Attic and the head invites comparison with the Acropolis korai [*152, 153*]. A Thebadas, probably Boeotian, signed a kore base in Athens.

The Cyclades had been important in the early history of the kore and there are several dedications on Delos late in the century, as [*181*], where a certain independently massive treatment of the hanging dress and novel handling of folds might betoken a Cycladic school, also perhaps represented in Athens (Acr. 594) and at Delphi. Some massive seated women, on Paros and Delos, are of the same stock. A drily modelled late kouros in London [*182*] may be from Anaphe, a small island near Thera.

In the Peloponnese Corinth, Sparta and Arcadia remain better known for minor works in bronze. Ancient authors tell us that the Sicyonian school flourished still, but its home has not proved informative archaeologically for this period. A limestone kore head [183] from Sicyon owes too much to Attic ionicizing styles (compare the 'folded' crown hair of [151]) to represent any decidedly Peloponnesian type, while the expression is almost Etruscan. The strange little kore from the Athenian Acropolis [184] has also been attributed to Sicyon and the Peloponnese. Her proportions are odd and the verticals of her chiton are carefully left undisturbed by the pull at her skirt. Kanachos of Sicyon is recorded as having made bronze, marble, wood and chryselephantine statues; in Sicyon, Thebes and Didyma. His cult statue of Apollo Philesios at Didyma was removed by Darius in 494, returned by Seleucus I two centuries later. The figure was like a kouros holding a bow and a stag, the animal so attached to the hand that a cord could be passed beneath each of its feet in turn, it being supported by the other three – a practical answer to Hephaistos' magic Perseus on the Shield of Herakles, who had no visible means of support at all. Late reliefs, gems and coins give an idea of the Apollo [185] which recalls the bronze [150] in pose and handling of attributes. If a Roman marble copy of the type is properly identified, it was posed in the new, relaxed Kritian stance.

Texts name Ageladas as an influential master and founder of the Argive school, attributing to him distinguished pupils even of much later date, but his athlete statues and other dedications for Olympia and Delphi are put explicitly in the years between 520 and about 490 and do not survive.

Corinth's role in developing major terracotta sculpture has been remarked already (and see p. 157). Several major works of the fifth century found at Olympia may be Corinthian in origin and the earliest is a clay Athena, three-quarters lifesize [186], whose painted features admonish us about the probable original appearance of her marble skin.

81 Kouros from Samos. The dedication is on the left thigh – 'Leukios dedicated (me) to Apollo'. (Samos 69; H. 1·0) About 560–550

Λευκιος ανεξηκε   ΓΕΥΚΙΟΞΑΝΕΘΗΚΕ
τωι Απολωνι   ΤΩΙΑΠΟΓΩΝΙ

83 Kouros head from Kameiros, Rhodes. (Rhodes; grey marble; H. 0·33) About 550

82 Kouros head from Samos, Heraion. The head, in Istanbul, was thought to be from Rhodes but it joins kouros fragments from Samos. The whole figure stood about 3·25 high. (Istanbul 530; H. 0·49) About 550–540

84 Dressed kouros from Samos, Cape Phoneas. (Samos 68; H. 1·79) About 540

85 Kore from Chios. The hands are placed beneath the hair, over the breasts, in an unusual gesture of prayer (?). The back is similar to the next. (Chios 225; H. 0·55, about 2·25 complete) About 580–570

86 Kore from Chios. Cf. 85; this figure held an offering before her breast. (Chios 226; H. 0·62) About 580–570

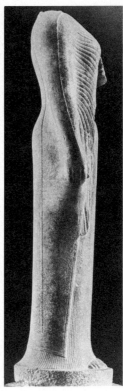

87 Kore ('Cheramyes' Hera') from Samos. She
wears epiblema, mantle and chiton. The dedication
by Cheramyes is written along the front edge of the
epiblema. He dedicated another kore and a kouros
at the same site. Both korai have round plinths and
it has been suggested that they were mounted on
columns with round egg-and-dart capitals. (Louvre
686; H. 1·92) About 560

ΧΗΡΑΜΥΗΣΜΑΝΕΘΙΚΕΝΤΗΡΗΙΑΓΑΛΜΑ

Χηρομυης μ'ανεδηκεν τηρηι αγαλμα

88 Ivory statuette from Ephesus, temple of Artemis.
She serves as handle to a wand surmounted by a hawk.
She wears a chiton and holds a jug and dish of Lydian
type. From below the Kroisos temple. (Istanbul; H. of
figure 0·107) About 560

89 Kore from Miletus. She holds a partridge.
(Berlin 1791; H. 1·43 About 570–560

90 Kore head from Miletus, temple of Athena. The epiblema is worn
over her hair. (Berlin 1631; H. 0·21) About 550–540

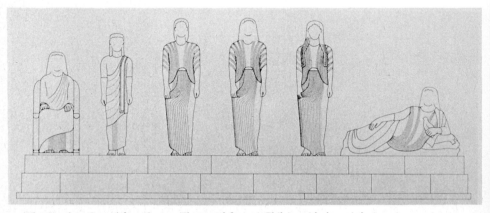

91 'The Geneleos Group' from Samos. The seated figure is Phileia, with the artist's signature
– 'Geneleos made us' – on her legs. The next figure is probably a dressed boy, then three
girls (unknown name: Philippe: Ornithe 92). The dedicator, -arches, reclines 93. (Samos,
except Ornithe; L. of base 6·08) About 560–550

92 (left) Ornithe, see 91. (Berlin 1739; H. 1·63)

93 (below) -arches, see 91. He wears chiton and himation, leans on a wineskin, holds a bird. (Samos 768; L. 1·58)

94 Seated figure from near Didyma.
(London B 271; H. 1·55) About 560

95 Seated figure from near Didyma.
Dedication – 'I am Chares, son of
Kleisis, ruler of Teichioussa. The
statue is for Apollo'.
(London B 278; H. 1·49) About 550

ΧΑΡΗΣΕΙΜΙΟΚΓΕΣΙΟΣΤΓΙΧΙΠΣΗΣΑΡΧΟΣ
ΣΟΝΩΤΊΟΓΑΘΤΑ·ΛΊΑΙΑ

Χαρης ειμι ο Κλεσιος Τειχιοσης αρχος
αγαλμα το Απολλωνος

96 Aiakes from Samos town. Seated lions support the throne arms. The dedication, on the side of the seat, reads – 'Aiakes, son of Brychon, dedicated (me). He secured the booty for Hera during his stewardship' – a civic pirate! (Samos, Tigani Museum 285; H. 1·48) About 540

ΑΕΑΚΗΣΑΝΕΘΗΚΕΜ
ΟΒΡΥ⟨ΩΝΟΣ:ΟΣΤΗ
ΗΡΗΙ:ΤΗΝΣΥΛΗΝ:Ε
ΠΡΗΣΕΝ:ΚΑΤΑΤΗΝ
ΕΠΙⱫΤΑΣΙΝ

Αεακης ανεθηκεν
ο βρυσωνος : ος τηι
Ηρηι : την συλην : ε-
-πρησεν : κατα την
επιστασιν

97 Kore from Samos. She holds a partridge. (Samos I. 217; H. 1·15) About 540–530

98 Kore from the Acropolis.
(Acr. 619; H. 1·43) About 560–550

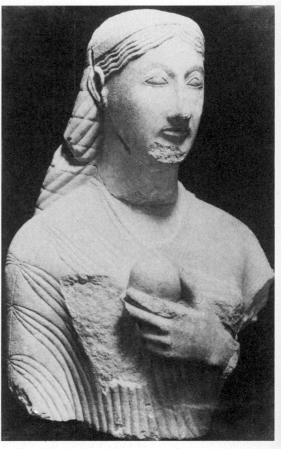

99 Kore from the Acropolis.
(Acr. 677; H. 0·545) About 560–550

100 Sphinx from Delphi. It stands on one of the earliest extant Ionic columns, about 10 m high. A later dedication on its base honours the Naxians with *promanteia* (priority with the oracle). (Delphi; H. 2·32) About 560

101 Kouros from Thera, cemetery. (Athens 8; H. 1·24) About 570–560

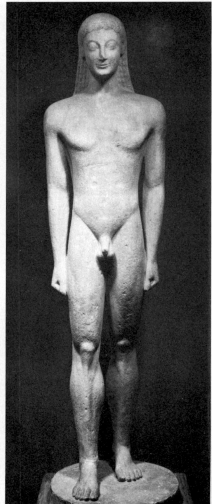

102 Kouros from Melos. (Athens 1558; H. 2·14) About 550

103 Nike from Delos. She has wings at back and heels and wears a chiton and peplos fastened by disc brooches at the shoulders. The inscription on the base reads – 'Farshooter [Apollo, receive this] fine figure [. . ., worked by] the skills of Archermos, from the Chian Mikkiades, . . . the paternal city of Melas'. (Athens 21; H. 0·90) About 550

Μικκια[δηι τωδ’ αγα.]λμα καλον Ν[..κην πτερωεσσαν?]
Αρχερμω σο[φ]ιεισιν ηκηβω[λε δεχσαι Απωλλων]
[τ]οι Χιοι, Μελαγος πατροιων ασ[τυ νεμωντι?]

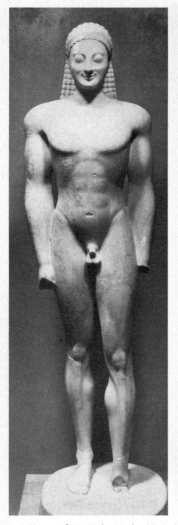

104 Kouros from Volomandra (Attica).
(Athens 1906; H. 1·79) About 570–560

105 Kouros from Greece, probably Attic.
(Florence; completed H. about 1·90)
About 560

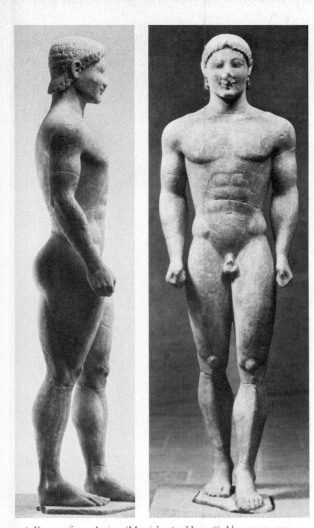

106 Kouros from Attica. (Munich 169; H. 2·08) About 540–530

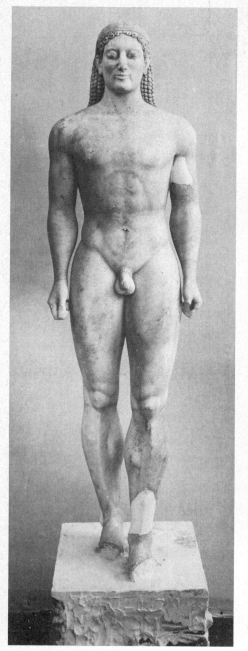

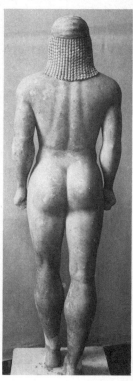

107 Kouros from Anavysos (Attica). This stood on a
stepped base inscribed – 'Stay and mourn at the
monument for dead Kroisos whom violent Ares
destroyed, fighting in the front rank'. He bore the
name of the Lydian king, deposed in 546. The statue
had been sawn in half and smuggled to Paris in 1937
before being returned to Greece. (Athens 3851; H.
1·94) About 530

στε̄θι : και οικτιρον : Κροισο
παρα σε̄μα θανοντος : hον
ποτ᾽ ενι προμαχοις : ολεσε
ϛυρος : Αρε̄ς

ΣΤΕΘΙ:ΚΑΙΟΙΚΤΙΡΟΝΚΡΟΙΣΟ
ΓΑΡΑΣΕΜΑΘΑΝΟΝΤΟΣΗΟΝ
ΓΟΤΕΝΙΓΡΟΜΑ+ΟΙΣ:ΟΛΕΣΕ
ΘΟΡΟΣ:ΑΡΕΣ

108 Kore (the 'Berlin kore', formerly '..goddess') from Keratea (Attica). Found wrapped in
protective lead, probably buried in antiquity at a time of threat, either of invasion (Persian?)
or through the unpopularity of the family in whose burial plot she stood. The crown is
painted with lotus-and-bud and maeander. She wears mantle and chiton, holds a
pomegranate; battlement pattern painted at neckline and skirt centre. (Berlin 1800; H 1·93)
About 570–560

108a Kouros and kore (Phrasikleia, by Aristion of Paros) on discovery (1972) in a pit at Merenda (Myrrhinous) in Attica, where they had been buried in antiquity. For Phrasikleia's base see p. 73. About 550

109 Kore from the Acropolis. She wears mantle, peplos and chiton, holds a wreath and pomegranate. The weighted belt ends hang at the front. This is one of the earliest sculptures to show use of the claw chisel. (Acr. 593; H. 0·995) About 560–550

110 Kore (the 'Lyons kore') from the Acropolis. The upper part reached France by 1719. The join with the lower part was observed by Payne only after some scholars had contrasted the 'Ionian' and 'Attic' character of each half. The crown is painted with lotus and palmette and her earrings are the eastern triple 'mulberry' type worn by Hera in *Iliad* 14, 182f. The upper part of the chiton is not rendered in folds but unrealistically shown as if with tailored sleeves. (Acr. 269+ and Lyons; H. 1·13) About 540. See also

111 Kore from the Acropolis. She wears mantle and chiton. (Acr. 671; H. 1·67) About 530

112 Calf-bearer (Moschophoros) from the Acropolis. He wears a light cloak, its folds ignored. Dedicated by Rh]ombos. By Phaidimos (?), and see on 193. (Acr. 624; restored H. about 1·65) About 560. See also frontispiece

113 Head of a man ('Sabouroff head')
from Athens or Aegina.
(Berlin 608; H. 0·23) About 550–540.
See also *133*

114 See next page

114 Horseman from the Acropolis. The 'Rampin head' is in Paris (see previous page), the rest in Athens. He wears a wreath of wild celery (the prize in the Isthmian and Nemean Games). Other fragments suggest that there was a pair of horsemen set side by side, the horses' heads inclined in, the riders' heads out. The suggestion that they are a dedication of the two 'horsy' (by name and nature) sons of Peisistratos would only be credible if the work is later than 546 (not quite impossible) when the tyrant returned to power. (Would they have survived the fall of the tyranny in 510?) They are too early to be a compliment to anti-tyrant Sparta, as the Dioskouroi, which is another suggestion. (Louvre 3104 and Acr. 590; H. of head 0·29) About 550

115 Kore (the 'Peplos kore') from the
Acropolis. She wears a peplos over chiton
(we see the sleeves and the bottom of the
skirt). The left forearm was made
separately; a wreath and shoulder brooches
were attached. Richly painted. By the Rampin
Master (?). (Acr. 679; H. 1·17) About 530.
See also *129*

116 Kore head from the Acropolis. By the Rampin Master (?).
(Acr. 654; H. 0·117) About 560–550

117 Diskophoros stele fragment from Athens. By the Rampin Master (?).
(Athens 38; H. 0·34) About 550

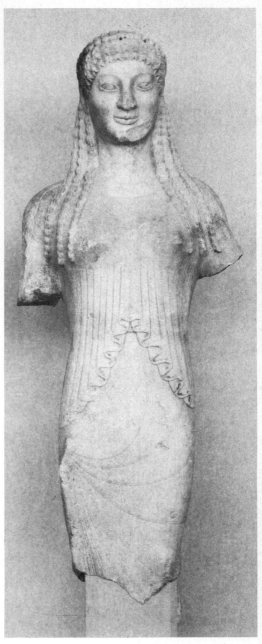

118 Kore from the Acropolis. A mantle hangs symmetrically over the chiton and is not divided at the flanks. (Acr. 678; H. 0·97) About 540–530

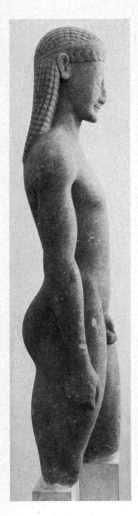
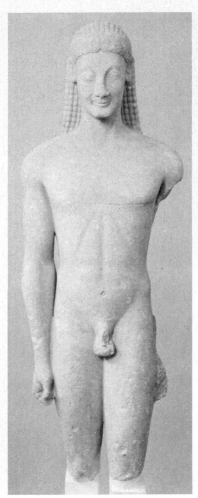

119 Kouros from the Ptoon
(Boeotia). (Thebes 3: H. 1·37)
About 550

120 Clay head of a sphinx
from a temple at Kalydon.
(Athens; H. of head 0·23)
About 580–570

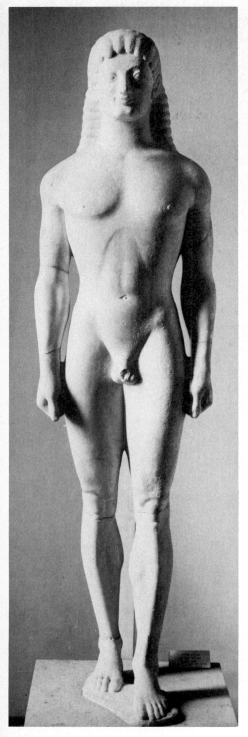

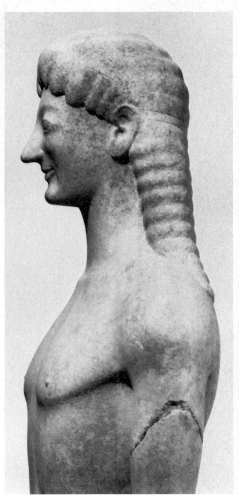

121 Kouros from Tenea. Found lying over part of a tomb, its head protected by a clay jar. (Munich 168; H. 1·35) About 550

122 Bronze head of a youth from Sparta (?). Hollow cast. (Boston 95.74; H. 0·69) About 540

123 Basis from Sparta. A – a man and a woman, his arm round her neck; she holds a wreath. B – as A but no wreath and he threatens her with a sword. On each narrow side a snake. Menelaos with Helen (?), wooing on A and threatening after Troy on B. The snakes suggest a votive for a hero rather than a grave relief; perhaps then from the Menelaion. (Sparta; H. 0·67) Second quarter of the 6th c.

A

B

124 Two-sided relief from Sparta, Acropolis. Apparently the blazoned shield of a warrior (there is another fragment with a head blazon), once associated with the later 'Leonidas' marble. The helmet type is east Greek. (Sparta) Late 6th c.

125 Bronze coin of the Emperor Gallienus showing the Athena of Gitiadas. (London)

126 Silver 'New Style' Athenian tetradrachm showing the Apollo of Tektaios and Angelion on Delos. (London)

127 Ivory head and foot fragments from Delphi. From chryselephantine figures. There are also fragments of seven other heads of various sizes and from sandalled feet and hands, as well as decorated gold plaques from the dress. (Delphi; two-thirds lifesize) About 550–540

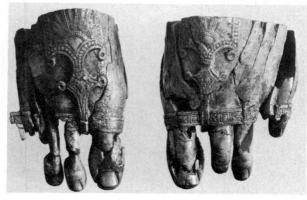

128 Painted cast of *28*, the Auxerre goddess.
(Cambridge, Museum of Classical Archaeology)

129 Painted cast of *115*, the Peplos kore
(Cambridge, Museum of Classical Archaeology)

130 Restoration of part of the Siphnian treasury frieze; cf. *212.2* (after *FDelphes*)

131–3 Painted photographs of casts of *227, 110, 113*

134 Bronze (sphyrelaton) bust of a winged goddess from Olympia. Hammered over a wooden core. (Olympia; nearly lifesize) About 580

135 Seated Athena from the Acropolis. Her aegis
bore a gorgoneion, totally effaced, and bronze
snakes were fitted at its edge. By Endoios, dedicated
by Kallias (?). (Acr. 625; H. 1·47) About 530–520

136 Kore from the Acropolis. Associated with a
column bearing the signatures of Endoios and
Philergos, dedicated by Ops[iades. (Acr. 602; H. 0·66)
About 530–520

137 Votive relief of a potter from the Acropolis. Beazley suggested for the dedicator's name Pampha]ios, a known potter of about 520–500. The sculptor's signature may be restored with the name En[dcios. (Acr. 1332; H. 1·22) About 510–500

138 Detail of *242*

139 Kouros head (the 'Rayet head') from Athens. Associated with fragments of a kouros
from the Piraeus Gate and perhaps belonging to one of the bases bearing signatures of
Endoios and Philergos found near by. (Copenhagen, Ny Carlsberg 418; H. 0·315) About 520

139 See opposite page

140 Bronze youth from the Acropolis. He probably held jumping weights (*halteres*), cf. *ARFH* fig. 85.2. (Athens 6445; H. 0·27) About 520–510

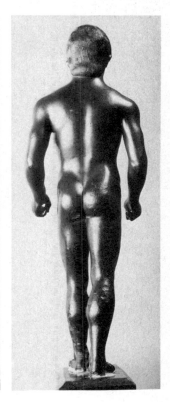

141 Kore ('Antenor's kore') from the Acropolis. Dedicated by the potter Nearchos (a Nearchos signs vases about 570–555 and his sons work to about 540) and signed by Antenor son of Eumares. The eyes are rock crystal set in lead. (Acr. 681; H. 2·155) About 530–520

ΝΕΛΡ+ΟΣΑΝ⊢ΘΕΚΕΙ
ΥΣΕΡΛΟΛΑΠΑΥ+ΕΙΥΙΑⴲ

ΑΝΤΕΝΟΡΕΓΓ
ΟΕΥΜΑΡΟΣΤ

Νεαρχος ανεθε̄κε[ν ho κεραμε]
υς εργον απαρχε̄ν ταϩ[ε̄ναιαι]
Αντε̄νο̄ρ επ[οιε̄σεν h]
ο Ευμαρος τ[ο αγαλμα]

142 Woman from the east pediment, temple of Apollo, Delphi. See also 203.1 (Delphi; H. 1·16) About 520–510

143 Head of a youth (the 'Webb head'). This has been thought a copy of the head of
Antenor's Harmodios in the tyrant-slayer group. (London 2728; H. 0·29) Roman copy of an
original of about 500

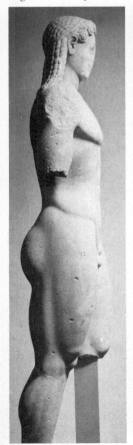

144 Kouros from Keos. Found in the
cemetery area near a pile of ash and
bone. (Athens 3686; H. 2·07) About 530

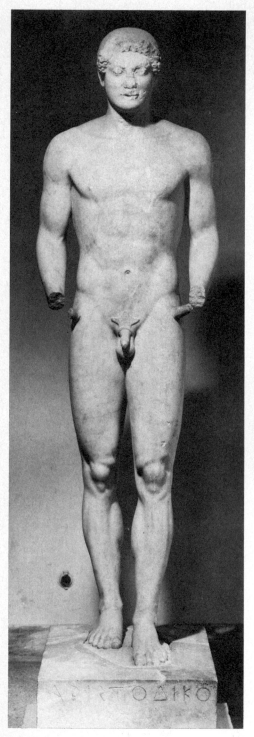

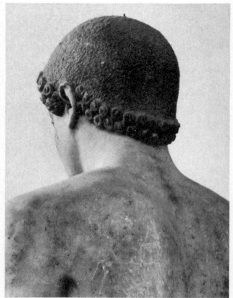

145 Kouros from near Mt Olympus (Attica).
The base is inscribed 'of Aristodikos'.
(Athens 3938; H. 1·95) About 510–500

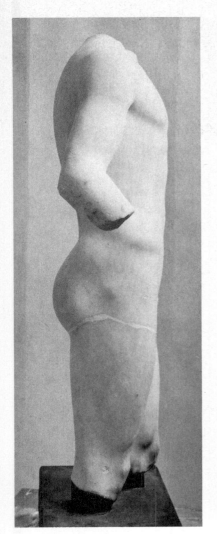 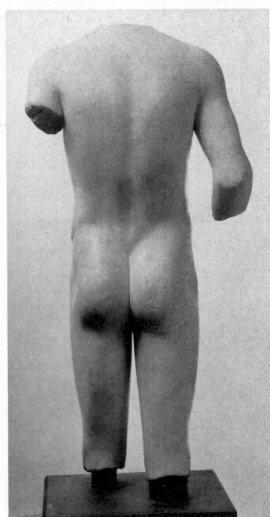

146 Kouros from the Acropolis. (Acr. 692; H. 0·87) About 490

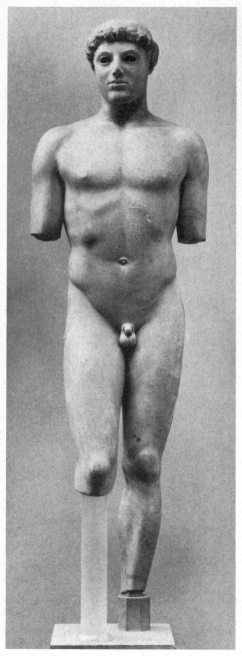
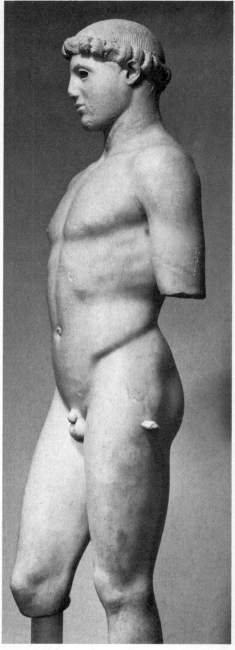

147 Youth from the Acropolis ('Kritian boy'). The sobriquet is given because of the similarity of the head to the head of Harmodios in the tyrant-slayer group by Kritios and Nesiotes, set up after 479 and known from copies. (Acr. 689; H. 0·86, about half lifesize) About 490–480

148 Youth from the Acropolis ('Blond boy'). Head
and part of loins. Traces of yellow-brown on the hair;
ringlets and side whiskers were also painted on.
(Acr. 689+; H. of head 0·25, loins 0·34; about three-
quarters lifesize) About 490–480

149 Worshipper from near the Ilissos. For the dress compare *112*. Possibly a Hermes. (Athens 3687; H. 0·65) About 500

150 Bronze Apollo from the Piraeus. Excavated in 1959 with a cache of later, Classical bronzes and marbles, possibly overtaken by Sulla's sack in 86 BC. He held a bow in the left hand, a phiale in the right. (Athens; H. 1·92) About 530–520

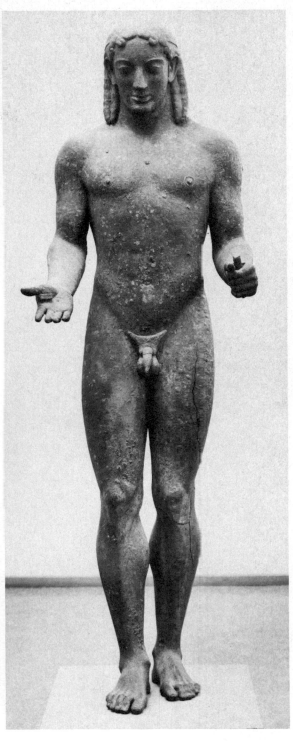

149 See opposite page

151 Kore from the Acropolis.
(Acr. 682; H. 1·82) About 530–520

152 Kore from the Acropolis. By the same hand
as 153. It has been thought (Karouzos) an
early work by the artist of Aristodikos 145.
(Acr. 673; H. 0·93) About 520–510

153 Kore from the Acropolis. By the same hand as 152 and cf. 180. (Acr 670; H. 1·15) About 520–510

154 Kore head from the Acropolis. The upper part was made separately, probably a repair. '. . . one of the great works of Attic sculpture' (Payne). (Acr. 643; H. 0·145) About 520–510

155 Kore from the Acropolis.
(Acr. 680; H. 1·15) About 520–510

156 Kore from the Acropolis
(Acr. 615; H. 0·92)
About 510–500

157 Kore from the Acropolis. Fragments of the body found also.
(Acr. 696+; H. of head 0·275) About 510–500

158 Kore from the Acropolis.
(Acr. 674; H. 0·92) About 500

159 Kore from the Acropolis.
(Acr. 684; lifesize) About 500–490

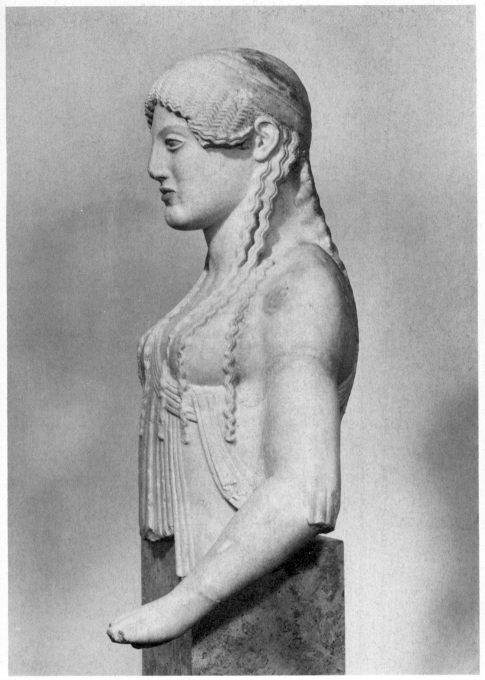

160 Kore ('Euthydikos' kore') from the Acropolis. Mounted on a column with a
hemispherical capital inscribed 'Euthydikos, son of Thaliarchos, dedicated (me)'. Euthydikos
dedicated another statue after 479 (pillar base found). The Blond boy *148* is probably by the
same artist. (Acr. 686, 609; H. 0·58, 0·42) About 490. See also next page

160 See last page

161 Kore from the Acropolis. (Acr. 688; H. 0·51) About 480

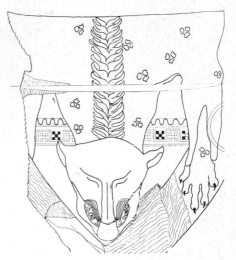

162 Seated Dionysos from Athens. The dress, sandals, stool cloth and panther skin are elaborately painted (see drawing). (Athens 3711; H. 1·07) About 520

163 Seated woman from Rhamnus. (Athens 2569; H. 0·44) About 530–510

164 Scribe from the Acropolis. Seated on a stool, wearing himation only and with an open writing tablet on his lap. The dedication of a bureaucrat of the new 'democracy' or a Treasurer of Athena (?). (Acr. 144; H. 0·45) About 500

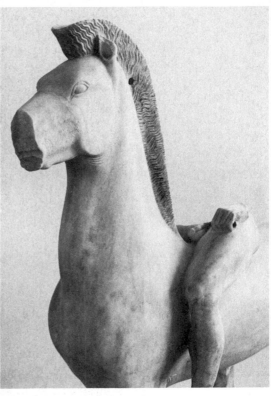

165 Horseman from the Acropolis. (Acr. 700; H. of whole horse 1·12) About 510

166 Horseman from the Acropolis. For the pose of head and body cf. *114*. This, however, is a miniature. (Acr. 623; H. 0·20) About 510

167 Nike from the Acropolis.
Set on a column bearing the
dedication of Kallimachos, the
general who commanded and
was killed at Marathon, set up
after his death. (Acr. 690; H. 1·4)
About 490–480

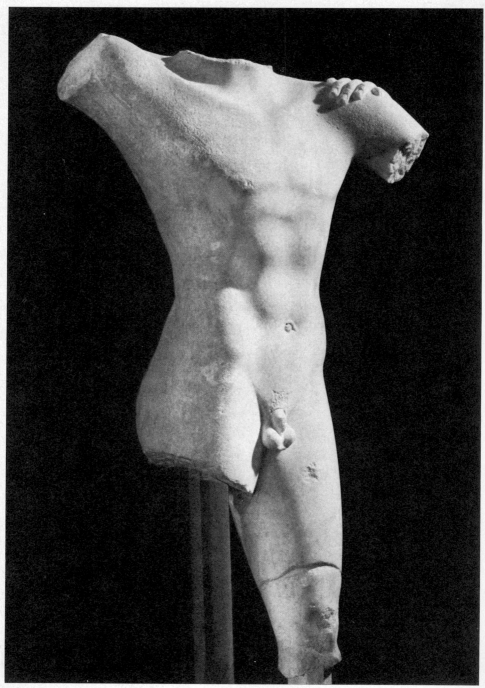

168 Theseus from the Acropolis. An action group in the round. His opponent's hand grasps his left shoulder from behind. A fragment with Theseus' hand seizing the throat of a bearded man must belong. Skiron or Prokrustes? (cf. *ARFH* figs. 90, 233.2). (Acr. 145; H. 0·63) About 510–500

170 Mask of Dionysos from Ikaria (Attica) where there was a shrine of the god. The richly plastic treatment of hair curls and features transcends its battered state. (Athens 3072; H. 0·41. About 520

169 Herm from Siphnos. (Athens 3728; H. 0·66) About 520

171 Mask of a god from Marathon. Horns were attached at the forehead. The style has been compared with that of the Euthydikos kore *160* and Blond boy *148*. (Berlin 100; H. 0·32) About 500–480

172 Fragments of an Athena from the Acropolis. The left foot was made separately. There is a cutting for a spear held upright, so an Athena. By Pythis, dedicated by Epiteles (the same combination on an Acropolis base). The capital of its column survives. (Acr. 136; H. of capital 0·25) About 510

Γ Υ Θ Ι S Ε Π Ο Ι Ε S Ε Ν
Ε Π Ι Τ Ε Λ Ε S Α Ν Ε Θ Ε Κ Ε Ν Α
Α Θ Ε Ν Α Ι Ρ Ι

Πυδις εποιεσεν
Επιτελες ανεδεκεν απαρχεν
Αδεναιαι

173 Athena from the Acropolis. She wears an aegis and once held spear and shield. Set on a column dedicated by Angelitos and signed by Euenor. (Acr. 140; H. 0·77) About 480

 \ Ν Λ Ξ V Ι Τ Ο S : Μ Α Ν Ε Θ ι
Α Θ Ε Ν Α Ι Α : Ι Ε ι
Ε V Ε Ν Ο Ρ Ε ι U Ι ε

Ανγελιτος : μ'ανεδε[κεν....]
[Ποτνι'] Αδεναια : χεχ[αριστο σοι τοδε δδρον ?]
Ευενορ εποιεσεν.

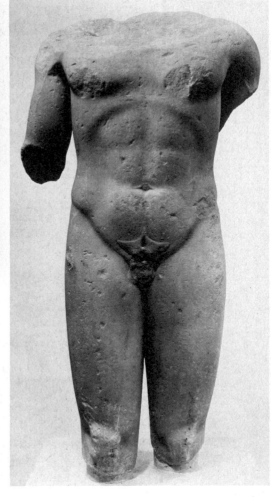

174 Youth. Dedicatory inscription on the broad vertical strip of the himation, worn over a chiton – 'I am Dionysermos, of the (genos?) of Tenor'. (Louvre MA 3600 H. 0·69) About 520

175 Kouros from Samos, the Heraion. (Samos 77; H. 1·07, lifesize) About 490–480

176 Warrior from Samos, the Heraion. The grey marble is as that for 75 but unlike the other
Heraion statues. Fragments of his buttock and a greaved shin also found. (Berlin 1752; H.
0·86) About 520

177 Kore from the Acropolis. Associated with the
column bearing a signature of Archermos of Chios. The
colour is well preserved – blue chiton with blue and red
patterns. The back is finished but without detail of dress.
The marble has been thought Chian. (Acr. 675; H. 0·55)
About 520–510

178 Kore head from Kyzikos (Troad). (Berlin
1851; H. 0·25) About 520

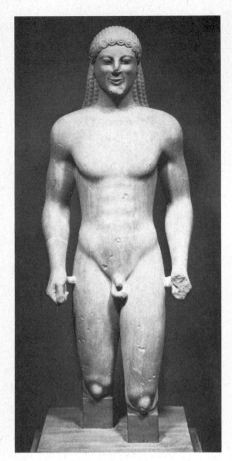

179 Kouros from the Ptoon. (Athens
12; H. 1·6 = about 2·16 complete)
About 530–520

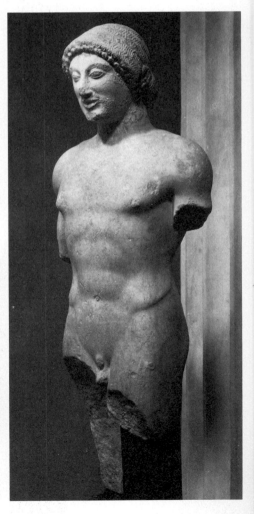

180 Kouros from the Ptoon. Dedicated
by Pythias of Akraiphia and Aischrion
(inscribed on thighs). See on 152, 153.
(Athens 20; H. 1·03 = about 1·47
complete) About 510–500

181 Kore from Delos. (Delos A 4064; H. 0·94)
About 520–510

182 Kouros from Araphe (?).
(London B 475; H. 1·01)
About 510–500

183 Limestone kore head from Sicyon.
(Boston 04.10; H. 0·175) About 530

185 Bronze coin of Miletus, 1st c. BC,
showing the Apollo Philesios of
Kanachos. (London)

186 Clay Athena head from Olympia. She was helmeted
and carried shield and aegis. Apparently from a votive group
including a fight, perhaps a Herakles adventure, of which
some scraps survive. (Olympia T 6; H. 0·22) About 490

184 Kore from the Acropolis.
(Acr. 683; H. 0·805) About 510

Chapter Seven

ARCHITECTURAL SCULPTURE

Placing and character

The architectural sculpture of seventh-century Crete was applied to simple one-roomed temples and disposed in an eastern manner, with dado friezes. In mainland Greece the second half of the century saw the inception of the stone Doric order of architecture for temples and at the end of the century the beginnings in east Greece, at Smyrna, of what was to become the Ionic order. These orders defined buildings which had colonnades around a central room for the cult image (*cella*) and low-pitched tiled roofs, leaving shallow gable ends. In Doric the entablature over the outer columns and sometimes over the inner porches was articulated by a frieze of triglyphs and metopes. This frieze is a translation of timbering into stone, presenting a series of plain rectangles (the metopes) with thinner vertically ridged dividers (the triglyphs). A frieze composed of separate panels like this was familiar in the east and in Greek Daedalic art [*31, 35*]. On some early Doric buildings the metopes have painted figures, as at Thermon in Aetolia. On developed Doric buildings relief sculpture could appear on the metopes, with relief or eventually free-standing sculpture in the gable pediments, and free-standing figures at the roof corners and apices (*acroteria*) as well as human or animal heads in clay or stone along the gutters. Minor friezes may be admitted in porches. The rendering of the order in stone was probably inspired by Egypt but the shape of the buildings was Greek and so was the disposition of the sculpture.

Ionic temples are confined to the east Greek world in this period, though elements of the style may appear on the mainland for votive monuments and for treasuries at Delphi. On Ionic buildings the placing of sculpture is rather less predictable than in Doric. There is normally nothing in the pediment [*211*] is an exception, on an exceptional building) but there are acroteria. The continuous frieze is an Ionic feature but not invariable and in fact rare on Archaic exteriors and not unknown even on Doric buildings. But the gutter (*sima*) may carry a frieze, there can be a frieze dado in porches and on the lower and perhaps upper drums of columns [*217–20*]. The continuous frieze devoted to a single developing theme, rather than with repeated identical or similar figures without dividers as on many seventh-century vases or at Prinias [*32*], is a foreign concept, already met in the strongly orientalizing Chania relief [*15*]. On vases such narrative friezes appear rarely in the seventh century, more often in the sixth. There is eastern precedent too for the 'Caryatid' korai replacing porch columns in treasuries [209, 210] and oddities like capitals with animal foreparts (Pegasi in Thasos and Chios) or the Chian anta bases in the shape of lions' paws, like massive furniture. (The Chian sculptor Boupalos was also an architect.)

Archaic architectural sculpture, then, appears on temples, on the temple-like treasuries, on Ionic altars, but rarely in other contexts until civic architecture rivals the religious in its use of the ornate orders.

The Doric pediment was called *aetos*, 'eagle', a Corinthian invention according to Pindar. It does resemble outspread wings and calls to mind the winged and tailed sun disc which crowns Egyptian and eastern stelai. The earliest pedimental decoration known to us is of large clay gorgon heads from temples at Selinus and Gela in Sicily. These rather heighten the resemblance to the sun disc, but gorgons, facing monsters and monster fights, are recurrent themes on Archaic temples – demonstrations of power not without an element of magical, apotropaic defence. The myth scenes that may accompany and which eventually replace them must relate to the cult or local myth although the connection is not always readily explained, and the symbolism or relevance of the subsidiary sculpture in friezes is often even more obscure. The pediment is an unhappy shape into which to force figure sculpture. Once more than a single gorgon was attempted for it the scheme begins to resemble that of some Greek vase friezes, with abrupt transitions between apparently unrelated subjects, but also with no unity of scale, though the shape naturally requires a roughly symmetrical composition. The scheme lasts even until the Apollo temple at Delphi [203], here to accommodate two of the last of the major pedimental animal-fight groups. Where there is a single theme unity of scale is at first ignored [187, 192], then realized with the help of falling or fallen figures to fit the narrowing wings [206], a constraint favouring battle subjects.

As in most other classes of stone carving the Greek treatment of relief soon displays an originality of execution and intention which far removes it from the shallow pictorial treatment of relief in the east and Egypt, where it covers wall areas rather than helps articulate architecture. At its simplest it is hardly more than drawing, lightly rendered in relief, though this can be infinitely subtle even in the shallowest field, and is naturally best suited to small monuments and not to architecture. Pedimental and eventually metopal figures become executed in the round and attached to, sometimes carved with, or set before the pediment wall or metope ground. An intermediate manner, best suited to friezes and smaller monuments, foreshortens the figures front to back, thus suggesting the whole figure and usually leaving just the head in high half-relief, not slicing through the fully rounded figures as happens in much later relief sculpture. As much detail as possible is carved on the forward plane (where it was drawn) and overlapping is suggested successfully by the slight recession of planes. There are virtuoso examples of this in the Archaic period [208.2, 212.1–2]: later frieze figures tend to be more discreet. Shadow, heightened by a dark painted back-ground, helped to project and distinguish the figures to the viewer, who was normally far more distant from the carving than the modern museum-goer.

The beginnings: Corfu

The earliest sculptural decoration on temples of the canonic orders was in clay – roof and gutter antefixes in the form of mould-made heads or figures. They appear in the Corinthian sphere in the second half of the seventh century, and it was at Corinth that the Sicyonian Boutades was said to have invented the practice. The island of Corfu (Kerkyra) lay within the area of Corinthian artistic influence, and it is there that we find the first major stone pediment in homeland Greece, on the temple of Artemis [187]. Unity of scale and theme have yet to be sought but the great central Gorgon and her two leopards make a brave trio. At this date there is inevitably still much linear detail to be defined in colour, with incised and compass-drawn outlines or low relief in the maeander-patterned dress. Much is conceived still in flat planes, but the smaller figures are almost in the round or only partly foreshortened front to back in what is to be the normal manner later. Chrysaor [187.2] is a notable figure, his features and body too advanced to allow the very early date once proposed for the pediment. His grotesque face suits his family background but the hooded lids and grimace are pleasanter when viewed from below. Sculptors are quick to make allowances for the unnaturally oblique viewpoints required for most architectural sculpture.

Athens

Most of the architectural sculpture found on the Acropolis is of limestone (*poros*), stuccoed and painted. It is generally now assumed to have been discarded after the Persian sack of 480/479, but since it all antedates the end of the Peisistratid tyranny in 510, since it was found in a fairly compact area immediately south and east of the later Parthenon, since there is a strong suspicion that there are originals and replacements for single buildings, and since only one major foundation is preserved (immediately south of the Classical Erechtheion, and still visible), and the idea that there was a second where the Parthenon now stands remains purely hypothetical, the older theory of the demolition of the tyrants' buildings after 510 and depositing of debris (*Tyrannenschutt*) thirty years before the Persian sack (producing the *Perserschutt*) should not be too readily abandoned. Peisistratos had promoted himself to live beside the gods on the Acropolis – the safest place for a tyrant – for at least some of his years in power, and so had his sons. It is understandable that his buildings, even perhaps sacred ones, might have been thought an affront to Athens and Athena, and it is always possible that some of the smaller pediments are not from sacred buildings at all. It would be unparalleled, so far as we know, in this period for a house or palace to be so decorated, but Peisistratos had posed virtually as a second Herakles, protégé of Athena, and Herakles is the dominant theme of the architectural sculpture of the dismembered buildings on the Acropolis. The only building that must have survived 510 was the temple of Athena with her sacred image, though the building had been newly furnished with marble pediments.

The earliest pieces are marble, the first use of the material on Greek buildings, if they are in fact architectural: a gorgon which may be an acroterion [188], possibly a Perseus and appliqué relief leopards [189]. The gorgon's hair, ears and eyes show some advance on the Dipylon head [62], the panthers some advance on the Corfu pediment [187]. The Athens pieces cannot be much later than 580–570, probably still too early for any temple constructed for the reorganized Panathenaia in 566. None of the limestone sculpture is near them in date though scholars have preferred to distribute the surviving pieces through the century and not subject them to the same general process of scaling down dates rightly applied to major works in marble. The tendency for some elements of the limestone sculpture to look primitive may be inherent in the treatment of the softer material, or the sculptor's different handling of figures to be viewed only at a distance. The reconstruction of pediments from the shattered fragments has provoked considerable speculation. Of the larger animals there is, at least, a lioness tearing a bull [190], a recumbent lion, and a lioness with a lion together tearing a bull [191]. The first may be somewhat the earlier but all are virtually in the round, not relief, of comparable though not uniform scale, and with no greater stylistic differences than are observed in the figures of other Acropolis groups. It is not altogether impossible that all except the first are from one building, which must be the Athena temple whose foundations we see. The animal threesome was certainly assembled with other figure groups beside it and the consensus seems in favour of the animals central, with a Herakles and Triton at the left, the three-bodied 'Bluebeard' [193] at the right [192.1]. A recent controversial suggestion for the other pediment [192.2] places a gorgon (of which there are possible scraps) between lion and lioness (compare Corfu), the snakes which are also available at the corners, promotes an Introduction of Herakles to Olympus [194] (hitherto taken as a small separate pediment), and restores a Birth of Athena (including [195]) to match the myth figures at the other end. The felines are far more developed than the Corfu or marble Acropolis leopards, the mass of their soft bellies realistically spreading on to the bodies of their victims, a treatment well in advance of, for instance, the Calf-bearer [112], let alone the architectural pieces named. The other figures too, in style and iconography, can hardly be earlier than about 550, despite some primitive-seeming features: additions, it may be, to the temple with the 'gorgon acroterion' in marble and perhaps replacing the limestone lioness and bull, and conceivably no earlier than Peisistratos' return to rule in 546. This view is supported by the assembly of the pediments indicated in [192] but does not depend on it.

Of the smaller pediments the exceptionally shallow relief of the Herakles and Hydra [196] may indicate an earlier date, unless it is a secondary, back pediment. A small Herakles and Triton [197] is more nearly in the round and the mysterious Olive Tree pediment [198] where the narrative is presented more as in a puppet theatre than with figures filling the pediment field, need hardly be earlier than the large limestone pediments, to judge from the developed treatment of dress folds.

In about 520 the Athena temple was provided with new pediments, of marble now. One end included lions with a bull, very close in style and composition to its limestone predecessor: another reason for not dating the latter too distantly. The other has a gigantomachy [199] where the fighting and falling figures can fit the gable without offending unity of scale. This is the work of a great sculptor, an artist who for the first time grapples with the problems posed by figures in the round (though for a single viewpoint) in twisting, violent action or collapse, but still far from success, still bound to the rigid axes on which figures and their parts are composed: 'in force of movement they are the only archaic statues really comparable with the west pediment of Olympia' (Payne). Fragments of a large frieze [200] must also have had an architectural setting but they are later than the temple, post-Peisistratid, and unlikely to have anything to do with it.

In the lower town of Athens there were large and small limestone pediments with lions, one with satyrs and women for the temple of Dionysos [201], and in marble a Herakles with the lion and another with two lions and a bull. To judge from vase paintings some of the new fountain houses built under Peisistratos carried acroteria and pedimental sculpture (animals, a satyr). At Eleusis the famous running girl [202] and a female winged figure are thought to be from the pedimental group of a small building overthrown by the Persians. The distinctive flat, flaring pleats and the treatment of features and eyes found on other works from the site suggest the existence of a local studio or influential local stylist in statuary.

Central and south Greece

The early Archaic temple of Apollo at Delphi was destroyed by fire. A subscription list for a new one was opened and the exiled Athenian family, the Alkmaionids, undertook the contract, themselves paying for marble to be used instead of limestone on the east façade. Herodotus says this was done after their abortive attack in Attica in 514 but some scholars have found difficulty in believing the temple sculptures to be so late. The building was in some respects a rival to the Peisistratid temple of Athena in Athens and borrowed from it the gigantomachy theme for the west pediment, of which very little survives. The east pediment [203] retains the old, disjointed composition of the older Athens pediments and Corfu, with animal fights at either side and a frontal centre piece with attendants and a chariot bearing the deity. The frontal chariot was repeated at the west for Zeus. The challenging frontality of the early gorgon pediments is divided now between the displays of power in the animal fights and a calm presentation or epiphany. In style and detail the kore attendants [142] in the east pediment and the Nike acroteria [204] so much resemble Antenor's kore in Athens [141] that it is most likely that Antenor designed the Delphi pediments.

The temple of Apollo at Eretria in Euboea was destroyed by the Persians on their way to defeat at Marathon in 490. The city had been closely associated with Athens, both under and after the tyrants, and despite the temple's occupant it is Athena [205.3] who stands at the pediment's centre (this seems to be the back pediment, however), another early example of the frontal–central–deity theme. The fight around her is of Greeks against Amazons with Theseus, new darling of the Athenian state, carrying off their queen [205.2]. Style and subject might suggest Athenian interest and perhaps patronage in post-tyrant years. The figures were carved in the round and fastened to the background by large square pegs. The cutting is sparkling and sharp, the postures well in advance of the experiments in the Athens temple but the figures comfortably rounded in a non-Athenian manner. One of the Amazons appears to have been salvaged in antiquity and carried off to Rome [205.1].

For the fullest expression of the fight motif as a pediment filler we turn to the island of Aegina. At the end of the sixth century a large Doric temple was built for a local goddess, Aphaia. Both pediments house fights, with a central Athena, probably as patroness of the Greeks at Troy where the action seems to be set, being chosen because of the involvement there of Aeginetan heroes Telamon and Ajax. The sculptures were excavated in 1811, bought by King Ludwig I of Bavaria and restored and improved by the neo-Classical sculptor Thorwaldsen. The restorations have been removed from the new display in Munich. The east pediment seems marginally later in style and more advanced in composition than the west. The earlier pediment [206.1], in the latest reconstruction proposed, presents duels beside Athena and symmetrical groups with the action moving towards the corners. The later, east pediment [206.2], has a more active Athena, the action moves rather towards the centre and the figures are more ambitiously posed with some falling, others poised to support. In some ways the contrast between the two is the contrast between the Archaic and the imminent Classical, yet little more than ten years may separate them. It seems that an east pediment had been designed and at least in part completed in the earlier phase of construction, but never installed and the figures were displayed on a base near the east end of the temple together with an acroterion (two korai and an anthemion; there were sphinxes at the roof corners). The subject and style are as for the west, and scraps have suggested that there might have been yet a third group prepared (possibly not for a pediment) involving women – perhaps Zeus pursuing Aegina. The twisting and falling figures of the east pediment are figures more familiar to us in vase painting, or in the high relief of the Megarian treasury [215], but here they are executed in the round, severely testing the sculptor's understanding of the anatomy of torsion. He had still, it seems, a little to learn, but these figures only suffer in comparison with the Athenian treasury at Delphi [213] through their scale and the artist's decision to attempt figures in action but off balance. Onatas of Aegina, whose attested works are slightly later, is a name often associated with the east pediment. An Aeginetan sculptor's signature appears on the Acropolis at Athens and his name, Kallon, was known to ancient writers who record many more from the island in the fifth century and remark their skills in bronze work. How far the sharp detail of the marble figures and their many metallic embellishments reflect this tradition it is hard to say, but a bronze head from Athens [207] in the style of the pediments conveys the quality of Aeginetan work in the metal, and its essential identity with styles in marble carving.

There are other important pediments of homeland Greece in the Archaic period, but smaller or less well preserved. I mention only a fine marble fragment of a small pediment with a fallen Amazon in the corner from Kopai in Boeotia; scraps of a terracotta Amazonomachy from Corinth, which reminds us of the city's earlier reputation in architectural sculpture in this material, and a recent find on Corfu, apparently from a temple of Dionysos, with an excellent limestone study of Dionysos and a lad at a symposium, with a dog and lion and, it seems, attended by satyrs. The style here is still broadly Corinthian [207a].

Treasuries

Treasuries are small, one-room, temple-like structures usually with columned porches, dedicated by states at the national sanctuaries both as rich tokens of thanksgiving and of ostentatious piety, and as repositories for rich offerings. The most elaborate are at Delphi and Olympia, and the majority date from the Archaic period. At Delphi they flanked the Sacred Way to the temple: at Olympia they overlooked the altars and the end of the stadium.

The earliest with sculptured decoration is the Sicyonian at Delphi, presumably dedicated by the tyrant Kleisthenes near the end of his rule, about 560. Its remains, with those of a strange round building, were found in the foundations of the later Sicyonian treasury. The earlier buildings, also Sicyonian, we assume (their stone seems to come from the area of Sicyon), may have been destroyed in the earthquake of 373. The treasury is unusual in having an all-round Doric colonnade of 5 × 4 columns, providing fourteen unusually broad metopes for relief sculpture [208], four of which are almost wholly preserved, with some scraps. Inscriptions painted on the background named the figures and an interesting design feature is the apparent continuation of a single object, the ship Argo, on two adjacent metopes, and the action carried across an intervening triglyph, if one with a boar shows the Calydonian creature and it is being attacked. The compositions are ambitious with the frontal horsemen severely foreshortened [208.1] and the brilliant impression of receding planes achieved in the cattle rustling [208.2]. Within the shallow field the sculptor finds room for considerable subtlety in modelling of anatomy and of dress, notably in the Europa relief [208.3].

Possibly more than one treasury at Delphi had Caryatid korai for porch columns. To the Cnidian parts of bodies only have been attributed. Of another there is a head [209] resembling the most ionicizing of the Athenian Acropolis. And there is the Siphnian, the most important of the Delphi treasuries. Siphnos had struck it rich in her gold and silver mines and the treasury was a tithe from her new wealth, built before the island was sacked by the Samians in 525 and the mines flooded; but only little before, we might judge, and there are signs of haste and incompletion. One beautiful Caryatid head is preserved [210] and enough of the bodies to show affinities with Cycladic korai. The relief decorated drum on her head is an architectural feature, to make an easy transition to the carved capital, not a formal polos head-dress, as sometimes described. The building is articulated by exquisitely carved Ionic mouldings and apart from the maidens in the porch had sculptured acroteria (Nikai), a frieze all round over the architrave, and two pedimental groups of which that on the back is preserved. The pediment [211] is unusual in having the lower parts of the figures engaged with the back wall, their upper parts in the round with the background deeply recessed. The scale of the centre group is uniform, with a slightly taller Zeus, reducing for the figures and horses at either side. The long friezes [212] are continuous compositions but the south has much missing. Of the short friezes that at the back (east) is bisected and each half, interrelated in theme – Olympus: Troy – symmetrically composed; that at the front is trisected to match the triple division of the porch. Painted inscriptions named the figures and were probably several times repainted, but few have survived. On a shield in the north frieze a signature has been severely recut but is just intelligible. The artist's name has been variously restored as Endoios or Aristion of Paros, but he claims to have carved 'these and those behind', i.e., the north and east friezes, which are the only ones on which painted inscriptions also survive. This is clearly true and we can add perhaps the surviving pediment and attribute to a second master the south and west friezes, with the Caryatids. The former artist cuts stockier, bigger-headed figures which look like early Athenian red figure vase painting rendered in the round, and he displays notable skill in cutting the roundness of figure and limb despite the shallow relief, and real virtuosity with overlapping figures which avoid becoming merely confused. Thus, the chariots in the Troy scene are shown in three-quarter view, not profile, the receding parts being painted on to the background [130]. His companion works on detailed forward planes cut abruptly back at the edges, and his high-crowned heads have seemed to some north Ionian beside his colleague's Cycladic. The building faced away from the visitor mounting the Sacred Way, who thus saw the east and north friezes first. If the 'islander' created the façade for the island treasury it was the more gifted eastern guest artist who secured the more conspicuous fields to decorate.

The Siphnian treasury is the high point of Archaic decorative sculpture, almost overwhelming in the elaboration of all surfaces and members which were by then deemed suitable to receive it. With colour and the many metal additions of weapons and jewellery it must have resembled more a large and glittering casket, less than nine metres long, than monumental architecture. Moreover, in the composition of the friezes it demonstrates Archaic narrative at its best, and the ingenuity with which Greek artists could face the problem of presenting complicated action in shallow relief. The gigantomachy theme, the Olympian defeat of the powers of primaeval earth, recurs often in Greek sacred sculpture and secular art. At Delphi it reflects as truly the quality of its age as it does over three centuries later, on the altar of Zeus at Pergamum.

Little later and of comparable quality is the sculpture from the Massilian (Marseilles) treasury at Delphi. The scraps that survive show that the style owed much to the north Ionian taste and origins of the settlers from Phocaea.

The Athenian treasury at Delphi, now rebuilt on the site, is the best known of these monuments, one of the latest of the Archaic series and, like the earliest, of the Doric order. Pausanias says it was dedicated after Marathon (490) but style and architecture point to a somewhat earlier date, and it is likely that he was misled by the immediately adjacent base, which *was* Athenian and for Marathon. The subject matter of its metopes, dividing the honours between Herakles and Theseus, makes it a good propaganda document of the new democracy, especially since Theseus is given the more conspicuous position, but does not chime with what we know of Athenian symbolism for Marathon. There are scraps of pediments including a fight at one end, chariots and perhaps a frontal Athena at the other, which would then be a direct further reference to the dedicating state. The acroteria were mounted Amazons, adversaries of both the heroes celebrated. The metope figures are wholly in the round or only tangentially attached to the background with which they are carved [213]. The figures are comparatively neat and small, not crowding the field, and the artist, dealing mainly with stock themes, occasionally creates for his subjects new compositions. Style and theme invite comparison with Athenian vases and suggest a date hardly much after 500. Athens itself offers no architectural sculpture of these years, so close sculptural comparisons are lacking since the shallow grave reliefs and major Acropolis dedications in the round, not all from Athenian hands, are different genres. But the treasury metopes own no other obvious home and we would expect an Athenian artist. The hard detail of hair, features, anatomy, is brilliant and the sharp pattern in no way hinders the effective vigour of the compositions. Limbs and torsos posed in triangles or oblique lines in the field present more thoughtful compositions than the horizontals and verticals of earlier metopal schemes, but are not yet as carefully balanced as they will be on, for instance, the temple of Zeus at Olympia. The sad state of preservation is tantalizing, yet wherever any major part of a figure survives it satisfies the eye as well as any late Archaic sculpture from anywhere in Greece. With the Aegina pediments, where composition is determined more by field than subject, they are the ultimate expression of Archaic narrative in sculpture. Single metopes can be securely placed architecturally on both the north and south sides and they suggest that the nine north metopes carried separate Herakles scenes, the south (more conspicuous) Theseus. At the back (west) one fallen metope suggests that the six showing the narrative of Herakles and Geryon go here, the action crossing the intervening triglyphs; leaving metopes with an Amazonomachy at the front, and of this we do not know whether it involved Herakles, or Theseus, or both, or neither.

The treasuries at Olympia are all Doric, more than half of them the gift of Greek colonies. From the pediment of the treasury of Cyrene is a fragment showing the eponymous nymph wrestling a tiny lion. Cocks and hens from this treasury and another, perhaps of Byzantium, suggest that the cock fight was a relevant symbol for a sanctuary devoted to sport, and this symbolism for courage in competition is met elsewhere in Greek art (cf. *ABFH* 167). A superb fragmentary relief [*214*] comes from another treasury but the only substantial sculpture surviving is from the pediment of the treasury of Megara (just possibly the Megara of Sicily, not Greece) with its gigantomachy in a high relief approaching that of the Athenian treasury at Delphi, but poorer in execution. It is composed in duels [*215*].

East Greece

We start with the least characteristic of all east Greek assemblages, the sculpture of the temple of Athena at Assos in the Troad [*216*]. Athens had dealings in this area in the sixth century and this may be the reason for it being the only Doric building on this coast and for the Herakles scenes upon it. It carries carved metopes, at least at the front, but the architrave below bears a frieze at front, back and sides (or for most of their length) in the Ionic manner and there is no pediment sculpture, another Ionic trait. The material is the local hard, brittle andesite. This partly accounts for the primitive appearance of the shallow relief which may be regarded as truly provincial and dates well into the second half of the sixth century.

The first massive Ionic temples of the rulers and tyrants of Ionia were built in the second quarter of the century, with important rebuilding or continuing work of decoration through the Archaic period. From buildings at the Heraion on Samos there are tantalizing scraps of high quality relief friezes including some over lifesize. The temple of Artemis at Ephesus is more rewarding. We are told by Herodotus that King Kroisos of Lydia paid for many of the columns and since he was deposed in 546 we have a terminus ante quem for the earliest sculptures, some of which were applied to the columns – to the lowest drums at the façade or, just possibly, the topmost drums. But none of the fragments of the dedicatory inscriptions naming the king are attached to the sculptured drums, the temple was long a-building and the surviving pieces are few. It is with a touch of optimism, then, that we regard the reliefs as an indication of the point reached in the rendering of dress in relief sculpture before 546. The figures on the columns are almost in the round [217]. The shape of heads and their soft, fleshy features are those of central and south Ionian sculpture, already discussed. There was no frieze on or over the architrave but there was a shallow one all round the gutter (0·88 high), apparently not begun before about 525 and being added to still in the fifth century.

At the temple of Apollo at Didyma we find the entablature frieze again but not a narrative one, as at Assos or on the Siphnian treasury. At the corners are flying gorgons and beside them massive reclining lions [218]. The lower column drums were decorated, however, not with a frieze of profile figures as at Ephesus, but with women facing outwards. Two heads are well preserved, wearing an epiblema veil held by a fillet. Their features are warm and velvety, a quiet enigma behind closed lids and lips, servants of a famous oracle [219]. The same scheme of out-facing women but with quite different intent appears on a smaller drum from Kyzikos, in the north, where they perform a ring dance [220].

The relief drum was one of the few recurrent features in the diverse record of architectural sculpture in east Greece. Another is the use of the relief frieze, not continuous, as at Assos, but in repeating slabs, a scheme inspired by the relief clay revetments widely used in both Greek and native regions of Anatolia and clearly related to a comparable Etruscan practice. Fine series of examples in stone relief, with the popular racing chariot motif, are found at Kyzikos [221] and earlier at Myus [222] and Iasos A relief with Europa from Pergamum may also be architectural, and others from Kyzikos with a Herakles and a heraldic group of lions over foreparts of bulls.

The Cyclades have virtually nothing to offer by way of architectural sculpture but on Thasos, the Parian colony in the north Aegean, we find a new genre, the relief decoration of city wall gateways with figures of deities in a robust late Archaic style [223], something much more in the manner of Hittite Anatolian architecture.

Chapter Eight

RELIEFS

The use of relief or painted slabs as grave markers or as votives was not peculiar to Archaic and Classical Greece but their manner of decoration there was novel. Comparable grave markers are not commonly found in the east or Egypt, but the royal tombs of Mycenae show the practice already established in Greece and the discovery of such monuments might have contributed to the ultimate choice of the relief grave stele. The barbarian knew votive reliefs and those which show an act of adoration find some parallel in Greece: what is new is the Greek monumentalizing in relief of more trivial symbols or of representations of the dedicator or deity. We deal here with relief work far shallower than that for contemporary architectural sculpture. At times it is hardly more than emphasized drawing, yet at times its subtlety of expression is exquisite. We have to remember that painted stone and wood may have been in common use for these purposes too, and occasionally painted clay.

In this chapter we look first at the grave markers – their shapes then their decoration, noting regional developments or taste where appropriate; then the votive reliefs. Athens dominates the first class more than the second. Some decorative reliefs from larger monuments will also be mentioned.

Grave reliefs

Plain and sometimes very rough hewn slabs served as grave markers in Geometric and seventh-century Greece. There is no unequivocal evidence that any bore figure decoration, although some are inscribed, and it seems likely that kouroi were serving as grave monuments before figure-decorated stelai appear.

In the sixth century Attica presents the fullest series [224] and must serve as our yardstick for practices elsewhere in Greece. The tall rectangular stelai are topped by splaying cavetto capitals [224.1, 2] – an Egyptian member which was also used in the Doric order. These capitals are decorated with incised and painted tongues, a variety of florals or, rarely, figures on front and sides [229]. About 550 this is replaced by a double-volute scroll [224.3], like a lyre, a type which is abandoned by about 530. All these capitals carried sphinxes, some perhaps a gorgon, in the round, the sphinxes' heads turned to the viewer. One early sphinx sits with haunches low and is carved in one piece with the capital [224.1]; later they raise their haunches and so require a smaller plinth set in to the stele top [224.2, 3; 226–8]. The shaft usually carries a single male figure in relief [230], but there may be a panel below [231], or above and below [224.3], decorated in relief or paint only, and stelai with the main figure only incised and painted, not cut in relief, are not uncommon.

The grave stelai of Ionia, best known on Samos, are not usually figure-decorated, but are plain shafts topped by elaborately carved palmette anthemia, some of the earlier being supported on lyre volutes. It is likely that these inspired the change from the cavetto in Athens and almost certain that, in common with so much else in Attic art, they inspired the stele type which follows those with sphinx crowns [224.4, 5]. These later Attic stelai have palmette crowns only, or double or single pairs of volutes, still with reliefs on the shaft but the whole monument is shorter and less elaborate. The type disappears at the end of the sixth century, presumably the result of legislation, hinted at by later authors.

The early stelai of Attica are not readily matched elsewhere but comparable monuments were certainly known. In Boeotia the Dermys and Kitylos stele [66] had a crown of some sort and later there is a lyre volute capital, very like the Attic, and some marble relief shafts. There are also stele crowns resembling the Attic from Aegina and, in clay, from Corinth, and a marble sphinx from Corinth, possibly from a grave stele. However, in the last decade of the sixth century and later, when the Attic series ceases, several slim stelai with palmette crowns are found throughout the Greek homeland and colonial world: far more than can be attributed to any diaspora of disappointed Athenian sculptors. The shape and decoration for stelai in these areas are retained into the early Classical period. The only important innovations are a more deliberately architectural setting for some reliefs [244], where on the Attic there was no frame, or only a simple narrow border which has the relief background rising gently to the forward plane and with a narrow 'shelf' as ground line and some examples of two-sided stelai in north Greece, a feature of a famous earlier stele from the borders of the east Greek world (Dorylaion).

All the stelai so far discussed have been tall and slim. A broader variety appears in the late Archaic period [236–8], in Athens and elsewhere, its shape determined by the seated figure or multi-figure group upon it. With some of these we approach problems of identifying function, funerary or votive.

In the last years of the Archaic Attic stele we find also in Athens rectangular bases with relief decoration on front and sides [241–3] which served to support grave stelai or statues, but the type goes back to near mid century with one example, carved on the front only [240]. A metope-like slab with a horseman (of which there is also an example on Chios) and the enigmatic 'Marathon runner' [239] may be from grave monuments of other types.

The commonest subject on the Attic stelai is a standing naked youth – a kouros [230–2]. He usually holds a staff or javelin but may be further characterized as an athlete by holding an oil flask (aryballos) or raised discus [117] and an older man raises the bound fist of a boxer [233] – a fine characterization with broken nose and battered ears where other heads convey the impersonal calm of the monumental kouroi, but more intimate, in a way, for the relief setting and the attributes held. Some later stelai carry a more mature bearded figure, fully armed [234, 235]. Occasionally there are pairs of figures – two youths, brother and sister [224.3], man and youth (this from Thebes), two warriors (one crouching) on a broader stone [236]. If we include painted stelai we can detect a tendency to dress on the later ones, both for men and youths, and an important theme continued on later, non-Attic stelai, is the older man leaning on his stick, with his dog [244]. The Attic stelai seem to present archetypes for the three ages of Archaic man – young naked athlete: warrior: man and dog – with javelin, discus or aryballos: with spear and armour: with a crutch. If the man-and-dog type originates, as has been suggested, in east Greece, it may be that all these variants identifying different ages and occupations were encouraged by east Greek artists, as much else in Attica of these years.

Seated figures such as appear also as grave markers are the subjects for a few broader stelai. The touching mother and child [237] was probably one but there are pieces of a male figure too, from Velanideza in Attica. The famous relief [238] may then very well be a grave monument, in which case we are brought very close to the subjects of Classical stelai, and a slightly later stele from Aegina shows the *dexiosis* handclasp between a standing man and a seated woman, a common motif later.

In subsidiary panels on stelai we have a minatory gorgon [231], but otherwise only horsemen or chariot scenes [229], which probably reflect upon the status of the dead, not without some hint of heroization. The stele or kouros bases likewise offer horsemen and chariot [240, 241] but also athletes [241, 242.1], a leisure scene [242.3] and once the animal confrontation [243] which recalls older fighting groups and displays of power.

Many of the stelai and bases from Athens were recovered from the 'Themistoclean wall', thrown up hurriedly after the departure of the Persians, in which, as Thucydides notes, grave monuments were incorporated. Inscriptions appear on the shafts or bases of stelai, or both, to name the dead, sometimes the artist, and we have noticed some stelai and bases already in discussing Attic sculptors. Stele and base are not often found together but on a famous exception [235] Aristokles signs on the stele ground line, with the dead Aristion's name appearing alone on the base. His name is found also on one, perhaps two other bases for broad stelai and on a kouros base for a Carian, Tymnes, which is inscribed in Carian script too. He was an artist of quality, not far short of his contemporary Endoios, so far as we can judge, but forgotten by ancient commentators on Greek art. (There is record of a Sicyonian sculptor of this name and date.)

The very wide use of stelai outside Attica at the end of the Archaic period has been remarked. The subjects are frequently like the Attic, often youths but more often clothed now [245], and the man-and-dog stele becomes especially popular. A notable example which demonstrates the continuing role of Naxos and mobility of artists is that made by the Naxian Alxenor for a grave at Orchomenos in Boeotia [244]. New motifs are the standing girl, alone on a stele [246] (Crete) and a child holding a cock and oil flask [247] (Kos). Broader stelai with unusual subjects include one from Kalchedon on the Bosporos perhaps commemorating death in childbirth [248], and one with an erotic subject from Kos [249] where the funerary connection is more questionable.

Votive and other reliefs

Seated figures on grave stelai we have found acceptable in Attica. Elsewhere they begin to pose the question whether they are not better regarded as votive for a goddess or, if a man or couple are involved, votives for a hero cult. We have then to ask whether the hero might be the recent dead and the stele serving as a grave marker also. Where figures of worshippers or attendants are added, often on a reduced scale in the Egyptian manner, the purpose clearly becomes votive whatever the association with a grave, recent or old. A seated figure of a woman appears as early as the mid-seventh century on Paros [250], and there are sixth-century examples from Paros her colony Thasos [251] and in Boeotia at Thespiae. The seventh-century incised stelai from Prinias in Crete [252] show a standing woman spinning or holding a bird; or a warrior, once accompanied by a tiny attendant; or, once, a seated figure. These are often taken for gravestones and must then have been embedded in standing masonry, but they might all be votive or even decorative like the other Cretan dado reliefs. This would explain why they seem all of roughly the same period, the slight differences of style not being of obvious chronological importance: in a cemetery we would expect a greater range. A seated man on a stele from Lebadea in Boeotia holds a kantharos cup and on one from Rhodes a drinking horn: these associations can be either Dionysiac or funerary. The kantharos appears also in the hands of the seated man on an important series of Laconian reliefs which begin about 550 and continue into the Hellenistic period. Here the man is seated beside a woman, a snake rears behind or under their thrones, and small worshippers approach [253]. These are clearly the heroized dead, and that the stele might serve for the recent dead in exceptional circumstances is suggested by one inscribed for Ch]ilon, the name of a sixth-century lawgiver, one of the Seven Wise Men of antiquity, who is known to have been worshipped as a hero. Most of the reliefs are in a dull, angular style of little merit but a late Archaic fragment is quite competent [254] and shows the relief with a pediment top, such as becomes the norm for broad reliefs from now on. Other Laconian votive reliefs show worshipper and snake or the Dioskouroi.

In the Classical period and later the hero at feast (*Totenmahl*) becomes a common votive subject. In the Archaic period it has an immediate funerary context only on the periphery of the Greek world, in Asia Minor and Etruria, and examples in Greece – from Tegea and a frieze slab on Paros [255] – are more probably votive or from *heroa*.

We turn to other relief work, votive or decorative. On the Acropolis at Athens an early marble relief carries a bold frontal chariot [256]. The goddess, alone or in action, is one theme for broad stelai, like metopes, but we find also relief-decorated bases, as in the cemetery (one with a chariot scene), and a two-sided stele. Illustrated are a fussily detailed scene of a family worshipping Athena [258], and a pleasing celebration of a festival [257] which demonstrates the use of the pediment over a broad stele to give an architectural setting. The girls engage us in their dance by looking out at us, like those on the east Greek columns [218–20]. The way such reliefs could be displayed is well shown by a contemporary vase painting where the votive tablet is mounted on a column and its façade is provided with doors [259]. As on the buildings of Athens Herakles was a subject for votive and decorative sculpture: a relief of him with the boar [260], and a base at Lamptrai in the countryside [261].

The islands have been cited for examples of early grave or votive reliefs. Paros offers others – slabs with the three Graces (one facing us), a gorgon [262], Artemis with Hermes, the last two in the flat foldless style of the seated woman stelai; and in her colony Thasos, where we saw the city gate reliefs, appears the seated goddess Kybele in a doorway, approached by korai [263]. The scheme is repeated in an Early Classical relief for the island, but Kybele alone in a niche or temple door is a type with a prolific later history in east Greece. An early example carved in the native rock on Chios has won spurious acclaim as 'Homer's seat'. Finally, an enigma from Samothrace [264]: a relief with a mythological scene, the figures named, closed at one side by a griffin head and neck, perhaps from a monumental throne or altar. As with the architectural sculpture, the myth and iconography of minor relief sculpture take us far beyond the range of more familiar and prolific classes of minor antiquities, such as bronzes and vases, and fragments like this are a sharp reminder of our ignorance.

Chapter Nine

ANIMALS AND MONSTERS

Greek artists were hardly less observant of the animal kingdom than they were of man, and the sculpture of the Archaic period includes several sympathetic and accurate studies of animals at rest or in action. In earlier years their presence in Greek art had been determined by their involvement in myth or cult; or, in the case of the horse, for its function as a status or heroizing symbol, whether ridden or harnessed to a chariot; or as symptoms of the orientalizing movement which introduced or re-introduced monsters like the sphinx and near-monsters like the lion, and which made of the 'animal frieze' a commonplace vase ornament.

Horses and horse-monsters, the centaurs, we have observed aplenty The horses in chariot teams (e.g. [203, 212]) are strictly subordinate to the main theme, although a chariot group alone [234, 241.2] may sometimes, perhaps, be used symbolically. The Acropolis horsemen dedications [114, 165, 166] show the artist as involved in his concern for the rendering of the beast as of the man, as excited by the pattern of muzzle and mane as, in a different way or with different effect, the Geometric bronze-worker had been [8].

Sphinxes have the heads of korai, the bodies of lions; and we have seen them as votive monuments [100] and on grave stelai [224–8], generally facing front and side respectively. The lion and its feline kin appears occasionally in a myth context, as with Herakles, or in major groups of architectural sculpture as a deity's familiar (the leopards at Corfu [187]) or with its prey [190, 191 203 243]; but it is also the one animal often presented alone, as grave marker or dedication, and since most Greeks knew it by report or representation rather than by sight, it left the artist more free to let his imagination run over pattern of limb, mane and muzzle, more susceptible also to the influence of foreign models.

Seventh-century vase painting demonstrates a progression in Greek approval from the round- or square-headed Hittite lion to the pointed-nose and shaggy Assyrian. The former, in its tamer aspect, we saw on the perirrhanteria [74, 75, 77, 78]. The latter is more ferocious, with gaping jaws and lolling tongue, and both painter and sculptor make great play with patterns of crinkled muzzle, mane and paws [265], and compare the rounder-headed [266].

In the sixth century the artist lightens the creature's limbs and body, taking as model the dog rather than any feline. One result is the crouching position, bottom in air, which is purely canine, and other mistakes are the placing of a lioness' dugs along the belly [*190, 191*], and giving her a heavy mane. In the sixth century regional types also become differentiated. The Peloponnese gives the head a heavy ruff of mane [*267, 268*], sometimes, as in Sparta, like a stiff round collar. The Cyclades offer a sleeker transition from small head to neck and long wiry body [*269*]. In east Greece, at Miletus and Didyma, we meet sleepy egyptianizing lions, set in pairs along the Sacred Way or as a grave marker. In the best preserved example [*270*] the artist has excelled in rendering the rough loose pelt, delighted in the languorous sweep of the spine, the pattern of mane, as consummate a compromise of pattern and observation as in any kouros. This differentiation of regional types diminishes with the end of the Archaic period. The head alone long continues to serve architectural sculpture as a water spout.

For other animal statuary the Athenian Acropolis offers the greatest variety: an owl for Athena, a fine dog of the breed met on several grave stelai [*271*], and one of the rarer monsters, a cock-horse ridden by a boy; nor should we forget the calf [*112*]. The horsemen have been introduced already with the Rampin rider [*114*] and there are pieces of others, being ridden [*114, 165, 166*] or led, including a rider in eastern dress and the early frontal chariot group [*256*]. An east Greek marble siren may be a grave monument.

Chapter Ten

CONCLUSION

The pictures and text of this book offer a view of the development of Greek sculpture over nearly three hundred years, from miniaturist works in the formal conceptual style of Geometric Greece, through periods in which the east, then Egypt, suggested new techniques and possibilities. to the sixth century in which the sculptor's own search for improved expression of canonic forms led him to the point at which he wished consciously to take life as his model. The overall development is clear and so is its chronology. In detail it is less clear, and in many respects the dates assigned are conventional. Often they depend on parallels with other, better dated arts, as that of the vase painter where the relative chronology is evident, the absolute chronology fairly well established (for the sixth and early fifth centuries see, on this, *ABFH* 193–5, *ARFH* 210 f.). Sometimes vase and 'sculpture' are combined [41] or there is a stratigraphic association in a grave [40] or votive deposit (Samos and much minor sculpture). There are fewer dangers in comparing, say, a drawn head with a sculpture which was once itself based on a sketch, than in comparing works in fundamentally different techniques, but the difference in scale can be misleading. Absolute dates for the sculptures themselves are few enough. The building of the Siphnian treasury [210–12] and the sack of the Athenian Acropolis (p. 62 f.) are historically attested and the relevant sculpture can be identified. So too with stelai built into the Themistoclean wall (p. 164). For the temple at Ephesus [217] the evidence is more circumstantial, and in dates suggested by the supposed occasions for the overthrow of temples or grave monuments we are in serious danger of seeing associations wilfully (e.g. [232]). For a few other individual monuments political circumstances suggest dates – the Apollo temple at Delphi [203–4], the Aiakes of Samos [96], Kallimachos' Nike [167]. But any stylistic sequence, local or general, deduced from such 'pegs' can never give us the confidence to date individual pieces to within, say, ten years, or to allow detailed historical conclusions such as are permissible, often, from the study of pottery.

   Almost all the major works of Archaic sculpture were created to serve the religious and spiritual life of the Greeks, from state-financed temple sculpture to the more personal commemorative monuments which immortalized the dead. But the secular constantly intrudes – an artist's signature; the epitaph which names the sponsor of the monument as well as the dead; the extravagant displays of personal or state wealth in sanctuaries, bribes for gods designed, no less, to provoke mortal envy or respect.

Of the sculptors themselves we know too little. They worked material which was difficult to come by rather than precious, and may have been rewarded for their time rather than their skills. Euthykartidas both made and dedicated a statue on Delos [56], but of the dedications on the Acropolis at Athens we can identify nearly thirty by painters or potters, none by sculptors except for Pollias, and his offering is a clay plaque painted for him by his son Euthymides! In early days the makers of magic images, the Telchines or a Daedalus, were themselves regarded as near-divine. Later in the Archaic period it is their creations alone which acquire sanctity. We know something of Archaic sculptors' careers because the signatures on their works survived to be recorded in later years when such artists enjoyed a higher social status, in an age of the artist not the artisan. In the sixth century, it seems, it was the potters who made money, the architects who won esteem and wrote books (some, like Theodoros of Samos, being sculptors also), while sculptors were less courted than poets, their works, once damaged, prized neither for their sanctity nor their merit (p. 64). Yet of all artists' signatures it is the sculptors' which speak most clearly of their pride in achievement, and in our eyes it is their work which expresses the zenith of artistic endeavour in any material in this age.

Whatever their status in the eyes of their contemporaries, their achievement in terms of the history of western art brooks no criticism. In Greece, as in the rest of the ancient world, before the end of the sixth century, figures and groups rendered in the round, in relief or indeed by other arts as that of the vase painter, were composed as one might compose a sentence: a succession or structure of separate members or clauses which can be reassembled in different ways for different purposes. For drawing and for writing the word in Greek is the same – *graphein* – and we 'read' an Archaic kouros or a narrative scene in the way we read a poem or epic, gathering the parts in succession until, finally, we learn the whole. In drawing and sculpture, and perhaps first in drawing, the artist comes to realize that the elements of his composition become the more effective symbols of his statement, of a figure or of narrative, the more closely they resemble life. So he looks at life, observes the interrelation of anatomy patterns on figures in repose or action, observes the interaction of figures, comes to understand that he can do what the writer cannot – present the whole in a single image: a single realistic image of a man or woman, now more than a sum of parts or dress, or a realistic expression of action which can abandon the 'literary' composition of 'A watched B fight C watched by D' for figure groups which 'freeze' the figures as on film, petrify them as with Medusa's head, and yet lose nothing of the advantages bestowed by older conventions of narrative, in gesture, pose or attributes, and abate nothing of the overriding demands of pattern, composition and proportion which long continue to inform Greek art. This is followed by us more easily, perhaps, in two dimensions than in three, on vases or in the composition of relief pediments. It led naturally enough to a better understanding of the field or space in which the figure or action is thought to operate, and this ambience too becomes part of the whole and not an embarrassment to be filled or trimmed away. For a single figure in the round it means that the rigid axes on which frontal images of parts are assembled are dismissed, and that for the satisfactory presentation of a unified study of a man life, perforce, becomes the model. What is achieved now in pose is improved later in exploration of expression and personality, and much of the remaining history of Greek sculpture is a study of the shifting dominance of interest in proportion and pattern or in expression and realism. The revolution effected by Greek artists at the end of the Archaic period was neither sought nor achieved by any other ancient people and it determined the future development of all European art.

187 Limestone pediment (west) from Corfu, temple of Artemis. At the centre is the Gorgon Medusa flanked by Pegasus and Chrysaor (rather than Perseus) who were supposed to have been born when she was decapitated by Perseus. Both Gorgon and Artemis are Mistresses of Animals, whence the leopards at either side. The small group at the right is Zeus striking down a Titan or giant with a thunderbolt. At the left a seated figure is threatened by a spearman: the scheme resembles that for the death of Priam at an altar, but this subject has no relevance here and it is more likely another display of divine power or retribution, and the seated figure may be female (Rhea, if the other victim is Kronos or a Titan). Stricken or dead Titans or giants in the corners. There are scraps of a similar Gorgon group from the east (main) pediment and of a metope (?) frieze from the porch, with a fight. (Corfu; pediment 3·15 × 22·16) About 580

187.1

187.2

187.3

187.4

187.5

187.6 See previous pages

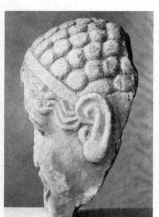

188 Gorgon head from the Acropolis, a temple acroterion. The figure's hands and snake belt also survive. (Acr. 701; H. 0·25) About 580–570

189 Leopard appliqué relief from the Acropolis. Probably from a frieze. Parts of two survive. (Acr. 552+554; H. 0·50) About 580–570

190 Limestone iones (much restored) and bull from the Acropolis. From a pediment, probably answered by a lion and bull in the other half. (Acr. 4; H 1·60) About 570–560

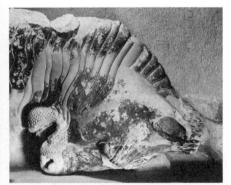

191 Limestone lion and lioness attacking a bull. From a pediment, see 192. (Acr. 3; H. 0·97) About 550–540

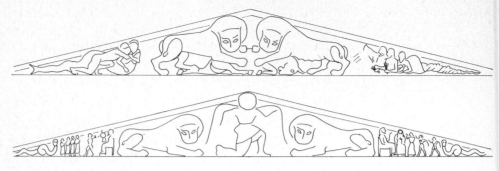

192 Pediments of the Athena temple on the Acropolis as restored by Immo Beyer (the drawings simplified). W. of gable floor 15·40. 1 – Herakles fights Triton; the bodies of the lion and lioness 191 are largely missing, as is the man before the three-bodied monster 193. 2 – the snakes, part of the lions and scraps of the wings of the Gorgon survive; also parts of few figures from the supposed Birth of Athena group 195 at the left; and more from the Introduction of Herakles to Olympus 194 at the right

193 Limestone triple-bodied monster (see 192) from the Acropolis, with wings, snake tails, holding water-symbol, corn, a bird. A symbolic rather than myth figure, of uncertain significance. Hair and beards are blue (the central head's hair is white), the flesh reddy, the scales blue, green and plain. Small snakes were attached to the figures' shoulders and arms. This has been attributed to the master of the Calf-bearer 112. (Acr. 35; H. 0·90) About 550–540

194 Limestone pedimental group from the Acropolis. Introduction of Herakles to Olympus (see *192*). Zeus and Hera (frontal) seated, Athena missing, Herakles, Hermes. Here with the possibly incorrect crowning moulding. (Acr 9; H. 0·94) About 550–540

195 Limestone man from the
Acropolis, perhaps from the
Birth of Athena group (see
192). (Acr. 55; H. 0·46)
About 550–540

196 Limestone pediment from the Acropolis. Herakles
and the Hydra. The crab at the left was sent by
Hera to attack Herakles. Iolaos waits with
the chariot. Very shallow (0·03) relief.
(Acr. 1; H. 0·79) About 560–550

197 Limestone pediment from the
Acropolis. Herakles fights Triton; cf.
192, which is later. The figures are
painted a dark brick-red. (Acr. 2; H.
0·63; H. of relief 0·18) About 560–550

198 Limestone 'Olive Tree' pediment from the Acropolis. A central building with a free-
standing girl carrying something on her head. Parts of another two women, and a man at the
left before the wall, behind which is an olive, incised and painted on the background.
Perhaps the myth-aition of a cult. The Ambush of Troilos has been suggested but the subject
is implausible here, the required Achilles and horses are wholly lacking, and the building
does not resemble a fountain house. (Acr. 52; H. 0·80) About 550–540

199.1 Athena from the Gigantomachy pediment on the Acropolis. The figures are all
slightly over lifesize. (Acr. 631) About 520

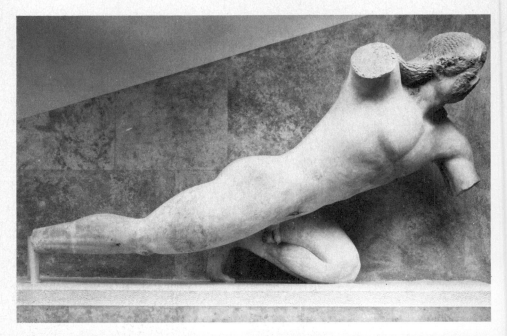

199.2 Giant

200 Frieze from the Acropolis. A charioteer mounting.
Other fragments include a 'Hermes' and a seated figure;
perhaps an assembly of gods. (Acr. 1342; H. 1·2) About
510–500

201 Limestone pediment, probably from the temple of
Dionysos, Athens. Satyrs and women. (Athens 3131; H. 0·54)
About 540–530

202 Running girl from Eleusis.
Possibly from a pediment.
(Eleusis; H. 0·65) About 490

203.1 Pediments of the temple of Apollo at Delphi, restored. E – the central chariot carries Apollo. Few fragments survive *142, 203.2*. The figures are carved in the round. W – gigantomachy with Zeus in the central chariot (this is far more hazardously restored). (H. of pediment 2·30; E – marble, W – limestone) About 520–510

203.2 Lion fighting a hind, from the temple of Apollo, Delphi. (Delphi; H. 1·1)

204 Nike acroterion from
the temple of Apollo, Delphi.
(Delphi; H. 1·13)

205.1 Temple of Apollo at Eretria.
Amazon archer. Found in the Villa
Ludovisi, Rome. The figure was angled
out from the pediment wall.
(Rome, Conservatori Mus. 12; H. 0·69)
About 510

205.2 Temple of Apollo at Eretria.
Theseus lifts the Amazon Antiope on
to his chariot. A low viewpoint
notably improves Theseus' features.
(Chalcis 4; H. 1·10) About 510

205.3 Temple of Apollo at Eretria. Athena; the gorgoneion on her aegis is exceptionally prominent (recall the earlier role of gorgons at pediment centres). (Chalcis 5; H. 0·74) About 510

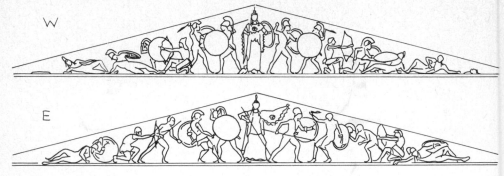

W

E

206 Temple of Aphaia on Aegina. Restored pediments (W. 15·0; H. 4·2). West: Probably fighting at Troy involving Ajax of Salamis (but of Aeginetan family). About 500–490. East: Probably fighting in the earlier attack on Troy, since a Herakles is identified *206.6* and he was accompanied by the Aeginetan Telamon (father of Ajax). About 490–480

206.2 Warrior's head from the earlier east pediment, Aegina. The hole in the chin is for the attachment of a beard. (Athens 1933; H. 0·28)

206.1 Athena from the west pediment, Aegina. (Munich 74; H. 1·68)

206.3 Torso of a warrior
from the west pediment, Aegina.
(Munich; cast in Oxford)

206.4 Fallen warrior from the west pediment, Aegina. (Munich 79; H. 0·47)

206.5 Fallen warrior from the east pediment, Aegina. (Munich 85; H. 0·64)

206.6 Herakles from the east pediment, Aegina. He wears a helmet fashioned as a lion mask (see also *213.8*; usually he never wears a conventional helmet in art). (Munich 84; H. 0·79)

207 Bronze head from the
Acropolis, Athens. Its helmet
is missing. (Athens 6446;
H. 0·25) About 490

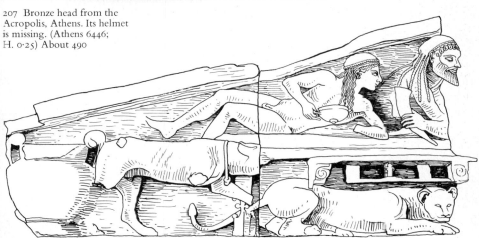

207a Limestone pediment from Corfu, temple of Dionysos (?). Discovered by A. Choremis
in 1973. It shows a feast, with Dionysos and a boy on a couch below which is a lion, the
god's familiar. To the left a mastiff and a wine crater. (Corfu; 2·73 × 1·3) Late 6th c.

208.1

208 Sicyonian treasury at Delphi. Limestone metopes. 1. The ship Argo (a fragment shows that it was completed on a second metope) with the mounted Dioskouroi at either side and on the ship two cithara players (Orpheus named, the left) and a third figure (...el..). 2. Lynkeus (missing) and Idas, Kastor and Polydeukes (these three named) steal cattle. They each hold two spears in the left hand, a spear or goad in the right. 3. Europa on the Zeus bull. Other fragments show: a boar, perhaps the Calydonian but not obviously attacked though the missing object below is a small hunting dog; Phrixos on the ram: another frontal horseman; a large animal, etc. The Dioskouroi are common to 1 and 2 and perhaps the boar hunt; they were worshipped at Sicyon. (Delphi; metopes 0·84–0·87 × 0·62–0·63) About 560

208.2

208.3

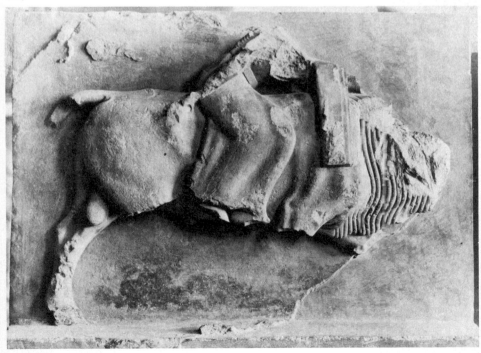

209 Head of a caryatid from an unknown treasury at Delphi. The 'drum' is carved with a group of women, a lyre-player and a syrinx-player. (Delphi; H. 0·66) About 530

210 Caryatid from the Siphnian treasury at Delphi. The 'drum' is carved with satyrs and nymphs (front missing; detail above from cast), the capital with lions attacking a stag. (Delphi). About 525

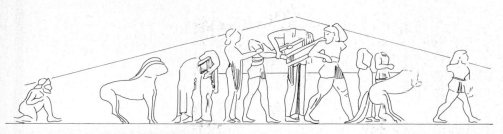

211 East pediment of the Siphnian treasury. Herakles makes to carry off the tripod; Apollo, supported by Artemis, to retain it. Zeus stands between restraining them. The other figures, chariots and horses seem not related to this theme, which may have been used to symbolize the First Sacred War at Delphi early in the century. (Delphi; H. at centre 0·74) About 525

NORTH

212.1 North frieze of the Siphnian treasury. (Figures named by inscriptions are italicized.) Gigantomachy. 1 – *Hephaistos* with bellows to heat coals. 2, 3 – Demeter and Kore, or the Moirai (?). 4 – Dionysos. 5 – Kybele in lion chariot. 6, 7 – Apollo, Artemis. 8, 9, 10 – giants *Kantharos* (note crest holder), *Ephialtas*, *Hypertas*. 11, 12 – Zeus with his chariot (and Herakles?) missing. 13 – *Hera*. 14 – *Athena*. 15, 16, 17 – giants *Berektas, Laertas, Astartas*. 18 – Ares. 19, 20 – giants *Biatas, Enaphas*. 21 – Hermes. 22 – Poseidon (?). 23 – a god. (Delphi; H. of frieze 0·64) About 525

4　5　　　　　　　　6　7　　8　　　9　10

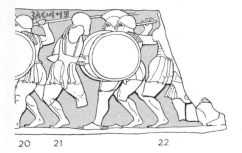

20　　21　　　　　22

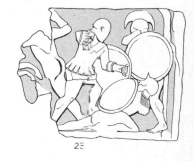

23

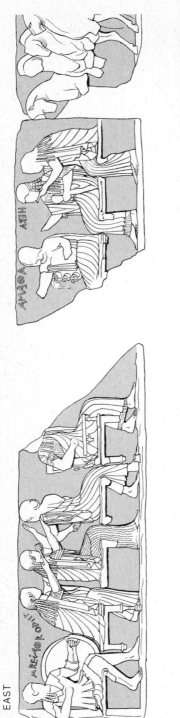

212.2 East frieze of the Siphnian treasury. Gods in Council: *Ares, Aphrodite, Artemis, Apollo* (these pro-Troy); *Zeus* (suppliant *Thetis?*); *(Poseidon?)*, *Athena, Hera, Demeter* (these pro-Greek). Fight at Troy: *Glaukos, Aineas, Hektor,* dead *Sarpedon* (a son of Zeus; *Iliad* 16), *Menelaos, Patroklos, Automedon, Nestor.* (Delphi) About 525. See also 130

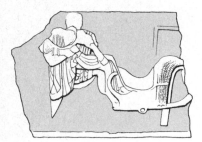

SOUTH

212.3 South frieze of the Siphnian treasury. A woman carried on to a chariot (the Dioskouroi with the Leukippidai?), chariots, a horseman, an altar

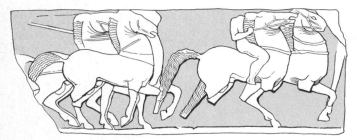

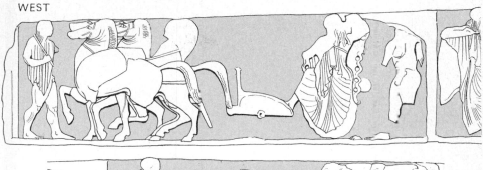

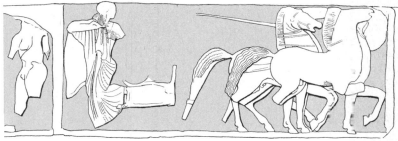

212.4 West frieze of the Siphnian treasury. Hermes before a chariot of winged horse being mounted by a winged Athena (an Ionian conception) with a companion. A woman (Aphrodite) dismounting from a chariot adjusting her necklace; at the right part of a palm tree. Chariot wheels, as elsewhere on the building, were added as separate pieces. The missing third slab must have shown Hera's chariot and Paris, on the occasion of the Judgement

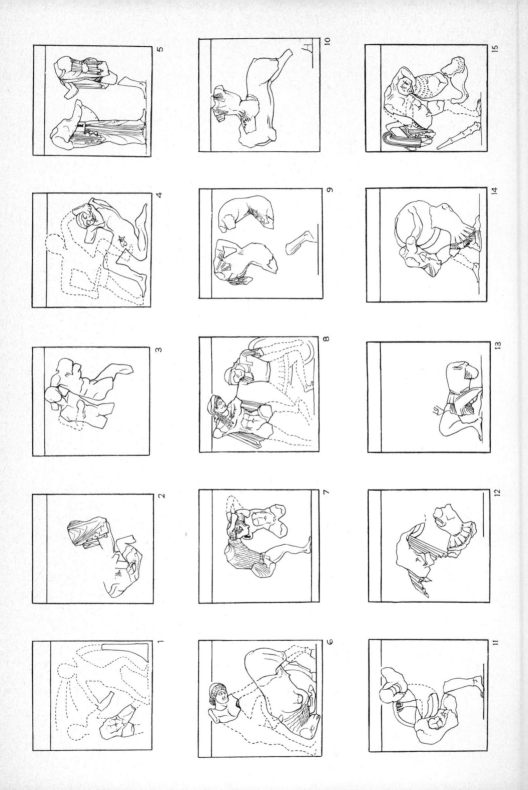

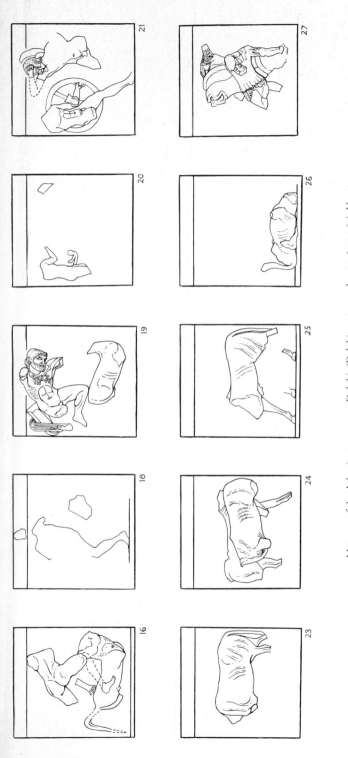

213 Metopes of the Athenian treasury at Delphi. (Delphi; metopes about 0·67 × 0·63) About 500–490. The numbering here follows *FDelphes* iv. 4. THESEUS (1–8): 1 – T. binds the robber Sinis to his pine tree (cf. *ARFH* figs. 115, 287); 2 – T. and a brigand wearing an animal skin; 3 – T. wrestles Kerkyon; 4 – T. fights Skiron, seizing his neck (cf. *ARFH* fig. 90); 5 – T. and Athena; 6 – T. binds the bull of Marathon (cf. *ARFH* fig. 201); 7 – T. and the Minotaur (cf. *ARFH* fig. 118); 8 – T. and Amazon Antiope. AMAZONOMACHY (9–14): 9 – an Amazon draws an arrow, another shoots; 10 – A. on horseback; 11 14 – Amazons v. Greeks. HERAKLES (15–22): 15 – H. v. lion, his useless weapons hang behind him; 16 – H. v. centaur; (17 – H. v. horses of Diomedes?); 18 – pursuit (H. and Apollo with tripod?); 19 – H. v. stag, probably breaking the antlers; 20 – Atlas and H. (?); 21 – H. v. Kyknos, H. wearing a lion-head helmet, cf 206.7; (22 – H. v. Amazon). HERAKLES and GERYON (23–27): 23–25 – Geryon's cattle; 26 – H. (foot) and the dead dog Orthros; 27 – Geryon, the triple warrior; one body raises a spear, one draws a bow, one collapses. Other unassigned metope fragments have parts of fights

213.1 Metope 5. Theseus and Athena

213.2 Metope 8. Theseus and Antiope

213.3 Metope 19. Herakles and stag

213.4 Metope 21. Herakles and Kyknos

213.5

213.8

213.5–8 From metopes 8, 19 (cast), 4, 21

213.6

213.7

213.9 Metope 7. Theseus and Minotaur

215.1 Pediment of the Megarian treasury at Olympia. Gigantomachy (after Bol and Herrmann). At the centre Zeus, to the left Athena and Poseidon (crushing a giant with a rock, the island Nisyros); to the right Herakles and Ares (?); each deity with a giant foe and with serpentine familiars of the giants in the corners (or, at the left, Poseidon's sea monster). (Olympia; W. 5·95, H. 0·84) About 510–500

214 Relief from an unknown treasury at Olympia. A chariot horse. The locks of the mane were alternately blue and red, the body yellow, the harness red, background blue. (Olympia; H. 0·47) About 540–520

215.2 Giant. Megarian treasury at Olympia, pediment

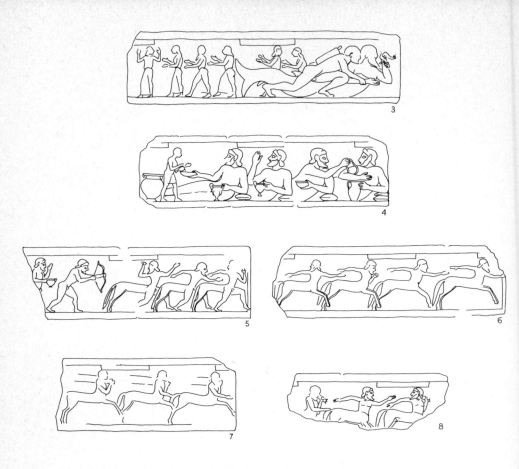

216 Temple of Athena at Assos. (The numbers follow those of Bacon *et al.*, *Assos* 151.) Frieze slabs 3–8: 3 – Herakles fights Triton while Nereids flee; 4 – feast, probably for Herakles; 5 – Pholos, with cup, watches Herakles shoot at the centaurs who flee or run with branches on 6–8

216.1 Frieze slab 3

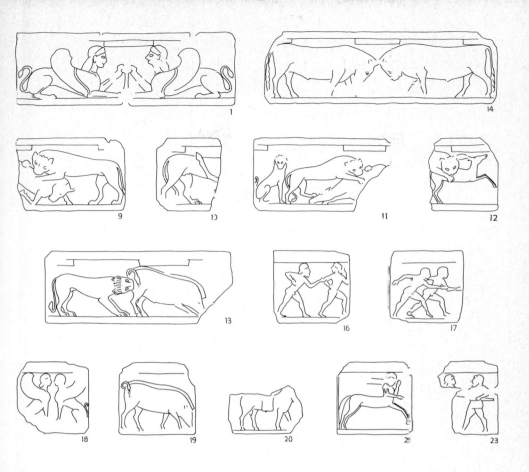

216 Temple of Athena at Assos. Frieze slabs 1–15 (2 and 15 are replicas of 1 and 14)
Metopes 16–23 (22 is a replica of 21): 20 – Europa on the Zeus bull; 23 – fight or struggle for
the tripod? (Istanbul, Boston and Paris) About 540–520

216.2 Frieze slab 4

216.3 Frieze slab 8

216.4 Frieze slab 13

217.1

217.2

217.3

217.1–5 Reliefs from the column drums of the temple of Artemis at Ephesus. 1 – woman's head (London B 91; H. 0·30); 2 – man wearing a panther skin (B 90; H. 0·59); 3 – man's legs (B 121; H. 1·0); 4 – dressed woman (B 119; H. 0·36); 5 – woman's hand and dress (B 118; H. 0·26) About 550–540

217.5

217.4

217.7 Relief from the parapet, Ephesus. Woman's head. (London B 215; H. 0·10) About 500

217.6 Relief from a column drum, Ephesus. Woman's head. (London B 89; H. 0·19) About 550–540

218.1 Temple of Apollo at Didyma. Restoration of upperworks and lower parts of columns to show relief sculpture (after Gruben). About 540–520

218.2 Architrave reliefs from the temple of Apollo at Didyma. Gorgons at the corners; recumbent lions. (Istanbul 239; H. 0·91) About 540–520

219 Column drum relief from the temple of Apollo at Didyma. (Berlin: H. 227)

220 Relief drum from Kyzikos. (Istanbul; H. 0·30) About 540

221 Relief slab from Kyzikos. (Istanbul 525; H. 0·55) About 520

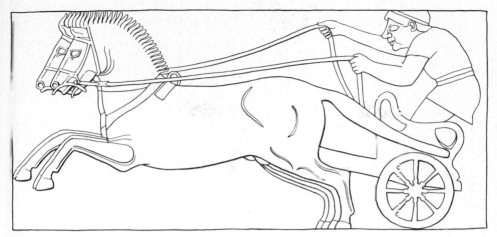

222 Relief slab from Myus. (Berlin; H. 0·70) About 540

223 Gateway relief on Thasos, in the city wall. An alert satyr, booted, holding a kantharos. The niche is for votive offerings. (H. 2·54) About 500

224 The sequence of Attic stelai (after Richter): 1 – New York; 2 – sphinx in Athens *226* and capital in New York, combined; 3 – New York *232*; 4, 5 – painted examples, Athens and New York

225 Limestone sphinx from Spata (Attica). A stele crown. The head is little more developed than that of the early Attic kouroi. (Copenhagen, Ny Carlsberg I.N. 1203; H. 0·84) About 580

226.1 Sphinx from Athens, Themistoclean wall. The cavetto capital, with painted flora, also survives. She wears a fillet with upstanding leaves (?). (Athens, Kerameikos Museum; H of sphinx 0·63) About 560. See also next page

226.2 See last page

227 Sphinx from Spata (Attica). A stele crown. She wears a *polos*. (Athens 28; H. 0·42)
About 550. See also *131*

228 Sphinx and capital from
Attica. The hair was black,
feathers green, black, red, blue;
breast scales red and blue; red
and black on the capital. This
has been associated with *234*.
(Boston 40.576; H. 1·42) About
540–530

229 Stele capital from Lamptrai (Attica). A
man and two women mourners at the sides.
On the front a mounted squire leads his
master's horse. (Athens 41; H. 0·73) About
550

230 Limestone stele from Athens,
Kerameikos. Man with sword and
spear. All later stele warriors
wear armour. The patterned border
is unusual. (Athens, Kerameikos
Museum; H. 1·81) About 560

232 Stele from Attica. Details, and see *224.3*. The boy carries a pomegranate and oil flask, the girl a flower. The panels above and below were once painted. The base inscription is in verse: 'To dear dead Me.... his father and dear mother raised this monument . . .'. Scholars wish to restore the name Megakles, of Alkmaionid family, and believe the monument was overthrown by the Peisistratids in 514. (New York 11.185; H. restored 4·23; the fragment with the girl's head is Berlin 1531) About 540

```
ΜΝΕΜΑΦΙΛΟΙ:ΜΕ
ΓΑΤΕΡΕΓΕΘΕΚΕΘΑΝΟΝ :
[    ΜΕΤΕΡ:
```

μνεμσ φιλοι : Με[γαλλει με ?]
πατερ επεθεκε θανοντ[ι]
χσυν δε φιλε μετερ : [...

231 Stele from Athens, Themistoclean wall. Youth with staff; a gorgon below. The block was cut back for re-use. This has been associated with Phaidimos and with the Rampin Master. (Athens 2687; H. 2·39) About 560–550

233 Stele fragment from Athens,
Themistoclean wall. The head and
raised bound fist of a boxer.
(Athens, Kerameikos Museum; H. 0·23)
About 540

234 Stele fragment from Attica.
Greaved legs and spear of a
warrior. A warrior mounts a
chariot in the shallow relief
panel below. Red, blue, green in
the cable border. Red background.
(New York 36.11.13; H. 1·42)
About 530

235 Stele of Aristion (name on base) from Velanideza
(Attica). Also restoration showing colour, and detail.
'The work of Aristokles' inscribed on the base line.
The upper part of the helmet and the beard tip were
made of separate pieces, missing. Red on hair and
background. Blue on helmet and corselet leaving
'ghosts' of patterns in other colours. (Athens 29; H. of
shaft 2·4) About 510

236 Stele fragment from near Athens. A standing and a kneeling warrior. Possibly not a gravestone. (Copenhagen, Ny Carlsberg I.N. 2787; H. 0·57) About 500

237 Stele fragment from Anavysos (Attica). A woman, probably seated, holds a child in her arms. The child's eyes are not closed, despite appearances. From a broad stele. The upper edge, top left, is finished and makes the outline of a painted volute finial. (Athens 4472; H. 0·38) About 530

238 Stele fragment from Attica. A seated woman and a girl. Both wear chiton, the woman a himation. Possibly a gravestone. By the artist of *258*. (Athens 36; H. 0·43) About 490

239 Stele from Athens. The palmette top is missing. The position of legs and arms indicates running, and the pose of the head has suggested to some that he is collapsing, dancing – both unlikely – or turning. It may have decorated one end of a brick grave monument. (Athens 1959; H. 1·02) About 510

240 Stele base from Athens. Four horsemen. (Athens, Kerameikos Museum P 1001; H. 0·32) About 550–540

241 Base for a seated figure (?) from Athens, Themistoclean wall. Front – 'hockey' players. Sides – warriors and chariot. (Athens 3477; H. 0·27) About 500

242 Kouros base from Athens, Themistoclean wall. 1 – front – a jumper, wrestlers, boy with javelin. 2 – side A – a ball game. 3 – side B – youths with cat and dog. Associated with the work of Endoios *138*, this and a base signed by Endoios bearing a painted seated figure were found close together near the Piraeus Gate (see on *139*). (Athens 3476; H. 0·32) About 510

243 Kouros base from Athens, Themistoclean wall. Lion and boar from one side. The other side has two horsemen and the front a ball game, as on *242.2*. The base seems to have been set on a narrower pillar or block. (Athens, Kerameikos Museum P 1002; H. 0·29) About 510

244 Stele from Orchomenos (Boeotia). The man offers a locust to a dog. Inscribed 'Alxenor of Naxos made this; just look!' (Athens 39; H. 1·97) About 490

ΑΛΧΣΗΝ϶Ͳ'Γ'ϹͰϟΕͰΗϽΝΑΧ϶ϽϽΑͲͲΕϟΙϤᴸ

Ἀλχσηνο̄ρ ἐποίησεν ℎο Ναχσιος· ἀλλ' ἐσιδε[ο̄σε]

246 Limestone stele from Eltyna (Crete). The girl holds a flower and wreath. (Heraklion 473; H. 1·85) About 490

245 Stele from Syme, near Rhodes. (Istanbul 14; H. 2·32) About 500

248 Stele from Kalchedon, on the Bosporos. The seated woman resembles figures on island stelai. The attendant figures recall assistants at childbirth (as for Zeus bearing Athena! cf. *ABFH* figs 62, 175) with a mourner at the right. Inscribed: '[Gravestone of]....ikos: ... had me put up'. (Istanbul 524; 0·38 × 0·57) About 550

247 Stele from Kos. (Kos; H. 0·42) About 490

249 Stele from Kos. On a couch a man holding a lyre with a naked girl in his lap (both heads gone, to the right); a child helps up a fallen man; at the left a piper. Not certainly a gravestone. (Kos; H. 0·72) About 500

250 Stele with a seated woman
from Paros. The stippled area
is only lightly recessed. The
drawing is approximate only.
(Paros; H. 1·19) About 650–625

251 Relief with a seated woman
from Thasos. The block is too
small and deep to be a grave
marker. (Louvre 3103; H. 0·24)
About 550

252 Incised limestone stelai from Prinias (Crete). 1 – a spinner, with traces of an inscription. 2 – kore with bird and wreath. 3 – warrior. 4 – seated man (?), a dog beneath the throne. 5 – detail of a warrior. The style resembles contemporary incised bronzes. (Heraklion 234, 396, 399, 397, 402; H. 0·725, 0·485, 1·06–1·09, 0·67) About 650–600

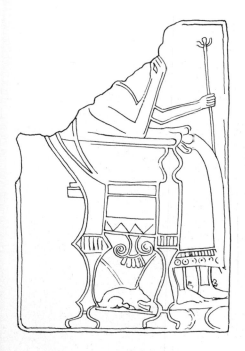

253 Hero relief from Chrysapha (Sparta). The man holds a kantharos, the woman a pomegranate. The worshippers hold a cock and flower. The throne type, with lion legs, is Egyptian.
(Berlin 731; H. 0·87) About 550–540

254 Hero relief, Spartan. The kore attendant pours into the kantharos held by a seated figure, missing.
(Copenhagen, Ny Carlsberg 23; H. 0·36) About 490

255 Death feast relief from Paros. The reclining 'hero' holds a phiale. Behind him a dog serving boy and dinos for the wine. Armour hangs on the wall. A companion relief has a lion attacking a bull. (Paros; H. 0·73) About 500

256 Frontal chariot relief, restored, from the Acropolis. Fragments of the horses and perhaps of the charioteer's head are preserved. The bodies are cut off rather than shown in the mock foreshortening of the Delphi metope *208.1*. (Acr. 575+; H. about 0·50) Second quarter of the 6th c

257 Relief from the Acropolis. A piper leads three dancing girls and a boy. The girls wear chiton with himation indicated only by paint. The acroteria of the 'pediment' were painted with palmettes. (Acr. 702: H. 0.39) About 500

258 Relief from the Acropolis. Athena, wearing helmet, himation and chiton, receives the offerings of a family of a father, mother, two boys (one holds up a phiale) and a girl. The pig is for sacrifice. By the artist of *238*. (Acr. 581; H. 0·66) About 490

259 From an Athenian black figure vase (Beazley, *ABV* 338, 3). The votive picture or relief is on a Doric column and is provided with doors. It shows two horsemen (in white paint, faintly) – the Dioskouroi. (Naples 3358) About 510

260 Relief from Athens, near the Agora. Herakles
shoulders the Erymanthian boar, to deliver to
Eurystheus (cf. *ARFH* fig. 89). He keeps hold of his
club (above) wears his lionskin on his head and
hanging from his left arm. The relief overlaps the
high pediment which must have been painted.
Perhaps from the sanctuary of Herakles Alexikakos.
(Athens 43; H. 0·76) About 500

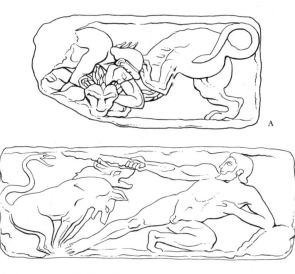

261 Statue base from Lamptrai
(Attica). A. Herakles and the lion.
B. Herakles and Kerberos. C.
Herakles reclines for a feast with
club and cup. The base may have
been for a statue of the god/hero.
(Athens 42 + 3579; H. 0·19)
About 500

262 Relief from Paros. A gorgon holding snakes. (Paros; H. 0·62) Second half of the 6th c.

264 Relief from Samothrace. Floral above, cable below. The figures are inscribed Agamemnon (seated), Talthybios with a herald's staff (Greek herald at Troy), Epe[ios (inventor of the Wooden horse). At the right a griffin's head (worn away but the gaping beak is clear) with spiral plume, and neck. (Louvre 697; H. 0·46) About 550

263 Relief from Thasos. Two korai with offerings approach a niche or door in which Kybele is seated. (Malibu, Getty Museum; H. 0·37) About 490

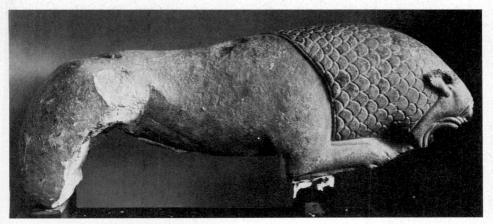

265 Limestone water spout from Olympia.
The reversed-scale mane and emphatic
ridges around the eyes and mouth are
remarkable. (Olympia; L. 0·79) Mid-7th c.

266 Limestone lion from Corfu. From
a grave monument, formerly associated
with the grave of Menckrates. (Corfu;
L. 1·22) About 600

267 Limestone lion from Perachora.
The type closely resembles that on
Corinthian vases of the first half
of the 6th c. (Boston 97.289; H. 0·95)
About 570–550

268 Limestone lion from Loutraki, near Corinth. One of an antithetic pair. (Copenhagen,
Ny Carlsberg 1297; L. 1·0) Second quarter of the 6th c.

269 Lions on Delos. They flank the approach to the Letoon sanctuary, in an Egyptian manner. Probably a Naxian dedication, deceptively primitive in appearance owing to their worn state and the sleek lion type favoured in the islands. Compare the Naxian sphinx at Delphi *100*. There were originally up to sixteen; one, with a new head, sits outside the Arsenal at Venice (below here). (H. of complete lion 1·72) Second quarter of the 6th c.

270 Lion from Miletus. Apparently one of a pair. (Berlin 1790; L. 1·76) Mid-6th c.

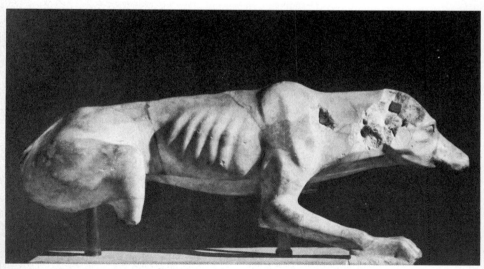

271 Dog from the Acropolis. One of a pair, possibly a dedication to Artemis Brauronia, as huntress. (Acr. 143; L. 1·25) Late 6th c.

ABBREVIATIONS

c.   century BC
H   height

AAA   Athens Annals of Archaeology
ABFH   J. Boardman, Athenian Black
            Figure Vases (1974)
Acr.   The Acropolis, Athens
AE   Archaiologike Ephemeris
AGSB   C. Blümel, Die archäisch
            griechischen Skulpturen de-
            staatlichen Museen zu Berlin
            (1963)
AJA   American Journal of
            Archaeology
AM   Athenische Mitteilungen
AMA   H. Schrader et al., Die
            archäischen Marmorbildwerke
            der Akropolis (1939)
Ann   Annuario della Scuola
            Archeologica di Atene
ARepts   Archaeological Reports
ARFH   J. Boardman, Athenian Red
            Figure Vases, Archaic Period
            (1975)
BCH   Bulletin de Correspondance
            Hellénique
Berger   E. Berger, Das Basler
            Arztrelief (1970)
BSA   Annual of the British School at
            Athens
CCO   J. Boardman, The Cretan
            Collection in Oxford (1961)
Deds.   A. Raubitschek, Dedications
            from the Athenian Acropolis
            (1949)
Didyma   K. Tuchelt, Die archäischen
            Skulpturen aus Didyma (1970)

FDelphes   Fouilles de Delphes
Gravestones G.M.A. Richter, The Archaic
             Gravestones of Attica (1961)
Ist.Mitt.   Istanbuler Mitteilungen
JdI   Jahrbuch des deutschen
             archäologischen Instituts
Jeffery   L.H. Jeffery, Local Scripts of
             Archaic Greece (1961)
Korai   G.M.A. Richter, Korai (1968)
Kouroi   G.M.A. Richter, Kouroi
             (1970)
Kurtz/   D.C. Kurtz and J.
     Boardman Boardman, Greek Burial
             Customs (1971)
Lacroix   L. Lacroix, Les reproductions
             de statues sur les monnaies
             grecques (1949)
Lullies   R. Lullies and M. Hirmer,
             Greek Sculpture (1960)
MWPr   Marburger
             Winckelmannsprogramm
ÖJh   Jahreshefte des österreichischen
             archäologischen Instituts in
             Wien
Payne   H. Payne and G.M. Young,
             Archaic Marble Sculpture from
             the Acropolis (1936)
RA   Revue Archéologique
Ridgway,
SS   B.S. Ridgway, The Severe
             Style in Greek Sculpture (1970)
RM   Römische Mitteilungen
Robertson   M. Robertson, History of
             Greek Art (1975)
Samos xi   B. Freyer-Schauenburg,
             Bildwerke der archäischen Zeit
             und des strengen Stils (Samos
             xi; 1974)

241

NOTES AND BIBLIOGRAPHIES

I INTRODUCTION

The relevant chapters in Robertson, *History of Greek Art* (1975) give the fullest and most recent, though selective, account of Archaic sculpture and may be referred to for fuller description and discussion of many pieces treated here. Richter's *Sculpture and Sculptors of the Greeks* (1970) deals with the figures by types rather than historically and is weak for the earlier Archaic period. W. Fuchs, *Die Skulptur der Griechen* (1969) also deals by types, more succinctly, C. Picard's *La sculpture antique* (1926 on) is full but sorely outdated for the Archaic period. An important study of Archaic Greek sculpture by B.S. Ridgway is forthcoming.

Essential monographs (see *Abbreviations*) are Richter's *Kouroi, Korai* and *Gravestones*; and Payne on the Acropolis sculpture; and there are apt observations on style and technique in R. Carpenter, *Greek Sculpture* (1960). There have been no comprehensive collections of pictures other than for the special monographs mentioned since F. Winter's *Kunstgeschichte in Bildern* (1900 on) or, for the eighth and seventh centuries, F. Matz, *Geschichte der griechischen Kunst* i (1950).

Minor sculptural work in other materials is noticed in this book where appropriate. For fuller treatment see R.A. Higgins, *Greek Terracottas* (1967); W. Lamb, *Greek and Roman Bronzes* (1929); a new comprehensive study of bronzes is being prepared by D. Mitten; J. Boardman, *Archaic Greek Gems* (1968).

The most useful historical account of the period is L.H. Jeffery, *Archaic Greece* (1976) and for foreign relations and effects on art see J. Boardman, *Greeks Overseas* (1973).

For ancient sources J. Overbeck, *Die antiken Schriftquellen* (1868, reprinted 1971) gives all texts and J.J. Pollitt, *The Art of Greece 1400–31 B.C.* (1965), select translations and commentary.

For the mythological subject matter see K. Schefold, *Myth and Legend in Early Greek Art* (1966) and the iconography chapters in *ABFH, ARFH*, with bibliographies.

II THE DARK AGES AND GEOMETRIC PERIOD

GENERAL

V. MÜLLER, *Frühe Plastik in Gr. und Vorderasien* (1929); E. Homann-Wedeking, *Die Anfänge der gr. Grossplastik* (1950); B. Schweitzer, *Greek Geometric Art* (1969) including [*5, 6, 9, 11, 12, 13*].

CLAY

R.A. Higgins, *Greek Terracottas* (1967), ch. 5; R.V. Nicholls in *Auckland Classical Essays* (ed. B.F. Harris) 1–37, also on bronzes. Lefkandi centaur [*4*] – *BSA* lxv, pls 8–10. Karphi [*1*] – *BSA* xxxviii, 75, pl. 31, and lv, 29. *Kerameikos* iv, pl. 26 [*3*], stag. Amyklaion – *AM* lv, Beil. 42–43. Piskokephalo [*2*] – *CCO* no. 472.

BRONZE

N. Himmelmann, *Bemerkungen zur gr. geometrischen Plastik* (1964) [*8, 11–13*]; H.V. Herrmann, *JdI* lxxix, 17 ff., local workshops; U. Naumann in *Opus Nobile* (Fest. Jantzen), 114 ff. and *Submin. und Protogeometrische Bronzeplastik auf Kreta* (1976); M. Weber, *AM* lxxxvi, 13 ff. and lxxxix, 27 ff. W. Lamb, *Greek and Roman Bronzes* (1929), ch. 2. *Olympia Bericht* vii, 138 ff. [*5*]. M. Comstock and C. Vermeule, *Bronzes, Boston* nos 3 [*9*], 15 [*10*]. Karditsa [*7*] – S. Karouzou, *AM* xci, 23 ff., as Achilles.

III THE ORIENTALIZING STYLES

EASTERN STYLES IN CRETE AND GREECE

Boardman, *CCO*, 79 ff., 134 ff., no. 378 [*18*]; *BSA* lxii, 57 ff. for date of [*21*] *et al.*; *Greeks Overseas* (1973), 56 ff.; in *Dädalische Kunst* (Hamburg Mus., 1970), 14 ff.; *Korai*, fig. 70–75 [*16*]. C. Davaras, *Die Statue aus Astritsi* (1972), incl. [*14, 15*]. R.A. Higgins, *BSA* lxiv, 143 ff., jewellery. P. Demargne, *La Crète Dédalique* (1947) general study. H.V. Herrmann, *Ol. Forsch.* vi, siren attachments [*21*]; and *Olympia, Heiligtum und Wettkampfstätte* (1972), 80 ff. [*20, 22*]. Afrati bronze [*17*] – *ARepts* 1973/4, 37. Ivory girls, Athens [*19*] – E. Kunze, *AM* lv, 147 ff.; Schweitzer, op. cit., pls 146–8, cf. 149, 150.

THE DAEDALIC STYLE

R.H. Jenkins, *Dedalica* (1936), classification (rather rigid) and chronology of clay and other works. R.A. Higgins, *Greek Terracottas* (1967), 25–29. Davaras, op. cit., incl. [*28–33*]. Boardman, *CCO*, incl. no. 496 [*26*]. T.J. Dunbabin, *Greeks and their eastern Neighbours* (1957), ch. 3, and Corinth plaques, pl. 8 [*23, 24*]. G. Rizza and V. Scrinari, *Gortina* i (1968), incl. [*25, 30, 31, 34*], also chronology. G. Rizza, *Ann* xlv/xlvi, 212 ff., Axos terracottas [*27*]. P. Kranz, *AM* lxxxvii, 1 ff., seated figures. Mycenae [*35*] – F. Harl-Schaller, *ÖJh* l, 94 ff. Prinias [*32*] – L. Pernier, *Ann* i, 18 ff. and *AJA* xxxviii, 171 ff.; C. Gottlieb, *AJA* lvii, 106 f. F. Grace, *Archaic Sculpture in Boeotia* (1939). J. Ducat,

242

Les Kouroi de Ptoon (1971), no. 46, signed. New York ivory [*39*] – G. Richter, *AJA* xlix, 261; F. Matz, *MWPr* 1948, 3ff. *Perachora* ii, pl. 171, A1 [*38*]. E. Karydi, *AA* 1964, 266ff., jewellery Thera [*40*] – Kurtz/Boardman 78f.; F. Poulsen, *dI* xxi, 188; N. Kontoleon, *AM* lxxiii, Beil. 104. *Dädalische Kunst* (supra), incl. [*36, 37*]. Dating by vase painting – H. Payne, *Necrocorinthia* (1931), 232–5, pl. 1.8–11 [*41*] and 47, and cf. K.F. Johansen, *Vases Siᵧyoniens* (1923), pl. 35.2 (Macmillan Painter, about 650).

OTHER EARLY ARCHAIC STATUARY

H.V. Herrmann in *Wandlungen* (Fest. Homann-Wedeking), 35ff. Tanagra [*42*] – *ADelt* xxiv A, pls 43–44. Crete – sphinx [*44*], E. Langlotz in *Corolla Curtius* i, 60ff.; lyre player [*43*], Schweitzer, op. cit., pl. 203; *kriophoros* [*45*], K. A. Neugebauer, *Kat. Br. Berlin* i, no. 158. Olympia [*46, 47*] – *Olympia Bericht* iv, 105ff. Boeotia [*48*] – D.K. Hill, *Catalogue, Bronze Sculpture, Walters Art Gallery* (1949), no. 237. Samos wood [*49, 50*] – D. Ohly, *AM* lviii, 77ff.; G. Kopcke, *AM* lxxxii, 100ff. Ivories – *Perachora* ii, pt 2, pl. 173, A9 [*51*]; B. Freyer-Schauenburg, *Elfenbeine aus dem samische Heraion* (1966), incl. [*54*]; A. Greifenhagen, *Jb. Berl. Mus.* vii, 125ff. [*53*], lyre figures; Delphi ivory [*52*] – K. Schefold in *Fest. von Lücken*, 769ff.; AA 1970, 574ff.; F. Salviat, *BCH* lxxxvi, 105 (base); E.L. Marangou, *Lakonische Elfenbein- und Beinschnitzereien* (1969).

IV MARBLE AND THE MONUMENTAL

THE FIRST MARBLE SCULPTURE

Marble analyses – C. Renfrew, *BSA* lxiii, 45ff.; B. Ashmole, *BSA* lxv, 1ff.; H.V. Craig, *Science* 176, 401–3 (isotopic analysis). Technique – S. Adam, *The Technique of Greek Sculpture* (1966), fundamental, replacing all earlier studies (Casson, Blümel). Quarries – S. Casson, *BSA* xxxvii, 21ff. (Naxos colossus) and *Technique of Early Greek Sculpture* (1933); A. Dworakowska, *Quarries in Ancient Greece* (1975). Egypt – E. Iversen, *Mitt. Inst. Kairo* xv, 134ff. (whence the drawing, p. 21); *Journ. Eg. Arch.* xlvi, 71ff. and liv, 215ff. (Diodorus); R. Anthes, *Proc. Amer. Phil. Soc.* 107, 62ff.; K. Levin, *AJA* lxviii, 13ff.; B.S. Ridgway, *AJA* lxx, 68f.; Boardman, *Greeks Overseas*, ch. 4; H. Schäfer, *Principles of Egyptian Art* (ed. Baines, 1974); Adam, op. cit., 5f. Cult statues – F. Willemsen *Frühe gr. Kultbilder* (1939); E. Vermeule, *Götterkult* (1974), 121f., 140, 158f. Funerary use – Kurtz/Boardman, 88f., 237ff. Bases – M. Jacob-Felsch, *Die Entwicklung gr. Statuenbasen* (1969). Euthykartidas [*56*] – G. Bakalakis, *BCH* lxxxviii, 539ff., also legs.

KOUROI

'Kouros', 'kolossos' – J. Ducat, *BCH* c, 239ff. *Kouroi*, figs 22–24 [*58*] (and on its sex, G. Daux,

BCH lxxxiii, 559ff.), nos 10 [*68*], 11 [*66*], 14 [*69*], 17 [*59*], 33 [*67*]. Delphi bronze [*57*] – *Kouroi*, figs 14–16; *FDelphes* v, no. 172. Naxian colossus [*60*] – *Kouroi* no. 15; P. Courbin in *BCH* Suppl. i, 157ff. (its fall) and *Mél. Hell . . . G. Daux*, 57ff.; N. Kontoleon, ibid., 239ff. (inscription); D. Pinkwart, *Bönner Jb.* clxxii, 12ff. and clxxii, 117 (the holes); *Archaeology* (1972), 213 (the drawing [*60*]). *Samos* xi, nos 29–34. Thera [*61*] – *Kouroi* no. 18B; N. Kontoleon, *AM* lxxiii, 117f. Attica – *Kouroi* nos 1 [*63*], 2 [*64*], 3 [*65*], 6 [*62*]; E. Harrison, *Hesperia* xxiv, 290ff.; Robertson, 45f. Inscribed Attic bases – L.H. Jeffery, *BSA* lvii, 115ff. Cretan statue at Delphi – G. Roux, *BCH* lxxv, 366ff. Kleobis and Biton [*70*] – *Kouroi* no. 12; inscription and placing, Jeffery, 154–6. Cf. the xoana of the Dioskouroi at Troizen by Hermon, which may have been Archaic and shown on coins – Lacroix, 220f.

KORAI

Nikandre [*71*] – *Korai* no. 1; Adam, op. cit., 44 (pierced hand; others have suggested a bow, for Artemis). *Samos* xi, no. 3 [*72*] – *Korai* no. 21. Olympia Hera [*73*] – *Korai* no. 3; H. V. Herrmann, *Olympia*, 96f.; Robertson, 47f.

PERIRRHANTERIA

[*74–79*] – J. Ducat, *BCH* lxxxvii, 577ff.; G. Hiesel, *Samische Steingeräte* 4ff. and in *Opus Nobile* (Fest. Jantzen), 77–81; F. W. Hamdorf *AM* lxxxix, 47ff., comprehensive; *Hesperia* xxvii, pls 10f., Isthmia; *Korai*, figs 35, 37–56. Cf. Laconian lions painted and relief on vases, *BSA* xxxiv, 25; and for the style, the Menelaion bronze, Matz, op. cit., pl. 62; Chalcis seated figure, Davaras, op. cit., figs 19–22; K. Schefold, *Meisterwerke* (1960), no. 89. Other Laconian sculpture, *BCH* xcv, 880f. Stone lamps – *CCO*, 123f. and especially the lion-head lamp from Brauron, *BCH* lxxiv, 301. Sparta kneeler [*80*] – M. Tod and A.J.E. Wace, *Cat. Sparta Mus.* no. 364. *ADelt* xxiv B, pl. 120.

ARTISTS AND AUTHORS

J.J. Pollitt, *Art of Greece* 3–15; F. Eckstein, *Handwerk* (1974). Daedalus – *Kouroi* 28 f. G. Rizza, *Cronache di Arch.* 1963, 5ff.; Boardman, *CCO* 158f. and *Acta 4. Kret. Synedr.*

V THE MATURING ARCHAIC STYLES

SOURCES

The Acropolis, Athens. The definitive publication of the sculpture is *AMA*. Payre gives an excellent narrative account and pictures. *Deds.* for types of bases, signatures and summaries of artists' careers. On the excavation G. Dickins' introduction to *Cat. of the Acr. Museum* i (1912), the Archaic Sculpture. Also M.S. Brouskari, *The Acropolis Museum, Descriptive Catalogue* (1974). The records are being restudied. Other problems, Ridgway, *SS* 31; and general, R.J. Hopper, *The Acropolis* (1971). Survivors of the Persian sack – Pausanias i 26.5, 27.7; *Deds.* 456. *Samos* xi; E. Buschor, *Altsamische Standbilder* (1934–61); *Didyma*. J. Ducat, *Les Kouroi de Ptoon* (1971). Local schools – E. Langlotz, *Frühgr. Bildhauerschulen* (1927), somewhat optimistic but a pioneer attempt.

KOUROI

Richter's *Kouroi* is basic. Older studies such as W. Deonna, *Les Apollons Archaïques* (1909) and E. Buschor, *Frühgr. Junglinge* (1950) are still valuable.

KORAI

Dress – *Korai*, 6ff.; Payne, 25f.

EAST GREEK SCULPTURE AND SCULPTORS

Korai nos 37 [*85*], 38 [*86*], 57 [*89*], 68 [*92*], 95 [*90*]. And *Ist. Mitt.* xvi, 95ff. *Kouroi* nos 49 [*101*], 77 [*81*], 86 [*102*], 125 [*83*], 127 [*82*], 124b [*84*]. For other east Greek see *Belleten* xxxi, 331ff.; xxxiv, 347ff.; *Ist. Mitt.* xiii/xiv, 73ff.; xvii, 115ff.; *Antike Kunst* xix, 81ff. *Samos* xi, nos 4–25 (korai; no. 20 [*97*]); nos 35–56 (kouroi); nos 58–63, Geneleos Group [*91*–*93*]; nos 72[*84*]–75 (dressed kouroi). G. Schmidt, *AM* lxxxvi, 31ff., works of Geneleos and the kolossos master; Robertson, 73–75; Lacroix, 207–16, cult statue of new temple shown on coins, with two peacocks? Cheramyes kore [*87*] – *Korai* no. 55; R. Heidenreich, *Forsch. u. Berichte* xii, 61ff., mounted on column; Robertson, 72f. Reclining figures – *AGSB* nos 66–68, Myus; *RA* 1976, 55ff., Didyma. Aiakes [*96*] – *Samos* xi, no. 67; R. Meiggs and D.M. Lewis, *Selection of Greek Historical Inscriptions* no. 16. Samian head type in alabaster in Egypt – *AA* 1952, 48ff. *Didyma passim* and nos K43 [*94*], K47 [*95*]. Ephesus ivories [*88*] – P. Jacobsthal, *JHS* lxxi, pls 34–36; *Korai* figs 257–62. Cyrene – E. Paribeni, *Cat. delle Sc. di Cirene* no. 6; *AJA* lxxv, pls 6–8. Kyzikos kouros – *Antike Kunst* viii, pls 26–28. Dressed kouroi – P. Devambez, *RA* 1966, 195ff.; K. Schefold, *Antike Kunst* xix, 116. 'Naxian' figures on Acropolis [*98, 99*] – *Korai* nos 58, 59; Payne, 12f. Naxian sphinx, Delphi [*100*] – *FDelphes* iv. 1. 41ff. Cycladic sculpture – N. Kontoleon, *Aspects de la Grèce Préclassique* (1970), 62ff.; *Epist. Epet. Ath.* (1957/8), 218ff. (Melos); *Praktika* (1972), pls 124–7, kouros with bent arms; head. G. Kokkorou-Alewras, *Archäische Naxische Plastik* (1975). Archermos and Nike [*103*] – Jeffery, 294f.; *Deds.* 484–6; *Korai* pl. xiva; O. Rubensohn, *Mitt. Inst.* i, 21ff. Acr. 659 – *AMA* no. 95; Payne, pl. 69. Chronology – N. Himmelmann, *Ist. Mitt.* xv, 24ff. E. Langlotz, *Studien zur nordostgr. Kunst* (1975).

ATTIC SCULPTURE AND SCULPTORS

Kouroi nos 63 [*104*], 70 [*105*], 135 [*106*]. *Korai* nos 43 [*109*], 89 [*110*], 111 [*111*]. Early korai – A. Ioannis

Rentis, *AAA* i, 34f. and *BCH* xcii, 754; followed by *Korai* nos 40 (Attica), 39 (Aegina). Berlin kore [*108*] – *Korai* no. 42; L. Alscher in *Fest. von Lücken*, 697ff., as archaizing late sixth c. It has also been thought false. Kroisos [*107*] – *Kouroi* no. 136; *AAA* vii, 215ff., the base. The Merenda find [*108a*] – E. Mastrokostas, *AAA* v, 298ff., and see below, Aristion. The kouros attributed by J. Frel to the master of the Lyons kore, *AAA* vi, 367ff. New kouroi – *AAA* iv, 137ff. and *ADelt* xxvii B, pl. 53, head, about 560. Scribes – L.H. Jeffery, *BSA* lvii, 151f. Artists' names etc.' – Deyhle, op. cit., 58ff.; *Deds.* 479ff.

PHAIDIMOS

J. Dörig, *AA* 1967, 15ff.; J. Frel, *AA* 1973, 193ff. Calf-bearer [*112*] – Payne, 1–3, pls 2–4; *AMA* no. 409; W. Deyhle, *AM* lxxxiv, 46; Robertson, 94–96. Sabouroff head [*113*] – *AGSB* no. 6; Robertson, 98f.

RAMPIN MASTER

Deyhle, op. cit., 4ff.; Robertson, 96–99. Horseman [*114*] – Payne, 4–9. *Korai* nos 113 [*115*], Peplos kore, and Payne, 18–21; 65 [*116*], 112 [*118*]. Diskophoros stele [*117*] – *Gravestones* no. 25.

ARISTION

Phrasikleia – E. Mastrokostas, *AAA* v, 298ff.; *Arch. Reports for 1972/3* 6f. On the base see also L.H. Jeffery, *BSA* lvii, 138f.; G. Daux, *Comptes Rendus Acad. Ins.* 1973, 382ff.; N. Kontoleon, *Archaiologike Ephemeris* 1974, 1ff.; Robertson, 100f.; C. Clairmont, *AA* 1974, 220–3.

OTHER AREAS

Boeotia – Ducat, op. cit., nos 141, 142, Attic dedications; *Kouroi* no. 94 [*119*]. Corinth – *Kouroi* no. 73 [*121*]; H. Payne, *Necrocorinthia* (1931), ch. 16, 17 (clay), pl. 49. 1–2 [*120*]; K. Wallenstein, *Kor. Plastik des 7 u. 6 Jhdts.* (1971). Laconia – M.N. Tod and A.J.B. Wace, *Cat. of the Sparta Museum* (1906), no. 1 [*123*]; *ADelt* xxiv, B, pls 124–5 two-sided reliefs [*124*]; M. Comstock and C. Vermeule, *Bronzes, Boston* no. 25 [*122*]; B. Schröder, *AM* xxix, 21ff.; E. Fiechter, *JdI* xxxiii, 107ff., Amyklai. Gitiadas – Lacroix, 217–20 [*125*]. Tektaios and Angelion – Lacroix, 202–4 [*126*]. Kypselid gold kolossos – J. Servais, *Ant. Class.* xxxiv, 144ff. Delphi chryselephantine [*127*] – P. Amandry, *BCH* lxiii, 86ff.; Suppl. 4, 273ff. (bull).

PROPORTIONS AND TECHNIQUES

Proportion and anatomy – *Kouroi* 17–25; M. Wegner, *RM* xlvii, 193ff.; L.D. Caskey, *AJA* xxviii, 358ff.; C. Karouzos, *Aristodikos* (1961) 9; A.F. Stewart, *Nature* 262 (1976), 155, scrotal asymmetry; J.J. Coulton, *BSA* lxx, 85ff., mensuration. E. Guralnik, *Computers and the Humanities* x,

153 ff. Technique (stone) – S. Adam, *The Technique of Greek Sculpture* (1966) supersedes all earlier works but S. Casson, *Technique of Early Greek Sculpture* (1933) is still useful and C. Blümel, *Greek Sculptors at Work* (1969) for pictures; B.S. Ridgway in C. Roebuck, *Muses at Work* (1969), 96 ff.; R. Anthes, *Mitt. Inst. Kairo* x, 79 ff., Egyptian guide sketches. Acrolith – C. Blinkenberg, *Die lindische Tempelchronik* C. 29 ff.; C. Blümel, *RA* 1968, 11 f., prostucco. Meniskoi – J. Maxmin, *JHS* xcv, 175 ff. Colour – G. Richter, *Met. Mus. Studies* i, 25 ff.; P. Reutersward, *Studien zur Polychromie der Plastik* (1960). Technique (bronze) – D. Haynes, *AA* 1962, 803 ff.; *RA* 1968, 101 ff.; *Art and Technology* (M.I.T., 1970); A. Steinberg in D. Mitten, *Master Bronzes from the Classical World* (1968); D.K. Hill in Roebuck, op. cit., 60 ff.; H.V. Herrmann, *Olympia* pl. 37, nn. 432–3 [*134*], sphyrelata; Robertson, 180 ff.

VI THE LATER ARCHAIC STYLES

ENDOIOS

Deyhle, op. cit., 12 ff.; *Deds.* 491–5; Robertson, 106–8. Seated Athena [*135*] – Payne, 46 f.; *AMA* no. 60. Kore 602 [*136*] – Payne, pl. 60. 1–3; *AMA* no. 7. Potter relief [*137*] – Payne, 48; *AMA* no. 422; J.D. Beazley, *Potter and Painter in Ancient Athens* 22. Rayet head [*139*] – *Kouroi* no. 138. Piraeus Gate kouros – G. Schmidt, *AM* lxxxiv, 6 ff.; U. Knigge, ibid., 76 ff. Bronze youth [*140*] – *Kouroi* no. 162.

ANTENOR

Deyhle, op. cit., 39 ff.; Payne, 31–33, 63–65; *Deds.* 481–3; *Korai* no. 110 [*141*] cf. no. 106 [*142*]. Tyrantslayers – A. Rumpf, *Festr. Mercklin* (1964) 131 ff.; *Athenian Agora* xiv, 155–60; J. Dörig, *Antike Kunst* xii, 41 ff., the Webb head [*143*] and on Roman copies of Archaic statues.

ATTIC SCULPTURE AND SCULPTORS

Kouroi nos 144 [*144*], 160 [*146*], 191 [*148*]. Ilissos [*149*] – Ridgway, *SS* 20, fig. 17. Kritian boy [*147*] – *Kouroi* no. 190; Payne, 44 f.; Robertson, 175 f. Aristodikos [*145*] – *Kouroi* no. 165; C. Karouzos, *Aristodikos* (1961); Athens 4489 head by same artist (?), V. Regnot, *BCH* lxxxvii, 393 ff. Piraeus bronze [*150*] – *Kouroi* no. 159 bis; N. Kontoleon, *Opus Nobile* 91 ff., copy of a marble; Robertson, 182 f. *Korai* nos 116 [*151*], 117 [*152*], 119 [*153*], 122 [*155*], 128 [*154*], 125 [*156*], 126 [*157*], 127 [*158*], 180 [*160*], 182 [*159*], 184 [*161*]; Payne, *passim*. Seated figures (grave) – *AM* lii, Beil. 25, 30; *AA* (1932), 225 f.; Kurtz/Boardman 89, 354. Dionysos [*162*] – W.H. Schuchhardt, *Antike Plastik* vi, pls 1–6; from Ikaria, *AM* xli, 169 (Athens 3897). Rhamnus [*163*] – *AM* xli, 119 ff., pl. 13. Acropolis scribes [*164*] – Payne, pl. 118; *AMA* nos 309–11. Riders (grave) – *AM* iv, pl.

3, Vari; *AA* (1933), 286; *AM* lxxxiii, 136 ff. Riders (votive) [*165, 166*] – Payne, 51 f., pls 133–9; *AMA* nos 312–21, and horses. Kallimachos' Nike [*167*] – *AMA* no. 77; Meiggs and Lewis, op. cit., no. 18; E. Harrison, *Greek, Roman and Byz Studies* xii, 5 ff. Other Acropolis figures – Payne, 43 f., pls 105–6, 107.4, Theseus [*168*]; pl. 121.4, 6 and 124.3, 6, Achilles and Ajax; Acr. 3715, *AMA* no. 306, Eros. Herms – *Athenian Agora* xi, 108 ff.; J. Crome, *AM* lx/lxi, pls 101–6 [*169*]; Payne, pl. 104. Cf. *ABFH* fig. 243, *ARFH* figs 278, 364. Masks [*170, 171*] – W. Wrede, *AM* liii, 66 ff.; Marathon mask [*171*] – ibid., Beil. 23; C. Blümel, *AA* 1971, 138 ff.; Robertson, 177; B. Ashmole, *Proc. Brit. Acad.* xlviii, 215 f. Euenor's Athena [*173*] – *AMA* no. 5; Ridgway, *SS* 29–31; Robertson, 179. Pythis' Athena [*172*] – Payne, 28 f., pls 43.3 and 44; *Deds.* no. 10.

EAST GREEK SCULPTURE AND SCULPTORS

Dionysermos [*174*] – P. Devambez, *RA* 1966, 195 ff. Samos xi, nos 138, 139 [*175*], warrior no. 78 [*176*]. Archermos and family – Jeffery, 294 f.; *Deds.* 484 ff. Chios – J. Boardman, *Greek Emporio* (1967) 181–3; *Korai* no. 123 [*177*]; *AMA* no. 68, the Nike. Seated women – von Graeve, *Ist. Mitt.* xxv, 61 ff.; N. Himmelmann, *Ist. Mitt.* xv, pls 2 ff.; *AGSB* nos 50–56, Miletus; *Forsch. u. Fortschritte* xxxv, 272 f., pair. Kyzikos head [*178*] – *AGSE* no. 31.

OTHER AREAS

Kouroi nos 145 [*179*], 155 [*180*], 159 [*182*]. *Korai* nos 147 [*181*], 99 [*183*], 120 [*184*]. Cycladic seated women – Berger, figs 47–48, Paros; *Arch. Epigr. Mitt.* xi, 156 f. Corinth, clay at Olympia – *Olympia Bericht* vi, 169 ff. [*186*]; poros kouros, *Hesperia* xix, pl. 91, Isthmia. Kanachos – E. Bielefeld, *Ist. Mitt.* xii, 18 ff., an eastern pose (?), and *Antike Plastik* viii, 13 ff., Roman copy (?); E. Simon in *Charites* (Fest. Rumpf) 38 ff.; Lacroix, 221–6 [*185*].

VII ARCHITECTURAL SCULPTURE

PLACING AND CHARACTER

Pediments – E. Lapalus, *Le Fronton sculpté en Grèce* (1947); W.H. Schuchhardt, *Archaische Giebelkompositionen* (1940), mainly Athens; A. Delivorrias, *Attische Giebelskulpturen und Akrotere* (1974), 177 ff.; M.S. Brouskari, *The Acropolis Museum* (1974). Friezes – R. Demangel, *La Frise Ionique* (1932); B.S. Ridgway, *Hesperia* xxxv, 188 f. Metopes – H. Kähler, *Das gr. Metopenbild* (1949). Chian architecture – J. Boardman, *Antiquaries Journal* xxxix, 193 ff. Relief types – Robertson, 56 f.

THE BEGINNINGS: CORFU

Clay revetments – H. Payne, *Necrocorinthia* (1931), ch. 17; E.D. van Buren, *Greek Fictile Revetments in the Archaic Period* (1926). Corfu [*187*] – C. Rodenwaldt, *Korkyra* ii (1939); Lullies, pls 16–19;

K. Schefold, *Myth and Legend* 52 ff.; E. Kunze, *AM* lxxvii, 74 ff. and J.L. Benson, *Gestalt und Geschichte* (Fest. Schefold) 48 ff. on subjects; Robertson, 63–67.

ATHENS

Tyrannenschutt – R. Heberdey, *Altattische Poroskulptur* (1919) 3 ff.; but see W.B. Dinsmoor, *AJA* xxxviii, 425. Temple foundations – W.H. Plommer, *JHS* lxxx, 127 ff. Gorgon, leopards [*189, 190*] – Payne, 10 f.; *AMA* nos 441, 463; Robertson, 48 f. Limestone pediments [*190–8*] – Heberdey, op. cit.; E. Buschor, *AM* xlvii, 1 ff., 81 ff.; W.H. Schuchhardt, *Archaische Giebelkompositionen* (1940) and *AA* 1963, 797 ff.; I. Beyer, *AA* 1974, 639 ff.; Robertson, 90–93. Marble gigantomachy [*199*] – Payne, 52 ff.; *AMA* no. 631; the new reconstruction in Athens has yet to be published; Delivorrias, op. cit., 178 f. K. Stähler, *Fest. H.E. Stier* (1972) 88 ff., dates animal pediment pre-510, gigantomachy (with centre frontal chariot as Delphi) 500. Marble frieze [*200*] – Payne, 47 f.; *AMA* nos 474–9. Lower town – *Athenian Agora* xi, nos 94–96; Heberdey, op. cit., 75 ff. [*201*]; G.M.A. Richter, *Catalogue of Sculpture, New York* no. 7. Eleusis [*202*] – F. Willemsen, *AM* lxix/lxx, 33 ff.; N. Himmelmann, *MWPr* 1957, 9 ff.; Ridgway, *SS* 26. Politics – J.S. Boersma, *Athenian Building Policy from 561/0 to 405/4 B.C.* (1970), 11 ff.; J. Boardman, *Rev. Arch.* (1972), 70 ff. and *JHS* xcv, 2, 10.

CENTRAL AND SOUTH GREECE

Delphi, Apollo temple [*203, 204*] – *FDelphes* iii; P. de la Coste Messelière, *BCH* lxx, 271 ff.; Robertson, 161 f.; west pediment, Euripides, *Ion* 205–18. Eretria, Apollo temple [*205*] – D. Bothmer, *Amazons in Greek Art*, 125 ff.; I. Konstantinou, *AM* lxix/lxx, 41 ff.; Robertson, 163 f. Aegina, Aphaia temple [*206*] – A. Furtwängler, *Aegina* i (1906); D. Ohly, *Die Aigineten* i (1972) 49 ff. *Glyptothek München: ein Kurzerführer* (1972) 49 ff.; Ridgway, *SS* 13–17, suggests that the bodies of the original east (front) pediment were mainly bronze and that the replacement is of 480–470; R.M. Cook, *JHS* xciv, 171, dating; Robertson, 165–7; Delivorrias, op. cit., 180 f. Kopai – *AM* xxx, pl. 13. Corinth, clay – R. Stilwell in *Studies . . . Capps* 318 ff. Corfu, Dionysos temple [*207a*] – A. Choremis, *AAA* vii, 183 ff.

TREASURIES

General – L. Dyer, *JHS* xxv, 294 ff.

DELPHI

Sicyonian and Siphnian [*208–12*] – P. de la Coste Messelière, *Au Musée de Delphes* (1936). Caryatids: 'Cnidian' – *Korai* nos 87, 88; Siphnian [*210*] – *Korai* no. 104; ex-Cnidian [*209*] – G.M.A. Richter, *BCH* lxxxii, 92 ff.; *Korai* no. 86. Siphnian [*212*] – inscriptions – Messelière, *BCH* lxviii/lxix, 5 ff.; E. Mastrokostas, *AM* lxxi, 74 ff.; Jeffery, 102

(Phocian ?). Signature – M. Guarducci in *Studi Banti* (1965), 167 ff. (Attic ?); L.H. Jeffery, *Archaic Greece* 185. Pediment subject – B.S. Ridgway, *AJA* lxix, 1 ff. and cf. *BCH* lxxxvi, 24 ff. M. Moore, *BCH* Suppl. 4, 305 ff. Robertson, 89, 152–9; Massalian – *FDelphes* iv. 2, pl. 29; E. Langlotz, *Studien zur nordostgriechischen Kunst* (1975), pls 8–12 and cf. pls 13, 14, 17. Athenian [*213*] – *FDelphes* iv.4; *BCH* xc, 699 ff.; *Athenian Agora* xi, 9–11, date; Robertson, 167–71; Delivorrias, op. cit., 181 f.

OLYMPIA

H.V. Herrmann, *Olympia, Heiligtum und Wettkampfstätte*, 97–104; *Olympia* iii, 5–25 [*214*]. Megarian [*215*] – P.C. Bol and K. Hermann, *AM* lxxxix, 65 ff.

EAST GREECE

General – E. Akurgal, *Die Kunst Anatoliens* (1961). Assos [*216*] – F.H. Bacon, J.T. Clarke *et al.*, *Assos* 145–53. Frieze slabs in Paris (*Enc. Phot.* 142 f.), Istanbul (Mendel, *Cat.* ii, nos 257–65), Boston; F. Sartiaux, *Les sculptures et la reconstruction* (1915) (=*Rev. Arch.* 1913–1914). Samos xi, nos 113–37. Ephesus [*217*] – *British Museum Catalogue of Sculpture* nos B86–268; *Didyma* 132–6. Didyma [*218, 219*] – *Didyma* nos K75–81 (columns), K82–4 (gorgons); G. Gruben, *JdI* lxxviii, 78 ff., reconstruction [*218.1*]; *AGSB* nos 59, 64 (altar). Pergamum – *AGSB* no. 29, Europa. Kyzikos [*220*] – *Antike Kunst* viii, pl. 28.2; *AJA* lxvi, pl. 100.21; other sculpture, *BSA* viii, pl. 4. Clay revetments – Å. Åkerström, *Die architektonischen Terrakotten Kleinasiens* (1966). Chariot reliefs – Kyzikos [*221*] – M. Schede, *Gr. und Rom. Skulptur des Antikenmuseums* (*Meisterwerke, Konstantinopel*, 1928) pl. 4; Myus [*222*] – *AGSB* no. 65 and *Ist. Mitt.* xv, pl. 29, Iasos – *Ann* l/li, 397 ff. Thasos [*223*] – *Études Thasiennes* i, Les Murailles.

VIII RELIEFS

GRAVE RELIEFS

Athens and Attica: Richter, *Gravestones* is the prime source; see *Gravestones* nos 3 [*225*], 11 [*226*], 12 [*227*], 38 [*228*], 20 [*229*], 23 [*230*], 27 [*231*], 37 [*232*], 31 [*233*], 45 [*234*], 67 [*235*], 77 [*236*], 59 [*237*], fig. 174 [*238*]. Further on Attic: E. Harrison, *Hesperia* xxv, 25 ff.; L.H. Jeffery, *BSA* lvii, 115 ff. on all inscriptions and 149 f. on stelai; Kurtz/Boardman, 84–86, general and on legislation; F. Willemsen, *AM* lxxxv, 34 ff., broad stelai, 'metopes', Aristokles [*235*]; F. Hiller, *MWPr* 1967 18 ff., dating and Ionia; G.M.A. Richter, *Mél. Mansel* i. 1 ff., Alkmaionid ? *AA* 1963, 431 ff., incised youth; *AAA* ii, 89 ff., warrior stele, Eleusis; D. Ohly, *AM* lxxvii, 93 ff., gorgon on stele; Robertson, 108–12. 'Marathon runner' [*239*] – M. Andronikos, *AE* 1953, 4.2, 317 ff.; K. Wiegartz, *MWPr* 1965, 46 ff., dancer. Bases [*240–3*] – F. Willemsen, *AM* lxxviii, 104 ff. Man-and-dog stelai [*244*] – B.S. Ridgway, *JdI* lxxxvi, 60 ff., claims origin for Ionia; *Antike Kunst* xix, pl. 17. Aegina: stele crown – *AA* 1938, 30; *dexiosis* – Berger, fig. 132; marble sphinx, now with head – *AAA* viii, 227 ff. Corinth: stele crown – *Corinth* xiii, pl. 82.X120; marble sphinx – *BCH* xcvii, 284 ff. Boeotia: *Gravestones* nos 28, 68, 75; *AM* lxxxvi, 67 ff., stele crown, Thebes; W. Schild-Xenidou, *Boiot. Grab- und Weihreliefs* (1972). Samos: E. Buschor, *AM* lviii, 22 ff.; J. Boardman, *Antiquaries Journal* xxxix, 201 f., date; *Samos* xi, 174 ff. Two-sided – Berger, figs 133–4. Chios rider metope – Berger, fig. 38. Syme stele [*245*] – Berger, fig. 58. Kalchedon stele [*248*] – *Ist. Mitt.* xix/xx, 177 ff.; *BSA* 1, 81–83; Jeffery, 366. Kos – C. Karouzos, *AM* lxxvii, 121 ff. [*249*]; Berger, fig. 140 [*248*]. Crete [246] – A. Lembessi, *Antike Plastik* xii, 7 ff. General non-Attic: *Gravestones* 53–55 K.F. Johansen, *Attic Grave Reliefs* (1951) 65 ff.; Berger, 36 ff., 102 ff.; H. Hiller, Ion. Grabreliefs (*Ist. Mitt.* Beiheft 12, 1975); *Antike Plastik* vii, 77, Ios, Tenos; *AReptsfor 1962/3*, 49, Phanagoria; *AAA* vi, 351, Amorgos.

VOTIVE AND OTHER RELIEFS

U. Hausmann, *Gr. Weihreliefs* (1960); Berger, 98 ff., 102 ff. Paros – *ADelt* xvi.B, pl. 215 [*250*]; *AGSB* no. 24; Berger, fig. 126; *Arch. Epigr. Mitt.* xi, 153, pl. 5 [*262*]. Thasos [*251*] – Berger, fig. 52 (51, 53, later). Prinias [*252*] – Johansen, op. cit., 80 ff.; A. Lembessi, *Steles tou Prinia* (1976). Laconia [*253, 254*] – M. Andronikos, *Peloponnesiaka* i, 253 ff.; A.J.B. Wace, *AE* 1937. 1, 217 ff., Chilon (Jeffery, 193; Pausanias iii, 16, 4); Johansen, op. cit., 82 ff., and fig. 39; K. Chrestou, *AE* 1955, 91 ff., Dioskouroi; *AGSB* no. 16 [*253*]. E.Guralnik, *Journ. Eg. Arch.* lx, 175 ff., on Egyptian connections of [*253*]. *Totenmahl* – Tegea, Athens 55; Paros [*255*] – N. Kontoleon in *Charisterion Orlandou* i, 348 ff.; Kurtz/Boardman, 234. Seated men – Berger, fig 120, Rhodes; Johansen, op. cit., fig. 56, Lebadea. Seated woman – Berger, fig. 27, Thespiae. Chian Kybele – Boardman, *Antiquaries Journal* xxxix, 195 f. Samothrace [*264*] – *Enc. Phot.* iii, 235; Jeffery, 299. Attica – Payne, pls 126–30; *AMA* nos. 418 [*256*], 424 [*257*], 430 [*258*]; Herakles and boar [*260*] – F. Brommer, *Herakles* pl. 14a; Lamptrai base [*261*] – *AM* lxvi, pls 62–65; M. Moore, *Getty Journal* ii, 37 ff., youth with horse, 'Cottenham relief'; J. Frel, *AA* 1973, 193 ff., on [*238, 258*].

IX ANIMALS AND MONSTERS

H. Gabelmann, *Studien zum frügr. Löwenbild* (1965), for all lions cited; F. Hölscher, *Die Bedeutung arch. Tierkampfbilder* (1972). Olympia [*265*] – H.V. Herrmann, *Olympia* 237; J.F. Crome in *Mnemosynon Wiegand* (1938), 47 f. Corfu [*266*] – Crome, op. cit., 50 ff.; C. Rodenwaldt, *Korkyra* ii, 176 ff. Corinthian lions [*267, 263*] – H. Payne, *Necrocorinthia* 243 f. Delos lions [*269*] – *Expl. Arch. Délos* xxiv, 26 ff. Acropolis animals [*271*] – Payne, 51 f., pls 16, 131–40. Siren – *Acta Arch.* v, 49 ff., playing kithara.

X CONCLUSION

Comparisons of sculpture and vases – G. von Lücken, *AM* xliv, 47 ff. Potters' dedications on the Acropolis – J.D. Beazley, *Potter and Painter in Ancient Athens* (1946), 21 ff.; *Deds.* Euthymides/Pollias – J. Boardman *JHS* lxxvi, 20 ff.

INDEX OF ILLUSTRATIONS

Italic numbers refer to figures

ATHENS, Acropolis Museum

1, *196*; 2, *197*; 3, *191*; 35, *193*; 55, *193*; 136, *172*; 140, *173*; 143, *271*; 144, *164*; 145, *168*; 269, *110, 132*; 552, *189*; 575, *256*; 581, *258*; 590, *114*; 593, *109*; 602, *136*; 609, *160*; 615, *156*; 619, *98*; 623, *166*; 624, *112*; 625, *135*; 631, *199*; 643, *154*; 654, *116*; 670, *153*; 671, *111*; 673, *152*; 674, *158*; 675, *177*; 677, *99*; 678, *118*; 679, *115, 129*; 680, *155*; 681, *141*; 682, *151*; 683, *184*; 684, *159*; 686, *160*; 688, *161*; 689, *148*; 690, *167*; 692, *146*; 696, *157*; 698, *147*; 700, *165*; 701, *188*; 702, *257*; 1332, *137*; 1342, *200*; ——, *190, 194, 198*

ATHENS, Kerameikos Museum

641, *3*; P1001, *240*; P1002, *243*; ——, *226, 230, 233*

ATHENS, National Museum

1, *71*; 8, *101*; 9, *67*; 12, *179*; 15, *68*; 20, *180*; 21, *103*; 28, *227, 131*; 29, *235*; 36, *238*; 38, *117*; 39, *244*; 41, *229*; 42, *261*; 43, *260*; 56, *66*; 776, *19*; 1558, *102*; 1906, *104*; 1959, *239*; 2569, *163*; 2687, *231*; 2720, *64*; 2869–70, *35*; 3072, *170*; 3131, *201*; 3372, *62*; 3476, *138, 242*; 3477, *241*; 3579, *261*; 3645, *36*; 3686, *144*; 3687, *149*; 3711, *162*; 3728, *169*; 3851, *107*; 3938, *145*; 4472, *237*; 6445, *140*; 6446, *207*; 12831, *7*; 16519, *38*; 16520, *51*; ——, *6, 54, 120, 150*

BALTIMORE, Walters Art Gallery

54.773, *48*

BERLIN, Staatliche Museen

100, *171*; 608, *113, 133*; 731, *253*; 1531, *232*; 1631, *90*; 1739, *92*; 1747, *75*; 1752, *176*; 1790, *270*; 1791, *89*; 1800, *108*; 1851, *178*; 7477, *45*; 31317, *8*; 31342, *44*; F724, *219*; 1964.36, *53*; ——, *222*

BOSTON, Museum of Fine Arts

95.74, *122*; 97.289, *267*; 98.650, *9*; 03.997, *10*; 04.10, *183*; 40.576, *228*; ——, *216*

CHALCIS, Museum

——, *205*

CHANIA, Museum

92, *15*; ——, *27*

CHIOS, Museum

225–6, *85–86*

COPENHAGEN, Ny Carlsberg Glyptotek

23, *254*; 418, *139*; 1297, *268*; I.N.1203, *225*; I.N.2787, *236*

CORFU, Museum

——, *187, 266*

CORINTH, Museum

KH1, *24*; MF4039, *23*; ——, *74*

DELOS, Museum

A333, *59*; A334, *58*; A728, *56*; A4064, *181*; ——, *60, 269*

DELPHI, Museum

467, *70*; 1524, *70*; 2527, *57*; ——, *52, 100, 127, 142, 203–4, 208–13*

ELEUSIS, Museum

——, *202*

ERETRIA, Museum

——, *4*

FLORENCE, Museo Nazionale

——, *105*

HERAKLION, Museum

47, *33*; 231–2, *32*; 234, *252*; 345, *14*; 379, *31*; 380, *30*; 396–7, *252*; 399, *252*; 402, *252*; 407, *29*; 473, *246*; 2064, *43*; 2445–7, *16*; 2448, *25*; 18502, *34*; ——, *1, 17–18*

ISTANBUL, Museum

14, *245*; 239, *218*; 524, *248*; 525, *221*; 530, *82*; ——, *88, 216, 220*

KARLSRUHE, Badisches Landesmuseum

F1890, *37*

KOS, Museum

——, *247, 249*

LONDON, British Museum

2728, *143*; B90–91, *217*; B118–19, *217*; B121, *217*; B215, *217*; B271, *94*; B278, *95*; B475, *182*; coins, *125–6*, *185*

LYONS, Museum

—, *110*

MALIBU, J. Paul Getty Museum

—, *263*

MUNICH, Glyptothek

74–85, *206*; 168, *121*; 169, *106*

NAPLES, Museo Nazionale

3358, *259*

NAXOS, Museum

—, *55*

NEW YORK, Metropolitan Museum

11.185, *232*; 17.190.73, *39*; 32.11.1, *63*; 36.11.13, *234*; 42.11.42, *11*

OLYMPIA, Museum

B1700, *47*; B4600, *5*; T6, *186*; —, *20–22, 73, 76, 134, 214–15, 265*

OXFORD, Ashmolean Museum

AE.211, *18*; AE.403, *26*; AE.1102, *2*

PARIS, Louvre

686, *87*; 697, *264*; 2828, *216*; 3098, *28, 71, 128*; 3103, *251*; 3104, *114*; CA931, *41*; MA3600, *174*; MNI910, *36*; —, *216*

PAROS, Museum

—, *250, 255, 262*

RHODES, Museum

—, *77, 83*

ROME, Conservatori Museum

—, *205*

SAMOS, Tigani Museum

H41, *49*; M285, *96*

SAMOS, Vathy Museum

68, *84*; 69, *81*; 77, *175*; 768, *93*; I.95, *72*; I.217, *97*; —, *12, 50, 91*

SPARTA, Museum

364, *80*; 1658, *79*; —, *78, 123–4*

THASOS, Museum

—, *69, 223*

THEBES, Museum

3, *119*; —, *42*

THERA, Museum

—, *40, 61*

VENICE, Arsenal

—, *269*

Acknowledgments

The publisher and author are indebted to the museums and collections named in many of the captions for photographs and permission to use them. Other important sources of illustration have been (brackets indicate the source for *one* of the views shown):
German Institute, Athens 5, 6, 22, 46, 47, 49, 50, (54), 72, 78, 79, 80, 81, 84, 85, 86, 93, 96, 97, 98, 109, (111), 116, (123), 134, 136. (137), (148), 149, 156, 161, 163, 167, 169, 170, 173, 175, 184, 186, 187, (191), (194), (195), (199), 201, 202, 214, 215, 230, 231, 237, 240, 243, 244, 247, 249, 255, 265, 266; German Institute, Istanbul 218.2; American School of Classical Studies, Athens 23, 24; French School at Athens 52, 56, (127), 213.1; E. Akurgal 220; J. Dörig 143; A. Frantz 64, 66, (226), 227, (235), (241); M. Popham 4; Hirmer Verlag 3, 7, 35, (70), 88, (100), 103, 112, (115), 118, (121), 145, 147, (148), (150), (151), 152, 154, 155, (158), (160), 162, 177, (193), 205.(2)–3, 206.1–3 & 6, 212 1–2, 242, 257, 258; Arts of Mankind 1, 16, 32.1, 65, (70), 73, (100), (104), (111), (115), 141, 142, (151), 153, 157, (158), 159, (160), 166, 168, 174, (194), 200, 204, 209, (210), 212.3–4, 213.2–4, (226), 233, 271; G. M. Young (Oxford) 57, 62, 67, 68, 101, 102, (104), 107, 110, 117, 119, 140, 144, 146, 179, 180, (188); F. von Matt (121); Edwin Smith 182; N. Kontos 108a; Author 29, 30, (31), (32.2), 55, 58, 59, 71, 76, 77, 85, 120, (137), 164, 165, 172, (188), (190), (193), (195), 196, 197, 198, (205.2), 206.4–5, (210), (211), 216.4, 252, 256, 260, (269).

249

INDEX OF ARTISTS

Italic numbers refer to figures; the bracketed are uncertain or for comparison

Ageladas 89
Alxenor 165; *244*
Angelion 76; *126*
Antenor 83, 156; *141, (143)*
Archermos 71–2, 88; *103, (177)*
Ariston 73–5, 158; *108a*
Aristokles 75, 164; *235*
Athenis 71, 88

Bathykles 76
Bion 74
Boupalos 71, 88

Daedalus 26, 76, 82, 170
Dipoinos 26, 76

Eleutheros 74

Endoios 26, 74, 82–3, 86, 158; *135–6, (137), (139), (242)*
Eudemos 72
Euenor 74, 87; *173*
Euthykartidas 21, 27; *56*

Geneleos 70; *91*
Gitiadas 76, 81; *125*
Gorgias 74

Kallon 74, 157
Kanachos 89; *185*
Kritios 83–7; *(147)*

. . . medes 24, 27; *70*

Onatas 74, 157

. . . otos 14

Phaidimos 74; *(112), (231)*
Philergos 74, 82–3; *136, (139)*
Pollias 170
Pythis 87; *172*

Rampin Master 73–5; *114, (115–17), (129), (231)*

Skyllis, see Dipoinos
Smilis 26

Tektaios, see Angelion
Telchines 26, 170
Terpsikles 72
Thebadas 88
Theodoros 20, 72, 170

GENERAL INDEX

Italic numbers refer to figures and captions

A. Ioannis Rentis 73
Aegina 26, 74, 156, 157, 163–4; *206*
aetos 152
Afrati 11; *17*
Agamemnon *264*
Aiakes 70, 169; *96*
Aineas *212*
Ajax 87 (and Achilles), 156; *206*
Alkmaionids 76, 83, 155; *232*
Amazons 156, 157, 159, 160; *205, 213*
Amnisos *14*
Amyklai 76; *6*
Anaphe 88; *182*
Anavysos *107, 237*
Angelitos *173*
Aphaia 156–7; *206*
Aphrodite 26, *212*
Apollo 11, 16, 22–3, 76, 85, 89, 155, 156, 161; *31, 52, 185, 203, 211–12*
Archaic smile 65, 86, 88
Archias 74
Ares *212*
Argo 158; *208*
Argos 24; *70*

Aristion 164; *235*
Aristodikos 79, 84; *145, (152)*
Artemis 24, 71, 82, 88, 153, 166; *52, 187, 211–12*
Assos 160–1; *216*
Astarte 12–13
Astritsi 14; *29*
Athena 14, 22, 24, 76, 81, 82, 86–7, 89, 153–4, 156, 159, 160, 166; *27, 34, 135, 172–3, 186, 192, 195, 199, 205, 206, 212–13, 258*
Athenian treasury 157, 159, 160; *213*
Athens *passim*; Acropolis 63–4, 153, 169, 170
Automedon *212*
Auxerre goddess 13–14, 25; *28, 128*
Axos 27

Bases 21; *56*
Berlin kore 73, 75; *108*
Blond boy 85, 87; *148, (160), (171)*
Boeotia 14, 16, 23–4, 76, 85–6, 88, 157, 163, 165; *36, 42, 67–8, 119, 179, 180, 244*
Boutades 153

Bowman 10–11
Boxer 163; *233*
Bronze 10–12, 15–16, 22–3, 26, 64, 76, 81, 83, 85, 89, 157
Bronze Age 9, 13, 16, 26, 162; *4*
Bulls 154–5, 161; *190–1, 213, 255*

Calf-bearer 74, 79, 168; *112, (193)*
Calydonian boar 158; *208*
Carian 70, 164
Caryatid 72, 152, 158; *209, 210*
Centaur 9, 167; *4, 13, 216*
Chairedemos 74
Chania 151; *15*
Chares 70; *95*
Cheramyes 69; *87*
Ch]ilon 165
Chios 24, 66, 69, 71–2, 74, 86, 88, 152, 163, 166; *85–6, 177*
Chronology 14–15, 169
Chrysaor 153; *187*
Chrysapha *253*
Chryselephantine 80, 89; *127*
Clay 9, 10, 13–14, 25, 69, 89, 153, 157, 163; *1–6, 23–4, 26, 34, 120, 186*

Cnidian treasury 158
Cocks 160
Cock-horse 168
Coins 76, 89; *125–6, 185*
Colour 80–1
Corfu 76, 153–4, 156–7; *187, 207a, 266*
Corinth 15, 25, 76–7, 88–9, 153, 157, 163; *23–4, 267–8*
Crete 9, 11–16, 22–3, 26–7, 151, 165; *1, 2, 14–18, 25–35, 43–5, 246, 252*
Cult statues 11, 20–1, 25–6, 76, 85, 151
Cyprus 9, 12, 25
Cyrene 70, 160
Cyriacus *60*

Daedalic 11, 13–17, 21–5, 80, 151
Deer/stag *3, 9, 203, 210*
Delos 23–5, 27, 64, 71–2, 76, 85, 88, 170; *56, 58–60, 71, 103, 181, 269*
Delphi 9, 16, 22–7, 63–4, 71–2, 76–7, 80, 83, 88–9, 151–2, 155–60, 169; *52, 57, 70, 100, 127, 142, 203–4, 209–13, 256*
Demeter 24; *212*
Dermys and Kittylos 163; *66*
dexiosis 164
Didyma 64, 69, 70, 72, 89, 161, 168; *94–5, 218–19*
Dionysermos 87; *174*
Dionysos 82, 86–7, 155, 157, 165; *162, 170, 207a, 212*
Dioskouroi 165; *114, 208, 212, 259*
Dipylon head 23, 154; *62*
Dodona 9
Dog 164, 168; *207a, 244, 271*
Doric 151–2, 162
Dorylaion 163
Dreros 11, 14, 81; *16*
Dress 13, 16, 66–9, 73, 85

Eastern art 11–17, 25, 66, 69, 161, 167; *19, 23, 73*
Egypt 18–20, 23, 26, 66, 77, 152, 162, 165, 168
Eleusis 24, 85, 155; *202*
Eleutherna 14; *33*
Eltyna *246*
Epe[ios *264*
Ephesus 17, 64, 70, 74, 82, 160–1, 169; *88, 217*
Epiteles *172*
Eretria 156; *205*
Eros 87
Erythrae 70, 82
Euboea 9; *4*

Europa 158, 161; *208, 216*
Euthydikos 85–6; *160, (171)*
Euthymides 170

Funerary 14, 22–4, 63–4, 66, 72, 74, 86, 162–5, 167–8

Geometric 9–12, 15–16, 26, 162
Giants *187, 212*
Gigantomachy 155, 159, 160; *199, 212*
Glaukos *212*
Gold 77
Gorgons 152–4, 161–2, 164, 166; *56, 135, 187–8, 205, 218, 231, 262*
Gortyn 14–15; *25, 30–1, 34*
Graces 88, 166
Griffins 12, 166; *22, 264*

Hair styles 13, 86
Harmodios and Aristogeiton 83; *143, (147)*
Hektor *212*
Helmet-maker 10; *11*
Hephaistos *212*
Hera 22, 24–6; *49, 50, 73, 110, 194, 212*
Herakles 76, 154–5, 159–61, 166; *186, 92, 194, 196–7, 206, 211–13, 216, 260–1*
Herm 87; *169*
Hermes 87, 166; *194, 200, 212*
Hipparchos 83, 87
Hipponax 88
Hockey *241*
Horses 10, 80, 167, 168; *8*
Hymettan 19

Iasos 88, 161
Idaean Cave 12; *18*
Idas *208*
Ikaria 86; *170*
Inscriptions 10, 22, 73–4, 157–8, 164
Ionic 151
Iphidike 88
Isthmia 25; *74*
Ivory 12, 14–17, 26, 70, 77; *19, 38–9, 5.–4, 88, 127*

Jewellery 11–12, 14

Kalchedon 165; *248*
Kallias *135*
Kallimachos 86, 169; *167*
Kalydon *120*
Karditsa *7*
Karphi *1*
Keos 84, 88; *144*

Keratea *108*
Klaros *24*
Kleisthenes 157
Kleobis and Biton 24, 79; *70*
Knossos 11
kolossos 26
Kopai 157
Kos 165 *247, 249*
Kritian boy 84–9; *147*
Kroisos *72; 107*
Kronos *187*
Kybele 166; *212, 263*
Kyzikos 59, 161; *178, 220–1*

Laconia 25–6, 76, 165
Lampito 83
Lamptrai 166; *229, 261*
Leanax 82
Lebadea 165
Lefkandi *4*
Leopards 153–4, 167; *189*
Lesbos 71 88
Leikippidai *212*
Leukios 69; *81*
Lions 12, 25, 154–5, 161, 167–8; *12, 52, 56, 73, 190–1, 203, 207a, 210, 218, 243, 255, 265–70*
Loutraki *258*
Lynkeus *208*
Lyons kore *73; 110, 132*
Lyre *53–4*
Lyre-player 16; *43, 209*

Magnesia *75*
Malesina *36*
Mantiklos *10*
Marathon 86–7, 159; *167, 171*
Marble sources 18–19, 23, 25, 27
Masks 87; *171–2*
Massilian treasury 159
Megakles *232*
Megarian treasury 157, 160; *215*
Melos 14, 71; *102*
Menekrates *266*
Menelaos 127, *212*
meniskoi 80
Merenda 72–3, 75; *108a*
Mikkiades 71
Miletus 24, 69, 70, 74, 168; *89, 90, 270*
Moirai *212*
Mycenae 14; *35*
Myus 70, 161 *222*

Naxos 18–19, 21, 23, 71, 165; *55, 60, 71, 100, 244, 269*
Nearchos *141*
Nelonides 82
Nestor *212*

Nikandre 25; *71*
Nike 71–2, 86, 88, 156, 158, 169; *103, 167, 204*
Nudity 13–14, 20, 22, 65, 69
Nymphs 24

Olive Tree pediment 155; *198*
Ops[iades *136*
Olympia 9, 10, 12, 14, 16, 25–6, 63–4, 76–7, 81, 89, 157, 160; *5, 13, 20–2, 37, 46–7, 73, 76, 134, 186, 214–15, 265*
Olympus 158
Orchomenos 165; *67*
Ornithe *92*
Orpheus *208*

Pampha]ios *137*
Pan 87
Paris *212*
Paros 19, 71, 74–5, 88, 165–6; *250, 255, 262*
Patroklos *212*
Pegasi 152
Peisistratos 63, 76, 82–3, 87, 153–5; *114, 232*
Pentelic 19
Peplos kore 75; *115, 129*
Perachora 14, 16; *38, 51, 267*
Pergamum 161
Perirrhanteria 25–6, 167; *74–9*
Perseus 89, 154
Phile 74
Phileia 70; *91*
Philippe *91*
Phocaea 69, 159
Phrasikleia 73, 75; *108a*
Phrixos *208*
Piraeus kouros 81, 85; *150*
Piskokephalo *2*
polos 10–11; *26, 49, 227*

Polykrates 63, 70, 72
Poseidon 22, 24; *212*
Potter 82–3; *137, 141*
Priam *187*
Prinias 14, 151, 165; *32, 252*
Proitos *39*
Proportions 20, 23, 65, 77–9, 84
Ptoon 14, 25, 64, 76, 86, 88; *68, 119, 179, 180*
Pythias and Aischrion *180*

Ram-bearer 16; *45, 69*
Rampin head 75; *114*
Rayet head 83; *139*
Rhamnus 86; *163*
Rhea *187*
Rhodes 14, 25, 69, 165; *77, 83*

Sabouroff head 74; *113, 133*
Samos 9, 16–17, 20–6, 63, 66, 68–72, 78, 83–4, 87–8, 160, 163, 169; *12, 49, 50, 54, 72, 75, 81–2, 84, 87, 91–3, 96–7, 175–6*
Samothrace 166; *264*
Sarpedon *212*
Satyrs 155; *201, 210, 223*
Scribes 86; *164*
Sicily 152, 160
Sicyon 76, 89, 153, 157, 164; *183, 208*
Sicyonian treasury 157; *208*
Siphnian treasury 80, 83, 158, 161, 169; *130, 210–12*
Siphnos 87; *169*
Sirens 12, 168; *21*
Smyrna 88, 151
Sounion 22, 24, 78; *64–5*
Sparta 25, 70, 74, 76, 89, 168; *78–80, 122–4, 253–4*
Spata *225, 227*

Sphinx 9, 14, 16, 21, 25, 71, 77, 162–3, 167; *31, 35, 44, 100, 224–8*
Syme *245*

Talthybios *264*
Tanagra 15; *42, 66*
Technique 18–20, 79, 80; bronze 10, 72, 81; *16*
Tegea 82
Telamon 156; *206*
Telekles 20, 72
Tenea 76, 79; *121*
Thasos 24, 78, 152, 161, 165–6; *69, 223, 251, 263*
Thebes 89, 164; *9, 10, 41, 48*
Themistoclean wall 164, 169; *226, 231, 233, 241–3*
Thera 14, 23, 24, 71, 88; *40, 61, 101*
Thermon 151; *39*
Theseus 87, 156, 159, 160; *168, 205, 213*
Thespiae 165
Thorwaldsen 156
Totenmahl 165–6
Treasuries 76, 151, 157; *208–15*
Troy 156, 158
Tyche 88
Tymnes 164
Tyrants 63, 82

Vase painting 15, 25, 76, 87, 158, 169–70; *41, 259, 267*
Velanideza 164
Volomandra 72–3, 75, 85; *104*

Webb head 83; *143*
Wood 16, 18, 20, 79–80; *49, 50*

Zeus 10, 16, 25, 77, 156–8; *50, 187, 194, 211–12*